D1320083

THE TRINITY & SUBORDINATIONISM

The Doctrine of God & the Contemporary Gender Debate

Kevin Giles

InterVarsity Press
Downers Grove, Illinois

InterVarsity Press
P.O. Box 1400, Downers Grove, IL 60515-1426
World Wide Web: www.ivpress.com
E-mail: mail@ivpress.com

InterVarsity Press® *is the book-publishing division of InterVarsity Christian Fellowship/USA*®,
*a student movement active on campus at hundreds of universities, colleges and schools of nursing
in the United States of America, and a member movement of the International Fellowship of
Evangelical Students. For information about local and regional activities, write Public Relations
Dept., InterVarsity Christian Fellowship/USA, 6400 Schroeder Rd., P.O. Box 7895, Madison,
WI 53707-7895, or visit the IVCF website at <www.ivcf.org>.*

Scripture quotations, unless otherwise noted, are from the New Revised Standard Version of the
Bible, *copyright 1989 by the Division of Christian Education of the National Council of the
Churches of Christ in the USA. Used by permission. All rights reserved.*

Cover illustration: Alinari/Art Resource, NY

ISBN 0-8308-2663-7

Printed in the United States of America ∞

Library of Congress Cataloging-in-Publication Data
Giles, Kevin.
   *The Trinity & subordinationism: the doctrine of God and the contemporary gender
  debate/Kevin Giles.*
     p. cm.
   Includes bibliographical references.
   ISBN 0-8308-2663-7
   *1. Trinity—History of doctrines. 2. Jesus Christ—History of doctrines. 3.
  Subordinationism. I. Title: Trinity and subordinationism II. Title.*
  BT109.G55 2002
  231'.044—dc21
                                                              2001051792

P	19	18	17	16	15	14	13	12	11	10	9	8	7	6	5	4	3	2	1
Y	17	16	15	14	13	12	11	10	09	08	07	06	05	04	03	02			

CONTENTS

Introduction

More than three years have passed since I decided to write a journal article of a few thousand words in response to the ever-growing number of evangelicals who were speaking of the eternal subordination of the Son in the Trinity. My areas of expertise are New Testament studies and hands-on pastoral ministry, not systematic or historical theology. But from what I remembered of my undergraduate studies, the subordination of the Son had been deemed a heresy in the early church. I imagined, as I began, that if I read widely from the books on the Trinity that have been accumulating over recent years at a nearby theological college library, I would soon have the information I needed to complete an essay. How wrong I was.

The learned tomes I turned to invariably said nothing about subordination in the Trinity, except in relation to the pre-Nicene fathers and the fourth-century debates about Arianism. What is more, they made no comment about "the headship" of the Father in the Trinity, they seldom discussed the significance of the Son's subordination to the Father in the incarnation, and they said nothing about the three persons' differences being grounded on their differing roles or functions—three matters central to the discussions on the Trinity in contemporary evangelical literature. As I reread what evangelicals who advocated the eternal subordination of the Son in the Trinity were saying, I noted that they were consistently and emphatically claiming that their position was historic orthodoxy. In support, they quoted theological luminaries such as Athanasius, Augustine, Calvin, Charles Hodge and Louis Berkhof as well as the Nicene and Athanasian

Creeds. It soon dawned on me that it would take a lot of effort to unravel the issues and work out an answer. I would need to read for myself Athanasius, Augustine and Calvin on the Trinity, in addition to the more important contributions by contemporary Protestant, Roman Catholic and Eastern Orthodox theologians. So began a fascinating journey of discovery that has culminated in this book.[1]

I began my work with one goal in mind—to determine what was the orthodox doctrine of the Trinity—but as I progressed in my reading, I discovered that the debate about the Trinity was in essence a debate about theological method, something right at the forefront of evangelical thinking today.[2] Behind this particular debate lay the interrelated questions, how does one settle a theological dispute when what is asked is not directly answered by the Bible, and how does one weigh differing arguments when both sides appeal to the Bible to substantiate their opposing conclusions? The moment I realized these issues were central in the historic discussion on the relationship between the Father and the Son in the Trinity, I immediately saw a profound and far-reaching connection between this debate and the contemporary discussion on the relationship between men and women in the home and the church.[3] Here too the problem is, how does one resolve a complex theological dispute that the Bible does not anticipate (e.g., what freedoms and responsibilities do women have in a culture that

---

[1] I would like to thank Gary W. Deddo, my editor at InterVarsity Press, who has been a constant encourager and help in preparing this book for publication. He has himself published an important scholarly work on the Trinity: *Karl Barth's Theology of Relations: Trinitarian, Christological and Human: Towards an Ethic of the Family* (New York: Peter Lang, 1999). He has constantly pushed me to sharpen my argument, tighten my logic and take into account matters I had passed over. He has been a hard taskmaster and a valued mentor. I would also like to thank my copyeditor, Jennifer Conrad Seidel, who worked through the manuscript in the final stage, making innumerable helpful suggestions and picking up dozens of slips of pen. She has an amazing eye for detail.

[2] See Alister McGrath, *The Genesis of Doctrine* (Oxford: Blackwell, 1990); Stanley J. Grenz, *Revisioning Evangelical Theology: A Fresh Agenda for the Twenty-First Century* (Downers Grove, Ill.: InterVarsity Press, 1993); Stanley J. Grenz and J. R. Franke, *Beyond Foundationalism: Shaping Theology in a Postmodern Context* (Louisville, Ky.: Westminister, 2001); Donald G. Bloesch, *A Theology of Word and Spirit: Authority and Method in Theology* (Downers Grove, Ill.: InterVarsity Press, 1992); Joel B. Green and M. Turner, eds., *Between Two Horizons: Spanning New Testament Studies and Systematic Theology* (Grand Rapids, Mich.: Eerdmans, 2000); and, earlier in the debate, Kevin N. Giles, "Evangelical Systematic Theology: Definition, Problems, Sources," in *In the Fullness of Time*, ed. D. Peterson and J. Pryor (Sydney: Lancer, 1992), pp. 255–76.

[3] I have been actively involved in the gender debate for thirty years. My first journal article was "Jesus and Women," *Interchange* 19 (1976): 131–36, and my first book was *Women and Their Ministry: A Case for Equal Ministries in the Church Today* (Melbourne, Australia: Dove, 1977). See also my book *Created Woman* (Canberra, Australia: Acorn, 1985).

has rejected patriarchalism), and how does one decide the issue when it is possible to quote verses that would support opposing viewpoints? It became apparent in the debate on the Father-Son relationship during the fourth century A.D.—as it has also become apparent during the debate on the woman-man relationship over the last thirty years—that quoting biblical texts and giving one's interpretation of them cannot resolve complex theological disputes. In the fourth century, this approach to "doing" theology had to be abandoned, and I believe this approach should also be abandoned today because it always leads to a "text-jam." The most recent scholarly book on what the Bible teaches on the ministry of women comes to just this conclusion.[4] What we have today is a bitter stalemate. A better way to understand how the Bible contributes to theology and what is involved in "doing" evangelical theology is obviously demanded.

Reading the Bible Theologically
Athanasius was one of the greatest theologians of all time. In reading his writings, I discovered that centuries before he had come to exactly the same conclusion: quoting texts cannot resolve complex theological debates. How these texts should be interpreted and how they relate to other texts in Scripture are the first questions; one must then ask, how does the teaching of these texts address the new question arising out of a new historical and cultural context? Arius accumulated an impressive number of texts to support his doctrine, but Athanasius was convinced Arius was in error. He argued that the texts Arius quoted to prove the subordination of the Son were selectively chosen and interpreted to give credence to what was already believed. Arius's methodology simply showed that given enough time, a clever theologian could find texts and interpretations to prove almost anything. Athanasius argued in reply that to "do" theology, one needed a profound grasp of what he called the "scope" of Scripture—the overall drift of the Bible, its primary focus, its theological center.[5] This gave a "double account" of the Son. It taught, on the one hand, that the Son is eternally one in being and action with the Father and, on the other hand, that the Son gladly and willingly subordinated himself temporally for us and our salvation. On the basis of this theological premise Athana-

---

[4]Craig L. Blomberg and J. R. Beck, *Two Views on Women in Ministry* (Grand Rapids, Mich.: Zondervan, 2001), esp. p. 13.
[5]Athanasius *Orationes contra Arianos* 3.26.28–29 (*NPNF* 4:409). As indicated by the abbreviation *NPNF,* this and other quotes from the writings of Athanasius are taken from *St. Athanasius: Select Works and Letters,* vol. 4 of *The Nicene and Post-Nicene Fathers of the Christian Church,* Series 2, ed. Phillip Schaff and H. Wace (Grand Rapids, Mich.: Eerdmans, 1971). I have made a few cosmetic changes to the English translation to modernize the language.

sius found that everything in Scripture made sense and spoke with one voice.

The "scope" of Scripture for Athanasius was to be seen in the Bible by those who had spiritual eyes to see, but it was made plain by the "tradition." "Our faith is right," he said, because it "starts from the teaching of the apostles and the tradition of the fathers."[6] For him, "tradition" was what those who preceded him believed the Bible taught, and this tradition agreed that the Son of God was eternally equal with the Father in divinity, majesty and authority; only in the incarnation did the Son assume an inferior or subordinate status for our salvation. It was on this given theological premise that Athanasius read the Scriptures. Later, as I read Augustine, I discovered that he too repudiated the quoting of texts in isolation to prove what was already believed. He demanded what he called a "canonical" reading of Scripture in the "doing" of theology.

Athanasius also saw that theological answers to questions asked by those living long after the completion of the New Testament invariably needed to go beyond what Scripture explicitly said. These questions demanded something more than reiterating what was in Scripture. Arius and, later, the "Arians" asked questions about the *being* of the Son, an idea taken from Greek philosophy. Beginning with a Greek understanding of God as pure spirit, they concluded that God could not enter this material world and take on human flesh. The Son must be therefore a subordinate god, of *different being or substance* from the Father. For the biblical writers, what God did and what he was like were the central issues. The *being* of God was something that did not gain their attention. To exclude Arius's presuppositions and teaching, Athanasius found he had to use the nonbiblical word *homoousios* (one in being or substance), which he maintained captured the trajectory set by Scripture. Thus he insisted that to be faithful to the tradition, one needed to confess the Son of God as *one in being* with the Father. Again we see the greatness of Athanasius as a theologian. He saw, more than a thousand years before any one else did, that as God's work in history moved forward and as culture changed, appealing to the Bible alone could not resolve the new questions a new age raised. To answer questions the Bible does not anticipate, the theologian must first determine what is primary and foundational in Scripture on the matter under consideration and then work out the implications of this in dialogue with those theologians of other opinions. I have come to be convinced that a similar approach is demanded today to resolve the debate on the woman-man relationship.[7]

---

[6]Athanasius *Epistula ad Adelphium* 6 (*NPNF* 4:577).

[7]In this introduction I do not intend to document what I discus later in detail. I give footnotes on only those matters not specifically mentioned later or not footnoted subsequently.

In the twentieth century, conservative evangelicals often discounted tradition, claiming that "our" theology comes directly from the Bible. More recently, however, as evangelicals have begun to reflect on the art and science of hermeneutics and on theological method, conservative evangelicals have recognized and affirmed tradition as an important "source" or contributor in theology.[8] Scripture remains the supreme authority for evangelicals, but tradition—understood as how the Scriptures have been interpreted or read by the best of theologians in the past—is accepted as an important, yet secondary, authority. It is not to be ignored, because it offers guidance in the present from the past. It tells us how theologians across the centuries have understood the Bible. Evangelicals on both sides of the contemporary debate on the Trinity are in complete agreement on this matter. Tradition so understood is important. This is demonstrated in that evangelicals on both sides of the Trinity debate claim their reading of the Bible's teaching on the relationship of the Father and the Son is supported by tradition.

Tradition should always be taken seriously and should never be ignored, but sometimes it needs to be corrected or rejected. The sixteenth-century Reformers gave to tradition, as understood above, great respect. They constantly appealed to the creeds and the fathers to substantiate their theology.[9] When the tradition was given by a decree of one of the great councils of the early church or enshrined in one or more of the three catholic creeds, the Reformers assumed this prescribed how the Scriptures were to be read. These traditions defined orthodoxy and directed the interpretative process. Nevertheless, when the Reformers were convinced on the basis of Scripture that the Church of Rome had erred, they did not hesitate to reject the traditional way Scripture had been read, for it supported ideas and practices excluded by clear biblical teaching. Thus, the Reformers insisted that salvation was by grace alone, not earned by works; that ministers of the gospel were not priests who made sacrificial offerings to God in the Eucharist; and that the pope did not speak for God. On these matters and others, the Reformers broke with tradition.

Because the dispute today among evangelicals on the Trinity—like that between Arius and Athanasius—cannot be resolved simply by quoting texts, both

---

[8]See the very fine discussion on tradition in Alister McGrath, *Christian Theology: An Introduction* (Oxford: Blackwell, 1994), pp. 188–91. See also McGrath, *Genesis of Doctrine,* passim; Richard Bauckham, "Tradition in Relation to Scripture and Reason," in *Scripture, Tradition and Reason,* ed. B. Drewery and Richard Bauckham (Edinburgh: T & T Clark, 1988), pp. 117–45; Giles, "Evangelical Systematic Theology," pp. 265–70.

[9]See the important and interesting study by A. N. S. Lane, *John Calvin: Student of the Church Fathers* (Grand Rapids, Mich.: Baker, 2000).

sides, as has been noted already, appeal to tradition to substantiate their understanding of the Father-Son relationship. Thus, to bring resolution to this matter we need to determine who is in fact accurately reflecting historical orthodoxy. Some evangelicals who have been taught that all theology springs immediately from the Bible may be inclined to reply along these lines: "Even if you can show that Athanasius, Augustine, Calvin, the creeds and confessions, and most modern theologians reject the eternal subordination of the Son in being or role, all you have done is outline historical information. We will continue to believe the Father is set over the Son as his authoritative 'head' because the texts we quote clearly prove this." It is possible for evangelicals to take this route, but if they do, they then set themselves outside of the orthodoxy the creeds and the Reformation confessions define and put themselves at odds with most other Christians, past and present. I very much doubt that any evangelical really wants to do this. Most evangelicals want to believe that the evangelical faith is historical orthodoxy. Thus the question remains, on whose side is the tradition?

Tradition in Relation to the Subordination of Women and Slavery
Once the importance of tradition in the debate on the Trinity is highlighted, another fascinating parallel with the man-woman debate comes into focus. Right at the heart of the hierarchical understanding of the man-woman relationship is an appeal to tradition. Those who adopt this position like to call it the "traditional" or "historic" position, and they accuse people such as myself of breaking with tradition, of advocating a "progressive hermeneutic" and of giving a "novel" reading of Scripture.[10] Most egalitarians seem to accept this charge and the self-designation their opponents use—I do not—and this puts them at a disadvantage. Just before beginning this book I wrote a two-part article for *Evangelical Quarterly* in which I maintained that the contemporary arguments for the ongoing subordination of women were in fact "novel," a radical break with tradition.[11] As I drew toward the end of my work on the Trinity, it became clear to me that what I had argued in this essay directly related to

---

[10]This is one of the main themes in the book *Women in the Church: A Fresh Analysis of 1 Timothy 2:9–15*, ed. Andreas J. Köstenberger, Thomas R. Schreiner and H. Scott Baldwin (Grand Rapids, Mich.: Baker, 1995).

[11]I would particularly like to thank Professor I. Howard Marshall, the editor of *Evangelical Quarterly*, for permission to reprint in revised form material from four articles I published in that journal (three are listed here; the fourth is given in the next footnote): "A Critique of the 'Novel' Contemporary Interpretation of 1 Timothy 2:9–15, Given in the Book, *Women in the Church*," parts 1 and 2, *Evangelical Quarterly* 72, no. 2 (2000): 151–67; no. 3 (2000): 195–215; and "Women in the Church: A Rejoinder to Andreas Köstenberger," *Evangelical Quarterly* 73, no. 3 (2001): 225–44.

my work on the woman-man relationship. I thus decided to rework this material, which now makes up part two of this book. Closely allied at all times with the contemporary debate about the woman-man relationship has been the question of what the Bible teaches on slavery, another matter on which I have published.[12] Again, the two sides hold diametrically opposed points of view on what the Bible actually says.

Egalitarians consistently argue that the Bible treats the issues of slavery and the subordination of women in much the same way. The writers of the Bible—as men living in cultures that accepted the institution of slavery and the subordination of women as unquestioned facts of life—depict both social realities as if they are agreeable to God. Neither are ever condemned or specifically questioned in Scripture. Given another cultural context, egalitarian evangelicals argue, slavery and the subordination of women are to be repudiated because, at a primary theological level, the Bible depicts every human as being of equal worth and dignity, never prescribing some social roles to men and others to women.

In contrast, *hierarchicalists* argue that the Bible treats the issues of slavery and the subordination of women very differently. The Bible regulates, but does not legitimate, slavery. It never suggests it is acceptable to God. The subordination of women on the other hand is depicted as prescribed by God. It is the ideal given in the creation stories before sin entered the world.

Who is right? Both sides assert their mutually exclusive alternatives ad infinitum. It is possible that tradition may be the deciding factor in the debate on slavery as well. In part three of this book I will explore this matter further.

What should be noted at this point is how evangelical thinking on these three matters relates to tradition. It is not the same. In regard to the Trinity both sides appeal to tradition to substantiate their position. It is my argument that tradition should be followed but that it does not support in any way the eternal subordination of the Son in being or function. One side has misread the tradition that is enshrined in the Nicene and Athanasian Creeds and the Reformation confessions of faith; the other has read it correctly.

In regard to male-female relations, the hierarchicalists argue that they represent the tradition and that egalitarians have broken with tradition. It is my argument that under the effect of the far-reaching and profound social change popularly called "women's lib," all Christians have abandoned the traditional in-

---

[12]Kevin N. Giles, "The Biblical Argument for Slavery: Can the Bible Mislead? A Case Study in Hermeneutics," *Evangelical Quarterly* 66, no. 1 (1994): 3–18. See also my *Women and Their Ministry,* pp. 97–104, and *Created Woman,* pp. 43–47.

terpretation that God has made women "inferior" to men, more prone to sin and incapable of leadership. One side readily admits this and maintains that their new theology for this changed world captures "the scope" of Scripture which makes primary an equal valuing of women and men that demands equality of consideration. This was previously hidden to theologians who wore the cultural spectacles of their patriarchal social world. The other side denies rejecting the tradition but, as we will show, actually does just this. They argue for the permanent subordination of women *in role,* building on ideas not found in Scripture or the tradition—an unchangeable created order, role theory and the idea that difference implies subordination.

On the matter of slavery, virtually all contemporary evangelicals deny the tradition. They simply ignore it as a general rule. They argue that the Bible regulates but does not legitimate slavery. It never endorses this cruel and inhuman institution. They begin with the altogether modern idea that slavery is an evil. If slavery is evil, they conclude, it cannot be endorsed in the Bible because the Bible cannot legitimate what is evil. The problem is that the tradition gives no support to such an idea. Until the latter half of the eighteenth century, virtually every theologian held that the Bible regulated *and* legitimated slavery, and the strongest advocates of this position were the nineteenth-century learned evangelical theologians of the Old South. It was only when cultural values changed as God's work in history moved forward that human beings for the first time came to see that slavery must be rejected and opposed. In this new social context teaching hitherto passed over in Scripture came to the fore: all people are made in the image of God, all are loved by God, all are to be set free in Christ. As a result, this change in culture led to a change in theology. The tradition was rejected and new ways of interpreting relevant biblical passages emerged.

The very close parallel with the contemporary women's debate cannot be missed. If such a turnaround could happen in the case of slavery, why not also in the case of women? I suggest an honest account of what took place with slavery may well open up the way forward in the debate on whether or not the Bible permanently subordinates women to men. Like slavery, this matter has come onto the theological agenda because God's work in history has made the tradition unacceptable to people of our age who judge the subordination of women to be ethically unjustifiable and in many cases practically unworkable.

The Hermeneutical Issue: Do Changed Historical-Cultural Contexts Demand and Provide New Interpretations of the Bible?
This book is predicated on the view that the Bible can often be read in more

than one way, even on important matters. This comment is uncontroversial because it is undeniable. History gives innumerable examples of learned and devout theologians who have differed from others in their interpretation of the Bible on almost every doctrine or ethical question imaginable. In relation to the doctrine of the Trinity my argument is that the tradition should prescribe the correct reading. This is claimed because this tradition is the fruit of deep and prolonged reflection by the best and most respected theologians across the centuries on what the Bible teaches on the Trinity, and their conclusions are now codified in the creeds and Reformation confessions of faith.

In contrast, I argue in the opposite way in the debate over what the Bible teaches on the status and ministry of women and on the issue of slavery. I hold that the tradition in these instances should be honestly acknowledged and categorically rejected. It reflects a reading of Scripture that was dictated by the world in which the interpreters lived. No other reading was open to them. This tradition is not the product of prolonged theological debate, and it was never endorsed by a universal church council, creed or confession. It is nothing more than the acceptance of what everyone in earlier times—Christian and non-Christian alike—believed on these matters. Only when God's work in history changed cultural values did another reading of Scripture become possible in both cases.

This claim is controversial for evangelicals because it allows that the Bible can be read in different ways in differing historical-cultural contexts. In one historical context an interpretation of Scripture can gain well nigh universal support and in another well nigh universal rejection. This suggests that the historical-cultural context is part of the exegetical outcome. Change the context, and matters closely related to culture in the Bible will be seen differently. Part of culture is, of course, the presumed scientific understanding of the world. Telling examples of changed interpretations of biblical teaching coming in the aftermath of a scientific discovery abound. Once the Bible was read as teaching that the Earth was flat, that the sun revolved around the Earth and that the world was created in six (literal) days about seven thousand years ago. The biblical writers at points reflect these views, and certainly most Christians for centuries with some justification thought this was what the Bible taught. No other interpretative possibility was open to the exegetes and theologians of earlier times. Yet new scientific discoveries have demanded that the old interpretations, with their good textual support, be abandoned. Only in a different cultural context could theologians discover a different reading of Scripture that made sense of the changed understanding of the world, an understanding that God himself had brought to pass.

The Bible's teaching on women and slavery illustrates this hermeneutical rule in regard to social ordering. Theologians living in a world that accepted without question the subordination of women and slavery, in exactly the same way as the biblical writers accepted these things, presumed that biblical teaching on these matters reflected the unchanging mind of God: he endorsed these social structures. Again, I say, no other options for interpreting the Bible were open to them. Then the world changed. For the first time in human history, slavery came to be seen as cruel and unjust; then women's subordination came to be seen as devaluing of women and unjust. In this new historical-cultural world theologians returned to the Scriptures to see what passages indicate that God's ideal was emancipation. In both instances, as I will show, all Christians—more specifically, all evangelicals—found new ways to read the Bible. They rejected the tradition, and rightly so, in the changed world in which they found themselves. The change in culture led to a change in interpretation.

Many conservative evangelicals find this argument very difficult because they have been lead to believe there can only be one correct interpretation of any given text, only one correct reading of the Bible on any particular matter. Modern discussions on hermeneutics, to which evangelicals have made very important contributions, have called this dogma into question.[13] It is now recognized that the human interpreter always reads through the "spectacles" given by his or her theological commitments, culture, scientific understanding of the world and much more. Given texts cannot mean just anything, but more than one interpretation is possible. The human author's intent is one limiting and controlling factor in determining what the text may mean, but with the Bible one must always remember that there are two authors—one human and one divine. God in his sovereign purposes may relativize what one biblical author intended by giving teaching elsewhere in Scripture that offers another perspective on the same matter.

Texts are not self-interpreting. They are only symbols on a page until a human agent gives them meaning. All texts, like all acts of communication, have to be interpreted. The interpreting agent, as has been noted, always reads through the "spectacles" given by the presuppositions she or he holds and takes for granted. There can be no interpretation in which the reader does not bring

---

[13]See in particular Anthony C. Thiselton, *The Two Horizons: New Testament Hermeneutics and Philosophical Description* (Grand Rapids, Mich.: Eerdmans, 1980); Thiselton, *New Horizons in Hermeneutics: The Theory and Practice of Transforming Biblical Reading* (Grand Rapids, Mich.: Zondervan, 1992); Kevin J. Vanhoozer, *Is There Meaning in the Text? The Bible, the Reader and the Morality of Literary Knowledge* (Grand Rapids, Mich.: Zondervan, 1998).

something to the text that becomes part of the interpretation. From this observation the following hermeneutical rule may be deduced: *Context contributes to meaning.* Once this is recognized, one can no longer think of the Bible as a set of timeless, transcultural rulings or as propositions that speak in every age with one voice. The Bible is to be seen rather as a book written in history by human authors, inspired and directed by the Holy Spirit, through which and in which the Holy Spirit speaks afresh time and time again. The Westminster Confession of Faith clearly reflects this pneumatic understanding of Scripture, which growing numbers of evangelicals have come to embrace in recent times.[14] It declares, "The supreme judge by which all controversies of religion are determined . . . can be no other but the Holy Spirit speaking in the scriptures."[15]

The effect of context on interpretation can be illustrated by imagining a town at the base of a high mountain. A traveler visiting the town only sees what is immediately before his eyes—buildings, streets, people. It is impossible for him to get an overall perspective on the town in that setting. But then he begins climbing a path up the mountain, and from every stopping point the town looks different. His changing context changes his perception of the town. The town does not change, but how he sees it changes. It would almost seem that God has purposely made the Bible like this. It is a Spirit-book that can speak for God in different contexts when things of necessity are seen in a different way.

The Key Issues in the Debate Among Evangelicals on the Trinity

Before I conclude this introduction, it may be helpful for me to explain the argument on the Trinity. The doctrine of the Trinity is the most important doctrine of all because it articulates what is most distinctive and fundamental to the Christian understanding of God: that he is triune. It is, however, the most difficult doctrine to comprehend in its developed expression. The first and major part of this book is not a general introduction to the doctrine of the Trinity, but rather a detailed study of one key aspect of the doctrine now dividing evangelicals: that is, the eternal subordination of the Son. In dealing with this issue, I have had to cover the history of the development of trinitarian doctrine and sought to unravel many complex ideas and opposing positions. To help my readers travel this path with me, I will give a brief overview of the development of the doctrine of the Trinity and explanations of the key issues.

---

[14]So Vanhoozer, *Is There Meaning,* pp. 424–28; Bloesch, *Theology of Word and Spirit,* passim; Grenz and Franke, *Beyond Foundationalism,* pp. 57–92.
[15] *Westminster Confession,* 1.10.

The Historical Development of the Orthodox Trinitarian Tradition
As a result of Jesus' ministry, death and resurrection and the subsequent giving
of the Holy Spirit, the first Christians were forced to rethink the doctrine of
God they had inherited from Judaism. They remained faithful to the Jewish
belief that there is one God, not least because Jesus himself affirmed this truth
(Mk 12:29–32); but they had to account also for Jesus and the Holy Spirit, who
they were sure made the one God present. The New Testament writers in complementary ways attempt the first answers to the questions raised by the
advent of Christ and the gift of the Holy Spirit. They agree on the following
points:

☐ There is only one God (1 Cor 8:4; Eph 4:6; Jas 2:19).

☐ This one God is Father, Son and Holy Spirit (Mt 28:19; 2 Cor 13:14).

☐ The Son, in taking human flesh and becoming the man Jesus, humbled himself as a servant and died on the cross (Phil 2:7–8; Jn 14:28; 15:8–9; Heb 5:8).

☐ God the Father raised him from death, exalting him to be Lord of all (Phil
2:9–11; Mt 28:18; Acts 2:36; Col 2:10).

☐ Jesus, the exalted Son of God, is now to be worshiped as God (Mt 28:17; Jn
9:38; 20:28; Heb 1:6; Rev 7:11–14).

☐ The Holy Spirit is God present with his people (Mt 28:19; Acts 5:3–4; 2 Cor
3:17).

These answers were adequate for the questions asked by the first generation
of Christians, but subsequent generations of Christians raised other questions
that these answers did not directly address. Often the answers offered to new
questions, though supported by biblical texts, appeared to contradict other
teaching in Scripture. In this centuries-long debate, the historic doctrine of the
Trinity was slowly and painstakingly developed, with a few key people making
the biggest contributions.

One of the first questions to be asked after the age of the apostles was, how
are the divine three really one? Some early Christians who were concerned
about safeguarding the unity of God argued that the Father, Son and Holy Spirit
were only successive *modes of revelation* of the one God. This answer, known
as *modalism,* was rejected because it undermined the eternal personal existence
of the three divine persons. Subsequent orthodox theologians, including contemporary theologians, seek to avoid modalism in their formulation of the doctrine of the Trinity. They are at pains to stress that each of the divine three is a
personal entity and, *as such,* eternally exists and so is eternally differentiated
from the others.

Early in the early third century, Arius, a presbyter in the Egyptian port city of

Alexandria, raised yet another profound question: is the Son of God really and truly God in human flesh? He answered in the negative. He held a Greek understanding of God as a pure spirit who could have no contact with this material world. For him the Son of God must be a secondary god, *different in being or substance* from the Father. Arius's teaching was a form of what theologians call *ontological subordinationism*. In Greek, the word *ontos* designates the *being,* the essential nature or essence, of something or someone. Arius argued that because the Son is subordinated eternally in his being/essence/nature, he was also subordinated in his work or role to the Father. The Son had to do as he was commanded. At the Council of Nicea in A.D. 325 the assembled bishops rejected Arius's teaching that the Son was different in being or substance from the Father, insisting instead that he was *one in being or substance* (Greek *homoousios*) with the Father. The publication of the Nicene Creed in A.D. 325 did not, however, silence the followers of Arius. They grew in numbers and their "proofs" from Scripture multiplied. One man—almost alone at first, and at great personal cost—stood against them: Athanasius. He saw that if there were a disjunction between the Father and the Son, then the Son could not perfectly reveal the Father for he was not truly God, nor could he make salvation possible because only God himself could save.

Athanasius gave profound answers to a number of fundamental questions on the Christian doctrine of God. His grasp of Scripture and his theological ability have been equaled by few others. I will highlight a few of the more important conclusions he reached.

The difference of the persons is indisputable for Athanasius because Father, Son and Holy Spirit are clearly distinguished in Scripture and they are differentiated by their relations with each other. The Father is eternally the Father *of* the Son; the Son is eternally the Son *of* the Father. For Athanasius this difference does not imply subordination. Repeatedly he says, "The same things are said of the Son which are said of the Father except him being said to be Father."[16] Building on what Scripture says about the Father and the Son's being "one" and about their each abiding in the other (Jn 10:30, 38; 14:10–11; 17:21), Athanasius

---

[16]Athanasius *Orationes contra Arianos* 2.20.54 (*NPNF* 4); 3.23.4; 3.23.5. See also *Contra Arianos* 3.23.5 where Athanasius continues, "What is said of the Father is said of the Son also"; *De Synodis* 3.49 (lines 3-4) where he says, "What is said of the Father is said in Scripture of the Son also, all but his being called the Father"; and *De Synodis* 3.49 (lines 66-67) where he states, "All that you find said of the Father, so much will you find said of the Son, all but his being Father." Cf. also *Illud Omnia* 3, "For what belongs to the Father belongs to the Son. For he that honours the Son honours the Father," and *Illud Omnia* 4, "For what belongs to the Father belongs to the Son."

spoke of the interpenetration, or coinherence, of the persons of the Trinity. Not surprisingly, given his profound emphasis on the unity of the persons, Athanasius rejected the idea that the Son was eternally subordinated either in his being or in his works or functions. For Athanasius the three divine persons are one in being and one in action. *Who they are* and *what they do* cannot separated. Thus, Athanasius never depicts the Father as commanding and the Son obeying.

The unity of being and action among the Father, Son and Spirit is a constant theme in the development of the orthodox doctrine of the Trinity. In humans it is possible to separate who we are (our being) from what we do (how we function). The best of theologians have always argued that this separation cannot be made with God. Who the triune God is (his being) and what the triune God does (his acts) are one.

Athanasius's key allies in the fight against Arianism in the later part of his life were the Cappadocian fathers (three learned theologians who were all born in Cappadocia in Asia Minor). They took as their starting point the divine three, whom they called in Greek *hypostases*. The three *hypostases* are one because they share the one divine being or nature (Greek *ousia*) in perfect fellowship together. The danger in this approach was not modalism but tritheism. In developing Athanasius's thinking, they underlined the distinctions by stressing the differing relations between the divine three, but in their case they grounded these differing relations on their eternal origins: the Father is "unbegotten," the Son "begotten" and the Spirit "proceeding." In contrast to Athanasius, the Cappadocians spoke of the Father as the "sole source or sole origin" (Greek *monarchē*) of the Son and the Spirit. They nevertheless categorically denied that derivation of being implied "a difference in being." The Son and the Spirit shared equally in the one being *(homoousios)* of the Father.

In the contemporary debate among evangelicals on the Trinity, a key issue is how the divine persons are differentiated. Those who think of God the Father (and men) as exercising "headship"—understood as "authority over"—insist that differentiation is indicated only if the subordination of the Son (or women) is upheld. Those who reject this approach argue that the tradition rejects the differentiation of the divine persons on the basis of their being, work or function. The general consensus is that differentiation can only be construed by stressing the personal identity of the divine three (Father, Son and Spirit), by stressing their differing relations (the Father is the Father of the Son, the Son is the Son of the Father, etc.) and by stressing their differing origins (the Father is unbegotten, the Son begotten, the Spirit proceeding). Any other differentiation inevitably opens the door to the errors of tritheism, modalism or subordinationism.

In A.D. 381, at the Council of Constantinople, Arianism was again rejected, the oneness of being of the Father and the Son was reaffirmed, and the divinity of the Holy Spirit was confessed.

Early in the fifth century, in the western part of the Roman Empire, another great theologian, Augustine of Hippo (a city in North Africa), gave his mind to restating the doctrine of the Trinity. In his presentation of this doctrine he begins with the unity of the triune God: he is one substance. Augustine then explains how the divine three are distinct "persons." Because the three persons are one in their inner life, this meant for Augustine that in their external operations, works or functions the three are also one. Particular works, he said, could be appropriated to each person, but they always acted as one. The Father, the Son and Holy Spirit in their external works functioned in perfect unison and harmony.

After Augustine's death, his conception of the Trinity was encapsulated in the so-called Athanasian Creed. This creed stresses the unity of the Trinity and the equality of the persons. It ascribes equal majesty, power and authority to all three divine persons: "In this Trinity none is afore, or after other; none is greater, or less than another; . . . the whole three Persons are . . . co-equal." The Son is only "inferior to the Father as touching his manhood." A more explicit rejection of the *eternal* subordination of the Son in being, function or authority is hard to imagine.

Among the sixteenth-century Reformers, Calvin gave the most thought to the doctrine of the Trinity. He was opposed to subordinationism of every kind known to him, insisting that texts that spoke of the subordination of the Son alluded only to his work as the mediator of our salvation. The Reformation confessions likewise all reject the eternal subordination of the Son.

Unfortunately, from this time on, Protestants and Roman Catholics marginalized the doctrine of the Trinity and often stated it in ways that were contrary to the Nicene and Athanasian Creeds. In the nineteenth and early twentieth centuries, conservative evangelicals were among those with a very weak and sometimes erroneous grasp of the historically developed doctrine of the Trinity.

The Contemporary Scene

In the last thirty years or so, the church has seen a widespread reawakening of interest in the doctrine of the Trinity. Karl Barth initiated this revolution for Protestants and Karl Rahner did the same for Roman Catholics. More has been written in this period on this doctrine than on any other doctrine. Those interested in this movement have returned to the historic sources and developed new insights that complement the best work from the past. In this process, many have found the contribution of Athanasius particularly instructive. The emphasis in this renewal of trinitarian theology has fallen on the unity of being and work among the divine three and on their perichoretic (interpenetrating) community.

Strangely, in the same period that most Roman Catholic and Protestant theologians have been stressing the divine three's unity of being and action, their communality and their mutual submission, conservative evangelicals who want to maintain the traditional pattern of male "headship" have begun speaking of the *eternal* subordination of the Son and the Spirit: just as man is *permanently* the "head" of the woman, so God is *eternally* the "head" of the Son.

Both sides agree that the doctrine of the Trinity should inform human relations. It is a practical doctrine with application to everyday living. The Trinity provides us with a model of relating that should direct our relationships. Those who depict the Trinity as three divine persons bound together in a unity of being and action, mutually indwelling one another and mutually subordinating to the others think that the doctrine of the Trinity makes egalitarian relations and flexibility in roles the ideal. In contrast, those who depict the Trinity as a hierarchy in some form think the ideal is seen in ordered relations where some are forever in the commanding role and others are forever in the subordinate role.

What seems to have happened is that contemporary conservative evangelicals who are opposed to women's liberation in the church and the home have read back into the Trinity their understanding of the subordination of women: God the Father has become the eternal "head" of Christ, and the differences among the divine persons have been redefined in terms of differing roles or functions. Rather than working as one, the divine persons have been set in opposition—with the Father commanding and the Son obeying.

Subordinationism

Those who argue that the Son (like the Holy Spirit) is *eternally* set under the Father are called *subordinationists,* and this point of view is called *subordinationism*. At least seven different arguments for the Son's eternal subordination can be delineated. Later I will outline each of them separately. The most common expression of subordinationism involves the ontological subordination of the Son and the Spirit, but even this idea can take many forms. In nineteenth- and early-twentieth-century American evangelicalism, ontological subordinationism was expressed in the idea that the Son and the Spirit were subordinated in their "subsistence"—that is, in their personal existence as the Son and the Spirit. Some evangelicals today endorse ontological subordinationism in one form or another, but the most popular expression of subordinationism found in contemporary evangelical literature rejects ontological subordinationism, arguing that the Son is only eternally subordinated in role or function. In this view, the Father is thought of as the (authoritative) "head" of the Son. The Father commands, and the Son obeys.

Role or functional subordination is based on the premise that the Son and, likewise, women can be permanently subordinated in function or role without in any way undermining their personal worth or equality. Role subordination, we are told, does not imply inferiority. This is generally true, but once the note of permanency is introduced and competence is excluded, this is not true. If one party is forever excluded from certain responsibilities—no matter what their competency may be—simply on the basis of who they are, then this indicates they lack something that only their superior possesses. In other words, they are inferior in some essential way.

The Immanent and Economic Trinity

Finally, in seeking to help readers understand the contemporary debate on the Trinity, I explain the common modern practice of distinguishing between the immanent Trinity (the eternal triune God as he is in himself that no human can ever fully comprehend) and the economic Trinity (the triune God as he has revealed himself in history). There is, of course, only one Trinity. This distinction between the immanent Trinity and the economic Trinity is simply a reminder that what can be known about God is given in his revelation of himself. There is no independent access to knowledge of God outside of God's interactions with creation, which reached its apex in Jesus Christ. Our Lord himself implied this when he said, "No one knows the Son except the Father, and no one knows the Father except the Son and anyone to whom the Son chooses to reveal him" (Mt 11:27).

Evangelicals who argue that the Son is in some way eternally subordinated to the Father endorse the principle that the economic Trinity reveals all that we may know of the Father-Son relationship, but they limit the historical (or economic) revelation to the incarnation. Thus they note that the Gospels depict the Son as sent by the Father, obedient to the Father and dependent on the Father. This temporal revelation, they conclude, discloses what is eternally true. The Father commands, and the Son obeys. Others who reject the idea that the Son is eternally subordinated to the Father also accept that the economic Trinity reveals all that we may know of the Father-Son relationship, but they do not limit this revelation to the incarnation nor to what the incarnation reveals of the Son alone. For them, the economy of God's self-revelation begins at creation and is consummated only at the end of time. So the revelation of the economic Trinity includes the triune God's work in creation, in salvation history and in the Son's present reign as Lord and "head over all things" (Eph 1:22; Col 2:10). Moreover, they believe the subordination of the Son in the incarnation reveals as much about the Father as it does of the Son. It discloses that the God of the Bible is a God who gladly stoops to save. Voluntary subordination is godlike.

Thus the primary question in this debate is, can any subordination in being or function be ascribed to the Son (and the Spirit) in the eternal or immanent Trinity? All agree that in the incarnation Christ temporally and voluntarily subordinated himself to the Father. Some evangelicals believe the subordination seen in the incarnation discloses the eternal relationship between the Father and the Son; other evangelicals and, I will argue, historical orthodoxy reject this deduction.

In what follows, this question is to be kept in mind at all times. This is the central issue in this debate.

PART 1

THE TRINITY TRADITION

Affirmed by All but Actually Rejected by Some

1

CONSERVATIVE EVANGELICALS HEAD OFF ON THEIR OWN

In the later part of the twentieth century and in the beginning of the twenty-first, the doctrine of the Trinity has captured the attention of theologians more than any other doctrine. Not since the theologically stormy days of the fourth century has there been so much discussion on this topic. Books on the Trinity by Protestant, Catholic and Eastern Orthodox theologians continue to be published. The Trinity is no longer thought of as an obtuse, secondary and impractical dogma. Rather it is recognized today as nothing less than a summary of the Christian understanding of God given in revelation. The Trinity is the foundation on which all other doctrines are built. It is of immense theological and practical significance.

In contemporary discussions of the doctrine of the Trinity, it is agreed that the God revealed in Scripture is by nature trinitarian. In this Trinity the three "persons" are reciprocally related: none is before or after another, none is less or greater than another, none is subordinated in being or function to another. The members exist as three equal yet differentiated "persons" in the most intimate communion.[1] David Cunningham, in his 1998 book, *These Three Are One:*

---

[1] Support for these claims will be presented in more detail later, when the contribution of modern-day theologians is discussed.

The Practice of Trinitarian Theology,[2] speaks of "a radical, relational, co-equality" in modern trinitarian thinking. Similarly, Ted Peters describes contemporary thinking about the Christian God as "antisubordinationist trinitarianism" in his 1993 book, *God as Trinity: Relationality and Temporality in Divine Life.*[3] The respected conservative evangelical systematic theologian Millard Erickson is of the same opinion. In his 1995 book, *God in Three Persons: A Contemporary Interpretation of the Trinity,*[4] Erickson sums up the modern understanding of the Trinity, which he endorses, in this manner:

> The Trinity is a communion of three persons, three centers of consciousness, who exist and always have existed in union with one another and in dependence on one another. . . . Each is essential to the life of the others, and to the life of the Trinity. They are bound to one another in love, *agape* love, which therefore unites them in the closest and most intimate of relationships. This unselfish, *agape* love makes each more concerned for the other than for himself. There is therefore a mutual submission of each to each of the others and a mutual glorifying of one another. There is complete equality of the three.[5]

After surveying past and present formulations of the doctrine of the Trinity, Wayne House, a leading conservative evangelical thinker and a contributor to the anthology *Recovering Biblical Manhood and Womanhood: A Response to Evangelical Feminism,*[6] also rejects all forms of subordinationism or hierarchical ordering in the Trinity. He concludes that orthodox trinitarianism "unhesitatingly sets forth Father, Son and Holy Spirit as co-equal and co-eternal in the Godhead with regard to both the divine essence and function."[7]

These theologians agree that the idea of eternal subordination of any of the persons to another in being or function should be repudiated. The Father, the Son and the Spirit are not ordered in a descending "chain of being" or "chain of command."

---

[2]David Cunningham, *These Three Are One: The Practice of Trinitarian Theology* (Oxford: Blackwell, 1998), p. 113.

[3]Ted Peters, *God as Trinity: Relationality and Temporality in Divine Life* (Louisville, Ky.: Westminster Press, 1993).

[4]Millard Erickson, *God in Three Persons: A Contemporary Interpretation of the Trinity* (Grand Rapids, Mich.: Baker, 1995).

[5]Ibid., p. 331.

[6]John Piper and Wayne Grudem, eds., *Recovering Biblical Manhood and Womanhood: A Response to Evangelical Feminism* (Wheaton, Ill.: Crossway, 1991); for Wayne House's contribution, see pp. 358–63.

[7]Wayne House, *Charts of Christian Theology and Doctrine* (Grand Rapids, Mich.: Zondervan, 1992), p. 47.

Paradoxically, in this same period of time many conservative evangelicals have been moving in the opposite direction in their understanding of the Trinity. The contemporary conservative evangelical case for the permanent subordination of women frequently asserts that the Son is *eternally* subordinated to the Father.[8] This "truth" is taken to be both a rationale for women's permanent subordination to men (i.e., the Trinity reflects the God-given ideal for male-female relationships) and an example of how equality in being/essence/nature/dignity and permanent subordination can both be endorsed without contradiction. Women, we are told, are equal with men in their essential being and dignity, yet they are subordinated to men in the home and the church.

---

[8]So George Knight, *The Role Relationship of Men and Women* (Grand Rapids, Mich.: Baker, 1977), pp. 33, 55-56; Susan Foh, *Women and the Word of God* (Phillipsburg, N.J.: Presbyterian & Reformed, 1980), pp. 41, 164–81; James Hurley, *Man and Woman in Biblical Perspective* (Grand Rapids, Mich.: Zondervan, 1981), p. 167; W. Neuer, *Man and Woman in Christian Perspective*, trans. Gordon J. Wenham (London: Hodder & Stoughton, 1990), pp. 111, 128; M. Kasslan, *Women, Creation and the Fall* (Wheaton, Ill.: Crossway, 1990), pp. 32–33; Piper and Grudem, *Recovering Biblical Manhood and Womanhood*, pp. 103–4, 128–30, 394–96, 457, 462; M. Harper, *Equal and Different: Male and Female in Church and Family* (London: Hodder & Stoughton, 1994), pp. 6, 14, 60, 153–63, 203–4; Wayne Grudem, *Systematic Theology: An Introduction to Biblical Doctrine* (Grand Rapids, Mich.: Zondervan, 1994), pp. 454–70; Andreas J. Köstenberger, Thomas R. Schreiner and H. Scott. Baldwin, eds., *Women in the Church: A Fresh Analysis of 1 Timothy 2:9–15* (Grand Rapids, Mich.: Baker, 1995), pp. 135–36; D. B. Knox, *The Ministry of Women: Report to General Synod of the Church of England in Australia* (Sydney: Anglican Information Office, 1977), pp. 29–33; D. B. Knox, *The Everlasting God* (Harfordshire, U.K.: Evangelical Press, 1982), pp. 69–72; Robert Doyle, "Sexuality, Personhood and the Image of God," in *Personhood, Sexuality and Christian Ministry*, ed. B. Webb (Sydney: Lancer, 1987), pp. 43–56; Robert Letham, "The Man-Woman Debate: Theological Comment," *Westminister Theological Journal* 52 (1990): 65–78; John V. Dahms, "The Subordination of the Son," *Journal of the Evangelical Theological Society* 37, no. 3 (1994): 351–64; E. L. Johnson, "Playing Games and Living Metaphors: The Incarnation and the End of Gender," *Journal of the Evangelical Theological Society* 40, no. 2 (1997): 271–85; Stephen D. Kovach and Peter R. Schemm, "A Defense of the Doctrine of the Eternal Subordination of the Son," *Journal of the Evangelical Theological Society* 42, no. 3 (1999): 461–76; Sydney Anglican Diocesan Doctrine Commission, "The Doctrine of Trinity and Its Bearing on the Relationship of Men and Women," 1999 report <www.anglicanmediasydney.asn.au/doc/trinity.html> (hereafter referred to as the Sydney Doctrine Report); Stephen D. Kovach, "Evangelicals Revamp the Doctrine of the Trinity," *The Council on Biblical Manhood and Womanhood News* 2 (1996): 1–7; D. W. Bercot, ed., *A Dictionary of Early Christian Beliefs* (Peabody, Mass.: Hendrickson, 1998), pp. 113–14; William D. Mounce, *Word Biblical Commentary: The Pastoral Epistles* (Nashville: Thomas Nelson, 2000), p. 148; Paul Barnett, *1 Corinthians* (Ross-shire, U.K.: Christian Focus, 2000), p. 200; Thomas R. Schreiner, "Women in Ministry," in *Two Views on Women in Ministry*, ed. Craig L. Blomberg and J. R. Beck (Grand Rapids, Mich.: Zondervan, 2001), pp. 215 n. 66, 343. Craig Keener ("Is Subordination Within the Trinity Really Heresy? A Study of John 5:18," *Trinity Journal*, n.s., 20 [1999]: 39–51) also endorses the eternal subordination of the Son but argues that it does not justify the permanent subordination of women.

Two differing approaches can be seen in the recent conservative evangelical literature advocating the *eternal* subordination of the Son: one is most fully enunciated in Wayne Grudem's 1994 *Systematic Theology: An Introduction to Biblical Doctrine;* the other in "The Doctrine of Trinity and Its Bearing on the Relationship of Men and Women," a report of the Sydney Anglican Diocesan Doctrine Commission in 1999. This report reflects the theological commitments of the largest seminary in Australia, Sydney's Moore Theological College, which is known for its conservative evangelical and Reformed stance and its opposition to the ordination of women.[9] Grudem insists that "the Son is eternally subordinated to the Father in role or function," not in being.[10] In contrast, the Sydney Doctrine Report argues that speaking of the functional subordination of the Son is only "true in so far as it goes."[11] The Son's functional subordination to the Father reflects "the essence of the *eternal* relationship between them"[12]— *"differences in being."*[13] The subordination of the Son and the Spirit "belongs to the very Persons themselves in *their eternal nature.*"[14] The Father is eternally "the head" of the Son: "The Son's obedience to the Father arises from the *very nature of his being* as Son."[15] His obedience is

---

[9]This commission was chaired by Bishop Paul Barnett, a member of Moore College Council and a trustee of the college, and was dominated by Moore College staff and lecturers. On this select committee were the then-principal of Moore College, Peter Jensen; the vice principal, Peter O'Brien; senior lecturer in systematics, Robert Doyle; visiting lecturers Robert Forsyth and John Woodhouse; and the former vice principal and former archbishop of Sydney, Donald Robinson. Behind this subordinationist teaching lies the very influential figure of the former long-term principal of Moore College, Dr. Broughton Knox. When I studied under Dr. Knox in the mid 1960s, he was opposed to subordinationism. In his lectures on the Trinity he made Calvin and Warfield both compulsory reading because of their total rejection of subordinationism. (I will outline the views of Calvin and Warfield in due course.) He was critical of Hodge and T. C. Hammond. Later, in the 1970s, as Dr. Knox increasingly gave theological leadership to those vehemently opposing the ordination of women, he became a subordinationist favoring Hodge's views. From then on the "headship" of God the Father and the "headship" of men became a characteristic feature of his theology. On his views see par. 26, 33 and 35 of the Sydney Doctrine Report and the quotations that I have taken from his writings, which appear later in this discussion.

[10]Grudem, *Systematic Theology,* p. 245 n. 27.

[11]Sydney Doctrine Report, par. 32. (See the full citation above in n. 8.) Other less-detailed examples of this approach from the North American scene will be outlined later. I thank Bishop Paul Barnett, the chairman of the Sydney Anglican Diocesan Doctrine Commission, for gaining permission from the committee for me to republish the report herein as appendix B. The report was published later in *The Sydney Diocesan Year Book, 2000* (Sydney: Diocesan Registry, St. Andrews House, 2000), pp. 538–50.

[12]Ibid., par. 32. I have added emphasis to key terms and phrases by putting them in italics.

[13]Ibid., par. 25. See also par. 18, 21, 26, 32.

[14]Ibid., par. 33. See also par. 17, 18, 21, 22, 32.

[15]Ibid., par. 18.

neither temporal nor voluntary.[16] In other words, the Son's functional subordination to the Father is grounded in his ontological subordination to the Father.

In seeking to make a response to my fellow evangelicals who subordinate the Son to the Father, I do not appeal directly to particular scriptural passages to establish who is right or wrong. I concede immediately that the New Testament *can* be read to teach that the Son is *eternally* subordinated to the Father. I seek rather to prove that orthodoxy rejects this way of reading the Scriptures. I will show that the tradition reflecting the conclusions of theologians such as Athanasius, the Cappadocian fathers, Augustine and Calvin, the formulations of the creeds and Reformation confessions, and the thought of most mainline Protestant and Catholic theologians today opposes the idea that the Son of God is eternally subordinated to the Father in being or function. If some evangelicals want to hold that the Son is eternally subordinated to the Father, I do not dispute that texts can be found to "prove" this opinion. What I dispute is their claim to represent historic orthodoxy, the tradition handed down to the church of our day.

Establishing *what* is the historic orthodox doctrine of the Trinity is of tremendous importance. The Christian doctrine of God is foundational to all Christian belief and practice. No other doctrine is so important. If we do not get this doctrine right, all of our doctrinal formulations will be vitiated.

The study of *how* this doctrine was established is also of great importance. The debate about the Trinity provides us with the classic example of how the right way to read the Bible was established even when it is possible to read it in more than one way. On this matter, as with others, Scripture appears to contain seemingly conflicting statements. Those on one side of this doctrinal dispute point to texts that subordinate the Son to the Father, and those on the other point to texts that speak of the oneness or equality of the Father and the Son. The quest for the orthodox doctrine of the Trinity is in part the story of how the best theologians across the centuries came to a common mind as to how the Scriptures should be read to inform and determine this doctrine. Interestingly, no other debate on what the Bible teaches stands as close to the present debate on the status and ministry of women now dividing evangelicals. Again, one side points to texts that subordinate women to men, and the other side points to texts that speak of their equality. Such proof-texting has led to an impasse. This study, I believe, provides some pointers that may well help us to agree on how the Scriptures should be read *in our culture* to inform and determine the Christian doctrine of the sexes.

---

[16]Ibid., par. 18, 32, 33.

Subordinationism

Conservative evangelicals who argue for the *eternal* subordination of the Son
in function or being insist that their theology of the Trinity is entirely orthodox. They reject the claim that they have fallen into the heresy of subordinationism. Grudem is particularly offended by R. C. and C. C. Kroeger's claim[17]
that subordinationism refers to the error of assigning an "inferiority of being,
status, or role to the Son or the Holy Spirit within the Trinity."[18] Grudem
replies that when they add the words *or role* to their definition, they condemn all orthodox Christology from the Council of Nicea onward, which has
always held that "the Son is eternally subordinate to the Father in role or
function."[19] Similarly, the authors of the Sydney Doctrine Report claim that
there is an orthodox subordinationism that affirms both the full divinity of the
Father and the Son and the subordination of the Son "from the very nature"
of his being as Son.[20] This, we are told, is supported by "Calvin and the Calvinists (Edwards, Berkhof, Hodge, Dabney, Packer, Knox)"[21] and the Nicene

---

[17]See R. C. and C. C. Kroeger, "Subordinationism," in *Evangelical Dictionary of Theology*, ed.
W. Elwell (Grand Rapids, Mich.: Baker, 1984), p. 1058.

[18]Piper and Grudem, *Recovering Biblical Manhood and Womanhood*, p. 539 n. 63; Grudem, *Systematic Theology*, p. 251 n. 35. Kovach and Schemm ("Defense," p. 462) are equally offended.

[19]Grudem, *Systematic Theology*, p. 245 n. 27, pp. 245, 251–52. For a similar claim see also Piper
and Grudem, *Recovering Recovering Biblical Manhood and Womanhood*, pp. 128, 457; and
Kovach and Schemm, "Defense," passim. The Kroegers are in fact totally correct, as this book
will show. It should also be noted that long before the contemporary debate about the ordination of women arose, *The Dictionary of Religion and Ethics* (ed. S. Matthews and G. Smith [Lon-
don: Waverley, 1921], p. 420) concluded that "subordinationism" is the error of setting the Son or
the Holy Spirit under the Father in "function or in essence" in the eternal or immanent Trinity.

[20]Sydney Doctrine Report, par. 18. M. E. Bauman ("Milton, Subordinationism and the Two-
Stage Logos," *Westminster Theological Journal* 48 [1986]: 177–82) also distinguishes between
heretical and orthodox forms of subordinationism. It is true, as I will show, that there are
many forms of subordinationism. This is clearly recognized by H. D. Major in "Subordinationism," in *Encyclopaedia of Religion and Ethics*, ed. J. Hastings (Edinburgh: T & T Clark,
1928), 11:910. See also Herman Bavinck, *The Doctrine of God*, trans. William Hendriksen
(Grand Rapids, Mich.: Baker, 1951), pp. 288–89; he distinguishes and discusses different
forms of subordinationism. I agree with Bavinck that all expressions of subordinationism
which entail the eternal subordination of the Son or the Spirit are to be rejected.

[21]Sydney Doctrine Report, par. 26; see also par. 14, 15. This assertion is not endorsed. Hodge,
as we will see, was definitely a subordinationist, but Calvin certainly was not. I asked Dr.
Robert Doyle of Moore College for references to support this claim, and he graciously sent
me eleven pages of quotes from twenty-eight theologians who supposedly endorse the *eternal* subordination of the Son. Some of those quoted are in fact opposed to this view (Wolfhart Pannenberg, Millard Erickson, G. L. Prestige, Alister McGrath); others, it seems to me,
only endorse temporal subordination (Donald Bloesch, Martin Lloyd-Jones); and yet others
simply reflect inadequate nineteenth- and early-twentieth-century ways of differentiating the
persons by order or derivation (Jonathan Edwards, Louis Berkhof, Otto Weber, Robert Louis
Dabney, E. A. Litton, John Beardslee, H. C. G. Moule, N. Jones, W. H. G. Thomas). None of

and Athanasian Creeds.[22] This is to be distinguished, the authors claim, from unorthodox "Subordinationism" (to be spelled with a capital *S*) represented by the Arians, "who over-emphasised the subordinationist elements of the NT presentation."[23] Stephen Kovach and Peter Schemm are also adamant on this point: "It cannot be legitimately denied that the eternal subordination of the Son is an orthodox doctrine believed from the history of the early church to the present day."[24] In support they quote the Nicene Creed, Athanasius, Gregory of Nazianzus, Augustine and Calvin, among others. They conclude their essay ("A Defense of the Doctrine of the Eternal Subordination of the Son") by saying, "Since the historical position of Christian orthodoxy is to accept the doctrine of the eternal subordination of the Son, it is not surprising that most evangelical systematic theologians in the twentieth century have adopted this position as reflecting both Scripture and church history."[25]

In reply to the contemporary conservative evangelicals who insist that the Son is *eternally* subordinated to the Father in *function* or *being,* this present study puts forth the case that those who take this position have in fact departed from orthodoxy at the most fundamental level, despite their pleas to the contrary: they deny—sometimes implicitly, sometimes explicitly—what is affirmed in the Nicene and Athanasian Creeds and in the Reformation confessions of faith; their teaching on the Trinity is in opposition to what the greatest theologians in Christian history, including Athanasius, Augustine and Calvin, have taught; their views are at odds with what most Catholic and Protestant theolo-

---

this last group of theologians develops a case, as far as I can see, for the eternal subordination of the Son, and none of them mentions "eternal role subordination." On Jonathan Edwards see Richard M. Weber, "The Trinitarian Theology of Jonathan Edwards: An Investigation of Charges Against Its Orthodoxy," *Journal of the Evangelical Theological Society* 44, no. 2 (2001): 297-318. We do not dispute others (Charles Hodge, Broughton Knox, Wayne Grudem and possibly J. I. Packer). Karl Barth, whose views will be discussed later, is also listed. So too is Gordon Fee. The authors of the Sydney Doctrine Report point out that in his exegesis of 1 Cor 8:6, Fee speaks of "the functional subordination of the Son" (*The First Epistle to the Corinthians* [Grand Rapids, Mich.: Eerdmans, 1987], p. 374). This observation is irrelevant. "Functional subordination" that is freely chosen and temporal is not problematic. Fee is not a subordinationist. This is seen in his invitation to participate in and contribute an essay on Paul's teaching on the Trinity to the high-level, ecumenical conference now published as *The Trinity: An Interdisciplinary Symposium on the Trinity,* ed. S. T. Davis, D. Kendal and G. O'Collins (Oxford: Oxford University Press, 1999). In reply to such lists, it must be said that the support of one or of one-hundred one people does not make something true. Good theology is not formulated by counting heads.

[22]Sydney Doctrine Report, par. 25.
[23]Ibid., par. 22.
[24]Kovach and Schemm, "Defense," p. 464.
[25]Ibid., p. 473.

gians today believe about the Trinity; and their interpretation of the Bible is contrary to how the Scriptures have been historically understood by most Christians. For these reasons, I reach the conclusion that they are to be judged as having fallen into theological error in regard to the most important Christian doctrine—the doctrine of God. They are guilty of subordinationism, understood as the error of reading back into the eternal Trinity the temporal and voluntary subordination of the Son seen in the incarnation. Their concern for upholding the permanent subordination of women, which they believe the Bible teaches, has led them to thinking that the Son is eternally subordinated to the Father, something the Bible definitely does not teach. The Son is the co-Creator (Jn 1:3; Col 1:16; Heb 1:2) from all eternity, and after Easter he is confessed not as the obedient servant of the Father but as the Lord who reigns as "the head over all things" (Eph 1:22; Col 2:10).

The Economic and Immanent Trinity

There is, and can only be, one Trinity. Nevertheless, since the eighteenth century[26] theologians have distinguished between the *economic,*[27] or revelational, Trinity and the ontological, *immanent,* or essential, Trinity. The former refers to the Trinity as revealed in God's unfolding work of creation and redemption in history; the latter refers to the essential being of the triune God, which no human could ever completely comprehend. Thus the term *the eternal Trinity* is simply another way of speaking of the immanent Trinity. This distinction between the immanent Trinity and the economic Trinity allows that there is more to God than what is revealed to us but that what is revealed is true and accurate. God is not other than he is in revelation. God is eternally triune and cannot be otherwise. He is not triune simply in the economy of creation and redemption.[28]

Most theologians today agree that all we know about the Trinity is given in God's unfolding (i.e., economic) self-revelation of himself in history. In the economic Trinity we have an accurate, though not exhaustive, revelation of the immanent Trinity. Athanasius, Calvin and Barth are particularly emphatic on this point. They insist that the doctrine of the Trinity is to be constructed solely on the basis of what is given in revelation, not on philosophical speculation.

---

[26]Wolfhart Pannenberg, *Systematic Theology* (Grand Rapids, Mich.: Eerdmans, 1991), 1:291 n. 111.

[27]On the origins and use of the term *economic,* see Catherine LaCugna, *God for Us: The Trinity and the Christian Life* (San Francisco: HarperSanFrancisco, 1991), pp. 24–30.

[28]Robert Jenson, in *Christian Dogmatics,* ed. Carl Braaten and Robert Jenson (Philadelphia: Fortress, 1984), p. 154.

The erudite Roman Catholic theologian Karl Rahner crystallized this epistemological principle in what is now known as "Rahner's rule": "The economic Trinity is the immanent Trinity and the immanent Trinity is the economic Trinity."[29] What Rahner wants to underline in this pithy maxim is that there is not a hidden God who is somehow different from the God disclosed in the historical revelation culminating in the incarnation, cross and resurrection. In Jesus Christ, "God's self-communication is truly a *self*-communication."[30] The Son is "the economic (historical) self-communication of the Father."[31] In his willing self-emptying of himself *for our salvation,* the Son reveals God*self.* The Christian God of revelation is the Almighty who gladly humbles himself as a "consequence of self-communication."[32]

For Rahner the subordination of the Son seen in the incarnation does not differentiate the Father from the Son. It does just the opposite. It reveals that the Father, like the Son, is willing to stoop to save. The incarnation tells us that subordination is godlike. Rahner consistently and unequivocally emphasizes the full equality of Father, Son and Holy Spirit. Following the Nicene Creed he insists that the three are "one in being." Only their "relations" differentiate the divine three. This human term, *relation,* he says, is used as a "negative and defensive" way of maintaining "how two things, which are identical with a third, are not identical with each other."[33] As far as he is concerned there can be no disjunction between the economic Trinity and the immanent Trinity nor between the Father, the Son and the Holy Spirit. In the Son we see the Father and anticipate the Holy Spirit. For Rahner, the Son reveals the truth of the whole Trinity, not just the truth concerning the Son.

Most conservative evangelicals who argue for the eternal subordination of the Son seem to have heard of Rahner's rule, but their understanding of what it teaches seems to be as mistaken as their understanding of historical theology. Robert Letham, John V. Dahms and the Moore College theologians think Rahner's rule logically implies the eternal subordination of the Son.[34] They reason

---

[29]Karl Rahner, *The Trinity,* trans. J. Donceel (New York: Herder & Herder, 1970), pp. 22, 34. For an excellent, concise summary of Rahner's views and a balanced critique of Rahner's rule, see J. Thompson, *Modern Trinitarian Perspectives* (Oxford: Oxford University Press, 1994), pp. 25–31; W. Kasper, *The God of Jesus Christ* (London: SCM Press, 1983), pp. 73–277; and Erickson, *God in Three Persons,* pp. 243–49, 291–95, 306–8.

[30]Rahner, *Trinity,* p. 35.

[31]Ibid., p. 63.

[32]Ibid., p. 101.

[33]Ibid., p. 69.

[34]Letham, "Man-Woman Debate," p. 68; Dahms, "Subordination," p. 364; Sydney Doctrine Report, par. 21.

that since the Son is subordinated to the Father in the economy of salvation, he must be subordinated eternally. That the Son's subordination in the incarnation is temporal and revelatory of what is true of all three divine persons of the Trinity is not recognized. Grudem in fact concludes that Rahner's rule teaches that in the Trinity there is "ontological equality but economic subordination"—exactly the opposite of what Rahner is arguing![35]

Kovach and Schemm audaciously claim that Grudem's conclusion "captures the foundational notion" behind the contemporary understanding of the Trinity[36] and that it lays "the groundwork for a trinitarian tension between ontological equality and economic subordination."[37] In the first claim, to put it bluntly, they are "dead wrong," and in the second, along with Grudem, they undermine the veracity of biblical revelation. If the biblical account of the revelation through the Son is in contrast with what is eternally true about the whole triune God, then the scriptural revelation cannot be trusted to accurately reveal the full truth about the whole triune God. This is tantamount to denying that the Son shows us the Father.

In answer to these misreadings of Rahner's rule, two things must be said. First, the incarnation on its own does not exhaust the revelation of the economic Trinity. The incarnation is only one scene in the unfolding, God-directed drama of creation, redemption and consummation. In other scenes the Son is revealed as preexistent God, the co-Creator, the Redeemer, the Judge and the Lord who is "the head over all things" (Eph 1:22; Col 2:10). In writing to the Philippians, Paul explains how the parts in this drama make a coherent story. As the preexistent Son, Christ had equality with the Father. Then he willingly "emptied himself, taking the form of a slave," after which he was exalted to the highest place to reign as Lord (see Phil 2:5–11). Thus, after Easter salvation is found in confessing Jesus as Lord (Rom 10:9), not in confessing him as the obedient subordinate servant under the eternal headship of the Father.

Second, differentiating the Father and the Son on the basis that the Son is subordinated in the incarnation is mistaken. Rahner's rule properly understood excludes this very idea. It is true that the incarnation clearly distinguishes the Father and the Son. It is the Son who takes human flesh, assumes the form of a slave and dies on the cross for our salvation, not the Father. However, in the work of salvation as in all divine activity, the persons of the Trinity are not to be separated or divided. The Father, the Son and the Holy Spirit are equally in-

---

[35]Grudem, *Systematic Theology,* p. 251.
[36]Kovach and Schemm, "Defense," p. 467.
[37]Ibid., p. 468.

volved in the work of salvation. In assuming a subordinate status and suffering on the cross, Jesus reveals what he and the Father with the Holy Spirit are willing to do together for the salvation of men and women. Rather than differentiating the Father and the Son, the incarnation indicates their unity. In assuming the form of a servant and suffering for our salvation, the Son reveals something essential about God*self.* It was Arius's error to think that the incarnation clearly differentiated the Father from the Son. For him the Son's servant role in the incarnation and his suffering proved that he was eternally subordinated in being and function to the Father. Athanasius and the authors of the Nicene Creed came to the opposite conclusion.

In suggesting that God's work in history can be likened to a God-directed drama that needs to be apostolically interpreted to gain the correct understanding of individual scenes, I have implied that what is at issue in the final analysis of this whole debate is, how should the text that tells the story—the Bible—be read? Both sides agree that the New Testament speaks of the subordination of the incarnate Son during his historic ministry. One interpretative tradition, beginning with the second-century "Apologists," argues that this discloses the *eternal* subordinate relationship of the Son to the Father. The Father is always set over the Son. The other interpretative tradition (crystallized in the Nicene and Athanasian Creeds) rejects this conclusion. It insists that the subordination of the Son seen in the incarnation is *voluntary* and *temporal.* Rather than indicating the eternal subordination of the Son to the Father, it speaks of their unity. The Father and the Son are one in being and act, and their love is so profound that no cost is too great for our salvation. The God of the Bible is a God who stoops to save. It is godlike to gladly subordinate oneself for the good of another.

2

THE HISTORICAL
DEVELOPMENT OF THE
ORTHODOX TRINITARIAN
TRADITION

T he doctrine of the Trinity has been the foremost concern of theologians in two periods of the church's history: the fourth century and the latter part of the twentieth century. In this chapter I will outline the conclusions reached by some of the most important theologians up to the time of the sixteenth-century Reformation, concentrating on those of most interests to evangelicals. I start with Athanasius, who developed a doctrine of the Trinity with such breadth and depth that contemporary theologians still turn to him for informative and suggestive insights for their work. In the next chapter I will discuss earlier attempts at constructing a doctrine of the Trinity that proved to be inadequate.

The ongoing historical quest to develop the doctrine of the Trinity has centered on two issues that are dynamically intertwined: first, how Christians may confess one God while affirming the eternal divinity and distinctions of Father, Son and Holy Spirit; and second, how to make sense of the diverse comments in Scripture that seem to teach, at some points, the full divinity and eternal equality of the Son with the Father and, at other points, the Son's subordinate status. The first of these issues we may call the *conceptual understanding* of the doctrine of the Trinity; the second we may call the *hermeneutical challenge*. The hermeneutical challenge involves finding a way of making sense of what is in Scripture so that it may both inform and confirm the developing conceptualization of the doctrine of the Trinity. These two matters moved forward in tandem in the early church, as they still do today.

In this conceptual and hermeneutical struggle, which has challenged the best of theologians, how the Bible, tradition and reason contribute in the building of this doctrine is instructive.[1] First, it was realized that quoting texts could not resolve anything. How the Scriptures were to be properly read, given that there were competing alternatives, had to be decided. Then it had to be agreed that theology could extrapolate from what is in Scripture, making objective advances on what is actually said in Scripture. In the process, tradition also played an important part. Theologians built on the work of their predecessors, and in the Nicene and Athanasian Creeds and the Reformation confessions these objective advances in the theology of the doctrine were codified. Reason also contributed. Every doctrine is a human construct; it is an ordering and interpretation of the data under consideration. Modern discussions on the nature of doctrine often suggest that a theological position is much like a scientific paradigm or model. Theological positions are creations of the human mind that seek to make sense of all the relevant information to answer a particular question asked at a particular time. A paradigm or model is always more than the sum of its parts. Human minds enlightened by the Holy Spirit actually contribute to theological outcomes. A century ago the conservative Reformed scholar B. B. Warfield clearly saw this. He maintained that "the mind brings to every science something which, though included in the facts, is not derived from the facts considered in themselves alone as isolated facts."[2]

At this present time, when evangelicals are thinking about theological method and the nature of theology, how the doctrine of the Trinity developed is of great interest. It is a reminder that theology (or doctrine, as it is often called) is far more than a reiteration of what is in the Bible. Thus as we study the development of the orthodox doctrine of the Trinity, we should keep in mind how Scripture, tradition and reason contributed, although this is not a matter we focus on in what follows.

Athanasius

In the development of the doctrine of the Trinity, Athanasius stands in a cate-

---

[1]On the objective development of doctrine in history, see the important study by Peter Toon, *The Development of Doctrine in the Church* (Grand Rapids, Mich.: Eerdmans, 1979).

[2]B. B. Warfield, "The Idea of Systematic Theology," in *The Necessity of Systematic Theology,* ed. J. J. Davis (Grand Rapids, Mich.: Baker, 1978), p. 131.

gory of his own. Thomas F. Torrance holds that Athanasius's contribution is of more importance than that of any other theologian.[3] In Athanasius's debate with the Arians, the question of how the Scriptures were to be interpreted was pivotal. Arius and his followers began with the premise that the Son could not share the same *being* as the Father. This meant the Trinity was understood as an ontologically ordered hierarchy. The Father, the "unoriginate," was first; the Son second, standing below the Father; and the Holy Spirit third, below the Father and the Son. They reasoned this way because they began with a Greek understanding of God, which excluded the possibility of God's having any direct communion or contact with creation. On this basis Jesus could not be *incarnate God* in the full sense of this term. He could only be thought of as a creature. Consequently, they searched the Scriptures to substantiate these presuppositions and conclusions. They pointed to texts that could be interpreted as teaching that the Son was created in time, and they noted the many passages that spoke of his human weaknesses, suffering and obedience to his Father. They then read back into the eternal Trinity these features of the Son's historic incarnate ministry. Athanasius, however, rejected their reading of the Scriptures as selective, "devious" and "irreligious."[4] Most of his *Orations Against the Arians (Orationes contra Arianos)* address the exposition of Scripture. He seeks to refute the Arians by appealing to the Bible. To grasp the true meaning of Scripture, he argues, the whole

---

[3]This is a constant theme in Thomas F. Torrance's important books, *The Trinitarian Faith* (Edinburgh: T & T Clark, 1988) and *The Christian Doctrine of God: One Being, Three Persons* (Edinburgh: T & T Clark, 1996). See also his essays "The Doctrine of the Holy Trinity According to Athanasius," in *Trinitarian Perspectives: Towards Doctrinal Agreement* (Edinburgh: T & T Clark, 1994), pp. 7–21, and "Athanasius: A Study in the Foundations of Classical Theology," in *Theology in Reconciliation* (Grand Rapids, Mich.: Eerdmans, 1975), pp. 215–66.

[4]Athanasius *Orationes contra Arianos* 1.1–5 (*NPNF* 4:188). T. Marsh argues that the essence of "the controversy was about the true interpretation of a corpus of biblical texts bearing on the relation of the Son to the Father" (*The Triune God: A Biblical, Historical and Theological Study* [Dublin: Columba, 1994], p. 115). On the debate over the interpretation of the Bible see R. P. C. Hanson, *The Search for the Christian Doctrine of God* (Edinburgh: T & T Clark, 1988), pp. 824–49. In relation to the key texts from John's Gospel, see particularly T. E. Pollard, *Johannine Christology in the Early Church* (Cambridge: Cambridge University Press, 1970). In addition to examining Pollard's book, one should reference Millard Erickson, *God in Three Persons: A Contemporary Interpretation of the Trinity* (Grand Rapids, Mich.: Baker, 1995), pp. 193–210, for a fair treatment on the Trinity in John's Gospel. Erickson lists other balanced scholarly works. The comments in the Sydney Doctrine Report about John's Gospel border on the absurd: see par. 19, 20. J. E. Davey is the sole authority quoted (see his *The Jesus of St. John's Gospel* [London: Lutterworth, 1987], pp. 78–79). In stark contrast to Davey, see R. G. Gruenler, *The Trinity in John's Gospel* (Grand Rapids, Mich.: Baker, 1986). C. K. Barrett concludes that John "more than any other writer in the New Testament lays the foundation for a doctrine of a co-equal Trinity" (*The Gospel of John* [London: SPCK, 1965], p. 78).

"scope" (Greek *skopos*) of the Bible has to be appreciated. He writes:

> Now the scope and character of Holy Scripture . . . is this: it contains a double
> account of the Savior; that he was ever God and is the Son, being the Father's
> *Logos* and Radiance and Wisdom; and that afterwards for us he took the flesh of a
> virgin. . . . This scope is to be found throughout inspired Scripture.[5]

On the basis of this "double account" of the ministry of the Son of God—the
eternal and the temporal—Athanasius postulated two basic theological presuppositions: the eternal oneness of being of the Father and the Son and the temporal subordination of the Son in becoming man. These two truths he
understood to be foundational to the Christian faith as prescribed by "tradition,"
that is, what he had received from those who had gone before him. He insisted
that Scripture was to be read in light of these truths and that, on this basis, the
Arian exegesis was wrong.

Athanasius opposed Arianism because it presupposed *a difference in being*
between the Father and the Son. Right at the heart of Arius's theology was ontological subordinationism. For Arius and his followers, the Son could only be
called God in a secondary sense. In reply, Athanasius argued that to deny that
the Father and the Son are eternally one in being is to deny what is essential to
Christian faith and salvation:

> For must not he be perfect who is equal to God? And must not he be unalterable
> who is one with the Father and his Son proper to his essence? . . . For this is why
> he who has seen the Son has seen the Father, and why knowledge of the Father is
> knowledge of the Son.[6]

Athanasius insists that the Trinity is eternal and unchanging. There was never
a time when God was a "monad."[7] "There is an eternal one Godhead in a Triad
and there is one glory of the Holy Triad," he wrote.[8] In answer to the Arians,
who argued that a human son is always less than his father, Athanasius replies
that while it may be said that the (divine) Son is the Father's "offspring" (Greek
gennēma), this in no way makes him subordinate or inferior to the Father.[9] A son
is of the same nature as his father, and this is true of the Son of God, yet the
human and the divine must not be compared. The Son of God is not created in

---

[5]Athanasius *Orationes contra Arianos* 3.26.29 (*NPNF* 4).
[6]Ibid., 1.10.35 (*NPNF* 4).
[7]Ibid., 1.6.17 (*NPNF* 4).
[8]Ibid., 1.6.18 (*NPNF* 4).
[9]In this paragraph I am following the wording and ideas in ibid., 1.7.

time, human passions are not involved, and he does not have a transitive nature. From all eternity he is the "image" of his Father; he is "his Word, Wisdom and radiance." Fundamental to Athanasius's theology from first to last is his belief that the Father and the Son are of one "being" or "substance" (Greek *ousia*). This term sums up for him what God is—what makes God, God. To illustrate this unity of being he repeatedly appeals to the analogy of light and its radiance, which, while distinguishable as two, are one and the same.

In his earlier writings Athanasius uses a number of terms[10] to denote the ontological unity of the Father and the Son, not needing to rely on the word *homoousios* (of one being or substance) that was so important at the Council of Nicea (A.D. 325). Even in his *Orationes contra Arianos*, written probably between 339 and 345, he only uses the word *homoousios* once. When this word was repudiated by Athanasius's opponents (c. 350), he came to see it must be defended at all cost to guarantee the apostolic faith. In reply to those who objected to the term *homoousios,* fearing that it implied modalism, which collapsed the distinctions within the Godhead, Athanasius argued that the term spoke both of the unity of being of the one God who is eternally a Triad, and of the eternal distinctions of the three persons—only differing things or persons can be said to be *homoousios*.[11] His insistence on this term to sum up the "scope" of Scripture discloses not only his theological concerns, but also his epistemological concerns. This word emphatically signifies that in and through the Son (and in the Spirit) God communicates himself. *How* we know and *what* we know of God the Father is through the Son. In Athanasius "the whole Godhead" is complete in the Son as much as it is in the Father.[12] God is God the Son as much as he is God the Father, so that the same things are said of each except that one is called Father and the other Son.[13] For Athanasius this one exception discloses the only difference he would allow between the Father and the Son.

In response to the Arians, who repeatedly appealed to the texts that spoke of the Son's frailties, ignorance and dependence on the Father to prove his subordination in being, Athanasius argued that these passages speak only of the reality of the incarnation.[14] Rather than being embarrassed by these passages, Athanasius emphasized them. The Son of God became one with us and

---

[10]For a list of these expressions see Hanson, *Search,* p. 437.

[11]Athanasius *Ad Serapionem de morte Arii* 1.16, 24.

[12]Torrance, "Athanasius," p. 252.

[13]Athanasius *Orationes contra Arianos* 3.23.4, 3.23.5 etc. (*NPNF* 4).

[14]In reply to Arius's arguments that an impassable God cannot suffer, Athanasius maintained that the incarnate Logos suffers only in his humanity, not in his divinity. This formulation allows for a dangerous dichotomy between the two natures of Christ.

one of us in order to be our Savior. As we have already noted, Athanasius argues that Scripture gives "a double account of the Savior," accounts of both his glory in heaven and his humility in the flesh on earth. One is eternal, the other temporal. Two texts more than any other show that this "double account" is presupposed throughout the "scope" of Scripture: first, the apostle John makes this plain when he juxtaposes the statements "the Word was God" and "the Word became flesh" in the opening chapter of his Gospel (Jn 1:1, 14); second, Paul says Christ was equal with God "but emptied himself, taking the form of a slave, being born in human likeness" (Phil 2:5–11).[15] These two texts, Athanasius maintains, give the interpretative key to the reading of the whole of Scripture:

> Any one, beginning with these passages and going through the whole of the Scriptures upon the interpretation they suggest, will perceive how in the beginning, the Father said to him, "Let there be light," "Let there be a firmament," and "Let us make man," but in the fullness of the ages, sent him into the world, "not that he might judge the world, but that the world by him might be saved."[16]

Athanasius maintained a clear distinction between God and creation, yet he argued that the God of the Bible is unceasingly and creatively present in the world. In the incarnation God actually assumed humanity and, in that sense, became man. He revealed himself in the world in the most profound way imaginable. He took human flesh and subjected himself to human frailty. The divine Son willingly subordinated himself. What this implied, says Torrance, was a "breathtaking understanding of God."[17] The God of Christian revelation was a God who could have communion and contact with creation. Epistemologically, this means that physical human beings can actually know God, who is immaterial, through Jesus Christ. This knowledge is a knowing of the very being of God because to know Jesus constitutes knowing the Father. Athanasius says, "Beholding the Son we see the Father, for the thought and comprehension of the Son is knowledge concerning the Father."[18] The Father is truly revealed in the Son, so what is true of the Son is true of the Father.

In Athanasius's writings the unity of the one Godhead is always at the fore. His two capital texts are John 10:30, "The Father and I are one," and John 14:9,

---

[15]Athanasius *Orationes contra Arianos* 3.3-4. He returns to these texts time and time again. In his exposition of key texts he begins with Phil 2:9–10. See *Orationes contra Arianos* 1.11– 19.

[16]Ibid., 3.26.30 (*NPNF* 4).

[17]Torrance, "Athanasius," p. 222.

[18]Athanasius *Orationes contra Arianos* 1.5.16 (*NPNF* 4). See also 3.25.22, 3.27.35–36, etc.

"Whoever has seen me has seen the Father." He did not, however, confuse the persons. "They are two, because the Father is Father and is not also Son, and the Son is Son and not also Father; but their nature is one."[19] In grounding the distinctions within the Godhead exclusively in the relations between the persons, Athanasius pioneered a path others would follow. For him the unity of the three divine persons was so profound that it implied their coinherence.[20] Building on the words of John 14:11, "I am in the Father and the Father is in me," he reasoned that at all times there is a complete mutual indwelling in which each person—while remaining what he is by himself as Father, Son or Holy Spirit—is wholly in the others as the others are wholly in him. Athanasius did not use the Greek word *perichoresis* (it had not yet been coined), but it was he who developed the conception of the coinherence of the persons within the Trinity, which was later recognized to be yet another of his many important pioneering contributions to trinitarian theology. Once this complete coinherence of the persons of the Trinity is recognized, it follows that the works of the three persons cannot be divided. Because the Father is always in the Son and the Son in the Father, their works are one.

What this last point makes plain is that Athanasius rejects not only any suggestion whatsoever that the Son is subordinate in *being* to the Father, but also any suggestion whatsoever that the Son is eternally subordinate to the Father in *function, role or work*. He is as opposed to ontological subordinationism as he is to functional subordinationism because he clearly saw that the latter implied the former, as demonstrated by the Arians. In contrast to his opponents, Athanasius never speaks of the Father commanding and the Son obeying. The wills of the Father and the Son are always in harmony. The idea that there is "chain of command" within the Trinity would have been an abhorrent thought to him. Wayne Grudem may imply that Athanasius teaches the subordination of the Son to the Father in role and function, but nothing could be further from the truth.[21] Such a suggestion shows little comprehension of Athanasius. For Athanasius the being *and* the functions of the Father and the Son are one. R. P. C. Hanson says that for Athanasius, "as the Son acts so the Father acts inseparably."[22] Time and time again, Athanasius insists that what the Father does, the Son does, and vice versa, and that the wills of the two are one:

---

[19]Ibid., 3.23.4 (*NPNF* 4).
[20]On the doctrine of *perichoresis* (coinherence), see particularly ibid., 3.23.
[21]Wayne Grudem, *Systematic Theology: An Introduction to Biblical Doctrine* (Grand Rapids, Mich.: Zondervan, 1994), p. 245.
[22]Hanson, *Search,* p. 427.

Wherefore through the Son does the Father create and in him reveal himself to whom he will, and illuminate them. . . . For where the Father is, there is the Son and where the light, there is the radiance, and what the Father works, he works through the Son, and as the Lord himself says, "What I see the Father do, that I do also"; so also when baptism is given, whom the Father baptizes, him the Son baptizes.[23]

When the Son works, the Father is the worker, and the Son coming to the saints, the Father is he who comes. . . . Therefore also . . . when the Father gives grace and peace, the Son also gives it.[24]

What God speaks, it is very plain. He speaks through the Word and not another, and the Word is not separate from the Father, nor unlike and foreign to the Father's essence, what he works, those are the Father's works.[25]

Since what the Father wills the Son wills also, and is not contrary either in what he thinks or in what he judges, but is in all respects concordant with him . . . therefore it is that he and the Father are one.[26]

In recognizing that the works of God reveal God, Athanasius once more demonstrates his profound grasp of biblical thought. He clearly saw that, in the Bible, what God does reveals what God is like and, in particular, that the works of the Son reveal the Father (Jn 5:36; 9:3–4; 10:25, 37; 14:10).

As we have noted, one of the ways the Arians differentiated the Father and Son was by speaking of the Father as the "unoriginate" and the Son as "originated."[27] This they took to mean that the Son was created in time, that he was a creature and that, as he was derived from the Father, he was less than the Father. In reply Athanasius insisted that there never was a time when the Son did not exist and that derivation of being did not imply diminution in being. He argued that to say "God is unoriginate does not show that the Son is a thing originated. . . . The Word is such as he who begat him."[28] He agrees that the Son is "begotten" of the Father, but he rejects that this can be construed as meaning the Son was created by, derived from or caused by the Father. The Son is the Son *of* the Father as the Father is the Father *of* the Son. There is mutuality in their relationship. Athanasius can

---

[23]Athanasius *Orationes contra Arianos* 2.18.41 (*NPNF* 4).

[24]Ibid., 3.15.11 (*NPNF* 4).

[25]Ibid., 3.15.14 (*NPNF* 4).

[26]Ibid., 3.15.10 (*NPNF* 4).

[27]I am following the argument in ibid., 1.9. See also 3.25.15 where Athanasius also rejects that the Father should be called "the unoriginate."

[28]Ibid., 1.9.31 (*NPNF* 4).

speak of the Father as the *archē* (origin) of the Son following tradition, but he prefers to speak of the Father and the Son together as the *monarchē* (one origin). In his *Orations Against the Arians,* he writes:

> And one is the light from the sun in the radiance; and so we know of but one origin *[archē]*; and the all-framing Word we profess to have no other manner of Godhead, than that of the only God, because he was born from him. . . . For there is but one form of Godhead, which is also in the Word. For thus we confess . . . one Godhead in a Triad.[29]

In his *Tome to the People of Antioch,* he reiterates this point. He says that there is "a Holy Trinity but one Godhead and one beginning" *(archē)* and that "the Son is coessential with the Father."[30] Thus he speaks of the Godhead as the *Triad* rather than as the *monad* and of the Triad as the *archē* rather than of the Father alone as the *archē*.[31]

To bring this discussion of Athanasius's own writings to a close, I quote one last passage that sums up eloquently his thinking on the Trinity. He argues that no one stands nearer to God than the cherubim and seraphim, yet no one has ever suggested that in

> the first utterance of the word, Holy, their voice is raised aloud, while in the second it is lower, but in the third, quite low,—and that consequently the first utterance denotes lordship, the second subordination, and the third marks a yet lower degree. But away with the folly of these haters of God and senseless men. For the Triad, praised reverenced and adored, is one and indivisible and without degrees *(aschematistos)*. It is united without confusion, just as the Monad also is distinguished without separation. For the fact of those venerable living creatures (Isa. vi; Rev. iv.8) offering their praise three times, saying "Holy, Holy, Holy," proves that the Three Subsistences are perfect, just as in saying "Lord," they declare the One Essence. They then that depreciate the Only-Begotten Son of God, blaspheme God, defaming His perfection and accusing him of imperfection, and render themselves liable to the severest chastisement. For he who blasphemes any one of the Subsistences shall have no remission.[32]

There is no uncertainty or ambiguity here. In Athanasius we find the most

---

[29]Ibid., 3.15.15 (*NPNF* 4). For more on this matter, see Torrance, *Christian Doctrine,* p. 183, and Torrance, *Trinitarian Faith*. pp. 78–79, 241–42.
[30]Athanasius *Tomus ad Antiochenos* 5 (*NPNF* 4). See the excellent discussion of Athanasius's position in Torrance, *Trinitarian Perspectives,* pp. 7–20.
[31]Torrance, *Trinitarian Faith,* p. 313.
[32]Athanasius *In illud Omnia mihi tradia sunt* 6.

thorough repudiation of the idea that the Son is in any way eternally subordinated to the Father. For Athanasius, without any caveats, the Father and the Son and the Holy Spirit are one in being *and* action. Wolfhart Pannenberg rightly concludes, "Athanasius vanquished subordinationism."[33] In answer to the Arians, Athanasius completely rejects the idea that the Trinity is to be understood as a hierarchy in any form whatsoever. He could not allow any diminution in the Son's divinity, majesty or authority—neither in who he is nor in what he does. Many times he repeats the principle, everything that the Father is, the Son is, except for being Father.[34] He does not think of the Father as "first," the Son "second" and the Holy Spirit "third." Indeed it may even be argued that for Athanasius the Son is "first." It is the Son who reveals the Father, and it is the Son who is the savior of women and men. He is the "fullness of the Godhead."[35] As far as Athanasius was concerned, the problem was not that the Arians merely "over-emphasised the subordinationist elements of the NT presentation," as the 1999 Sydney Doctrine Report states;[36] the Arians were "heretics" of the most dangerous kind. He refuses them the name "Christian."[37] Their doctrine of the Son undermined the very foundations of Christianity. By arguing that the Son is *different in being* from the Father, they impugned the full divinity of the Son of God, the veracity of the revelation of God in Christ and the possibility of salvation for men and women.[38]

The Cappadocians

In the subsequent ongoing debate over Arianism, the Cappadocian fathers[39] sought to take conceptual trinitarian thinking even further. They took as their starting point not the one being of God but the three divine "persons," whom they called *hypostases*. The three are one because at an intratrinitarian level they share the one being or substance *(ousia)*.[40] The unity of the three

---

[33]Wolfhart Pannenberg, *Systematic Theology* (Grand Rapids, Mich.: Eerdmans, 1991), p. 275.

[34]Athanasius *Orationes contra Arianos* 3.23.4, 3.23.5, etc. (*NPNF* 4). See further on this Torrance, *Trinitarian Perspectives,* p. 18 and n. 47.

[35]Athanasius *Orationes contra Arianos* 3.23.1 (*NPNF* 4).

[36]Sydney Anglican Diocesan Doctrine Commission, "The Doctrine of Trinity and Its Bearing on the Relationship of Men and Women," 1999 report, par. 22 <www.anglicanmediasydney. asn.au/doc/trinity.html>. See appendix B of this book.

[37]This is the center of Athanasius's argument in the opening chapter in *Four Orations Against the Arians (Orationes contra Arianos).*

[38]See Athanasius *Orationes contra Arianos,* chaps. 1–3.

[39]The Cappadocian fathers were Basil (330–397); his brother, Gregory of Nyssa (d. 394); and their friend Gregory of Nazianzus (329–390).

[40]Catherine LaCugna, *God for Us: The Trinity and the Christian Life* (San Francisco: HarperSanFrancisco, 1991), p. 8.

hypostases is conceived as an intimate personal communion *(koinōnia)*. This
suggests to them—and here they develop Athanasius's ideas of coinherence—
that each hypostasis "inheres in the other two"[41] (cf. Jn 10:30, 38; 14:11; 17:21).
On the basis of this principle they argue that every divine attribute is fully
expressed in each of the *hypostases*. So the Father, Son and Holy Spirit are
omnipotent, omniscient and eternal, and the three always work in perfect harmony. For the Cappadocians if the three *hypostases* share the one nature and
are bound together in their common life, they must be one in being and
action. Basil wrote, "All things are performed equally among the worthy by the
Father and the Son and the Holy Spirit."[42] Gregory of Nyssa similarly said, "We
are not told that the Father does anything by himself in which the Son does not
cooperate or that the Son has any isolated activity apart from the Spirit."[43] In
his debate with Eunomius, he reiterates Athanasius's thesis that the Father is
not the Father apart from the Son, and vice versa. He writes, "The Father exists
from all eternity as Father and so too does the Son. Without the Son the Father
is not Father."[44]

By beginning with the three persons (Greek *hypostases*), the Cappadocians
could never be accused of modalism. Their theology of the Trinity emphasizes
personal (Greek *hypostatic*) distinctions within the Godhead. Like Athanasius,
however, they could not allow that these distinctions were in being or action.
The one *ousia* the persons of the Trinity shared excluded this possibility. For
the Cappadocians, like Athanasius, this oneness in being implied a oneness in
work or function. The being and the acts of the divine Trinity could not be separated, although they could be distinguished. Gregory of Nyssa wrote, "All action that impacts the creature from God . . . begins with The Father and is actual
through the Son and is perfected by the Spirit."[45] In speaking in this manner, the
Cappadocians allow for an "order" in the operations or works of the three *hypostases,* but this order does not imply an hierarchy in being or function. Their
answer to the problem of how the three are to be differentiated was to argue
that the three are distinguished solely by their relations of origin: the Father is
"unbegotten" *(agennēsia)*, the Son "begotten" *(gennēsia)*, and the Holy Spirit
"proceeding" *(ekporeusis,* cf. Jn 15:26). In other words, the Father is differenti-

---

[41]Basil *Epistulae* 38.8. See also J. N. D. Kelly, *Early Christian Doctrine* (London: A & C Black,
    1977), p. 264.
[42]Basil *Epistulae* 189.7.
[43]Gregory of Nyssa *Ad Ablabium, quot non sint tres dei* 124.
[44]Gregory of Nyssa *Contra Eunomium* 2.2. For more on this, see LaCugna, *God for Us,* pp. 62–
    63.
[45]Gregory of Nyssa *Ad Ablabium, quod non sint tres dei* 125.

ated by his relation to the Son as is the Son to the Father and the Spirit to the Father and the Son.

The Cappadocian fathers explicitly wanted to exclude subordinationism, but because they were wedded to thinking that the Father was the *monarchē* (one source or origin) of the Son and the Spirit, they were not completely successful in doing this.[46] In their doctrinal expressions of the Trinity there is a tension between their insistence that all three persons share the one divine *ousia* and their insistence that the *hypostasis* of the Father alone is God in the absolute sense—and as such is the sole cause or origin of the Son and the Holy Spirit. In contrast, for Athanasius the idea that the Father alone was *archē* in this sense lent itself to the Arian error.[47] As we have noted, Athanasius held that since the whole Godhead is in the Son and in the Spirit, they must be included with the Father in the one originless *archē*.

Here it is to be recalled that in the Bible and in the early church, the title "Father" is used in two cognate ways: in reference to the Godhead and to the person of the Father. Torrance argues that the Cappadocians' error was to completely conflate these two meanings of the title "Father." In the former sense, the Father (i.e., the Godhead) may be thought of as the source or font of all being. In the second sense, the Father (i.e., the Father of the Son) is he who is coequal and coeternal with the person of the Son and the person of the Holy Spirit. [48]

The Creed of Nicea and the Nicene Creed

Soon after his conquest of the East, the Emperor Constantine called an ecumenical council, primarily to deal with the Arian controversy. The council convened on June 19, 325, in the city of Nicea in Bithynia, with 318 bishops present (as tradition has it). A creed with four anti-Arian anathemas attached was accepted and signed by all but two of the bishops. The longest paragraph in this creed explains what it means to confess belief in "one Lord Jesus Christ, the Son of God."[49]

---

[46]So G. L. Prestige, *God in Patristic Thought* (London: SPCK, 1952), p. 249; Thompson, *Modern Trinitarian Perspectives,* p. 24; Pannenberg, *Systematic Theology,* 1:279–80; LaCugna, *God for Us,* p. 69; Torrance, *Trinitarian Faith,* p. 241, etc.

[47]Athanasius *De synodis* 16.

[48]Torrance, *Christian Doctrine,* pp. 137, 181; Torrance, *Trinitarian Faith,* p. 241. See also LaCugna, *God for Us,* p. 71.

[49]The full text in Greek and English is given in J. N. D. Kelly, *Early Christian Creeds,* 3d ed. (New York: McKay, 1972), pp. 215–16. Hanson (*Search,* p. 163) gives a slightly different English translation. I am quoting from Kelly's translation.

In opposition to Arianism this creed declares that the Son is "begotten" (not made); "from the Father's substance"; "God from God, light from light, true God from true God"; "of one substance [homoousios] with the Father," "through whom all things came into being." It also adds that this one Lord Jesus Christ, "because of us . . . and because of our salvation came down and became incarnate."

In affirming that the Son is "true God from true God" and is of "one substance with the Father," the bishops at Nicea categorically endorsed the eternal equality of the Father and the Son as well as the reality of the temporal coming down of the divine Son to become incarnate for our salvation. In other words, they agreed that the temporal subordination of the Son to the Father within the economy of salvation did not entail the subordination of the Son in the life of the eternal and immanent Trinity.

Torrance holds that an "absolutely fundamental" step was made in the Christian understanding of God when the words *one in being with the Father (homoousion tō Patri)* were included in the Nicene Creed. It was, he says, "a turning-point of far-reaching significance."[50] These words "clearly asserted, not only that there is no division between the being of the Son and the being of the Father, but also that there is no division between the acts of the Son and the acts of God."[51] The creed makes this unity of action explicit by stating that the Father and the Son are the Creator of "all things." They share identically in the authority of creation. If the Father and the Son are one in being and act, then the idea that the Son is eternally set under the Father, ontologically or functionally, is categorically excluded. When two people are true equals the permanent and necessary subordination of one party to the other in being or function/work is excluded.

David Cunningham says the Council of Nicea intentionally excluded all expressions of subordinationism known at that time:

> In order to rule out Arianism and other forms of subordinationism, the Nicene Council rejected a whole variety of attempts to place the three in hierarchical order—logical, causal, temporal or otherwise. The Council's clarity on this point is especially visible in the Nicene anathemas, which claim that there was no time when the Word "was not." And to make it clear that the "begetting of the Son" need not imply temporal order, the Creed states that this begetting takes place

---

[50]Torrance, *Trinitarian Faith,* p. 144. On the significance and implications of the inclusion of these words in both the Creed of Nicea and the Nicene-Constantinopolitan Creed, see the full discussion in Torrance, ibid., pp. 132–45.

[51]Ibid., p. 137.

eternally. Nor is there any logical hierarchy among the Three; they all imply one another and are dependent on one another, so that no one of them can be understood in a position of primacy over the others.[52]

At the Council of Constantinople in 381, the "faith of Nicea" was reaffirmed in a creed with different wording at key points and with an additional clause spelling out the full divinity of the Holy Spirit. This is the so-called Nicene Creed that is used in Western and Eastern churches today.[53] It is accurately designated "the Nicene-Constantinopolitan Creed." This creed, ratified in 381 and again at the Council of Chalcedon in 451, is the fruit of fourth-century Eastern theology.

The wording of the Creed of Nicea is not identical to the Nicene Creed of 381, but in their Christology the theology of the two creeds are in full agreement. The phrase "from the substance of the Father" was omitted in 381, possibly simply because it was redundant alongside the more explicit affirmation "of one being with the Father." What was theologically new was the confession of the Holy Spirit as "the Lord and life-giver, who proceeds from the Father, who with the Father and the Son is together worshipped and together glorified." In these words the complete divinity of the Holy Spirit is affirmed to make the Nicene Creed a fully trinitarian confession. In both creeds, it is to be noted, the threefold structure is determined by the economy of revelation, which has as its goal "our salvation."

In both creeds the key phrases in the confession of Jesus Christ as the Son of God are that he is "one in substance or being *[homoousios]* with the Father" and that "for us and our salvation he came down from heaven." Once these two truths were established as theological principles, they became hermeneutical principles. Those who confess Christ in these words are agreeing that these two clauses accurately encapsulate what the Bible as a whole teaches about the eternal oneness in being of the Father and of the Son and what it teaches about the Son's voluntary and temporal subordination—his coming down from heaven for our salvation. This confession then becomes for them an interpretative guide in the understanding of individual passages in Scripture that could be read to deny either of these basic truths.

We thus conclude that those who speak today of the eternal subordination of the Son in function or being not only contradict the theology of the Nicene Creed, but also reject the interpretive principles it enshrines. In failing to note

---

[52]David Cunningham, *These Three Are One: The Practice of Trinitarian Theology* (Oxford: Blackwell, 1998), p. 112.

[53]There is one notable exception to its universality. See the following discussion on the Western addition of the *Filioque* clause that the Eastern Churches have never accepted.

the hermeneutical guidance the Nicene Creed offers, they wrongly conclude that texts which speak of the temporal subordination and obedience of the incarnate Son define his eternal status and role. Thus no matter how many texts they quote in support of their case, this creed judges their efforts to be mistaken. They have failed to grasp what Athanasius calls "the scope of scripture," by which he means "the overall drift," "the theological center," of Scripture.

Augustine

In book 1 of his great work *De Trinitate,* Augustine seeks to prove—almost entirely by appeal to the Bible—the complete equality of the divine persons.[54] His hermeneutical approach is to be noted. He begins with the Scriptures, which he believes affirm the full divinity of the Son and the Holy Spirit (e.g., Jn 1:1; 5:21; Rom 11:36; 1 Cor 1:24; 1 Tim 6:14–16). Then he turns to the passages that speak of the subordination of the Son to the Father. In dealing with these he makes it "a canonical rule," what we would call today a "hermeneutical principle," to interpret them as referring exclusively to the incarnate Son who took "the form of a servant."[55] The one text through which all else in Scripture about the Son should be understood is, for Augustine, Philippians 2:6. Here Paul declares that the Son, "who, though he was in the form of God, did not regard equality with God as something to exploited, but emptied himself, taking the form of a slave, being born in human likeness."

In book 2 Augustine moves on to discuss the texts that speak of the Son's being "sent," which he says many "in error" quote to prove the Son is "less than the Father." He notes that some presume "the one who sends is greater than the one sent."[56] In reply Augustine argues firstly that sending does not necessarily entail inequality: only that the one sent comes "from" the sender. And he argues secondly, and more importantly, that the temporal *mission* (sending) of the Son and the Spirit are to be distinguished from the eternal *procession* of the Son and the Spirit. This leads him to formulate a second rule of interpretation: namely, the temporal mission of the Son and the Holy Spirit are revelations in time, whereas the procession of the persons is eternal. In making this distinction Augustine denies that it is possible to understand the eternal Trinity solely by what is revealed in the temporality of the economy of salvation.

---

[54]On Augustine see particularly E. Hill, *The Trinity* (Brooklyn: New City, 1991). All the references below are taken from Hill's translation of *De Trinitate,* as noted. Augustine discusses the Trinity in a number of his writings, but his most profound and extended discussion is given in *De Trinitate.*

[55]Augustine *De Trinitate* 1.14.

[56]Ibid., 2.27.

Having laid down the ground rules for correctly understanding the Scriptures and, on the basis of these rules, having shown that the Scripture insists on the unequivocal equality of the three divine persons, Augustine moves on in books 4 through 6 to develop his theology of the Trinity, aiming to completely exclude subordinationism. His goal, says E. Hill, is "to safeguard the absolute equality of the Son and the Holy Spirit with the Father, while still maintaining their real distinctions from each other."[57] Augustine's starting point is not the *monarchē* of the Father but the one divine substance shared by the three persons. With this starting point there can be no questioning of the equality of the three, for they "share the inseparable equality of one substance present in a divine unity."[58] This unity of substance, he insists, indicates "the supreme equality of Father, Son and Holy Spirit."[59] Thus everything said of one member of the Trinity can be said of any of the others: "So total is the equality in this triad that not only is the Father not greater than the Son as far as divinity is concerned, but also Father and Son together are not greater than the Holy Spirit."[60]

Because the three share (subsist in) the same divine essence, they have one will and work as one. Augustine never depicts the Father as commanding and the Son obeying. He writes, "The Father and the Son have but one will and are indivisible in their workings."[61] "Just as Father, Son and Holy Spirit are inseparable, so do they work inseparably."[62] Thus this often-quoted maxim sums up accurately Augustine's thought: "the external works of the Trinity are one" (Latin *opera trinitatis ad extra sunt indivisa*).[63] This unity of action, Augustine insists, does not obliterate the distinctive contribution of each of the persons in their united working. Although Father, Son and Holy Spirit are involved in every external operation of the Godhead, the Scriptures are said to "appropriate" particular works to particular persons.[64]

Michel Rene Barnes argues that behind Augustine's emphatic insistence that the three persons of the Trinity work inseparably lies a commitment to "the fundamental doctrine of catholic (which is to say Nicene or pro-Nicene) trinitarian theology."[65] This takes as an axiom that

---

[57]Hill, *The Trinity*, p. 186.
[58]Augustine *De Trinitate* 2.15.
[59]Ibid., 6.15.
[60]Ibid., 8.1.
[61]Ibid., 2.9.
[62]Ibid., 1.7 and 2.99.
[63]This phrase is not actually found in his writings.
[64]Ibid., 6.1-7.
[65]Michel Rene Barnes, "Rereading Augustine's Theology of the Trinity," in *The Trinity: An Inter-*

whatever shares the same nature performs the same actions, and what performs the same actions must have the same nature; the Father and the Son perform the same actions so they must have the same nature, and sharing the same nature they act in unity.[66]

In Augustine's approach to understanding the Trinity, how the three persons are distinguished is a key issue. For the Cappadocians, who begin with and emphasize the divine three, this is not a major issue, for they assume the distinction of persons (*hypostases*). Their problem was explaining the unity. For Augustine, who begins with and emphasizes the divine unity, differentiating the persons is a major issue: he has to be careful to avoid modalism. The idea that the divine three are differentiated by difference in being or works is excluded on principle right from the start. The three are of one substance and work as one. Following Athanasius, Augustine first insists that the Father is not the Son, and the Son not the Father, and the Spirit is not the Father or the Son, while allowing that the same things can be said of all three.[67] But he is aware that more than this needs to be said. He thus concludes, like the Cappadocians, that the persons of the Trinity are to be differentiated primarily by their relations to one another.[68] For him the terms *Father, Son* and *Holy Spirit* are names given to three distinct "subsistent relations" within the Godhead, which he reluctantly concedes may be designated "persons." The Father is distinguished as Father because he "begets" the Son; the Son is distinguished because as the Son he is "begotten"; the Spirit is distinguished from the Father and the Son because he "proceeds" from them both.[69]

Augustine thought of the Holy Spirit as the mutual love of the Father and the Son and as the communal bond that unites them. This meant that for him the Holy Spirit could be the Spirit of not just one of them but rather of the two in relationship. He found this theological insight taught in Scripture: he noted that the Bible spoke of the Holy Spirit as both the Spirit of the Son and the Spirit of the Father. The Father and the Son, he therefore reasoned, must be a single principle in relation to the Holy Spirit. He writes:

> We must confess that the Father and the Son are the origin of the Holy Spirit; not two origins, but just as the Father and the Son are the one God, and with refer-

---

disciplinary *Symposium on the Trinity,* ed. S. T. Davis, D. Kendall, G. O'Collins (Oxford: Oxford University Press, 1999), p. 164.
[66]Ibid., p. 160.
[67]Hill, *The Trinity,* pp. 69, 241, 227, etc. (Augustine *De Trinitate* 2.5, 8.1, 7.9., etc.).
[68]For more on this matter, see H. Lancaster, "Divine Relations of the Trinity: Augustine's Answer to Arianism," *Calvin Theological Journal* 34 (1999): 327–46.
[69]Hill, *The Trinity,* pp. 197, 209, 432–33 (Augustine *De Trinitate* 5.12, 6.7, 15.47–48).

ence to creation one Creator and one Lord, so with reference to the Holy Spirit they are one origin; but with reference to creation Father, Son, and Holy Spirit are one origin, just as they are one Creator and one Lord.[70]

In struggling with the issue of how the New Testament authors can use the one term *God* of both the Father and the Trinity, Augustine finds 1 Corinthians 11:3—where Paul says, "God is the head of Christ"—possibly the most perplexing text. If "God" here refers to the Trinity, how, he asks, can the whole Trinity be the head of just one of the divine persons? He suggests it may be better to think of this verse as simply referring to the Father's position in relation to the Son in the incarnation, when the Father "is the head of the man mediator which he [Christ] alone is."[71] It is not surprising that Augustine finds this verse troublesome, for in his understanding of the Trinity it is impossible to think of he who is confessed as Lord as set under the Father in any way whatsoever in their eternal relations. They are equal in all respects, although the Father is always the Father and the Son always the Son.

In drawing to a conclusion this brief outline of Augustine's doctrine of the Trinity, it is to be noted that in *De Trinitate* the Son and the Spirit do not derive their divinity from the Father; the Father, the Son and the Spirit are not ordered numerically or hierarchically; the Father, the Son and the Holy Spirit are not exclusively responsible for particular works or roles; and they have but one will, so that in the eternal Trinity, it is impossible to think of the Son as the servant who must always obey the Father, who is forever his head. J. N. D. Kelly concludes that by placing the unity of the Trinity "squarely in the foreground," Augustine "rigorously excluded subordinationism of every kind."[72] Similarly, Louis Berkhof says Augustine "entirely eliminated" any element of subordination within the Trinity.[73] There are aspects of Augustine's doctrine of the Trinity that can be questioned,[74] but for those who argue for the eternal subordination of the Son in essence (ontologically or in subsistence) or in his works, operations or role, it should be quite clear that Augustine stands in opposition to them.

---

[70]Augustine *De Trinitate* 5.15.

[71]Ibid., 6.1.

[72]Kelly, *Early Christian Doctrine*, p. 272. E. J. Fortman is equally emphatic that Augustine's theology of the Trinity excludes eternal subordinationism in any form (*The Triune God: A Historical Study of the Doctrine of the Trinity* [Grand Rapids, Mich.: Baker, 1972]).

[73]Grudem, *Systematic Theology*, p. 83. This is a strange assertion to make if Berkhof is a subordinationist, as some conservative evangelicals argue.

[74]For more on this, see Colin Gunton, *The Promise of Trinitarian Theology* (Edinburgh: T & T Clark, 1991), pp. 1–50; Robert Jenson, *Systematic Theology: The Triune God* (Oxford: Oxford University Press, 1997), 1:110–14.

The *Filioque* Clause

The Nicene Creed in its A.D. 381 wording spoke of the Spirit as "proceeding from the Father." In seeking to relate the three persons of the Trinity, Augustine suggested that the Holy Spirit was the bond of love between the Father and the Son that united them. It was a small step from this to thinking of the Spirit as proceeding from the Father and the Son,[75] especially since John's Gospel spoke of Jesus as the giver of the Spirit (e.g., Jn 14:16; 15:26; 16:7, 13–15; 20:22). At the third Council of Toledo in 589 the words *and the Son* were added to the Nicene Creed. (These three English words translate one Latin word, *Filioque*). The procession of the Spirit "from the Father and the Son" had been endorsed in the East by Epiphanius and Cyril of Alexandria in the fourth and fifth centuries, and in the West by the Roman Pontiffs Leo the Great and Gregory the Great in the fifth and sixth centuries. This teaching was also endorsed by the Athanasian Creed. Much later it was solemnly reaffirmed at the Fourth Lateran Council of 1215, the Council of Lyons in 1274 and the Council of Florence in 1439. However, from the time of Photios, the ninth-century patriarch of Constantinople who made the *Filioque* clause a matter of contention with the Western church, this addition to the creed has been rejected by the Eastern Orthodox churches.[76]

This addition safeguards the vital truth established in the Nicene Creed that the Father and the Son are one in being/substance, and it disallows any disjunction between the Son and the Spirit that would be contrary to Scripture, where the Spirit can be called "the Spirit of Jesus" (Acts 16:7) or "the Spirit of Christ" (Rom 8:9; Gal 4:6). Moreover, in making the Father and the Son the *archē* or source of the Spirit, the idea that the Father is the one source (Greek *monarchē*) of the Son and the Spirit is challenged. In contrast to the Eastern church, the Western church has always been more concerned about the danger of subordination implied by making both the Son and the Spirit dependent on the Father than it has been concerned about maintaining the *monarchē* of the Father.

We may thus infer that the continuing endorsement of these added words to the creed represents the Western church's concern for emphasizing the equality

---

[75]So Bertrand de Margerie, *The Christian Trinity in History* (Petersham, Mass.: St. Bede, 1982), pp. 164–65.

[76]His primary theological criticism was that this implied the subordination of the Spirit, an argument Western theologians have never accepted. See Ted Peters, *God as Trinity: Relationality and Temporality in Divine Life* (Louisville, Ky.: Westminster Press, 1993), pp. 63–66.

of the Father and the Son that is basic to the Nicene faith, without ever intending or wishing to suggest the subordination of the Spirit. Behind the *Filioque* clause lies the theological principle that just as no difference in act (role or function) can be allowed in the external works or acts of the Father, Son or Holy Spirit, so too none can be allowed between the Father and the Son in the internal procession of the Spirit.

The Athanasian Creed

In about A.D. 500, probably in the south of France, the most complete formal statement of trinitarian doctrine was composed as a test of orthodoxy: this we know as the Athanasian Creed.[77] Essentially, it is a summary of Western trinitarian theology, reflecting the thought of Augustine more than anyone else but clearly reaching back to the foundation laid by Athanasius. For Lutherans, Roman Catholics and Anglicans (such as myself), it is a binding doctrinal norm.

The creed begins by declaring that to be saved one must "hold the Catholic Faith," which is identified with the trinitarian and christological affirmations that follow. In regard to the Trinity, "the Catholic Faith is this: That we worship one God in Trinity, and Trinity in Unity; neither confounding the Persons, nor dividing the Substance." The confession of the "Unity" of the Trinity involves belief that the three persons are identical in substance and have identical attributes. To underline this point the creed declares that "such as the Father is, such is the Son, and such is the Holy Ghost" and "none is afore, or after other; none is greater, or less than another. But the whole three Persons are co-eternal together and co-equal."[78] These words, says Leonard Hodgson, "express rejection . . . of all subordinationism."[79] There can be no disputing, says Kelly, that "the dominant idea [is] the perfect equality of the three persons."[80] The distinctions are limited solely to the differing relations they bear to each other as a result of their differing origins: "The Father is made of none. . . . The Son is of the Father alone . . . begotten. The Holy Ghost is of the Father of and the Son . . . proceeding." There is no suggestion that their distinctions are based on differing roles, as Gru-

---

[77]See further J. N. D. Kelly, *The Athanasian Creed* (London: A & C Black, 1964).

[78]In this book I quote the wording of the Athanasian Creed given in *The Book of Common Prayer* (New York: The Church Hymnal Corporation, 1979). The Athanasian Creed is an agreed text in ecumenical discussions. The only variations allowed are cosmetic changes to modernize the language. See further John H. Leith, *Creeds of the Churches: A Reader in Christian Doctrine from the Bible to the Present* (Atlanta: John Knox, 1973).

[79]Leonard Hodgson, *The Doctrine of the Trinity* (London: Nisbet, 1955), p. 102.

[80]Kelly, *Athanasian Creed,* p. 79.

dem suggests, let alone "differences in being," as the Sydney Doctrine Report maintains.[81]

In the briefer christological section of the creed that follows, the Son is confessed as "equal to the Father as touching his Godhead; and inferior to the Father, as touching his manhood." "Inferior" is one possible translation of the Latin word *minor,* which literally means "less than."[82] Kelly sees the wording of this phrase as reflecting Augustine's premise that the Son is inferior or subordinated[83] only while in human form.[84]

In contrast to the Nicene-Constantinopolitan Creed, where the economy of revelation in history gives the structure of the creed, the Athanasian Creed is basically a theological statement about the eternal Trinity with an additional section on Christology. Right at the heart of this Creed we have an explicit condemnation of those who say the Son is eternally subordinated to the Father in any way. What the Creed emphasizes is the unity of being and action of the three persons, the full divinity of the Son and the reality of the incarnation. It can be accepted that some may choose to reject in part or in whole the Athanasian Creed for one reason or another, but the claim by Charles Hodge, Wayne Grudem and the Sydney Doctrine Report that this creed endorses their subordinationistic teaching cannot be accepted. This creed condemns their theology.

Calvin

For evangelicals of Reformed persuasion, Calvin's contribution to any question is of great interest. He has many important things to say on the doctrine of the Trinity.[85] On this matter, as with all others, Calvin seeks to enunciate the teach-

---

[81]See par. 25. Here we are told that by distinguishing the persons of the Trinity, the Athanasian Creed makes "most clear" their "differences of being."

[82]The original and authoritative Latin reads, *"aequalis Patri secundum divinitatem, minor Patri secundum humanitatem,"* which Kelly (*Athanasian Creed,* p. 19) translates as "Equal to the Father in respect of his divinity, less than the Father in respect to his humanity."

[83]It is important to note that the words *inferior* and *subordinate* can be used synonymously in English. Time and time again we find evangelicals insisting that they do not hold that the Son is inferior to the Father or that women are inferior to men. They are simply subordinated. This is far too subtle a distinction. In the *Concise English Dictionary* ([Oxford: Clarendon, 1964], p. 623), the word *inferior* is defined as "situated below, lower in rank," which is exactly the meaning of the word *subordinate.* A subordinate employed in a business is an inferior.

[84]Kelly, *Athanasian Creed,* p. 80.

[85]See further B. B. Warfield, "Calvin's Doctrine of the Trinity," in *Calvin and Augustine* (Philadelphia: Presbyterian & Reformed, 1956), pp. 189–284; Thomas F. Torrance, "Calvin's Doctrine of the Trinity," in *Trinitarian Perspectives: Towards Doctrinal Agreement* (Edinburgh:

ing of Scripture, listening attentively to how others before him have understood it. In his hermeneutical methodology he is neither a naive biblicist who thinks that doctrines can be formulated apart from tradition, like the radical anti-Nicenes of his day, nor a committed traditionalist who appeals to the Scriptures simply to substantiate church teachings, like the Catholics of his day. What is particularly noteworthy is that in his appeal to the church fathers, Calvin draws on the best of both Eastern and Western trinitarian thought. His reading and comprehension of these writings is impressive.

Calvin begins his study of the Trinity with a discussion of what to call "the three." He is aware that some have objected to the term *person*. For this reason he allows that the Greek equivalent word, *hypostasis,* or its Latin translation, *subsistentia* (subsistence), may be used as alternatives.[86] How the term *person* is understood, however, is for Calvin the key issue. His definition is given in a carefully worded paragraph:

> "Person," therefore, I call a "subsistence" in God's essence, which while related to the others, is distinguished by an incommunicable quality. By the term "subsistence" we would understand something different from essence. For if the Word were simply God, and yet possessed no other characteristic mark, John would have wrongly said that the Word was always with God (John 1:1). When immediately after he adds that the Word was also God himself, he recalls us to the essence as a unity. But because he could not be with God without residing in the Father, hence emerges the idea of subsistence, which even though it has been joined with the essence by a common bond, and cannot be separated from it, yet has a special mark whereby it is distinguished by it.[87]

In this important paragraph Calvin makes three matters explicit. First, the word *person* when used in trinitarian discourse is to be defined as a "subsistence in God's essence." Second, each of the three in their individual subsistence is to be distinguished from the others. It is important to note that what differentiates them as Father, Son and Holy Spirit, Calvin says, is an "incommunicable quality." What this is he does not say, because we presume he recognizes that the Scriptures do not answer this question; but whatever it is, it is unique to each. Third, the three subsistences share one divine being or essence. In making these points Calvin excludes

T & T Clark, 1994), pp. 41–76; P. W. Butin, *Revelation and Redemption and Response: Calvin's Trinitarian Understanding of the Divine-Human Relationship* (Oxford: Oxford University Press, 1995).

[86]John Calvin *Institutes of the Christian Religion* 1.13.2–3. I will be following the edition edited by J. Neil and translated by F. L. Battles (London: SCM Press, 1960).

[87]Ibid., 1.13.6.

modalism, tritheism and subordinationism all at the same time. The persons are distinguished, the one being of God is affirmed, and the equality of the three is established by stressing that they all share in the one divine essence or being. Thus he insists that "in the absolutely simple unity of God these three hypostases or subsistences coexist in one being without being confused with one another."[88] The word *subsistence* for Calvin, rather than implying the subordination of the Son or the Spirit to the Father, excludes this very idea. For him it would be logically impossible for the equality of the three subsistences, who are one "being-in-itself," to be diminished when the three are differentiated as "being-in-relation."[89]

Following this discussion Calvin moves on to argue explicitly for the full divinity of the Son and the Holy Spirit. Four arguments for the deity of the Son, entirely based on Scripture, are given:

☐ He is identified as the eternal Word, which "abides everlastingly one and the same with God, and is God himself."[90]

☐ He is frequently called "the Lord," the very title also given to God, the Father.

☐ He is said to do things that are the prerogatives of God alone (save, create, heal, raise the dead, etc.).

☐ To him we address our prayers and offer our worship.

He deploys basically the same arguments to establish the deity of the Spirit.

Time and time again Calvin warns against any dividing of the one Godhead. He allows only for "a distinction not a division" between the three. He writes, "Let us not then be led to imagine a Trinity of persons that keeps our thoughts distracted and does not at once lead them back to that unity."[91] His stress on the divine unity naturally leads him to endorse the doctrine of perichoresis, although he does not use this term: "The Father is wholly in the Son, the Son wholly in the Father, even as he himself declares: 'I am in the Father, and the Father is in me' (John 14:10)."[92] This unity and coinherence within the Trinity means that the wills of the three are one. Calvin rejects the conventional division of labor within the Trinity, according to which the Father is the Creator, the Son is the Redeemer and the Holy Spirit is the Sanctifier—as if each person had separate and distinct roles. Calvin holds that the whole Trinity is involved in cre-

---

[88]Calvin, *Ioannis Calvini Opera quae supersunt omnia* 7.312, ed. G. Baum, E. Cunitz and E. Reuss, 55 vols. (Berlin: 1863-1890), quoted in Torrance, *Trinitarian Perspectives,* p. 70.
[89]Torrance, "Calvin's Doctrine," p. 70.
[90]Calvin *Institutes* 1.13.7.
[91]Ibid., 1.13.17.
[92]Ibid., 1.13.19.

ation, redemption and sanctification, although each of the three makes a distinctive contribution. Thus he notes that in Scripture,

> to the Father is attributed the beginning of activity, and the fountain and well-spring of all things; to the Son, wisdom, counsel and the order and disposition of all things; but to the Spirit is assigned the power and efficacy of that activity.[93]

This means that, like the Cappadocians, Calvin accepts an "order" or structuring in how the three persons operate but rejects any thought that this order implies hierarchy or a division of action. At first thought, this conclusion would seem to stand in tension with his willingness (adopting traditional phraseology) to speak of the Father "as first, then from him the Son and finally from both the Spirit," if it were not that he explained that this is simply how "the mind of each human being is naturally inclined to contemplate God."[94] His complete rejection of hierarchical ordering is made explicit when he says that there can be "*in eternity* no before or after" within the Godhead.[95]

Calvin's case is that in both *being* and *action* the Son and the Holy Spirit are one with the Father. In who they *are* and what they *do,* the Father, the Son and the Holy Spirit are equals—equals in deity, majesty and authority. In other words, Calvin never suggests that in their operations/functions/roles the Son and the Holy Spirit are eternally subordinated to the Father, but just the opposite: the *works* or *functions,* to use his words, of the Son and the Holy Spirit indicate that they work as one with the Father. For this reason, Calvin, in contrast to many modern-day conservative evangelicals, never depicts the Father as being at the top of a chain of command. I can find no instance where he differentiates the eternal relationship between the Father and the Son in terms of differing authority (e.g., the Father commands, the Son obeys). He does not accept that the Father is eternally "the head" of the Son.[96]

In dealing with the biblical texts that can be read to imply the eternal subordination of the Son, Calvin determines to let tradition rule his interpretative decisions.[97] Like Athanasius and Augustine, he will not concede an interpretation

---

[93]Ibid., 1.13.18.

[94]Ibid.

[95]Ibid., italics mine.

[96]See below for his comments on 1 Cor 11:3.

[97]Robert L. Raymond is, however, of a different opinion (see *A New Systematic Theology of the Christian Faith* [Nashville: Thomas Nelson, 1998], pp. 317–42). He argues that at points Calvin actually breaks with the Nicene tradition. In reply see Paul Owen, "Calvin and Catholic Trinitarianism: An Examination of Robert Raymond's Understanding of the Trinity and His Appeal to John Calvin," *Calvin Theological Journal* 35, no. 2 (2000): 262–82.

of any text that might suggest any diminution in the eternal divinity, majesty or authority of the Son. Calvin reads passages where the Son is depicted as being subordinated or inferior to the Father as speaking only of the mediatory work of the Son.[98] He interprets them soteriologically, not ontologically. He emphatically refuses to read back into the immanent or eternal Trinity the subordination of the Son seen in the incarnation. I give three examples where we can see that Calvin's commitment to the tradition—the faith expressed in the Nicene and Athanasian Creeds—is controlling his exegesis.

In commenting on John 14:28, "the Father is greater than I," which Calvin maintains is often "twisted in various ways"[99] by those who want to "prove" that the Son is in some way subordinated to the Father, he says, "He places the Father in the higher rank, seeing the bright perfection of splendor that appears in heaven differs from that measure of glory which was seen in him when he was clothed in flesh."[100] He also writes, "Christ is here not drawing a comparison between the divinity of the Father and of himself, nor between his own human nature and the divine essence of the Father, but rather between his present state and his heavenly glory to which he was shortly to be received."[101]

In contemporary conservative evangelical subordinationism Paul's comment that "God is the head of Christ" (1 Cor 11:3) is a key text. It is read to teach that the Father *eternally* rules over the Son. Calvin asks, what "preeminence" do these words give to the Father in relation to the Son?

> The answer is, since he has made himself subject to the Father in our flesh, for, apart from that, being of one essence with the Father, he is equal with him. Let us bear in mind, therefore, that this is said about Christ the mediator. My point is that he is inferior to the Father because he has clothed himself with our nature, so that he might be the first born among many brothers.[102]

For Calvin, the Father is only "the head" of Christ during the time Christ "made himself subject to the Father" to be our mediator by taking "our flesh." In his eternal being and role he is one with the Father. The great Reformer does not see in this comment any hint that the Father eternally rules over the Son.

Calvin's exegesis of 1 Corinthians 15:24—where Paul says, "Then comes the

---

[98]Calvin *Institutes* 1.13.26; see also 1.13.25.

[99]John Calvin, *The Gospel According to St. John,* trans. T. H. L. Parker (Edinburgh: Oliver & Boyd, 1959), p. 89.

[100]Calvin *Institutes* 1.13.26.

[101]Calvin, *Gospel,* p. 90.

[102]John Calvin, *The First Epistle of Paul the Apostle to the Corinthians,* trans. John Faser (Grand Rapids, Mich.: Eerdmans, 1960), p. 229.

end, when he [Christ] hands over the kingdom to God the Father"—is also instructive:

> Surely the kingdom of the Son of God had no beginning and will have no end.
> But even as he lay concealed under the lowliness of flesh and emptied himself,
> taking the form of a servant (Phil. 2:7), laying aside the splendor of majesty, he
> showed himself obedient to his Father (cf. Phil. 2:8). Having completed this sub-
> jection, "he was at last crowned with glory and honor" (Heb. 2:9), and exalted to
> the highest lordship that before him "every knee should bow" (Phil. 2:9). So then
> will he yield to the Father his name and crown of glory, and whatever he has
> received from the Father, that "God may be all in all" (1 Cor. 15:28). . . . Here we
> cannot excuse the error of the ancient writers who pay no attention to the person
> of the mediator, obscure the real meaning of almost all the teaching one reads in
> the Gospel of John and entangle themselves in many snares. Let this, then, be our
> key to right understanding: those things which apply to the office of the mediator
> are not spoken of simply either of the divine nature or of the human. Until he
> comes forth as judge of the world Christ will therefore reign, joining us to the
> Father as the measure of our weakness permits. But when as partakers in heav-
> enly glory we shall see God as he is, Christ having then been discharged the
> office of mediator. . . . Then he returns the lordship to his Father so that—far from
> diminishing his own majesty—it may shine all the more brightly. Then also God
> will cease to be the head of Christ, for Christ's own divinity will shine of itself.[103]

Following Augustine, Calvin interprets this difficult passage in the light of Philippians 2:5–11, stressing that Christ willingly laid aside his majesty in the incarnation and that at the end he will again willingly hand back rule to the Father. His view is that Paul is teaching that the rule of Christ continues until the day of judgment, when his work as the mediator of redemption will cease. From then on Christ has no further soteriological work to accomplish. He thus hands back the rule of the world to the Father.[104] In this change Christ is in no way diminished—indeed his majesty will "shine all the more brightly," says Calvin.

In Calvin's interpretation of both 1 Corinthians 11:3 and 1 Corinthians 15:24, as we have just seen, the "headship" of the Father in relation to the Son is taken to be temporal. It does not belong to the eternal relations within the Trinity. This observation raises the question of how Calvin deals with the problematic idea that the

---

[103]Calvin *Institutes* 2.14.3. See also *First Epistle of Paul,* pp. 324–28.
[104]So J. F. Jensen, "1 Cor. 15:24–28 and the Future of Jesus Christ," *Scottish Journal of Theology* 40 (1987): 543–70. On Augustine's interpretation of this text see Barnes, "Rereading August-ine's Theology," pp. 169–74.

Father is the *monarchē* (the sole origin, the beginning or the *principium*) of the Son (and the Spirit). Calvin rejects vehemently the idea that the Father alone is "truly and properly the sole God who in forming the Son and the Spirit infused into them his own deity."[105] He insists that the Father, the Son and the Spirit are fully divine from all eternity since they share in the one divine essence or being. In regard to their deity, the Father is not the *monarchē* of the Son or the Spirit. Nevertheless Calvin affirms that the Father is the *monarchē* of the Son "in respect of his person."[106] He is the Son *of* the Father. Calvin summarizes his case in this way:

> Christ in respect to himself is called God; with respect to the Father, Son. Again, the Father with respect to himself is called God; with respect to the Son, Father. In so far as he is called Father with respect to the Son, he is not the Son; in so far as he is called the Son with respect to the Father he is not the Father; in so far as he is called Father in respect to himself, and Son with respect to himself, he is the same God. Therefore when we speak simply of the Son without regard to the Father, we well and properly declare him to be of himself; and for this reason is called the *sole beginning*. But when we mark the relation that he has with the Father, we rightly make the Father the *beginning* of the Son.[107]

In these words Calvin both emphatically differentiates the Son from the Father in respect to his person (he is the Son *of* the Father) and rejects any differentiation between the Son and the Father in respect to his being (the Father and the Son are eternally ontologically one).

As we conclude our brief exposition of Calvin's doctrine of the Trinity, we are left wondering how so many evangelicals can claim that Calvin is an advocate of the eternal subordination of the Son in being or function. Nothing would seem further from the truth. It must be presumed that those who make this claim have not read Calvin closely, or that they have not understood him or that they are being disingenuous. B. B. Warfield and Thomas F. Torrance, in their scholarly studies of Calvin's doctrine of the Trinity, are agreed that the great Reformer is opposed to subordinationism in any form. Warfield argues that Calvin wrote seeking the "elimination of the last remnants of subordinationism,"[108] being consistently in "inexpugnable opposition to subordinationists of all types."[109] As far as Torrance is concerned, Calvin "leaves no room for any element of subordinationism."[110]

---

[105]Calvin *Institutes* 1.13.23.
[106]Ibid., 1.13.25.
[107]Ibid., 1.13.19, italics mine. See also 1.13.23, 1.13.25.
[108]Warfield, "Calvin's Doctrine," p. 230.
[109]Ibid., p. 251.
[110]Torrance, *Trinitarian Perspectives,* p. 66.

Reformation Confessions

All of the Reformation confessions of faith seek to exclude modalism and subordinationism, but as these two errors were rejected by the Roman Catholic Church and by the Nicene and Athanasian Creeds, what is said on the Trinity in these confessions is usually brief and to the point. The agreed understanding of the Trinity is conceptually Western: God is one divine essence or substance in three persons who are to be distinguished but not divided, being "equal in power and alike eternal."[111] A lengthier section on the Trinity is found in the Belgic Confession of 1561. Here we are told that within the Trinity, "all three are co-eternal and co-essential. There is neither first nor last; for they are all three one, in truth, in power, in goodness, and in mercy" (art. 8). Then follow three more clauses: the first clause gives scriptural proofs for this doctrine of the Trinity; the second states what is to be believed about Jesus Christ (he is the "true, eternal, and almighty God, whom we evoke worship and serve"); and the third is entitled, "The Holy Ghost is the true and eternal God." The Second Helvetic Confession of 1566, "the most widely received among Reformed Confessions,"[112] which was composed by Heinrich Bullinger, likewise expands on the brief paragraph on the Trinity found in most Reformation confessions of faith. This confession opposes the "blasphemies" of those who teach that any person within the Trinity is "subservient or subordinate, . . . unequal in it, are greater or less, . . . [or] different with respect to character or will." The term *subservient* condemns those who teach that the Son must always obey the Father as a servant (i.e., he is eternally subordinate in role/function/operations) whereas the term *subordinate* condemns those who teach the Son is subordinate in being/essence/substance.

Like the Nicene and Athanasian Creeds, the Reformation confessions of faith exclude subordinationism in any form. They are doctrinal statements outlining Reformation trinitarian orthodoxy and rulings on how the Bible should be read by those who would claim to stand in the Reformation tradition.

---

[111]So the Augsburg Confession, art. 1; the Tetrapolitan Confession (1530), art. 2; the First Confession of Basle (1534), art. 1; the First Helvetic Confession of Faith (1536), art. 6; the Confession of Faith Used by the English Congregation in Geneva (1556), art. 1; the French Confession of Faith (1559), art. 6; the Scots Confession (1560), art. 1; the Thirty-Nine Articles of Religion (1563), art. 1.

[112]So A. C. Cochrane, *Reformed Confessions of the Sixteenth Century* (London: SCM Press, 1966), p. 220.

3

SUBORDINATING
TRADITION

I n his substantial study *The Christian Trinity in History,* Bertrand de Margerie says subordinationism is "a perpetual temptation and one, which should not surprise us."[1] Over the centuries many have argued that in one way or another the Son is eternally subordinated to the Father. I outline below seven examples of differing expressions of subordinationism. They are treated as discrete approaches, but usually those who major on one form of subordinationism embrace others as well. Except for the first two examples, which are limited historically, all the other examples can be found in conservative evangelical literature today, as I will demonstrate.

Ante-Nicene Subordinationism

It is generally conceded that the ante-Nicene Fathers were subordinationists. This is clearly evident in the writings of the second-century "Apologists." Their challenge as ardent monotheists was to show, without falling into tritheism, how the Son and the Holy Spirit could be confessed as God alongside God the Father, who for them was God in the absolute sense. In seeking

---

[1]Bertrand de Margerie, *The Christian Trinity in History* (Petersham, Mass.: St. Bede, 1982), p. 74.

to resolve this problem they were the first Christian theologians to attempt an intellectual explanation of the relationship of the three divine persons. The unfolding historical revelation of Father, Son and Holy Spirit given in the Bible provided them with the answers they needed. They developed their trinitarian thinking solely on the basis of the economy of revelation. They proposed that Christ was the eternal Logos (the thought, mind or word) of God. In creation he was first made manifest. Justin calls the Logos God's "off-spring" *(gennēma)*,[2] or "child" *(teknon)*.[3] For him it is quite clear that the Son is "in second place" and the Holy Spirit is "third in order."[4] He even speaks of the Son as the "second God" to be worshiped "in secondary rank."[5] Irenaeus follows a very similar path. In his writings, we find the same stress on monotheism, the same identification of God with God the Father and the same understanding of Christ as the Logos. What Irenaeus adds is extended reflection on what was involved in the economy of salvation and a deeper interest in the Holy Spirit. For him the Logos and the Spirit are the two hands of God at work.[6]

The theological enterprise begun by the Apologists and Irenaeus was continued in the West by Hippolytus and Tertullian. Tertullian is of particular importance because he was first to use the word *Trinity* (Latin *Trinitas*), and it was he who developed the terminological definition of the Trinity as "one substance—three persons" (Latin *una substantia, tres personae*), which would determine Western trinitarian theology for centuries. These two theologians found themselves confronted with modalism: the idea that the one God manifested himself in three ways, or modes, of being. In rejecting modalism they both stress the real distinctions between Father, Son and Holy Spirit, whom they call "persons"; but both of them subordinate the Son and the Spirit. They begin their exposition of the Trinity by affirming that God, who they identify with God the Father, was originally one. Tertullian—writing against Marcion—exclaims, "If God is not one, then there is no God."[7] It was at creation that the Son and the Spirit, who were forever with the Father, were made manifest. Like the Apologists, Tertullian reasons from what is disclosed in God's unfolding (economy of)

---

[2]"The First Apology of Justin," in *Ante-Nicene Fathers,* ed. Alexander Roberts and James Donaldson (Grand Rapids, Mich.: Eerdmans, 1979), 1:21; "Dialogue with Trypho a Jew," in *Ante-Nicene Fathers,* 62.4.

[3]"Dialogue with Trypho" 125.3.

[4]"First Apology" 14.32.60

[5]Ibid., 13.3.

[6]Irenaeus *Against Heresies,* ibid 4.6.6; 2.30.9.

[7]Tertullian *Against Marcion,* in *Ante-Nicene Fathers,* 1.3.

revelation. He affirms that the divine three are eternally distinct persons and so excludes modalism, but he accepts the subordination of the Son and the Spirit, whom he sees as creations of the Father. Thus he speaks of the Son as "second to the Father" and of the Spirit as "third from God."[8] Edmund Hill concludes that Tertullian, along with the Apologists, envisages the Son and the Holy Spirit like "lieutenants of the sole monarch, the Father."[9]

The ante-Nicene Fathers did their best to explain how the one God could be a Trinity of three persons. It was the way they approached this dilemma that caused them insoluble problems and led them into subordinationism. They began with the premise that there was one God who was the Father, and then they tried to explain how the Son and the Spirit could also be God. By the fourth century it was obvious that this approach could not produce an adequate theology of the Trinity. Those who followed them took other paths. In the East the approach was to begin with the three divine persons and then show how they were one; in the West the approach was to begin with the one God and then explain how God is three persons. Perhaps rather than calling them "subordinationists," it would be fairer and more accurate to call them "naive subordinationists." This adjective is suggested because although they did subordinate the Son and the Spirit, they were doing their best to be faithful to the teaching of Scripture as it was understood in the historical period in which they found themselves.[10] Bernard Lonergan is even more circumspect. He writes,

> If the term, subordinationism, is used to describe a certain fact, namely that the ante-Nicene authors were not well up on the theology of a later age, then of course its use is both legitimate and useful. For before anything can be understood one must know what is to be understood and explained. On the other hand, if we consider the proper goal of scientific inquiry, which is understanding, then the term, subordinationism, becomes a source of the greatest obscurity and confusion. For it is anachronistic to conceive the doctrine of the ante-Nicene authors according to the criteria of later theology, and anachronism precludes correct historical understanding.[11]

---

[8]Tertullian *Against Praxeas*, in *Ante-Nicene Fathers*, 7.15.

[9]Edmund Hill, *The Mystery of the Trinity* (London: Chapman, 1985), p. 52.

[10]W. Marcus insists that the subordinationism of the pre-Nicean period must be sharply distinguished from Arianism (*Der Subordinationismus: als historisches Phanomenon* [München: M. Hubner, 1963], p. 171). He says it was not ontological but *"heilsgeschichtlich-kosmologische oder oikonomische"* subordinationism.

[11]Bernard Lonergan, *The Way to Nicea* (London: Darton, Longman & Todd, 1976), p. 41.

Arian Subordinationism

Turning to the East we meet the dominating presence of Origen of Alexandria. He is very much a transitional figure. His contribution was both positive and negative. On a positive note he insisted on the eternal generation of the Son. This excluded the idea that the Son was created in time (i.e., he is one of God's creatures). His understanding of the Father as the "fountainhead of deity" *(pēgē tēs theotētos)*, who alone was "intrinsically God" *(autotheos)* was his negative contribution. This led him to depict the Son as different in being to the Father. On the basis of his largely Greek understanding of God he concluded that the Son (and the Spirit) must be ontologically subordinated to the Father. For him the Son could only be called God in a secondary sense.

Arius's teaching on the Trinity may be seen as a development and popularization of the ontological subordinationism of Origen.[12] Arius thought of God the Father as unitary, absolute, transcendent and the unoriginate source of all reality. His *being* was unique. He could not share it or communicate it with any other. On this basis the one who became incarnate as the Son of God, or Logos, had to be a creature whom the Father begat in time—of *different being* to the Father. Arius's basic premise was a Greek view of God, yet he was able to support his ideas by an impressive appeal to Scripture. He began with those texts that he thought, or did, speak of the Son's subordination (e.g., Prov 8:22; Jn 14:28; 17:3; 20:17; 1 Cor 15:28; Heb 3:2; 5:8), and then, in the light of these, he minimized the force of the texts that spoke of the full divinity of the Son and the "oneness" of the Father and the Son.[13] Arius began with the belief that the Son is subordinated to the Father, and then he found evidence for this in the many texts that spoke of the Son's subordination in the incarnation.[14]

Because the Son was hierarchically set under the Father in being, he was understood to be set under the Father in authority. As for a human son, his father stood above him in glory and power. In the few texts we have from Arius's pen

---

[12]I speak of "Arianism," but it is to be noted that the so-called Arianism of the fourth century took many forms. On this see R. P. C. Hanson, *The Search for the Christian Doctrine of God* (Edinburgh: T & T Clark, 1988), pp. 3–59; and, in brief, Marsh, *The Triune God: A Biblical, Historical and Theological Study* (Dublin: Columba, 1994), pp. 102–4.

[13]On the use of Scripture in the Arian debate, see Hanson, *Search*, pp. 824–48 and T. E. Pollard, *Johannine Christology in the Early Church* (Cambridge: Cambridge University Press, 1970).

[14]I think this is a better way to understand Arius's reasoning than that suggested by Catherine LaCugna, who says, "Arius concluded that the subordination of Christ to God according to the economy implied subordination at the level of God's being" (*God for Us: The Trinity and the Christian Life* [San Francisco: HarperSanFrancisco, 1991], p. 35). The pro-Nicenes, she adds, "argued in the opposite fashion."

and in the later "Arian" writings, the Son is consistently depicted as subject to the Father's will.[15] He does as the Father commands. The logic was that ontological subordination presupposed functional subordination and that functional subordination indicated ontological subordination. R. Gregg and E. Groh, in their innovative study of Arianism, claim that the functional subordination of the Son was in fact a key element in Arian theology. The Son's obedience to the Father illustrates what is needed to earn salvation. As they see it, "At the center of the Arian soteriology was a redeemer obedient to his Father's will, whose life of virtue modeled perfect creaturehood and hence a path of salvation for all Christians."[16] In reply to the Arians, as we have seen, Athanasius and the Cappadocian fathers taught that the Father and the Son were one in being and act/ function. Their teaching was codified in the Nicene Creed.

Arianism was a specific heresy, predicated on a Greek understanding of God. In the subsequent history of the church many others would advocate the eternal subordination of the Son, but usually they would do so on other premises and in other ways. Partly on the basis of ignorance about the true nature of historic Arianism, and partly because Arianism was thought to be the worst of heresies, those who deliberately (or in ignorance) broke with what was understood to be trinitarian orthodoxy were called "Arians."[17] In this usage the charge of being an "Arian" was not limited to those who spoke of the ontological subordination of the Son (and the Spirit) to the Father. It became a synonym for what is called "antitrinitarianism,"[18] which included also the errors of modalism and unitarianism.

Derivative Subordinationism

Basic to Arius's teaching was the absolute uniqueness and transcendence of God the Creator, who was identified with God the Father. For Arius the Father was "the unoriginate source" (*agennētos archē*) of all reality. In contrast, the Son was "begotten" (*gennētos*) or created (*genētos*) in time. This Arian teaching involved three closely related ideas: God the Father is the *monarchē* (the sole source or origin) of the Son; the biblical terminology of "begetting" implies the

---

[15]Hanson, *Search,* pp. 5–15, 19–43; R. Williams, *Heresy and Tradition* (London: Darton, Longman & Todd, 1987), p. 98.

[16]R. Gregg and E. Groh, *Early Arianism: A View of Salvation* (Philadelphia: Fortress, 1981), p. x.

[17]See Maurice Wiles, *Archetypal Heresy: Arianism Through the Centuries* (Oxford: Clarendon, 1996).

[18]See B. B. Warfield, "Antitrinitarianism," in *The New Schaff-Hertzog Encyclopaedia of Religious Knowledge,* ed. S. Jackson (Grand Rapids, Mich.: Baker, 1949), 1:203–5.

Son's creation in time; and creation or begetting presupposes subordination in being and function.

The idea that the Son was created in time had already been rejected by Origen, and when the words *eternally begotten of the Father* were included in the Nicene Creed of 381, the Son's creation in time found virtually no support in orthodoxy. However, apart from this specific matter, Arius's ideas on the relationship between the Father and the Son have proven to be amazingly resilient, appearing time and time again to substantiate differing expressions of subordinationism. Because the primary idea is that derivation of being implies diminution of being and authority, I call this error "derivative subordinationism." In the sixteenth century Calvin speaks of "certain rascals" who claim that the Father is God *par excellence* because he alone is "the fountainhead and beginning of deity."[19] The great Reformer vigorously opposed this idea, arguing that it involved ontological subordinationism.[20] The Arminians in the seventeenth century also held that the Son and the Spirit were subordinate because they were derived from the Father. The leading Arminian, Episcopius, wrote,

> It is certain from these same scriptures, that to these three persons divinity and divine perfections are attributed, but not collaterally or co-ordinately, but subordinately. So that the Father alone has the divine nature and those divine perfections for himself. . . . He is first in order . . . as it is more honorable to generate, to cause to proceed, than to be caused.[21]

In seventeenth-century England derivative subordinationism flourished. Bishop George Bull, in his famous and widely read *Defensio Fidei Nicaenae,* taught that the Son "in respect to his divinity, is a degree subordinate to the Father, insomuch as he is *from* him."[22] Likewise John Pearson in his also widely read book *The Exposition of the Creed* says, "In respect of his nature, the Father is greater (than the Son) in reference to the communication of the Godhead."[23] On the basis of the exegesis of 1,251 biblical passages, Samuel Clarke concluded

---

[19]John Calvin *Institutes of the Christian Religion* 1.13.23. On this debate in more detail, see B. B. Warfield, "Calvin's Doctrine of the Trinity," in *Calvin and Augustine* (Philadelphia: Presbyterian & Reformed, 1956), pp. 233–84.

[20]See our earlier discussion on Calvin's teaching on the Trinity.

[21]Quoted in H. C. Sheldon, *History of Christian Doctrine* (New York: Harper, 1886), 2:98.

[22]George Bull, *Defensio Fidei Nicaenae* (London, 1683). The English translation of the Latin text is taken from Sheldon, *History of Christian Doctrine,* p. 99.

[23]John Pearson, *The Exposition of the Creed* (London: Ward, Lock & Co., 1854), p. 198. This claim is repeated several times. This book was first published in 1659; the fifth printing was in 1683. More data on Pearson's explicit subordinationism is given in Wiles, *Archetypal Heresy,* p. 139.

in his book *Scripture Doctrine of the Trinity* (1712) that the Athanasian Creed was wrong. The Father alone is self-existent; the Son and the Spirit owe their divinity to the Father, who is uniquely true God. Clarke thus concluded that the Son and the Spirit are subordinate to the Father and therefore must obey him.[24] He was one of the most learned biblical scholars of his day, but in the end "the lower house of convocation" of the Church of England judged his ideas to be heretical.

In contemporary conservative evangelical writings, derivative subordinationism is often endorsed. John V. Dahms, in his essay "The Generation of the Son," published in the *Journal of the Evangelical Theological Society,*[25] argues that "the derivation of the Son from the Father" demands the "ontological subordination" of the Son to the Father because this alone explains the "ontological basis for the dissimilarity" of the two divine persons.[26] Similarly, Stephen Kovach and Peter Schemm writing in the same journal ten years later say, "The idea that the Son is begotten and the Father unbegotten means that the Father is primary and Sonship *[sic]* secondary."[27] "The eternal begottenness of the Son" indicates "the eternal subordination" of the Son.[28] This, they claim, is what the creeds teach.[29] The 1999 Sydney Doctrine Report makes the same claim: "In the creeds, the Son and the Spirit are asserted to be equal with the Father, but it is a derived equality. With the second and third persons, the mode of derivation and the relationship of being is distinct."[30]

The continuing recurrence of derivative subordinationism is surprising when it was so forcibly repudiated by Athanasius, the Cappadocian fathers and Augustine.[31] In reply to the Arians, Athanasius argued that the God of the Bible was not a "Monad" who begat a Son in time but a Triad from all eternity. He gladly endorsed the biblical terminology of the "begetting" of the Son but ac-

---

[24]Samuel Clarke, *Scripture Doctrine of the Trinity* (London, 1712). See further, Wiles, *Archetypal Heresy,* pp. 110–16.

[25]John V. Dahms, "The Generation of the Son," *Journal of the Evangelical Theological Society* 32, no. 4 (1989): 493–501.

[26]Ibid., p. 497.

[27]Stephen D. Kovach and Peter R. Schemm, "A Defense of the Doctrine of the Eternal Subordination of the Son," *Journal of the Evangelical Theological Society* 42, no. 3 (1999): 497.

[28]Ibid., p. 465.

[29]Ibid., p. 470.

[30]Sydney Anglican Diocesan Doctrine Commission, "The Doctrine of Trinity and Its Bearing on the Relationship of Men and Women," 1999 report, par. 25 <www.anglicanmediasydney.asn.au/doc/trinity.html>. (See appendix B of this book.)

[31]The evidence for these assertions has already been given. On the rejection of derivative subordinationism, see also LaCugna, *God for Us,* pp. 30–37, 61–65, 85–86; D. MacLeod, *The Person of Christ* (Leicester, U.K.: Inter-Varsity Press, 1998), pp. 121–28.

cused the Arians of reading literally what we would call today "metaphorical" language. They argued that men became fathers in time and that their sons were less than them and obedient to them. In reply, Athanasius argued that all human fathers have fathers and all human sons have the potential to be fathers. God the Father alone is intrinsically Father, and God the Son intrinsically the Son. Then turning the tables on them, he pointed out that their appeal to the human father-son relationship, rather than supporting their case, proved the very opposite. A human father's son is of the same being as his father. The Cappadocians built on Athanasius's reasoning by making a clear distinction between being "begotten" and being "made" and between the titles "Ungenerate" and "Father." They argued divine begetting implies a Son; divine creation or making implies a creature. The first is to be endorsed, the second rejected. The Son in Scripture is begotten not made. In regard to the titles "Ungenerate" and "Father," they insisted that they were not synonyms. The title "Ungenerate" differentiates the Father from the Son and the Son from the Father. In contrast the title "Father" speaks primarily of relationship. The Father is the Father of the Son. The Father cannot be the Father without the Son, and vice versa.

The Cappadocians differed from Athanasius in speaking of the Father as the *monarchē* (the sole source or origin) of the Son (and the Holy Spirit). However, they sought to exclude completely ontological subordinationism by arguing, firstly, that the three "persons" *(hypostases)* share equally in the one divine nature or being *(ousia)* and, secondly, that the three persons fully coinhere in each other. For them, in contrast to Arius, derivation in being did not entail diminution in being. Their opposition to ontological and functional subordinationism cannot be questioned. However, many Western theologians have argued that in continuing to speak of the *monarchē* of the Father, the Cappadocian fathers, metaphorically speaking, left the back door ajar for subordinationism to reenter.[32] Even one of the Cappadocian fathers, Gregory of Nazianzus, saw the dangers of speaking of the person of the Father as the *monarchē:* "I am alarmed at the term the source *[tēn archē]*, lest I make him [the Son] the principle of inferiors. . . . To subordinate any of the three is to overthrow the Trinity."[33]

Augustine develops another model of the Trinity. He begins with the one di-

---

[32]So G. L. Prestige, *God in Patristic Thought* (London: SPCK, 1952), p. 249; Wolfhart Pannenberg, *Systematic Theology* (Grand Rapids, Mich.: Eerdmans, 1991), 1:279–80; LaCugna, *God for Us,* p. 69; J. Thompson, *Modern Trinitarian Perspectives* (Oxford: Oxford University Press, 1994), p. 24; Thomas F. Torrance, *The Trinitarian Faith* (Edinburgh: T & T Clark, 1988), p. 241.

[33]Gregory of Nazianzus *Oratio in laudem Basilii* 43.30.

vine substance and then moves to the three divine persons. For him the Father *and* the Son are the *archē* (origin, source) of the Holy Spirit. In contrast to the Cappadocians, the *monarchē* of the Father is not the unifying principle. Augustine also clearly distinguishes between the *eternal* "generation" of the Son and the *eternal* "procession" of the Spirit and the *temporal* "mission" of the Son and the Spirit. For him the *temporal* missions of the Son and the Spirit do not have an effect on the *eternal* relations they share with the Father in the divine unity.

There is, nevertheless, a sense in which the *monarchē* of the Father may be affirmed without suggesting subordinationism, and some contemporary mainline Protestant and Roman Catholic theologians continue to speak of the Father in this way.[34] In the Nicene Creed the Son is confessed to be "begotten of the Father" and "true God from true God."[35] He is the Son *of* the Father, yet he is fully God.[36] He does not derive his divine *being* from the Father: he is eternally one in being with the Father, but apart from the Father he is not the Son (any more than the Father is the Father without the Son). Speaking this way of the *monarchē* of the Father thus underlines the distinctiveness of the persons. The Son's distinct *person* is defined by his relation to the Father, and vice versa.

Some contemporary Western theologians, however, are opposed to speaking of Father as the *monarchē* of the Son and the Spirit. They note that this idea is called into question by the Western version of the Nicene Creed—which speaks of the Spirit proceeding from the Father *and* the Son—and they argue it is problematic for a doctrine of the Trinity where the complete equality of the three distinct divine persons is affirmed. In rejecting the *monarchē* of the Father, they follow Athanasius. For him the idea that the Father alone was the *monarchē* of the Son was an Arian error. Since the whole Godhead is in the Son and the Spirit, they must be included with the Father in the *monarchē* of the Trinity.[37]

Millard Erickson gives eloquent expression to the contemporary rejection of

---

[34]For example, Leonardo Boff, *Trinity and Society,* trans. Paul Burns (Maryknoll, N.Y.:Orbis, 1986), pp. 83, 146; Pannenberg, *Systematic Theology,* 1:324–27; W. Kasper, *The God of Jesus Christ* (London: SCM Press, 1983), p. 295.

[35]Torrance says these words exclude "any difference in Deity, Glory, Power and Being between the Father and the Son. The deity of the Son is as true and as unqualified as the Deity of the Father. While the Son is begotten of the Father, he is, with the Spirit, equal in every respect to the Father, apart from being Father" (*The Christian Doctrine of God: One Being, Three Persons* [Edinburgh: T & T Clark, 1996]), p. 189).

[36]Torrance says this does not mean that "the Son is to be thought of as proceeding from the *Person* of the Father (ἐκ τῆς ὑποστάσεως τοῦ Πατρός) but from the *Being* of the Father (ἐκ τῆς οὐσίας τοῦ Πατρός) as in the pronouncement of the Council of Nicaea" (*Christian Doctrine of God,* p. 141). Torrance's discussion of the doctrine of the *monarchē* of the Father deserves careful reading. See ibid., pp. 141, 176, 180–90.

[37]See my earlier exposition of this point and also Torrance, ibid., p. 181.

the idea that the Father is the *monarchē* of the Son and the Spirit. He writes:

> To speak of one of the persons as unoriginate and the others as either eternally
> begotten or proceeding from the Father is to introduce an element of causation
> or origination that must ultimately involve some type of subordination among
> them. . . .
>
> While the Father may be thought of as the cause of the existence of the Son
> and the Spirit, they are mutually the cause of his existence and the existence of
> one another. There is an eternal symmetry of all three persons.[38]

Numerical Subordinationism

Very closely related to derivative subordinationism, and often integral to it, is
what I call "numerical subordinationism." As noted earlier, Justin and Tertullian, as an expression of their naive subordinationism, describe the Son as "second" to the Father and the Holy Spirit as "third." This same numerical
subordinating, now with ontological intent, appears in Origen. He speaks of
the Son as "secondary in rank" and of the Spirit as "of the third rank."[39] This is
not surprising for the background of thought in the East was Neo-Platonic par-
ticipationism, where "order" implied a descending scale of "being": a hierarchy
of superordinate to subordinate.

Trinitarian orthodoxy has allowed that the Father may be spoken of as "first,"
the Son as "second" and the Holy Spirit as "third" in relation to economic or revelational order as in the Apostles' and Nicene Creeds.[40] However, temporal ordering has been consistently rejected: the Father, the Son and the Holy Spirit are
all eternal and therefore not temporally subordinated.

Ordering in rank, status and function has nevertheless been commended or
implied from time to time. Thus Pearson concludes in his *Exposition of the Creed*
that since the Father is "first," he is "pre-eminent."[41] Many contemporary conservative evangelicals reason in the same way. For example, as noted above, Kovach and Schemm say, "The idea that the Son is begotten and the Father
unbegotten means that the Father is primary and Sonship *[sic]* secondary."[42]
"There is," they continue, "order and ranking in the Godhead, thus the name of

---

[38]Millard Erickson, *God in Three Persons: A Contemporary Interpretation of the Trinity* (Grand
Rapids, Mich.: Baker, 1995), pp. 309–10.

[39]Origen *Contra Celsum* 5.9. See also W. Hill, *The Three-Personed God* (Washington, D.C.:
Catholic University of America Press, 1982), p. 40.

[40]See Torrance's very helpful comments on economic or revelational order in *Christian Doctrine*, p. 176.

[41]Pearson, *Exposition of the Creed*, p. 59.

[42]Kovach and Schemm, "Defense," p. 465.

Father is given to 'the First,' of Son to 'the Second,' and of Holy Spirit to 'the Third.' "[43]

It seems that this deduction is made by way of an analogy with fallen human relationships, where the word *order* usually suggests an ordering in rank, status and function. The one who is first is over others; those who are in lower numerical order are subordinates or inferiors. The word *subordinate* means to be "ordered under." In this usage the word *order* implies hierarchical ordering. Most orthodox theologians past and present are agreed that the relationship of the three divine persons is ordered and structured. This order is not, however, conceptualized hierarchically. It need not be because the word *order* does not entail, by necessity, hierarchy. People seated evenly around a circular table, or a room with everything in its proper place, may be said to be "in order." Moreover, where perfect love prevails none need be first, second or third in being/status or in function/work.

Divine order involves both how the three divine persons relate to one another and how they relate to humans and humans to them. In the intradivine life, the Father always relates to the Son as Father, and the Son to the Father as Son, and the Spirit as he who proceeds from the Father or from the Father and the Son. On these ordered relations orthodoxy distinguishes the persons. There is, however, order also in divine-human interaction. The great Athanasius spoke repeatedly of an order *(taxis)*, or observable pattern *(eidos)*, in how we come to the triune God and how he comes to us. In respect to the God-to-human relationship the order is "from the Father, through the Son and in the Holy Spirit." In the human-to-God relationship the order is "in the Spirit, through the Son, to the Father."[44]

It should also be noted that neither Paul nor other New Testament authors always preserve the order of Father, Son, Holy Spirit. The reverse order is found in 1 Corinthians 12:4–6 and Ephesians 4:4–6; in 1 Peter 1:2 the order is Father, Spirit, Son; in 2 Corinthians 13:14 and Galatians 1:1 the Son is named before the Father. In the light of these texts B. B. Warfield, the learned American Reformed scholar, asks

> whether the order Father, Son, Spirit was especially significant to Paul and his fellow-writers of the New Testament? If in their conviction the very essence of the doctrine of the Trinity was embodied in this order, should we not anticipate that

---

[43]Ibid., p. 468.

[44]Athanasius *Ad Serapionem de morte arii* 1.6, 9, 12, 14, 28, 30f; 3.5; 4.6, etc. See further on this Marsh, *Triune God,* p. 170.

there should appear in their numerous allusions to the Trinity some suggestion of this conviction?[45]

Contemporary discussions of the Trinity by Roman Catholic and mainline Protestant theologians generally reject numbering the members of the Trinity "first," "second" and "third." This terminology, says David Cunningham, obscures "the radical co-equality of the Three [for] it suggests a logical or temporal sequence" where the one called "first" is in some way set over the others.[46]

Nineteenth- and Twentieth-Century Ontological Subordinationism

The subordinationism that flourished in the seventeenth century on the continent and in England found supporters in America. It is not surprising to find these ideas among Arminian and more liberal theologians in the United States,[47] but it is surprising to find them firmly established in the writings of conservative Reformed theologians[48]—most notably in the work of the learned nineteenth-century Presbyterian Charles Hodge. In his detailed discussion on the doctrine of the Trinity in his widely read *Systematic Theology,* he repeatedly affirms the divinity of the Son but at the same time, in no less than thirteen instances,[49] speaks of the subordination of the Son.[50] For him, "three essential facts" sum up the doctrine of the Trinity: "unity of essence, distinction in persons and subordination."[51] This involves "the principle of subordination of the Son to the Father and the Spirit to the Father and the Son"[52]—a hierarchi-

---

[45]B. B. Warfield, *Biblical Foundations* (London: Tyndale Press, 1958), p. 108.

[46]David Cunningham, *These Three Are One: The Practice of Trinitarian Theology* (Oxford: Blackwell, 1998), p. 113.

[47]See on this G. P. Fisher, *History of Christian Doctrines* (Edinburgh: T & T Clark, 1902), pp. 418–45.

[48]See also A. H. Strong, *Systematic Theology* (Philadelphia: Judson, 1907), p. 342. The Sydney Doctrine Report, par. 26, claims that "the Calvinists" Jonathan Edwards and Robert Louis Dabney also endorsed the subordination of the Son in "personal subsistence." I personally could not find this in their writings.

[49]Charles Hodge, *Systematic Theology* (Philadelphia: Judson Press, 1907), 1:455, 460-62, 464-65, 467-68, 474.

[50]In his *A Commentary on the First Epistle to the Corinthians* [(London: Banner of Truth, 1958), p. 63], Hodge says, "The Scriptures speak of a threefold subordination of Christ. 1. A subordination as to the mode of subsistence and operation of the second, to the first person of the Trinity; which is perfectly consistent with their identity of substance, and equality in power and glory. 2. The voluntary subordination of the Son in his humbling himself to be found in fashion as a man. . . . 3. The economical or official subordination of the the anthropos [God-man]. That is, the subordination of the incarnate Son of God, in his work of redemption and as the head of the church."

[51]Hodge, *Systematic Theology,* 1:467.

[52]Ibid., 1:460.

cal ordering of the Trinity. This subordination, he says, is in "the mode of subsistence and operation of the persons."[53] Hodge claims emphatically that his
understanding of the Trinity exactly reflects "the facts" revealed in Scripture,
the teaching of the Nicene and Athanasian creeds, and that of Augustine and
Calvin.[54]

Subordination in "modes of operation" indicates that the Son does as the Father directs and the Spirit does as the Father and Son direct. In their functions,
works or operations, the Son is set under the Father and the Spirit under the
Father and the Son. The Father is first, the Son is second, and the Spirit is third
in authority.[55] How the eternal subordination of the Son to the Father in his operations, functions or works can be reconciled with the confession "Jesus is
Lord," Hodge never explains. The concept of subordination in "subsistence" is
a little more complex. Hodge's definition of the Trinity as "one divine being
[who] subsists in three persons, Father, Son and Holy Spirit," explains what he
means.[56]

Hodge presupposes the Western model of the Trinity, which was given its
classic definition by Augustine. This begins with God as a unity of essence/sub-
stance/being before moving to the persons who are said to "subsist" in or as
Father, Son and Holy Spirit. "To subsist" is "to exist in or as." Hodge is thus arguing that in his personal existence as the Son, the second person of the Trinity
is subordinated to the person of the Father, and that in his personal existence
as the Holy Spirit, the third person of the Trinity is subordinated to the first and
second persons. The Father is first not only in his operations or works (functional superiority) but also in his "subsistence"—individual existence as the Father (ontological superiority); the Son is second and the Spirit third. Hodge thus
speaks of the Son as "inferior in rank."[57] In other words Hodge is depicting the
eternal Trinity as a hierarchy. Paul Jewett says that Hodge's understanding of
subordination in subsistence is "remarkable in its confusion."[58]

Hodge never explains why he holds that the three members of the Trinity are
ordered hierarchically in being and function. He presents his case as if it is what
all orthodox Christians in the past have believed. His endorsement of derivative

---

[53]Ibid., 1:445, 461.
[54]Ibid., 1:464, 467.
[55]Ibid., 1:445. See Warfield, *Biblical Foundations,* pp. 110-11 for a clear and concise explanation of what is meant by "operational subordination" (something Warfield rejects in the eternal Trinity).
[56]Hodge, *Systematic Theology,* 1:444-55.
[57]Ibid., 1:469.
[58]Paul Jewett, *God, Creation and Revelation* (Grand Rapids, Mich.: Eerdmans, 1991), p. 317.

subordination would seem to be the answer: He maintains that "the Son is of the Father": "he is from another."[59] He quotes, with approval, Bishop Pearson, who speaks of the "pre-eminence of the Father" since "he is from none" while the Son is "from him."[60] This view, Hodge says, is endorsed by the Nicene fathers, who, he claims, teach that sonship "means derivation of essence." The first person of the Trinity is Father, because he communicates the essence of the Godhead to the second person; and the second person is Son, because he derives that essence from the first person.[61] This suggests that divine being (essence) flows downward from the Father in diminishing measure. For this reason the Son is subordinated ontologically and functionally to the Father, and the Spirit is likewise subordinated to the Father and the Son. However, the Nicene fathers, as we have seen, totally rejected the idea that derivation of being implies diminution in being. The Father and the Son, the Nicene Creed asserts, are *one in being*.

In arguing for the eternal subordination in subsistence and operations of the Son and the Spirit, Hodge parts company with historic orthodoxy, despite his many claims to the contrary. The subordination of the Son (and the Spirit) in subsistence and operations is excluded by the Nicene and Athanasian Creeds, the Reformation confessions of faith, and, interestingly, by Warfield, Hodge's successor at Princeton. He says it is "thoroughly illegitimate . . . to suggest any subordination for the Son or the Spirit which would in any manner impair that complete identity with the Father in being and that complete equality with the Father in powers."[62] Even if one can find texts to support the subordination of the Son, these technically named kinds of eternal subordinationism can hardly be called "facts" found in Scripture. Rather than being supported by Augustine, subordination in subsistence directly contradicts what is essential to Augustine's doctrine of the Trinity. The divine unity absolutely excludes for Augustine the possibility that any of the persons can be subordinated in any way. In *De Trinitate*, he writes, "It is the same for God to be as to subsist."[63] He continues, saying, "We talk of three persons of the same being, or of three persons of the one being, but we do not talk about three persons out of the one being, as though what being is were one thing and what person is another."[64]

---

[59]Hodge, *Systematic Theology*, 1:469 and 465.

[60]Ibid., 1:465.

[61]Ibid., 1:468.

[62]Warfield, *Biblical Foundations*, p. 112. Warfield never indicates he is opposing Hodge's theology. Indeed, he implies he is in agreement with Hodge. As this is not the case, an apologetic motive must be presumed in Warfield's writings.

[63]Augustine *De Trinitate* 7.9.

[64]Ibid., 7.11.

Early in the fifth century, Rufinus of Aquileia seems to have been the first to use the Latin word *subsistentia* as the translation of the Greek word *hypostasis* to distinguish clearly between the one divine being and the three persons.[65] For him as a Western theologian, the three subsistences or persons could not be subordinated ontologically or functionally because they shared equally in the one divine substance. Augustine saw clearly that the use of the word *person* (Latin *persona*)—understood as "individual thinking subject"—to designate the three subsistences was not the ideal term. The understanding of the word *person* he had inherited was the problem. It was only in the late Middle Ages that it was seen that "differing relations" was a better way to define the word *person*. Thomas Aquinas built on this insight, arguing that the three mutually opposed relations in God—fatherhood, sonship and passive spiration—actually constitute the divine persons in their particularity.[66] On this basis a divine "person" is defined as "a subsistent relation in God." This understanding of a divine person even more firmly shut the door on ontological subordination. The divine being common to the three, the divine "being-in-itself," remains intact when the three are distinguished as divine "being-in-relation." There could be no subordination whatsoever of the divine persons in their subsistence as Father, Son and Spirit, for at all times they are of one substance.

It is interesting to note that two of the theologians Hodge lists at the end of his chapter on the Trinity as his sources are George Bull and John Pearson, two men Maurice Wiles calls "Arian."[67] Another factor that also certainly distorted Hodge's reasoning was his social context. He was part of a small, educated, male elite in a hierarchically ordered society in which black slaves were "in perpetuity" subordinated to white masters—a system Hodge endorsed unashamedly, claiming it was supported by the clearest teaching of Scripture.[68] It seems that this pervasive reality had a greater effect on his thinking than did the Scriptures or the creeds. So he wrote, "Order and subordination pervade the whole universe, and [they are] essential to its being."[69] We are thus not surprised that with these social and political commitments, Hodge read back into the Trinity the fixed hierarchical ordering of his cultural setting.

---

[65]For what follows see de Margerie, *Christian Trinity*, pp. 122–39; Kasper, *God of Jesus Christ*, pp. 280–81, and the detailed exposition of the thought of the Cappadocians, Augustine and Calvin already given.

[66]On Aquinas see W. Hill, *Three-Personed God*, pp. 62–80.

[67]Wiles, *Archetypal Heresy*, p. 482. See Hodge, *Systematic Theology*, 1:482.

[68]See more on this in chapter ten, "The Tradition: The Bible Endorses the Institution of Slavery."

[69]Hodge, *Commentary*, p. 206.

Dutch Reformed theologian Louis Berkhof, an American living early in the twentieth century, also speaks of "a certain subordination as to the manner of personal subsistence" in the Trinity.[70] Evangelicals who advocate the permanent subordination of women frequently quote these words.[71] Berkhof's support of the *eternal* subordination of the Son and the Spirit is, however, at best ambiguous. His treatment of the Trinity is far more balanced than Hodge's. He knows nothing whatsoever about "eternal role subordination," and he repeatedly rejects the ontological subordination of the Son.[72] In fact, given in full, the quotation above reads, "[there is] a certain subordination as to the manner of personal subsistence, but no subordination as far as possession of the divine essence is concerned." In one problematic sentence, Berkhof uses phraseology reflecting nineteenth-century American Reformed discussions of the Trinity. His words in these few lines cannot be easily harmonized with his overall exposition of the Trinity, which stresses the equality of the persons in their being and work.[73]

Hodge never explicitly says that the Son and the Spirit are subordinated in their person, nature or being (ontology), nor does he speak openly of hierarchical ordering in the Trinity, although his conclusions clearly suggest both of these things. Contemporary evangelicals are less circumspect. George Knight, who is famous in conservative evangelical circles for developing the novel argument that women and men are equal in being yet subordinated in *role,* explicitly speaks of the "ontological" subordination of the Son.[74] It is his view that the Bible teaches a "chain of subordination" within the Godhead—which must mean a hierarchical order.[75] Dahms, in two separate articles published in the *Journal of the Evangelical Theological Society,* also speaks unambiguously of the

---

[70]Louis Berkhof, *Systematic Theology* (London: Banner of Truth, 1958), p. 89.

[71]See, e.g., Thomas Schreiner in *Recovering Biblical Manhood and Womanhood: A Response to Evangelical Feminism,* ed. John Piper and Wayne Grudem (Wheaton, Ill.: Crossway, 1991), p. 130; Sydney Doctrine Report, par. 26.

[72]Berkhof, *Systematic Theology,* note p. 84 line 1, p. 83 par. c. See also Berkhof, *The History of Christian Doctrines* (London: Banner of Truth, 1969), pp. 83–97.

[73]The Sydney Doctrine Report, par. 15, also quotes T. C. Hammond as a supporter of the ontological subordination of the Son (*In Understanding Be Men: An Introductory Handbook on Christian Doctrine* [London: Inter-Varsity Press, 1936], p. 57). Hammond does mention the subordination of the Son in this brief summary of doctrine, but at this point he seems simply to be reflecting Hodge. In the 1960s Dr. Broughton Knox told me and other students that Hammond wrote this book on the boat that first brought him from Ireland to Australia before the Second World War. The only texts he had before him were the Bible and Hodge's *Systematic Theology.*

[74]George Knight, *New Testament Teaching on the Role Relationship of Men and Women,* (Grand Rapids, Mich.: Baker, 1977), p. 56.

[75]Ibid., p. 21.

ontological subordination of the Son. In the first of these essays, "The Generation of the Son" (quoted previously), he argues that the doctrine of the "generation of the Son" implies that the Son's divinity is "derived" from the Father.[76]
This must be accepted, he tells us, if the "ontological basis for the subordination
of the Son to the Father, which the NT emphasizes," is to be upheld.[77] This subordination, he adds, is not merely economic or functional.[78] In a personal letter
to me he says that he emphatically rejects the idea that "the Son simply has a
subordinate role." It is "my view," he writes, that "the role of the Son is preceded
and determined by his *being* [essence precedes existence]."[79] In his second article, "The Subordination of the Son," he sets out his case in more detail for the
"ontological basis for eternal subordination [of the Son]."[80] The Son must be ontologically subordinated, he reasons, for "if the Father and the Son are essentially alike in every respect, the Son could never subordinate himself to the Father
without denying his own nature."[81] What is so startling about Dahms's articles
in this prestigious conservative evangelical journal are his unambiguous assertions that the Son is *ontologically* subordinated to the Father.

In his essay "The Man-Woman Debate: Theological Comment," published in
the *Westminster Theological Journal,* Robert Letham adopts a similar position
but is less consistent.[82] He wants to have it both ways: the three persons of the
Trinity are ontologically equal, and the Son and the Spirit are subordinated in
"the ontological relations of the persons of the Trinity."[83] This, he explains, involves the eternal subordination of the Son and the Spirit "in the order of subsistence."[84] Subordination in subsistence, an idea we have already found in
Hodge, alludes to a subordination in essential personhood, a difference in being
between the Father and the Son. This is ontological subordinationism. Letham
bases his case for the eternal subordination of the Son in the immanent Trinity
on the subordination of the Son seen in the incarnation—what he calls "the eco-

---

[76]Dahms, "Generation," p. 499.

[77]Ibid., p. 497.

[78]Ibid.

[79]John V. Dahms, letter to author, dated July 12,1995.

[80]John V. Dahms, "The Subordination of the Son," *Journal of the Evangelical Theological Society* 37, no. 3 (1994): 351–64; see p. 363.

[81]Ibid., p. 364.

[82]Robert Letham, "The Man-Woman Debate: Theological Comment," *Westminister Theological
Journal* 52 (1990): 65–78.

[83]Ibid., p. 68. See further G. Bilezikian, *Community 101* (Grand Rapids, Mich.: Zondervan,
1997), pp. 195–97. He highlights Letham's contradictory assertions. Bilezikian's argument
was published earlier as "Hermeneutical Bungee Jumping: Subordination in the Godhead,"
Journal of the Evangelical Theological Society 40, no. 1 (1997): 57–68.

[84]Letham, "The Man-Woman Debate," p. 73.

nomic Trinity." So, he writes, "the revelation of the economic Trinity truly indicates the ontological Trinity."[85] To prove that the Son is subordinated to the Father he cites John 5:19–43; 17:1ff. and Hebrews 5:8; 10:5–10,[86] texts quoted by the Arians. In a quite amazing assertion he says that if the subordination seen in the incarnation does "not reflect the eternal relation of the Father and the Son then we are left with modalism."[87] His premise is that the divine persons can only be differentiated from one another by subordinating the Son to the Father and the Spirit to the Father and the Son. This is a slip in logic, for the word *difference* does not imply, let alone demand, subordination. Two human beings can be fully equal and yet be distinct and different persons. If this is so, why cannot it also be so in the divine Trinity? What drives Letham's case for the eternal subordination of the Son is his concern to uphold the permanent "headship" of men. His basic premise is that just as there is a hierarchical order in the eternal Trinity, "which includes a relation of authority and obedience," so too such an order prevails between men and women.[88]

Later in 1999, the *Journal of the Evangelical Society* also printed an article by Stephen Kovach and Peter Schemm arguing that "the Son is eternally subordinated to God the Father both in relation and role."[89] The authors concentrate on role subordination but insist that this indicates an eternal hierarchical ranking in the Godhead and a "subordination as to the mode of subsistence."[90] In other words, in ontological relations the Son is eternally set under the Father. Again we find this case supported by appeal to Athanasius, Augustine, Calvin and the Nicene Creed and by the claim that the best of evangelical and Reformed theologians, past and present, endorse the eternal subordination of the Son. Kovach and Schemm tell us that theologians who affirm the equality and symmetry of the divine persons in the Trinity reflect "an agenda that wants to redefine women's roles outside of biblical revelation." They are guilty of introducing "new ideas on the Trinity."[91]

In Australia, this same concern to uphold the "headship" of men has led Moore College theologians also to depict the eternal Trinity as an ontological hierarchy. Thus D. B. Knox, the former principal, argues in his case for the exclusion of women from ordination that the Father-Son relationship within the

---

[85]Ibid., p. 68.
[86]Ibid., p. 69.
[87]Ibid. See also the Sydney Doctrine Report, par. 21.
[88]Letham, "The Man-Woman Debate," p. 65.
[89]Kovach and Schemm, "Defense," p. 472.
[90]Ibid., pp. 469, 475.
[91]Ibid., p. 476.

immanent Trinity is to be understood in terms of "superiority-inferiority"—an order of "headship and subordination."[92] Similarly, Robert Doyle, the senior lecturer in systematic theology at Moore College, in an article opposing the ordination of women, maintains that "there is an ontological order in the Trinity. Order does mean hierarchy."[93] Another Sydney evangelical theologian, Tony Payne, makes much the same point. He concludes, "The hierarchy and submission within the Godhead belongs to eternity."[94]

It is, however, in the 1999 Sydney Doctrine Report on the Trinity that we find the most detailed presentation of the case that the Son is eternally subordinate to the Father in being and role. The controlling premise of this report is that just as God the Father is eternally "the head" of God the Son, so man is permanently "the head" of woman. The report begins by affirming "the unity and equality of the three persons of the Godhead," but the emphasis in the document falls on the view that

the Scriptures thus themselves bear witness to a subordination which belongs to

---

[92]D. B. Knox, *The Ministry of Women: Report to General Synod of the Church of England in Australia* (Sydney: Anglican Information Office, 1977), pp. 30, 31. See also his book *The Everlasting God* (Harfordshire, U.K.: Evangelical Press, 1982), pp. 69–72, where he stresses that there is "order" within the Godhead and between men and women that is characterized by the "headship" of the Father and of men. His wording is much more careful in *Everlasting God* than in *Ministry of Women*. Only when one perceives that "order"—by definition for Knox—means "hierarchical order" can one understand what is being said in this section. In both writings he quotes Jn 14:28, "the Father is greater than I," to explain his understanding of the order in the eternal Trinity. It is to be admitted, nevertheless, that many of his comments in this section that speak of the equality of the Father and the Son, and on the transforming power of love in relationships, are orthodox and helpful. The problem is, some of his comments and the logic of his argument imply subordinationism. The writings of Dr. Knox are being collected and reprinted by Sydney evangelical Anglicans. His study on the Trinity just quoted now appears in *Broughton Knox: Selected Works,* ed. Tony Payne (Sydney: Matthias, 2000), 1:37–170. This collection includes an appendix written by Knox titled "The Implications of the Doctrine of the Trinity for Theology and for Ordinary Life" (pp. 153–72), which contains a section on order in the Trinity and order in the man-woman relationship. Again equality is affirmed, yet at the same time we are told that this order implies a "priority of responsibility" and that in the Godhead the order must always be Father, Son and Holy Spirit—an order the New Testament does not always follow! See, e.g., 2 Cor 13:13.

[93]Robert Doyle, "God in Feminist Critique," *Reformed Theological Review* 52, no. 1 (1993): 21; and "Sexuality, Personhood and the Image of God," in *Personhood, Sexuality and Christian Ministry,* ed. B. Webb (Sydney: Lancer, 1987), pp. 43–46.

[94]Tony Payne, *The Briefing* 164 (September 1995): 7. For a similar opinion from another Sydney Anglican theologian, see Paul Barnett, *1 Corinthians* (Ross-shire, U.K.: Christian Focus, 2000), p. 200, who describes 1 Cor 11:3ff. as "a powerfully hierarchical statement" that speaks of the "eternal subordination" of the Son and the permanent subordination of women.

the eternal relationship between the persons of the Trinity, and not only to the humanity of Jesus in the incarnation, or even in the broader work of redemption. This applies to the Spirit as well as the Son. . . . Unity, equality and subordination characterise the life of the Trinity.[95]

This hierarchical ordering in the Trinity, the report emphasizes, is ontologically grounded. We are told that role subordination is "only true as far as it goes." The subordination of the Son reflects "the *essence* of the eternal relationship between them" (the Father and Son).[96] It bears witness to their differing *"mode of being"* and *"differences of being."*[97] It "belongs to the *very Persons* themselves in their *eternal nature.*"[98] The Eastern tradition's emphasis of the "priority of the Father" is commended because it "ensures a hierarchical mode of conceiving God."[99] Because the Son is subordinated to the Father in his being/nature/essence/person, the idea that his obedience to the Father is " 'voluntary, temporal and personal' is both inadequate and untrue."[100] The Son's obedience to his "head," the Father, "arises from the very nature of his *being* as Son. . . . He is incapable of doing other than his Father's will."[101] The Son is eternally bound to do what his "head," the Father, commands.

Basic to the whole argument of the Sydney Doctrine Report is the view that unless the Son is subordinated to the Father and women to men, their differences cannot be maintained.[102] It is repeatedly stressed that the distinction between the persons of the Godhead and between women and men are based on a difference in essence, nature or being—an unchanging and unchangeable hierarchical ordering—not just on differences in role or function. Thus the charge is made that to endorse the " 'egalitarian' case" for the persons within the Trinity, or between the sexes, "logically leads to a claim for undifferentiated equality."[103] "This subordination in the Godhead," we are told by the authors of this report, "is part of orthodox Christian teaching and . . . it expresses the truth of Scripture."[104] Time and time again it is claimed that the position taken on every issue

---

[95]Sydney Doctrine Report, par. 17.
[96]Ibid., par. 32. In this quote and the ones that follow, I have added the emphasis by putting key terms in italics.
[97]Ibid., par. 24, 25.
[98]Ibid., par. 32.
[99]Ibid., par. 23.
[100]Ibid., par. 33; see also par. 32.
[101]Ibid., par. 18; see also par. 32, 33.
[102]Ibid., par. 24, 25, 32, 40, 44.
[103]Ibid., par. 44.
[104]Ibid., par. 29.

raised is "biblical" or reflects "the whole teaching of Scripture." What is more, the authors assert "subordination in the Godhead" is taught in the Nicene and the Athanasian Creeds and by "Calvin and the Calvinists (Edwards, Berkhof, Hodge, Dabney, Packer, Knox)."[105] The error of the Arians, it is maintained, was that they merely "over-emphasised the subordinationist elements" of the New Testament.[106]

In the light of the growing trend among conservative evangelicals to speak of the Trinity in terms of hierarchical relationships,[107] Doyle's conclusion, quoted above, is significant. He sees with absolute clarity that an *eternal* hierarchical order within the Trinity has ontological implications. When these two words—*eternal* and *hierarchical*—are used together, there is no other option. The word *hierarchy* speaks of graded relationships: a descending order of superordinate to subordinate, of superior to inferior. The word *eternal* speaks of an attribute belonging solely to the Godhead.[108] In depicting the order within the Trinity as eternally hierarchical, one claims that this order reflects God as he is. Within the immanent Trinity there are "differences in being."

Although conservative evangelical theologians who speak of the subordination in *being* of the Son would insist on their orthodoxy and would claim that they are not Arians in the classic sense, their assertions that the Son is subordinated in his person/nature/essence/being (or in his "subsistence"), and that the three persons in the Trinity are set in an *eternal* hierarchical order, leaves them in a very ambiguous situation at best. In arguing, or implying, that the Son is eternally differentiated in *being* from the Father, they contradict the Nicene Creed, which affirms that the Son is "one in being *[homoousios]* with the Father." If the Son is *one in being* with the Father, then he cannot be subordinated ontologically, and there is no reason why he must eternally be subordinated to the Father in his work or role. If the Father and the Son share equally in divinity, they must share equally in authority, power and majesty. They are to be equally worshiped along with the Holy Spirit. To assert the equality in person and in

---

[105]Ibid., par. 25, 26.

[106]Ibid., par. 22.

[107]So James Hurley, *Man and Woman in Biblical Perspective* (Grand Rapids, Mich.: Zondervan, 1981), p. 167; M. Harper, *Equal and Different: Male and Female in Church and Family* (London: Hodder & Stoughton, 1994), pp. 6, 14, 83, 153–63; P. Barnett, *1 Corinthians*, p. 200; Piper and Grudem, *Recovering*, pp. 104, 130, 163, 394, 396. Elisabeth Elliot ("The Essence of Femininity: A Personal Perspective," *Recovering*, p. 394) speaks of a "glorious hierarchical order of graduated splendor, beginning with the Trinity."

[108]In contemporary studies on the Trinity the meaning of the term *eternity* is much discussed. See Ted Peters, *God as Trinity: Relationality and Temporality in Divine Life* (Louisville, Ky.: Westminster Press, 1993), pp. 146–70.

work of the Father and the Son in no way confuses the persons. The Father and the Son are never interchangeable because they eternally remain distinct in their persons and in the relations of origin that constitute them the persons they are.

It is to be conceded, nevertheless, that none of these evangelicals is a true Arian. They all repeatedly insist that they believe in the full divinity of the Son and the Holy Spirit. They want to have it both ways: the Son and Holy Spirit are equal with the Father, and they are also subordinated to him. The question is not whether they are Arians but whether their position is true to the most faithful doctrinal formulations of historical orthodoxy and whether their position as stated is theologically coherent. Historically speaking, I think it is safe to say that such contemporary formulations represent no historically promulgated position. They are certainly not in line with the concerns of Nicene faith that seeks to avoid any subordinationism of the Son in his being or acts.

Notwithstanding the issue of historical orthodoxy, their reasoning is incoherent. In their concern to uphold the subordination of women they have departed not only from historical orthodoxy expressed in the creeds and Reformation confessions but also from sound logic. They make mutually contradicting assertions about the Trinity. It is impossible to hold at one and the same time that the three persons of the Trinity are "one in being" and that there are "differences in being" between the three divine persons. To add a denial that the subordination of the Son and the Spirit does not imply that they are "inferior" to the Father does not help. Someone who is eternally or permanently subordinated in an involuntary way can only be regarded as an inferior. He is not the equal of his superior in any essential way. In their concern to uphold the permanent "headship" of men, they claim that God the Father is eternally the "head" of the Son, forgetting that in the New Testament the most fundamental confession after Easter is "Jesus is Lord." In "highly exalting him," the Father makes the Son the "head over all things" (Eph 1:22; Col 2:10).

Operational Subordinationism

As we have noted, Hodge speaks of the subordination of the Son in his "mode of subsistence *and* operations." By "operations," Hodge means his works or "functions."[109] For Hodge the subordination of the Son in his operations arises from the fact that he is subordinated in his subsistence: in other words, operational or functional subordination is grounded in ontological subordination.

---

[109]This is the word Warfield uses to explain what is meant by theologians when they speak of the "operational subordination" of the Son and the Spirit. See Warfield, *Biblical Foundations*, p. 110.

Dahms and the authors of the Sydney Doctrine Report, as we have seen, are exactly of the same opinion. In this report we are told, "The Son's obedience to the Father arises from the very nature of his *being* as Son."[110]

Warfield accepts that in the economy of salvation, the Son (and the Spirit) operate subordinately to the Father; but he insists this is "due to convention, an agreement, between the persons of the Trinity—a covenant as it is technically called—by virtue of which a distinct function in the work of redemption is voluntarily assumed by each."[111] This subordination, he says, does not imply any subordination in subsistence or in the eternal operations or works of the Son.[112] His logic works in the opposite direction to that of Hodge and of contemporary evangelicals who think the eternal subordination of the Son *explains* his functional subordination. For Warfield, the Father and the Son are one in their subsistence and therefore one in their operations, even if in the work of redemption each voluntarily assumes distinct functions.

In classic orthodox formulations of the Trinity, the distinctive work, or operations, of the persons of the Trinity are not divided. Athanasius and the Cappadocians insist that all three persons coinhere and work as one in all that they do (cf. Jn 10:30, 38; 14:11). In a similar vein, but within a different framework of thought, Augustine holds that the external works of the three persons of the Trinity are indivisible. There is a unity of will and action, grounded in the simplicity of the Godhead. Thus in both the Eastern and Western trinitarian traditions, *being* and *action* are held together. The intratrinitarian equality of the persons excludes on principle the idea that any one of the three is eternally set under another in their operations, works or functions.

But above all the *eternal* operational subordination of the Son is to be rejected because it cannot be reconciled with Scripture. At the resurrection, following his temporal and voluntary subordination demanded by the incarnation, the Son is exalted as Lord. He now sits at the right hand of God as the ruler of the universe. He has become "the head over all things" (Eph 1:22; Col 2:10). In Matthew's Gospel, Jesus says, "All authority in heaven and on earth has been given to me" (Mt 28:18). Rather than depicting the Son as eternally and compulsorily set under the Father, the New Testament consistently depicts the exalted Christ as equal to the Father in divinity, majesty and authority.

Conservative evangelicals who argue that the Son is eternally bound to obey the Father build on the premise that where two or more people live or work

---

[110]Sydney Doctrine Report, par. 18.
[111]Warfield, *Biblical Foundations*, p. 111.
[112]Ibid.

together one person must be in charge. This is how they envisage marriage, especially among Christians. They seem to forget that where love prevails there can be a harmony of wills and a gladly accepted mutual subordination. They err in seeking to explain how the persons of the Trinity relate to one another by appealing to a common feature of fallen human relationships.

Eternal Role Subordinationism

"Operational subordination" is simply a way of speaking of functional subordination, or "role subordination." The contemporary conservative evangelical case for the functional subordination of the Son, however, differs from nineteenth-century arguments for operational subordination on one very important matter. Hodge believed operational or functional subordination was a consequence of subordination in subsistence. Today the argument is made that you can have functional subordination *without* subordination in being or subordination in subsistence. In other words, *being* and *action* can be separated. Significantly, the terminology has also changed. No one ever spoke of the subordination in *role* of the Son (or of women) prior to the mid 1970s.[113]

Role subordination is the most common expression of subordinationism found in evangelical literature today. In this approach the Father is depicted as the "head" who commands, and the Son is depicted as the one who obeys. There is, we are told, within the eternal Trinity "a chain of command." Letham says the Father and the Son are related in "an order of authority and obedience."[114] Similarly, Wayne Grudem says that "the Father has the role of commanding, directing and sending" and the Son has the "role of obeying, going as the Father sends, and revealing God to us."[115] Raymond Ortland writes, "Within the Holy Trinity the Father leads, the Son submits to him, and the Spirit submits to both."[116]

The case for the eternal role subordination of the Son, without a subordination in being, is given most developed expression in Grudem's *Systematic Theology*. In this popular conservative evangelical publication, Grudem maintains that the Bible teaches both the equal divinity of the three persons and "the eter-

---

[113]For proof of this assertion see chapter seven, "Women in Contemporary Hierarchical-Complementarian Literature."

[114]Letham, "Man-Woman Debate", p. 69.

[115]Wayne Grudem, *Systematic Theology: An Introduction to Biblical Doctrine* (Grand Rapids, Mich.: Zondervan, 1994), p. 250.

[116]Raymond Ortland, "Male-Female Equality and Male Headship: Genesis 1—3," in *Recovering Biblical Manhood and Womanhood: A Response to Evangelical Feminism,* ed. John Piper and Wayne Grudem (Wheaton, Ill.: Crossway, 1991), p. 103.

nal subordination in role of the Son" and the Holy Spirit. This, it is claimed, is
what the church (Protestant, Catholic and Eastern Orthodox) has believed "at
least since Nicea (A.D. 325)."[117] Eight chapters later, when Grudem comes to discuss "man as male and female," we find that his "equal in essence but eternally
subordinate in role" understanding of the Trinity perfectly matches and confirms
his thesis that men and women are equal in essence yet differentiated in roles.
Later, when discussing "church government," Grudem again concludes that his
understanding of the Trinity confirms and endorses his view of the differing role
of women and men in church. Men have been given the ruling role, and women
have been given the subordinate role—they are to submit to male "headship."[118]

    Following the introduction of the word *role* by Knight to describe permanent-
ly fixed, hierarchically ordered gender relations, it was a small step to begin
speaking of "the eternal role" subordination of the Son to the Father. This was
an ingenious move. On this basis it was claimed, firstly, that the role subordination of women was reflective of, and endorsed by, the role subordination of the
Son and, secondly, that role subordination and equality (of essence/being)
could exist together. The former did not impinge on the latter. This new way of
speaking of the eternal Trinity, especially in regard to the Father-Son relationship, which is now so common in conservative evangelical circles, implies the
following:

☐ The temporal role subordination of the Son seen in the incarnation should
be read back into the immanent or eternal Trinity.

☐ The eternal role subordination of the Son to the Father is consistent with the
ontological equality of the Father and the Son.

☐ The differences between the divine persons should be understood entirely
in terms of differing roles or functions.

☐ There is a stark separation in the operations, works and functions of the
three divine persons.

☐ A relationship of authority and obedience exists between the Father and the
Son in their eternal relations.

    Historical orthodoxy gives no support to any of these ideas.[119] The second
point in the above list—the eternal subordination in role of the Son to the Father
is consistent with the ontological equality of the Father and the Son—is of particular interest, for it is on this premise that Grudem and many other conserva-

---

[117]Grudem, *Systematic Theology*, p. 251.
[118]Ibid., pp. 455–68.
[119]For another critique of "role subordination" within the Trinity see the excellent chapter in
    Bilezikian, *Community 101*, pp. 187–202.

tive evangelicals ground their case that women are equal in essence or being yet are permanently subordinated in role or function. In regard to human beings, the *permanent and necessary* role subordination of one sex, race or social group implies that they are in some way inferior in "being,"[120] and this is true on the divine level as well. If the Son must *always* obey the Father, then he must in some ways be less than the Father. He lacks something possessed solely by the Father. His role is determined by his being. Historic orthodoxy has long seen this conclusion and has argued in the opposite direction. Because the Father and the Son are one in being, they act as one. It is thus impossible to avoid the conclusion that the *eternal* role subordination of the Son implies the ontological subordination of the Son despite any protestations to the contrary. Thus, much more consistently the Sydney Doctrine Report boldy says that the eternal role subordination of the Son is only "true as far as it goes." It has to be recognized that eternal role subordination implies a difference in the "Persons themselves in their eternal nature."[121]

In asserting that the eternal role subordination of the Son must have ontological implications, the Sydney Anglican theologians are to be commended for the logical force of their reasoning. The coherence of their position is above reproach. Athanasius, the Cappadocians and most orthodox theologians across the centuries have recognized that if the Son is eternally set under the Father in his works, roles or function, this implies that he is less than the Father in his person, nature or being; he is a subordinate God. They have thus rejected the eternal role or functional subordination of the Son since their starting point is the eternal oneness of being of the Father and the Son.

---

[120]This is demonstrated by Rebecca Groothuis, *Good News for Women: A Biblical Picture of Gender Equality* (Grand Rapids, Mich.: Baker, 1997), pp. 41–45. Role differentiation on its own does not imply inferiority. If roles are based on training or competence and they can change, personal equality is not called into question. If, however, one's role is permanent and training or competence does not count, then this suggests the subordinated one lacks something given only to the superior. The subordinated one is inferior in some way. I return to this matter in part two of this book.

[121]Sydney Doctrine Report, par. 32, 33.

4

THE RETRIEVAL &
REFINEMENT OF THE NICENE
TRINITARIAN TRADITION
IN THE TWENTIETH CENTURY

W ith the flowering of scholarly interest in the doctrine of the Trinity
in the second half of the twentieth century, a doctrine that had been marginalized and often deficiently expounded for centuries came onto center stage
again and gained the attention it deserved. I have heard these years of neglect
called "the age of the exile for the Trinity." Wolfhart Pannenberg says this
neglect led to a "decay of the doctrine of the Trinity."[1] In the seventeenth and
eighteenth centuries in England and on the continent, many leading divines
embraced subordinationism.[2] Charles Hodge in nineteenth-century America is
a classic example of the "decay" Pannenberg mentions. Karl Rahner lays the
blame for this retreat in the history of Western theology at the feet of Aquinas,
who discussed first and separately *De Deo uno* (The one God) before discussing *Deo trino* (God the Trinity). This order suggests that the trinitarian nature
of God is a secondary feature of the Christian understanding of God.[3] It was
not until the first volume of Karl Barth's *Church Dogmatics* was published in

---

[1]Wolfhart Pannenberg, *Systematic Theology* (Grand Rapids, Mich.: Eerdmans, 1991), 1:291.
[2]See in detail Maurice Wiles, *Archetypal Heresy: Arianism Through the Centuries* (Oxford:
  Clarendon, 1996).
[3]Karl Rahner, *The Trinity*, trans. J. Donceel (New York: Herder & Herder, 1970), pp. 9–21.

1936 that there was any change of direction.[4] In this seminal work the doctrine of the Trinity was given pride of place and developed in ways faithful to the Nicene tradition for the first time in centuries. A parallel retrieval and renewal of the doctrine of the Trinity was initiated among Roman Catholics by Rahner, who published in 1967 an epoch-making study on the Trinity, which was translated into English in 1970 and called *The Trinity*.[5] From this point on, books on the Trinity flowed from the presses. No other doctrine has gained so much attention from so many first-rate theological minds in the last thirty years. Now it is agreed that the doctrine of the Trinity, as Athanasius and Augustine saw so clearly, is the primary and foundational doctrine of Christianity. The undisputed trend has been to retrieve Nicene orthodoxy and to refine it. The goal has been to eradicate any implications in the primitive tradition that could detract from the full equality and unity of the three distinct persons of the Trinity.

Most of the evangelicals who argue for the eternal subordination of the Son seem oblivious to this whole development—or if they are aware of it, they dismiss it summarily. This is tragic because, as Alister McGrath rightly says, "the most significant restatements of the doctrine of the Trinity within the Western tradition date from the twentieth century."[6]

Karl Barth

Karl Barth's reformulation of this crucial doctrine is provocative and imaginative. In his extensive treatment of the Trinity in *Church Dogmatics* 1/1, Barth enunciates the contours of his trinitarianism. Basic to his distinctive approach is his argument that the Trinity is disclosed in revelation, not just in the words of revelation found in Scripture. The Father is the *Revealer,* the Son is the *Revelation* and the Holy Spirit is the *Revealedness.* In Jesus Christ, God does not just impart information about himself, he imparts himself. "If he [Jesus] reveals God," Barth reasons, "he must himself be God."[7] In the confession "Jesus is Lord," the full divinity of the Son is affirmed, as is his distinction from the Father. To make sure none doubt his endorsement of these twin truths, Barth gives several pages to explicitly refuting the errors of both "subordinationism"

---

[4]Karl Barth, *Church Dogmatics* 1/1, trans. G. T. Thomson (Edinburgh: T & T Clark, 1936), 1:338–560.

[5]Karl Rahner, "Der dreifaltige Gott als transzendeter Urgrund der Heilsgeschichte" in *Mysterium Salutis: Grundriss heilsgeschichtlicher Dogmatik,* ed. J. Feiner and M. Lohrer (Einsiedeln: Benzinger, 1967), 2:317–97. See also n. 3.

[6]Alister McGrath, *An Introduction to Theology* (Oxford: Blackwell, 1994), p. 260.

[7]Barth, *Church Dogmatics* 1/1, 1:465.

and "modalism."[8] His consummate assertion is that "the Church doctrine of the Trinity is a self-enclosed circle."[9] This completely excludes any thought that the Trinity is a threefold hierarchy. It comes as somewhat of a surprise that when speaking of the subordination of the Son to the Father in the incarnation, Barth allows the possibility that this may say something of an eternal "difference in the mode of existence of the Son," though "not [of] any difference in being."[10] What this might mean is left open. For these comments Thomas F. Torrance accuses Barth, at this early stage in his writings, of allowing an "element of subordinationism in his doctrine of the Holy Trinity," despite all else Barth says on the subject.[11]

Dealing with the doctrine of reconciliation some twenty-five years after the publication of the first volume of *Church Dogmatics,* Barth faces squarely the paradox of how Jesus Christ—who is truly God—could take the form of a servant, humbling himself for the salvation of humankind.[12] It is, he says, "a difficult and even an elusive thing to speak of obedience which takes place in God himself."[13] The Son's obedience, he says, means we must accept that there is "an above and a below, a *prius* and a *posterius,* a superiority and a subordination in God."[14] Having said this, Barth then wrestles with the implications of what he has written. First of all, he reasons that if Jesus is subordinated to the Father in the incarnation, then this only occurs "in the forecourt of the divine being, with a divine dispensation (economy) in favor of, and with respect to, the particular nature of the world, not therefore with the true and proper and non-worldly being of God."[15]

In arguing along these lines, albeit in tortuous language, he follows Athanasius, Augustine and Calvin, who all held, as we have noted, that the Son's subordination seen in the incarnation was entirely temporal, related only to the economy of salvation. But Barth is not content with this explanation. He seeks a more profound answer. Building on his emphasis on the unity of the Godhead, characteristic of Western trinitarianism, he suggests that the subordination of the Son may in fact reveal something of the very being of the Godhead. He

---

[8]Ibid., 1:437–43.

[9]Karl Barth, *Church Dogmatics* 1/1, trans. G. W. Bromiley and T. F. Torrance (Edinburgh: T & T Clark, 1975), p. 380.

[10]Barth, *Church Dogmatics* 1/1, p. 473.

[11]Thomas F. Torrance, *Karl Barth: Biblical and Evangelical Theologian* (Edinburgh: T & T Clark, 1990), p. 131.

[12]Karl Barth, *Church Dogmatics* 3/1, esp. pp. 157–210.

[13]Ibid., p. 195.

[14]Ibid., p. 196.

[15]Ibid.

thus speaks in the above quote not of the subordination of the Son, but of *"a subordination in God."* He continues:

> We have to draw no less an astounding deduction that in equal Godhead the one God is, in fact the One and also Another, that he is indeed a First and a Second. One who rules and commands in majesty and the one who obeys in humility. The one God is both . . . in perfect unity and equality.[16]

In other words, for Barth what is revealed in the obedience and humiliation of the Son is a revelation of something in the "inner life of God"—"Godself."[17]

In expounding his distinctively Christian anthropology Barth takes up yet again the question of why the Son is depicted as subordinate to the Father in the incarnation, and he gives another complementary answer. The Son, in taking our humanity, becomes one with us and at the same time becomes the exemplar of faith:

> Jesus has let his Being, Himself, be prescribed and dictated and determined by an alien human being, and by the need and infinite peril of this Being. He is not of Himself. . . . No, the glory of His humanity is simply to be fully claimed and clamped by His fellows, by their fate and state, by their lowliness and misery. . . . He is pleased to be the One who is supremely compromised.[18]

For Barth the being *and* acts, the essence *and* functions, the person *and* the work of Christ are inseparable. Both equally reveal God in all his majesty. Who Jesus is and what he does are inextricably bound together.[19] Only of Jesus may it be said

> that His work itself is one with His active person, and therefore that He the doer and His deed are indissolubly one. . . . The point which interests us here is that we cannot separate His person from His work, if only for the same reason that it is in His person, because he gives nothing more nor less than Himself, that He accomplishes His work—the work of self-sacrifice with which He brings life and salvation to the world.[20]

---

[16]Ibid., p. 202.

[17]Ibid., p. 201.

[18]Barth, *Church Dogmatics* 3/2, p. 215. This theme is developed and reiterated throughout chapter 44, "The Man for Other Men."

[19]I follow the excellent exposition of this matter in Gary W. Deddo, *Karl Barth's Theology of Relations: Trinitarian, Christological and Human: Towards an Ethic of the Family* (New York: Peter Lang, 1999), pp. 44–50.

[20]Barth, *Church Dogmatics* 3/2, p. 19.

Barth's development of this matter is grounded in his exposition of John's Gospel, where the work of Christ is made coincidental with the work of the Father. Commenting on John 5:17–22, "the Son can do nothing on his own, but only what he sees the Father doing; for whatever the Father does, the Son does likewise," Barth says:

> The works done by the Son are those of the Father Himself, of the One who has sent Him, for the Father has given to Him these works to accomplish in the Father's name and for the manifestation of His name. . . . The converse is also true. Because the Father dwells in Him, the Son, it is the Father who performs the works through Him (John 14:10).[21]

At every turn of his relentless probes into the implications of the incarnation, coming to each question time and time again, Barth finds in Christ the revelation of "Godself." In Jesus, God is seen as he is: "He acts towards us [in Christ] as the same triune God that he is in Himself."[22] "The man Jesus in His being for man, repeats and reflects the inner being or essence of God."[23] The revelatory trajectory is from the person of Jesus Christ historically revealed on earth to the unseen Father above. The temporal revelation of the Son in the incarnation is the revelation of whole eternal triune being of God, not just a revelation of the eternal nature of the Son alone. Without using the same words, Barth anticipates Rahner's rule: "The economic Trinity is the immanent Trinity and the immanent Trinity is the economic Trinity." In this christocentric trinitarianism, subordinationism in the end is excluded absolutely by Barth. The Son reveals the Father.

What constantly surprises us as we read Barth is that his Christology, and thus his doctrine of the Trinity, is depicted almost exclusively in personal and relational terms.[24] The Father, the Son and the Holy Spirit are related in a personal perichoretic union; the Father and the Son are related as one in their being and work; Jesus and humankind are related by their common humanity; and man and woman made in the image of God are related in their sexual polarity. The outcome of this is that the doctrine of the Trinity becomes, in Barth, the most practical doctrine of all. It is the basis for all other doctrines and for the ethical imperatives for Christian living in the world.

Barth accepts that there is an analogous relationship between the divine life and human life, but he rejects totally an *analogia entis*—an analogy of being—

---

[21]Ibid., p. 63.
[22]Barth, *Church Dogmatics* 2/1, p. 51.
[23]Ibid., 3/2, p. 219.
[24]Again I draw on Deddo, *Barth's Theology*, pp. 36–41.

between humans and God.[25] When a consideration of humanity becomes the basis of doing theology, Barth insists, theologians end up depicting God in their own likeness. They fall into the sin of idolatry. The transcendence of God, his absolute otherness, is called into question. For Barth the doctrine of the Trinity is discovered *only* by the divine revelation given in Jesus Christ. He nevertheless accepts that if there were no correspondence whatsoever between the creature and the Creator, the Creator's revelation of himself could not be understood by the creature. Barth thus speaks of an *analogia relationis*—an analogy of relation. The "I" and the "Thou" in the divine triune relations correspond analogically to the "I" and the "Thou" of human relations. However, even this *analogia relationis* for Barth is not a way of doing theology; it is not a methodological starting point. His thesis that human relations in some way correspond to the relations within the Trinity is a *conclusion* flowing from his Christology and thus his doctrine of the Trinity; it is *not a presupposition* with which he begins his thinking about Christ or the Trinity. The movement can never be from the human to the divine. The imperative is that human relations should conform to divine relations, not vice versa. In the Trinity we see the three differentiated divine persons honoring each other, loving each other, giving of themselves to the others and working together in perfect cooperation. This is a paradigm for human relations, especially those between woman and man.[26]

After Barth

Barth's creative and insightful discussion of the Trinity has greatly affected the best of contemporary trinitarian theology. His work stimulated others to return to the study of the Trinity to rediscover the riches of the Christian doctrine of God. At this juncture I do not intend to enter into an extended discussion of contemporary trinitarian thought. I will simply highlight the contribution of a select number of important modern mainline Protestant, Roman Catholic, Eastern Orthodox and conservative evangelical contributions to the doctrine of the Trinity that bear on this study.

---

[25]See Barth, *Church Dogmatics* 1/1, p. 383–99; 3/2, pp. 220–21, etc.

[26]Barth's treatment of the man-woman relationship should be studied carefully by both sides in the contemporary evangelical debate about the status and ministry of women. See *Church Dogmatics* 3/4, pp. 116–225. Barth's stress on the polarity of the sexes, their equality and reciprocity lifts his case above anything else in the literature. Too much has been made of his exploration of what the apostolic exhortations to wives to be subordinate might mean (pp. 168–73). Nothing he says on this detracts from what he has said previously of the equality, dignity and freedom of women. If Barth were alive today he may word this point differently, but he is right in recognizing that husbands are called to give a lead in loving, sacrificial service for their wives. See Deddo, *Barth's Theology,* pp. 119-30 and n. 55.

Contemporary Mainline Protestant Trinitarianism

Among mainline Protestant works on the Trinity since Barth, Thomas F. Torrance's book *The Christian Doctrine of God: One Being, Three Persons* is, I believe, the best and most profound.[27] If anyone wanted to explore at greater depth the classical doctrine of the Trinity in general and in particular why subordinationism in any form is to be rejected, then I could recommend no book more strongly. For Torrance the doctrine of the Trinity is to be accorded primacy over all other doctrines. It is "the nerve and centre of them all," informing and integrating every other doctrine.[28] He begins his study of the doctrine of the Trinity by turning to Scripture. The Bible is for him "a coherent witness to God's trinitarian self-revelation."[29] From this basis the formal doctrine of the Trinity is to be "derived," "grounded" and "controlled."[30] In seeking to articulate the trinitarian faith as it has been developed in history, Torrance says he is "heavily influenced" by Greek patristic theology, as enunciated especially by Athanasius and the Cappadocian fathers, and by Reformed theology, especially as expounded by Calvin, Barth and Hugh Ross Mackintosh, his first mentor in trinitarian theology.[31] Speculative and innovative contemporary developments in trinitarian thought are not discussed in this book. In addition to his impressive breadth of reading in patristics, Torrance's exposition of the Trinity is characterized by three features:

1. A christocentric focus. For Torrance everything to be known about the Christian God is given by revelation, and this revelation is centered in Christ. The following quote sums up his position well:

> In Christ alone, the only-begotten Son of God, who is of one and the same Being as God the Father, is God's self-revelation perfectly identical with himself. Only in Christ, God become man for us, does he communicate his self-revelation to us by the power of the Spirit in such a redeeming and enlightening way that we may apprehend it and, human beings though we are, really know God in himself, both in his oneness as the Lord God and in his differentiation as Father, Son and Holy Spirit, one Being, three Persons.[32]

---

[27]Thomas F. Torrance, *The Christian Doctrine of God: One Being, Three Persons* (Edinburgh: T & T Clark, 1996). On Torrance as a theologian, see the biography by Alister McGrath, *Thomas F. Torrance: An Intellectual Biography* (Edinburgh: T & T Clark, 1999).
[28]Torrance, *Christian Doctrine,* p. 31.
[29]Ibid., p. 49.
[30]Ibid., p. 50.
[31]Ibid., p. ix.
[32]Ibid., p. 15.

In his earlier book *The Trinitarian Faith,* he makes the same point, possibly more starkly in different words: "In Christ we know God as he is in his own inner being, as Father, Son and Holy Spirit. Jesus Christ is the *arche* (ἀρχή), the Origin or Principle, of all our knowledge of God, and of what he has done and continues to do in the universe."[33]

2. *A stress on the oneness of being of Father, Son and Holy Spirit.* For Torrance the most monumental development in trinitarian theology was made when the Council of Nicea decreed that the Father and the Son were *one in being (homoousios).* When the oneness of being of the three persons Father, Son and Holy Spirit was affirmed, he argues, the errors of tritheism, modalism and subordinationism in any form were banished forever from orthodox trinitarianism.[34] For him the term *homoousian* underlines the full deity of the Son and the Spirit, excluding any "disjunction" between the Father, Son and Holy Spirit or any thought that the economic and the immanent Trinity can be held apart. In Christ we meet with the one being of God, and in Christ the triune God as he is in himself is revealed. Thus not only does this one word capture what is central to the biblical understanding of Father, Son and Holy Spirit, but it also safeguards salvation in Christ. If Christ is not one in being with the Father, then in him we do not meet with God.

> What God is toward us in his revealing and saving acts in the Gospel he is in himself, in his own eternal Being as God. Unless that is the case, any disjunction between the self-revelation of God the Father through Christ and the Spirit could only mean in the last analysis the Gospel is empty of any divine reality or validity. This is why the faith of Christians rests upon the supreme truth of the Deity of Christ and the Holy Spirit, for only through God himself is saving communion with God accessible to us.[35]

3. *A unity in being and action within the Trinity.* For Torrance the *homoousian* principle reinforced by the doctrine of perichoresis means that there can be no separation between the being and the acts of God, between the one divine nature of the three persons and their functions. Since they are one in being, they act as one. It could even be said that in Torrance, Rahner's rule becomes "What God is in his acts he is in his being, and vice versa."[36] For this reason

---

[33]Thomas F. Torrance, *The Trinitarian Faith* (Edinburgh: T & T Clark, 1988), p. 7.

[34]Torrance, *Christian Doctrine,* p. 115.

[35]Ibid., p. 21.

[36]I thank Graham James for this suggestion. I could not find these words as a quote anywhere in Torrance, but time and time again he says the equivalent. See ibid., pp. 4, 6, 22, 24, 30, 95, 115, 149, 152, 194, 236, 243.

Torrance never speaks of the Father's commanding and the Son's obeying as if
they were not always totally of one mind and will. Like Athanasius he excludes
on principle operational or role subordination. If they are one in being, then
they act as one:

> *Jesus Christ the incarnate Son is one in Being and Act with God the Father. What
> Jesus Christ does for us and to us, and what the Holy Spirit does in us, is what God
> himself does for us, to us and in us.*[37]
>
> Since God's Being and Activity completely interpenetrate each other, we must
> think of his Being and his Activity not separately but as one Being-in-Activity and
> one Activity-in-Being. In other words, the Father, the Son and the Holy Spirit always
> act together in every divine operation whether in creation or redemption, yet in
> such a way that the distinctive activities of the Father, the Son and the Holy Spirit
> are always maintained, in accordance with the propriety and otherness of their Per-
> sons as the Father, the Son and the Holy Spirit. This may be called the "perichoretic
> coactivity of the Holy Trinity."
>
> In every creative and redemptive act the Father, the Son and the Holy Spirit oper-
> ate together in fellowship with one another but nevertheless in ways peculiar to
> each of them. It is not possible for us to spell that out in terms of any demarcation
> between their distinctive operations, if only because within the coactivity of the
> three divine persons those operations perichoretically contain one another and pass
> over into one another while remaining what they distinctively are in themselves.[38]

Many other mainline Protestant studies on the doctrine of the Trinity written
by well known theologians are far more innovative and speculative than Torrance's. Few evangelicals would want to embrace all that they say. Two examples, however, are of relevance to this study.

Jürgen Moltmann has written extensively on the Trinity.[39] Barth's relational
understanding of the Trinity and his stress on the practicality of this doctrine is
influential in Moltmann's thinking. He differs, however, from Barth by adopting
a more "social" understanding of the Trinity, drawing on the Eastern tradition.
The individuality of the persons in this social model of the Trinity is to the fore,
their unity being grounded in their perichoretic relations. In regard to divine action Moltmann insists that we should think of three subjects, or centers of activity, who live in perfect harmony and work together as one: "The three persons

---

[37]Ibid., p. 95. Italics in the original.
[38]Ibid., pp 197-98.
[39]See further Richard Bauckham, *The Theology of Jürgen Moltmann* (Edinburgh: T & T Clark,
  1995).

are equal; they live and are manifested in one another and through one another."[40] He categorically rejects "all subordinationism." For him the triune God's relationship with the world is defined in terms of love. This suggests to him that God relates to human beings not as monarch to subject but as one who seeks a loving fellowship with those with whom he identifies himself.

For Moltmann, the Bible's account of God's unfolding trinitarian relationship with the world is not a mythological story, but a history of changing trinitarian relations in which the relations between the divine persons both affect the world and are affected by the world. For him, "the starting point for the Christian doctrine of the Trinity must be the salvation history attested in the Bible: the history of the Father, the Son and the Spirit."[41] This history, he insists, always has an eschatological orientation. In this unfolding story the three divine persons are not constituted in a fixed order for all eternity. Instead, their roles or work overlap and change:

> In the historical and eschatological testimony of the New Testament, we do not find one, single form of the Trinity. We find a trinitarian co-working of Father, Son and Spirit, but with changing patterns. We find the order Father-Spirit-Son; the order Father-Son-Spirit; and finally the order Spirit-Son-Father. Up to now, however, dogmatic tradition has only worked with a single pattern. And in the West this pattern has always been Father-Son-Spirit.[42]

In summing up the basis of all his theological work, Moltmann says, "I am trying to reflect a theology, which has a biblical foundation, an eschatological orientation and a political responsibility."[43] In a moment I will take up his interest in the connection between trinitarian theology and social justice issues.

Wolfhart Pannenberg provides the second example of more speculative mainline Protestant discussions of the Trinity.[44] Ted Peters says Pannenberg is "navigating at the point where the flow of trinitarian discussion is currently cresting."[45] Pannenberg is relevant to this study because conservative evangeli-

---

[40]Jürgen Moltmann, *The Trinity and the Kingdom of God*, trans. M. Kohl (London: SCM Press, 1981), p. 176.

[41]Jürgen Moltmann, *History and the Triune God*, trans. John Bowden (London: SCM Press, 1991), p. 82.

[42]Moltmann, *Trinity*, pp. 94-95.

[43]Ibid., p. 182.

[44]On Pannenberg more generally, see Stanley J. Grenz, *Reason for Hope: The Systematic Theology of Wolfhart Pannenberg* (Oxford: Oxford University Press, 1990), pp. 44-78.

[45]Ted Peters, *God as Trinity: Relationality and Temporality in Divine Life* (Louisville, Ky.: Westminster Press, 1993), p. 135.

cals often quote him as teaching the eternal subordination of the Son. This claim is made because Pannenberg speaks of the Son's being dependent on the Father for his sonship and being differentiated from the Father by being subject to him. He makes these comments in the context of outlining his distinctive way of differentiating the persons of the Trinity.

Pannenberg rejects the traditional way of differentiating the persons by their differing relations or origins. Instead he argues that their distinctions are to be seen in how they depend on one another. He argues that self-differentiation is bound up with dependence. For him the term *person* is a correlative concept. Personhood is found in the self-giving of oneself to another whereby one's identity is established by the other. This leads him to speak of the Son's subjecting himself to the Father and the Spirit's subjecting himself to the Son and the Father.[46] However, he then immediately goes on to speak of the dependence of the Father on the Son and Spirit.[47] This, he says, discloses the "mutuality in their relationships."[48] The Father's dependence on the Son takes place, Pannenberg argues, after Christ's resurrection, when he is given all power and authority, being made head over all things (Mt 28:18; Lk 10:22; Jn 5:23; Phil 2:9–11). Only on the last day will Christ hand back to the Father his rulership of the world (1 Cor 15:28). Pannenberg writes:

> In the handing over of lordship from the Father to the Son, and in its handing back from the Son to the Father, we see mutuality in their relationship. . . . By handing over lordship to the Son the Father makes his kingship dependent on whether the Son glorifies him and fulfills his lordship by fulfilling his mission. The self distinction of the Father from the Son is not just that he begets the Son, but that he hands over all things to him, so that his kingdom and his own deity are now dependent on the Son.[49]

Evangelical theologian Stanley Grenz believes that in this picture, "the subordination of the Son to the Father . . . [is] balanced by the subordination of the Father to the Son."[50] Pannenberg read holistically does not support the idea that the Son is unilaterally and eternally subordinated in being or role to the Father. His emphasis falls on the mutuality and changing nature of the relationships among the persons of the Trinity.

---

[46]Pannenberg, *Systematic Theology,* 1:308–13, 321.
[47]Ibid., 1:313–314, 322.
[48]Ibid., 1:313, etc.
[49]Ibid., 1:313.
[50]Stanley J. Grenz and Denise Kjesbo, *Women in the Church* (Downers Grove, Ill.: InterVarsity Press, 1995), p. 154.

Contemporary Roman Catholic Trinitarianism

The contemporary renewal of Roman Catholic trinitarian theology is usually attributed to Rahner, whose work we have already discussed. Since his book *The Trinity* was published in English in 1970, there has been an unending stream of well-researched and well-argued books on the Trinity by Roman Catholics. The scholarship seen in most Catholic books on the Trinity is impressive. In their discussions of the development of the doctrine of the Trinity and in their contemporary expressions of this doctrine, these books do not differ significantly from Protestant works.[51] Most of them interact in a positive manner with recent non–Roman Catholic contributions to the doctrine of the Trinity and come to very similar conclusions. The Trinity is a communion of three distinct divine persons who interpenetrate one another and work as one, none being set over or under the others. Here it is to be remembered that the sixteenth-century Reformers did not differ from the Catholic Church on this doctrine. Indeed, when discussing the Trinity the Reformers were at pains to show that they agreed with the church fathers and the historic creeds; they held to the catholic doctrine of the Trinity. What surprised me as I came to research this study was that none of the Catholic books I read discussed subordinationism in any detail. They uniformly agree that the pre-Nicene fathers naively subordinated the Son and the Spirit to the Father and that Arius and those who followed him ontologically subordinated the Son and the Spirit to the Father. Subordinationism is not given a hearing by Roman Catholic theologians because their doctrine of the Trinity is emphatically "Western." It presupposes the Augustinian principle, elaborated on by Aquinas, that any discussion of the Trinity must begin with the unity of the three persons. Whenever the divine unity is to the fore, subordinationism is excluded. The Western *Filioque* clause also precludes any suggestion that the Son is subordinate to the Father. When one depicts the Holy Spirit as proceeding from the Father and the Son, the first two persons are envisaged as standing side by side. Conservative evangelicals have compiled a long list of Protestant theologians who have taught the subordination of the Son, or who are thought to do so; but I have not come across any quotations supporting

---

[51]Two excellent recent introductions to contemporary Catholic scholarship on the Trinity are T. Marsh, *The Triune God: A Biblical, Historical and Theological Study* (Dublin: Columba, 1994), and G. O'Collins, *The Tripersonal God: Understanding and Interpreting the Trinity* (New York: Paulist, 1999). In preparing this study I have constantly drawn on Catholic works. In the footnotes I have appealed to books by Bertrand de Margerie, Edward J. Fortman, Bernard Lonergan, Edmund Hill, William Hill, John Thompson, Leonardo Boff, Karl Jasper and Catherine LaCugna.

the subordination of the Son from a Roman Catholic theologian—except Rahner, whose "rule" is mistakenly thought to endorse the eternal subordination of the Son. Roman Catholic theologians are not quoted because Roman Catholic theology consistently and univocally rejects ontological and functional subordinationism.

Contemporary Eastern Orthodox Trinitarianism

The late-twentieth-century renewal of interest in and reflection on the doctrine of the Trinity among Western theologians has its parallel among Eastern Orthodox theologians. This has opened up a most fruitful exchange in ecumenical discussions. Both sides have learned from the other. Most of the differences between Eastern and Western trinitarian theology do not bear on our study of subordinationism, but one key matter does.[52] Following the Cappadocians, Eastern theologians generally continue to speak of the Father as the *monarchē* of the Son and the Spirit.[53] Some of their number opposed to the ordination of women have taken this to imply a carefully prescribed subordination of the Son,[54] but in drawing this conclusion they set themselves in opposition to the great Cappadocian theologians, who were adamantly opposed to the subordination of the Son in being or function, and to the best of twentieth-century Orthodox theologians.

The Russian émigré Vladimir Lossky is possibly the most influential Eastern Orthodox theologian of the twentieth century. For him the *monarchē* of the Father and the rejection of the Filioque clause have to be upheld at all cost. He does not, however, countenance any subordinationism. The following quote makes this clear:

> The Father is called the cause of the Persons of the Son and the Holy Spirit. . . .
> This unique cause is not prior to his effects. . . . He is not superior to his effects.
> . . . We have to confess not only the unity of the One Nature in the Three, but
> also the unity of the Three Persons of the one identical nature. By defending the
> Personal procession of the Holy Spirit from the Father alone, Orthodoxy makes a

---

[52]On this whole matter see Duncan Reid, *Energies of the Spirit: Trinitarian Models in Eastern Orthodoxy and Western Theology* (Atlanta: Scholars Press, 1997).

[53]For a good, brief summary of twentieth-century Eastern Orthodox trinitarianism, see E. J. Fortman, *The Triune God: A Historical Study of the Doctrine of the Trinity* (Grand Rapids, Mich.: Baker, 1972), pp. 275–83. In a more popular vein, see Timothy Ware, *The Orthodox Church* (Harmondsworth, U.K.: Penguin, 1978), pp. 216–23.

[54]So T. Hopko, *Women and Priesthood* (Crestwood, N.Y.: St. Vladimir's, 1983), pp. 93–127. See also Catherine LaCugna, *God for Us: The Trinity and the Christian Life* (San Francisco: HarperSanFrancisco, 1991), pp. 397ff., for other examples.

profession of faith in the "Simple Trinity," wherein the relations of origin denote
the absolute diversity of the Three, while also indicating their unity.[55]

In more recent times, the Greek Orthodox theologian and bishop John Zizioulas has reiterated many of Lossky's concerns. He too insists that the person
of the Father be understood as constituting the divine unity:

> The being and life of God does not consist in the one substance of God (as in
> Western theology) but in the *hypostasis,* that is, the person of the Father. The One
> God is not the one substance but the Father, who is the "cause" both of the gener-
> ation of the Son and the procession of the Spirit.[56]

Because, Zizioulas insists, the unity of God is found in a person, the Father,
trinitarian relations are characterized by love and the most profound *koinonia.*
For this reason, he says:

> it is impossible to say that in God any of the three persons exist or can exist in
> separation from the other persons. The three constitute such an unbreakable unity
> that individualism is absolutely inconceivable in their case. The three persons of
> the Trinity are thus one God because they are so united in an unbreakable com-
> munion *(koinonia)* that none of them can be conceived apart from the rest. The
> mystery of the one God in three persons points to a way of being which pre-
> cludes individualism and separation.[57]

In the light of this emphatic stress on divine unity in a communion of love
within the Trinity, we are not surprised that Zizioulas is as opposed to modalism
as he is to subordinationism. In discussing the Cappadocian fathers' contribution
to the development of trinitarian theology, he outlines their (and his) opposition
to these two errors in terms of the historical forms known to them, "Sabellianism"
and "Eunomianism."[58] Sabellianism is to be rejected, he argues, because it denies
that the divine three are full persons for all eternity. Eunomianism is to be rejected, firstly, because it denies that the Father and the Son are one in being *(homoousios)* and, secondly, because it divides the persons, suggesting that they do
not exist and work as one. He says, "The Cappadocians called the persons by
names indicating *schesis* [relationship]: none of the three persons can be con-

---

[55]Vladimir Lossky, "The Procession of the Holy Spirit in the Orthodox Triadology," *The Eastern Churches Quarterly* 7 (1948): 45. Emphasis added.
[56]John D. Zizioulas, *Being in Communion* (Crestwood, N.Y.: St. Vladimir's, 1993), pp. 40–41.
[57]John D. Zizioulas, "The Doctrine of the Holy Trinity: The Significance of the Cappadocian
Contribution," in *Trinitarian Theology Today,* ed. C. Schwöbel (Edinburgh: T & T Clark,
1995), pp. 44-60 (quote on p. 48).
[58]Ibid., pp. 45–50.

ceived without reference to the other two, both logically and ontologically."[59]

In this Eastern Orthodox picture of the Trinity it is impossible to think that there is a "chain of command" within the Trinity, that the Father gives orders and the Son obeys. The three divine persons are so intimately related and so profoundly coexistent that there is the most perfect unity of will and work. The Father is the *monarchē*, the one source of the Son and the Holy Spirit, but he is not thought of as the "monarch" who has authority over the Son and the Spirit, as some evangelicals seem to imagine.[60]

Western theologians, as has already been noted, are often critical of the Eastern *monarchē* model of the Trinity, arguing that although subordinationism is excluded, the conceptual framework is hierarchical: it envisages the Father as having some preeminence. However, the 1991 "Agreement Between Reformed and Orthodox on the Doctrine of the Trinity" overcomes this objection, following Athanasius, by making the Godhead the *archē* of the Trinity. Moreover, this document confirms what has just been argued—that Eastern Orthodox trinitarian theology does not allow for any subordination within the Trinity. Here we are told that the three persons are "coeternal and coequal," that "the entire and undivided Godhead resides in each person," that the divine three act together "in creation, providence, revelation and salvation" and that "there is only one indivisible Godhead and *archē*."[61] The following paragraph, taken from the agreement, could not be more explicit.

> Of far-reaching importance is the stress laid upon the Monarchy of the Godhead in which all three divine Persons share, for the whole indivisible Being of God belongs to each of them as it belongs to all of them together. This is reinforced by the unique conception of coinherent or perichoretic relations between the different Persons in which they completely contain and interpenetrate one another while remaining what they distinctively are in their otherness as Father, Son and Holy Spirit. God is intrinsically Triune, Trinity in Unity and Unity in Trinity. There are no degrees of Deity in the Holy Trinity, as is implied in a distinction between the underived Deity of the Father and the derived Deity of the Son and the Spirit. Any notion of subordination is completely ruled out. The perfect simplicity and indivisibility of God in his Triune Being mean that the Arche (ἀρχή) or Monarchia (μοναρχία) cannot be limited to one Person.[62]

---

[59]Ibid., p. 50.

[60]See in particular Michael Harper, who repeatedly makes this claim (*Equal and Different: Male and Female in Church and Family* [London: Hodder & Stoughton, 1994]).

[61]See Torrance's commentary in Thomas F. Torrance, *Trinitarian Perspectives: Towards Doctrinal Agreement* (Edinburgh: T & T Clark, 1994), pp. 115–43.

[62]Quoted in Torrance, *Christian Doctrine*, p. 185.

Contemporary Evangelical Trinitarianism

Contemporary, conservative evangelical discussions of some substance on the Trinity generally do not countenance any kind of subordination in the immanent or eternal Trinity. Christopher Kaiser, Charles Sherlock, Gerald Bray and Millard Erickson, in their excellent discussions of the Trinity, all argue that the Bible and creedal orthodoxy disallow any suggestion that the Son or the Spirit are eternally subordinated to the Father.[63] Many other respected contemporary evangelical theologians, in briefer discussions on the Trinity, also insist on the full equality of the three persons, rejecting all forms of subordinationism.[64] Wayne Grudem and other evangelicals who argue for the eternal subordination of the Son and the Spirit do not represent informed, mainstream evangelical opinion.

In this discussion, Erickson's work commands the most interest. Many regard Erickson as the foremost conservative evangelical systematic theologian alive today. The adjective "conservative" may be stressed because he admits that he is uneasy about what he calls "the Evangelical Left."[65] J. I. Packer describes Erickson's *Christian Theology* as "the most widely used" text on systematics in evangelical seminaries, and he says this "masterly piece of work" is "robustly evangelical, essentially conservative and gently Calvinistic."[66] In 1995 Erickson published the most scholarly and detailed study of the Trinity from the pen of a conservative evangelical this century: *God in Three Persons: A Contemporary Interpretation of the Trinity*. In this book he gives an excellent overview of the debates about the Trinity in the early church; a penetrating critique of various biblical, theological and philosophical objections to this doctrine; and a masterful outline of the biblical teaching on the Trinity, with a whole chapter on John's Gospel. He concludes with a compelling presenta-

---

[63]Christopher Kaiser, *The Doctrine of God* (London: Marshall, Morgan & Scott, 1982); Charles Sherlock, *God on the Inside* (Canberra, Australia: Acorn, 1991); Gerald Bray, *The Doctrine of God* (Leicester, U.K.: Inter-Varsity Press, 1993); Millard Erickson, *God in Three Persons: A Contemporary Interpretation of the Trinity* (Grand Rapids, Mich.: Baker, 1995).

[64]So Donald G. Bloesch, *God the Almighty* (Downers Grove, Ill.: InterVarsity Press, 1995), pp. 199–204; Paul Jewett, *God, Creation and Revelation* (Grand Rapids, Mich.: Eerdmans, 1991), pp. 322–25; D. Macleod, *The Person of Christ* (Leicester, U.K.: Inter-Varsity Press, 1998), pp. 75–78, 83, 86–89, 146–52; Wayne House, *Charts of Christian Theology and Doctrine* (Grand Rapids, Mich.: Zondervan, 1992), p. 47; G. Bilezikian, *Community 101* (Grand Rapids, Mich.: Zondervan, 1997), pp. 187–202; Grenz and Kjesbo, *Women in the Church,* pp. 114, 151–56, etc.

[65]See Millard Erickson, *The Evangelical Left: Encountering Postconservative Evangelical Theology* (Grand Rapids, Mich.: Baker, 1997).

[66]Millard Erickson, *Christian Theology,* 2nd ed. (Grand Rapids, Mich.: Baker, 1998). These quotes are taken from the dust cover of the book.

tion of what he believes is the best way to express the doctrine of the Trinity in the light of Scripture and the best of theological thought past and present. In doing this he sympathetically interacts with the most important contributors to the debate on the Trinity in recent years—such as Barth, Rahner, Moltmann, Pannenberg, Leonardo Boff and Catherine LaCugna—yet he never hesitates to differ from them when he thinks they have not accurately reflected the teaching of the Bible, which for him is the ultimate norm by which all theology must be tested.

Erickson agrees that all thinking about the God of Christian revelation must begin with the trinitarian being of God. He unequivocally endorses the "social" understanding of the Trinity insisting that the unity of the persons lies in their perichoretic union:

> The closeness of the three is accentuated through the fact that the goals, intentions, values, and objectives of each of the three is the same as each of the others. There is no difference in these respects that would draw any away from either of the others.[67]

Erickson maintains that the God of Christian revelation should not be thought of as either male or female. He is particularly critical of those who depict God the Father in patriarchal terms. He argues that those who do this seek to impose their own values by selectively quoting from Scripture and by absolutizing the cultural world of the Bible.

> God is not bound by gender and sex; he transcends both. It is quite possible that the patriarchal depiction of God that we find in much Christian theology is an illicit development of the masculine motifs in isolation from other qualities and from the biblical contexts in which they were originally given.[68]

Erickson considers attempts to hold simultaneously the full ontological equality of the three divine persons and the eternal role subordination of the Son (or the Spirit) to be a logical impossibility.

> A temporal, functional subordination without inferiority of essence seems possible, but not an eternal subordination. And to speak of the superiority of the Father to the Son while denying the inferiority of the Son to the Father must be contradictory.[69]

---

[67]Erickson, *God in Three Persons,* p. 226.
[68]Ibid., p. 281.
[69]Ibid., p. 309.

Furthermore, he will not allow that the generation of the Son and the procession of the Holy Spirit imply any superordination and subordination within the Trinity.

> There is no permanent distinction of one from the other in terms of origination. While the Father may be the cause of the existence of the Son and the Spirit, they are also mutually the cause of his existence and the existence of one another. There is an eternal symmetry of all three persons.

This implies, he says, "a mutual submission of each of the members of the Trinity to each of the others," characterized by "*agape*, self-sacrificial, giving love"—a "complete equality of the three."[70]

Professor Shirley Guthrie, in his book *Christian Doctrine,* sums up what he believes is the emerging, contemporary way of understanding the Trinity:

> The oneness of God is not the oneness of a distinct, self-contained individual; it is the unity of a *community* of persons who love each other and live together in harmony. . . . They are what they are only in relationship with one another. Each only exists in this relationship and would not exist apart from it. Father, Son and Holy Spirit live only in and with and through each other, eternally united in mutual love and shared purpose. Behind this understanding of the Trinity lies . . . the *perichoresis* doctrine.
>
> There is no solitary person separated from the others; no above and below; no first, second, third in importance; no ruling and controlling and being ruled and controlled; no position of privilege to be maintained over against others; no question of conflict concerning who is in charge; no possible rivalry or competition between competing individuals; no need to assert independence and authority of one at the expense of the others. Now there is only the fellowship and community of equals who share all that they are and have in their communion with each other, each living with and for the others in mutual openness, self-giving love, and support; each free not from but for the others. That is how Father, Son and Holy Spirit are related in the inner circle of the Godhead.[71]

Practical and Ethical Implications

Not surprisingly, contemporary mainline Protestant, Roman Catholic and evangelical theologians have seen the practical and ethical implications of a doctrine of the Trinity that stresses mutuality, community and equality. This is a

---

[70]Ibid., p. 333.
[71]Shirley Guthrie, *Christian Doctrine* (Philadelphia: Westminster Press, 1994), pp. 92–93.

very positive development, since the lack of attention to the practical implications of the doctrine of the Trinity is often blamed for the doctrine's long neglect. Catherine LaCugna tells us one of the reasons she wrote her book *God for Us: The Trinity and Christian Life* was to show that "the doctrine of the Trinity is ultimately a practical doctrine with radical consequences for the Christian life."[72] Barth paved the way for this development, but Moltmann was one of the first to spell out in some detail what such an understanding of the Trinity might mean relationally and politically. Moltmann's understanding of the Trinity becomes the ground for his social agenda. At the heart of this vision is "a community of men and women without supremacy and without subjection."[73] This social agenda, predicated on a doctrine of the Trinity that emphasizes the equality of the three divine persons and their perichoretic community, is even more forcefully and consistently worked out by Leonardo Boff in his book *Trinity and Society*. For him the Trinity, understood as a community of differentiated divine equals, is

> extremely rich in suggestion in the context of oppression and desire for liberation. . . . For those who have faith, the trinitarian communion between the divine Three, the union between them in love and vital interpenetration, can serve as a source of inspiration, as a utopian ideal. . . .
>
> The community of Father, Son and Holy Spirit becomes a prototype of the human community dreamed of by those who wish to improve society and build it in such a way as to make it an image and likeness of the Trinity.[74]

One particular practical and ethical issue that many contemporary theologians have thought is informed by reference to the Trinity is that of the man-woman relationship. On the basis of a symmetrical and communal understanding of the Trinity, patriarchy has been challenged. We see examples of this in the writings of LaCugna, an orthodox Roman Catholic,[75] in the work of more radical feminists such as Elizabeth Johnson[76] and in books by egalitarian evan-

---

[72]LaCugna, *God for Us,* p. 377.

[73]Moltmann, *Trinity,* p. 192.

[74]Leonardo Boff, *Trinity and Society* (Maryknoll, N.Y.: Orbis, 1986), pp. 6, 8.

[75]See LaCugna, *God for Us,* pp. 266–89, and her essay, "God in Communion with Us: The Trinity," in *Freeing Theology: The Essentials of Theology in Feminist Perspective* (San Francisco: HarperSanFrancisco, 1993), pp. 83–114. She argues for the continuing use of the traditional names for the divine persons—Father, Son and Holy Spirit—despite the dangers of reading into these names patriarchy.

[76]Elizabeth Johnson, *She Who Is: The Mystery of God in Feminist Theological Discourse* (New York: Crossroad, 1992). She wants to introduce such titles as Mother and Sophia alongside the traditional names for the three divine persons to affirm feminist insights.

gelicals. Thus evangelicals Stanley Grenz and Denise Kjesbo—in their book *Women in the Church*—appeal to the Trinity to support the full emancipation of women. For them the contemporary orthodox understanding of the Trinity suggests "the mutual dependence and the interdependency of male and female," and "rather than barring women from leadership roles in the church . . . encourages mutuality at all levels in the life of Christ's community."[77]

Of special interest are the conclusions reached by Erickson in *God in Three Persons*. We have already seen that he endorses a symmetrical and communal understanding of the Trinity. From this, Erickson argues, a number of practical outcomes follow. In particular, we are given a model or pattern for our relationships:

> Thus the type of relationship that should characterize human persons, particularly believing Christians who have accepted the structure of intratrinitarian relationships as the pattern of their own relationships to others, would be one of unselfish love and submission to the other, seeking the welfare of the other over one's own. Humility, then, in the best sense of the word, will be one of the prized virtues.[78]

This understanding of the Trinity, he believes, should also inform church life.

> Whatever the form of (church) government no one will seek to dominate, to force his or her views and desires on the group. . . . There will be no coercion, no political bargaining, no seeking to restrict the power to a small group. . . . Anyone who wants to be a leader should become the servant of all.[79]

Contemporary conservative evangelicals who appeal to the doctrine of the Trinity to support the "headship" of men also believe that the Trinity should inform human relationships, especially in the church and the home. They differ only in how they understand the Trinity and the consequential social implications. For them the Trinity is basically a hierarchy with the Father at the top. As "the head," he commands and the Son obeys. This patriarchal image of the Godhead is taken as exemplifying how relationships within the Christian home and the church should be structured. Men are to command, women are to obey.

---

[77] Grenz and Kjesbo, *Women in the Church,* p. 154. Their discussion of these issues (pp. 151–56) is highly commended.

[78] Erickson, *God in Three Persons,* p. 333.

[79] Ibid., p. 335.

5

EVANGELICALS AT
THE END OF A VERY
THIN BRANCH

Although all evangelicals would insist that the inspired words of the Old and New Testaments are the ultimate basis for doctrine, most would concede that how these texts have been understood on any matter in the past is also of great importance. It is for this reason that Charles Hodge and contemporary evangelicals claim that their teaching on the eternal subordination of the Son represents historic orthodoxy. They want to have "tradition" on their side. It is of course true that the historical interpretation of any passage, or the understanding of the Bible's teaching on any matter, is not absolute. Revision is always possible on the basis of a better exegesis that wins over the mind of the church. But this has not happened in the case of the Trinity. Evangelicals who argue for the eternal subordination of the Son to the Father may be able to quote a few verses in support, but they have not been able to convince most other evangelicals, or the best of mainline Protestant and Roman Catholic theologians, that their position reflects the overall teaching of Scripture. The truth of the matter is that the conservative evangelicals who argue for the eternal subordination of the Son, claiming that this is what the Bible teaches, are a small minority, sitting out on the end of a very thin branch.

"Tradition," rather than being on their side, is their strongest opponent. What they claim is "the biblical" understanding of the Trinity is condemned by the

Nicene and Athanasian Creeds and the Reformation confessions of faith; it is rejected absolutely by Athanasius, Augustine and Calvin; and it stands in stark contrast to what is taught by contemporary Roman Catholic and mainline Protestant theologians and the majority of conservative Reformed and evangelical theologians. They do have Hodge on their side, as well as the Protestant subordinationists in the period between the Reformation and the mid twentieth century—when the doctrine of the Trinity went into "exile" and a state of "decay"—but appealing to those who are patently mistaken and in error does not give weight to their case. Two wrongs don't make a right.

The 1999 Sydney Doctrine Report claims that "Calvin and the Calvinists" endorse subordinationism, but this is simply not true, despite the exceptions, such as Hodge. No one could be more emphatically opposed to all forms of subordinationism than Calvin, as has been shown.[1] The most scholarly evangelicals of Reformed persuasion in the twentieth century have likewise rejected subordinationism. No one more clearly illustrates this truth than B. B. Warfield, who tells us he writes to "vigorously reassert the principle of equalization" in the Trinity.[2] In his essay "The Biblical Doctrine of the Trinity," he readily admits that there are passages in the Scriptures that speak of the subordination of the Son in his incarnate ministry, but he insists that it is "thoroughly illegitimate to press such passages to suggest any subordination for the Son or the Spirit" in the immanent or eternal Trinity.[3] This means that Warfield rejects the subordinationism of Hodge. In his book *The Doctrine of God,*[4] Herman Bavinck enumerates a number of forms of subordinationism besides Arianism and repudiates all of them.[5] It is his view that Augustine once and forever "banished all subordinationism."[6] Likewise Herman Hoeksema in his *Reformed Dogmatics* opposes a hierarchical understanding of the Trinity. He says that "there is no division, no

---

[1] One of Calvin's students, the erudite Caspar Olevian (1536–1587), who taught in Heidelberg, carefully restates his master's trinitarian theology: "God is three distinct, co-eternal subsistences, but he is one essence." It is his goal to exclude all forms of subordinationism and to show that Reformed theology is catholic orthodoxy. See R. Scott Clark, "The Catholic Trinitarianism of Caspar Olevian," *Westminster Theological Journal* 61 (1999): 15–39. Sometimes it is claimed that Jonathan Edwards taught the eternal subordination of the Son, but this is not true. See Richard M. Weber, "The Trinitarian Theology of Jonathan Edwards: An Investigation of Charges Against Its Orthodoxy," *Journal of the Evangelical Theological Society* 44, no. 2 (2001): 297-318.
[2] B. B. Warfield, *Biblical Foundations* (London: Tyndale, 1958), p. 116.
[3] Ibid, p. 112.
[4] Herman Bavinck, *The Doctrine of God,* trans. William Hendricksen (Grand Rapids, Mich.: Eerdmans, 1951).
[5] Ibid., see pp. 280–81, 283, 288, 314.
[6] Ibid., pp. 281, 283.

separation, no subordination between the three persons" and that "the most absolute equality exists between Father, Son and Holy Spirit."[7] Lastly, Cornelius
Van Til is quoted. He says, "A consistently biblical doctrine of the Trinity would
imply the complete rejection of all subordinationism."[8] In his many writings Van
Til always stresses the full equality of the three divine persons in their being and
work.

Conservative evangelicals who claim that their doctrine of the eternal subordination of the Son is historical orthodoxy show both an ignorance of what the
great theologians of the past and the creeds and confessions actually teach and
an ignorance of the recognized inadequacies of many expositions of the doctrine of the Trinity from the time of the Reformation to the 1960s.[9] Quoting selectively from nineteenth- and early-twentieth-century discussions of the Trinity
only proves that much of the work on this matter from this period was sadly
deficient. For many centuries the primary doctrine of Christianity—the doctrine
of the triune God—was marginalized and deficiently expounded. The legacy of
this deficiency is unfortunately clearly evident among conservative evangelicals.
Hodge is the classic example, but he is not alone. In the famous twelve-volume
work *The Fundamentals,* produced between 1910 and 1915, which purported
to be in part an exposition of "the central doctrines" of Christianity, the Trinity
is not even discussed. In 1982 Carl Henry, who some call "the father of modern
conservative evangelicalism," wrote that conservative evangelicals have not yet
"contributed significant literature to the current revival of trinitarian interest."[10]
Although his theology, *God, Revelation and Authority,* fills six large volumes,
his own treatment of the Trinity is a brief summary of others' opinions rather
than an original contribution of any substance. In an aside without comment
that appears in his one chapter outlining the doctrine of the Trinity, he takes
over the language of Hodge, speaking of the subordination of the Son in his
"mode of subsistence and mode of operations."[11] For Henry the doctrine of God

---

[7]Herman Hoeksema, *Reformed Dogmatics* (Grand Rapids, Mich.: Reformed Free, 1966), p.
151, 152.

[8]Cornelius Van Til, *A Christian Theory of Knowledge* (Philadelphia: Presbyterian & Reformed,
1969), p. 104.

[9]Karl Rahner, *The Trinity,* trans. J. Donceel (New York: Herder & Herder, 1970), pp. 10–21;
Millard Erickson, *God in Three Persons: A Contemporary Interpretation of the Trinity* (Grand
Rapids, Mich.: Baker, 1995), pp. 11–29.

[10]Carl Henry, *God, Revelation and Authority: God Who Speaks and Shows,* vol. 5 (Waco, Tex.:
Word, 1982), p. 212.

[11]Ibid., p. 207. I notice R. L. Lightner also endorses the eternal subordination of the Son, pre-
suming this is orthodoxy (*Evangelical Theology: A Survey and Review* [Grand Rapids, Mich.:
Baker, 1986], p. 49).

is not the primary doctrine; the doctrine of Scripture as the inerrant word of God is the primary doctrine. As late as 1995 Millard Erickson says, "There really has been no major scale doctrine of the Trinity produced for some time by persons of distinctively evangelical persuasion."[12] His excellent treatise makes a good beginning to what may be hoped is a transition point in evangelical theology.

The Root Cause of This Error

We now ask, why is it that some evangelicals in the latter part of the twentieth century have embraced subordinationism? It certainly did not arise out of an independent reconsideration of the doctrine of the Trinity. This innovative form of subordinationism arises entirely in connection with attempts to preserve what to them is a fundamental truth: namely, male "headship." In their concern to more securely ground their teaching on the male-female relationship, they have embraced an old error that undermines the most fundamental truth of all—the Christian doctrine of God. Their starting point has been their understanding of the woman-man relationship: women and men are equal yet different, and so too are the Father and the Son. So far, so good. But for these evangelicals *difference* is defined almost exclusively in terms of subordination.[13] The key difference between men and women is that men are to lead and women are to obey; God has given to the man an (authoritative) headship. The relationship between the Father and the Son is drawn in these terms. This hierarchical understanding of the Trinity is then quoted to illustrate and confirm the subordination of women. We are told that the man-woman relationship should be modeled on the relationship between the Father and the Son. The circular nature of this reasoning cannot be missed.

The argument that the doctrine of the Trinity should inform all human relationships is an argument based on analogy. It presumes that there is a degree of correspondence between divine relations and human relations, but not identity. Both sides in this debate accept this. Regarding the term *analogy,* Karl Barth's profound discussion of this matter is invaluable.[14] His thesis is that the most common and deleterious cause of theological error is to reason analogically from humankind to God. When this is done, God is created in human terms, which is idolatry. Barth insists that the movement must always be in the

---

[12]Erickson, *God in Three Persons,* p. 14.

[13]See chapter seven, "Women in Contemporary Hierarchical-Complementarian Literature," where I explain more fully this distinctive usage of the word *difference.*

[14]See our earlier discussion of this in chapter four, at the end of the section on Barth's doctrine of the Trinity.

opposite direction—from God to humankind. God as he is, is not understood by any other means than the revelation in Jesus Christ. In Christ the triune God is disclosed as a God in communal relation with himself and with men and women. Barth thus speaks of an "analogy of relations." The revelation in Christ supplies the imperative for human relations, especially between man and woman. This revelation directs the two sexes, who alike are created in the image of God, to live "in correspondence with the image of God," Jesus Christ.[15]

Evangelicals who speak of the eternal subordination of the Son have fallen into the very error of which Barth warns: they have read back into the Trinity their prior beliefs about the sexes.[16] Instead of moving from relations in God to human relations by analogy, they move from fallen human relations to divine relations. They reverse what is an acceptable theological tool. In their zeal to uphold male leadership in the home and the church, they corrupt the doctrine of God—the doctrine on which all other doctrines, including the doctrine of salvation, rest. At least three strands of evidence indicate that those who argue for the permanent subordination of women and the eternal subordination of the Son are moving analogically from the human to the divine.

The first strand of evidence is given in the substance of what has so far been written. I have argued that historical orthodoxy rejects absolutely the eternal subordination of the Son. The Son is not subordinated to the Father either in being or function. The Nicene and Athanasian Creeds and the Reformation confessions of faith not only reject subordinationism but also establish an orthodox

---

[15]Karl Barth, *Church Dogmatics* 3/1, trans. J. W. Edwards, D. Bussey and H. Knight Bussey (Edinburgh: T & T Clark, 1957), p. 201.

[16]An interesting parallel to our debate is to be seen in Miroslav Volf's important study *After Our Likeness: The Church as the Image of the Trinity* (Grand Rapids, Mich.: Eerdmans, 1998). He finds that almost everyone says the church should correspond analogically in some way with the Trinity. What he discovers, however, is that in the two test cases he examines, prior beliefs determine how the Trinity is understood. Roman Catholic Cardinal Joseph Ratzinger argues that the Trinity should be conceived primarily monistically. Unity is prior to diversity. His ecclesiology perfectly corresponds to his Western doctrine of the Trinity: the one Holy Catholic Church is primary, and congregations are secondary. In contrast, John Zizioulas, an influential Greek Orthodox theologian and bishop, holds that the local church led by its bishop is primary, although it always represents the whole church. For him, wherever the Eucharist is celebrated by the bishop, the church is found in all its fullness. This understanding of the church likewise corresponds to his Eastern understanding of the Trinity, where the Father constitutes the many (the Son and the Spirit) and at the same time is conditioned by them. Volf concludes that both men read back into the Trinity their prior beliefs. Whenever this is done, he maintains, there invariably follows a distortion of the fundamental dogma of Christianity, the Trinity. In brief comments, he criticizes both Ratzinger (p. 72) and Zizioulas (p. 114) for allowing traces of subordinationism into their doctrine of the Trinity (see also p. 217), but I suspect both would reject this charge.

hermeneutic to be followed for understanding the biblical texts that speak of the Son's subordination in his incarnate ministry. If these authorities are taken as guides for the interpretation of Scripture, then the Trinity is to be understood as a community of equals who work together in perfect harmony and love: "None is before or after: none is greater or less than another. . . . (All) are co-equal." Those who read the Bible otherwise, arguing for the eternal subordination of the Son, read the Bible in a way rejected by orthodoxy. Their failure to acknowledge the historically orthodox conclusion and proper hermeneutic for formulating the doctrine of the Trinity has led them into error.

The second strand of evidence builds on the first. Those who argue for the permanent subordination of women claim that the modern stress on the equality of the persons in the Trinity is a reading back of contemporary egalitarian social ideals into the Godhead. However, the reverse is the truth. It is they who have read back into the Trinity their hierarchical understanding of the male-female relationship. As previously shown, the equality of the trinitarian persons in their being and acts is not a theological innovation. It was consummately argued by Athanasius in the fourth century, Augustine in the fifth century and Calvin in the sixteenth century, when society was hierarchically ordered and patriarchy was the norm. The orthodox doctrine of the Trinity that excludes any subordination in being or act was developed counterculturally. Since these doctrinal convictions have been well established in the life of the church for centuries, evangelicals who believe women and men should grant to each other equality of consideration are not the innovators. Their understanding of the Trinity was already there for use in illuminating the man-woman relationship. While there have been several significant modern expositions of the Trinity that in some ways refine or restate the historic tradition, none of them overthrows the normative core of the orthodox understanding, nor can they provide anything like a secure basis for the truly innovative notion of the *eternal* subordination of the Son to the Father.

We find a third strand of evidence in the *details* of the argument made by the conservative evangelicals for the eternal subordination of the Son. Those who argue for the permanent subordination of women depict the triune God of Christian revelation in exactly the same ways as they view the woman-man relationship. Those who argue for the permanent subordination of women use novel language and concepts developed only in the last thirty years,[17] which are then transferred to discussions regarding the Trinity. Thus their beliefs about

---

[17]In chapter seven I show how the foundational arguments and constructs in post-1970s cases for the permanent subordination of women stand in contrast with the historical arguments. They are "novel."

women come to be mirrored detail by detail in their beliefs about the Son. In this way the orthodox doctrine of the Trinity is subverted by a prior agenda.

To illustrate this phenomenon I have selected the six most important elements in the conservative evangelical case for the subordination of women. I outline each of these using subheadings to compare three aspects of the debate: what those who argue for the permanent subordination of women generally believe about women in relation to men; what they believe about the Son in relation to the Father; and what orthodoxy affirms about the Trinity.

Headship

☐ *Their view of the man-woman relationship.* The most important truth to be upheld in relation to the ordering of the sexes is the "headship" of men in the church and husbands in the home.

☐ *Their view of the Father-Son relationship.* In the Trinity the Father is the "head" of the Son. The Father exercises authority over the Son and assumes the leadership role.[18]

☐ *The orthodox view of the Trinity.* Western and Eastern orthodoxy do not speak the Father as the eternal "head" of the Son, and Athanasius and the Western tradition in general think the idea that the Father is the *archē* (source) of the Son is problematic. As far as the apostle Paul is concerned, after the resurrection Christ has "first place in everything" (Col 1:18), having become "the head over all things" (Eph 1:22; Col 2:10). Thus in the post-Easter age, salvation is found not in confessing Jesus is the obedient Son but in confessing that "Jesus is Lord" (Rom 10:9; Phil 2:11) and that therefore he is equal in divinity and equal in divine authority with the Father.

A Chain of Command

☐ *Their view of the man-woman relationship.* The headship of men must be preserved not only because it is prescribed in the Bible but also because in the church and the home someone must have the final say. In human relations there is always the possibility of a clash of wills. God has given authority to men, not women. Men should have the "casting vote."

---

[18]Wayne Grudem, *Systematic Theology: An Introduction to Biblical Doctrine* (Grand Rapids, Mich.: Zondervan, 1994), pp. 250, 257, 459; Sydney Anglican Diocesan Doctrine Commission, "The Doctrine of Trinity and Its Bearing on the Relationship of Men and Women," 1999 report, par. 18, 33, 38 <www.anglicanmediasydney.asn.au/doc/trinity.html>. (See appendix B of this book.) On this point and those to follow I do not intend to document in detail the points made, for the ideas I set out are pervasive in the literature and I have documented them in detail earlier.

□ *Their view of the Father-Son relationship.* In the Trinity, God the Father commands and the Son obeys. There is a "chain of command." The Son "is to submit to his Father."[19]

□ *The orthodox view of the Trinity.* Orthodoxy, in contrast, depicts the Father and the Son in such perfect harmony that the idea of a clash of wills is excluded on principle. The divine persons so profoundly interpenetrate one another (the doctrine of perichoresis) that their wills are one. Athanasius, Augustine and Calvin never differentiate the Father and the Son on the basis of differing authority, nor do the creeds. The idea that the Father commands and the Son obeys is an Arian error. After his resurrection. Jesus himself said, "All authority in heaven and on earth has been given to me" (Mt 28:18). He now reigns as Lord.

Role Subordination

□ *Their view of the man-woman relationship.* Women are equal to men in being, but they are subordinated in role. The idea of "role subordination" of women first appeared in the 1970s.[20] It is now one of the foundational pillars of the contemporary case for male leadership in the church and the home.

□ *Their view of the Father-Son relationship.* In the 1980s this novel role terminology was transferred to the Trinity. Before this time no one had ever mentioned *role* subordination in the Trinity. In making the role subordination of the Son the most fundamental aspect of trinitarian theology and the basis for a theology of the sexes, Wayne Grudem's *Systematic Theology* pioneers a path no one has taken before.

□ *The orthodox view of the Trinity.* Orthodoxy knows nothing of "role" subordination in the Trinity. The terminology and attendant theology is novel. It is not found in any of the classic texts on the Trinity. More importantly, the concept is foreign to orthodoxy. Orthodoxy insists that the Father, the Son and the Holy Spirit are one in being *and* in work; they are equal in essence *and* function/role. The Father and the Son act or work as one.

Difference Necessitates Subordination

□ *Their view of the man-woman relationship.* The distinction between the sexes is grounded in their God-given differences in roles (Grudem) or in their "differences of being" (Sydney Doctrine Report). If the permanent headship of

---

[19]Sydney Doctrine Report, par. 18, 32, 33; Grudem, *Systematic Theology,* pp. 250, 257, 459.
[20]See chapter seven, where this point is fully substantiated.

men and the subordination of women are denied, then sexual differentiation
cannot be preserved. The error of egalitarians is that by negating this God-
given subordination, they confuse or obliterate the differences between the
sexes.[21]

☐ *Their view of the Father-Son relationship.* The distinctions between the
persons of the Trinity cannot be preserved unless the subordination of the Son
and the Spirit is upheld. If the subordination of the Son is denied, their differences are denied. So Grudem writes that if the eternal subordination of the Son
to the Father and of the Spirit to the Father and the Son is rejected, "then there
is no inherent difference in the way the three (divine) persons relate to one
another, and consequently we do not have the three distinct persons existing
as Father, Son and Holy Spirit for all eternity."[22]

☐ *The orthodox view of the Trinity.* Orthodoxy does not ground the distinctions between the divine persons on differences in being or roles. The historic tradition holds that the Father, the Son and the Spirit are differentiated
only and essentially by their relations one to the other. The Father is the Father
of the Son, the Son is the Son of the Father, and the Spirit is the Spirit of the
Father and the Son. As these relationships can never change, the persons can
never be confused. If the persons of Father, Son and Spirit are constituted by
their roles, this would lead to the heresy of modalism. If they are constituted
by their "differences in being," this would lead to the heresies of tritheism and
ontological subordinationism. Thus orthodoxy insists that the differences
among the persons are essential to the Godhead and that the persons are one
in being and work. Who they are and what they do are one.

Eternal Subordination

☐ *Their view of the man-woman relationship.* Women's subordination is
grounded in an unalterable constitutive order given in creation before the Fall.
For this reason it is a transcultural principle that does not change when culture
changes. It is permanent.

☐ *Their view of the Father-Son relationship.* In regard to the Trinity, the
Son is eternally subordinated to the Father. The corollary of women's *permanent* subordination is the *eternal* subordination of the Son.

☐ *The orthodox view of the Trinity.* Historic orthodoxy accepts the tempo-

---

[21]Again, refer to chapter seven, where examples of such claims are given.
[22]Grudem, *Systematic Theology,* pp. 251, but see pages 248–51. Robert Letham starkly puts the
case that the difference within the Godhead demands subordination ("The Man-Woman
Debate: Theological Comment," *Westminister Theological Journal* 52 [1990]: 65–78).

ral subordination of the Son in the incarnation for us and our salvation; it rejects the eternal subordination of the Son and subsequently interprets Scripture with this in mind.

Tradition

☐ *Their view of the man-woman relationship.* Christians have always believed that the Bible teaches the subordination of women in the home and the church. Those who preserve this truth are the only ones upholding the "traditional" or "historic" position on women. The egalitarians are the innovators.

☐ *Their view of the Father-Son relationship.* Likewise, Christians have always believed that the Son is eternally subordinated to the Father. This is what Athanasius, Augustine and Calvin and the Nicene and Athanasian Creeds teach. Tradition is on "our" side.

☐ *The orthodox view of the Trinity.* Historic orthodoxy supports exactly the opposite belief regarding the trinitarian persons. The authorities quoted all explicitly oppose the eternal subordination of the Son. In part two of this book I will demonstrate that the so-called contemporary traditional or historic case for the subordination of women is also innovative. On this matter both sides in the debate have rejected the tradition.

*   *   *

I could go on, but the case has been made. The recent impetus to understand the Trinity as equal in divinity but subordinate in function or role has arisen exclusively in the context of arguing for the permanent subordination of women, not in the context of a review of the history of the doctrine or a reconsideration of biblical texts and their historic interpretation relating to our understanding of the Trinity. In virtually every aspect of this hierarchical presentation of trinitarian theology, the determining force is not the Bible as it has been understood across the centuries but rather an all-consuming concern to maintain the "headship" of men. This passion has led to the most dangerous of all errors—the corruption of the primary doctrine of Christianity, the doctrine of God. The eternal subordination of the Son has been postulated on the basis of a belief that women are permanently subordinated to men. The relationships between members of the Trinity have been conceived in terms of fallen human relationships, where the more powerful rule over the less powerful. We are then told that this hierarchical understanding of the Trinity supports and informs the permanent subordination of women—an improper analogical argument from the creaturely to the divine. The whole approach is to be rejected not because it makes the Trinity a model for human relationships, but because it makes fallen human relationships the model for divine relationships. God is depicted in human terms. Barth argues that this constitutes idolatry.

Conclusion

In our study of the early church's controversy over the Trinity, we have seen the hermeneutical importance of grasping what is central to Scripture as a key element for doing evangelical theology. Athanasius, Augustine and Calvin all recognized that quoting individual verses proved nothing. The overall drift of Scripture and theological center had to be rightly discerned. Orthodox tradition has been found to faithfully capture this sense of perspective, and so the best of theologians and exegetes have relied on it in their attempts to interpret Scripture across the ages.

In the historically developed orthodox tradition, one text more than any other, Philippians 2:5–11, has been taken to disclose the right way to understand the whole "scope" of Scripture in regard to the Son. He is eternally equal with God, yet he voluntarily and temporarily subordinated himself in the incarnation for the salvation of men and women. In the contemporary debate this same text is again of tremendous significance. The original intent of these words speaks to the questions we are addressing in our present context. Paul penned these words not because he was concerned that some thought the Son was eternally subordinated to the Father. His concern at this time was the behavior of Christian women and men. He wanted both sexes to emulate Christ's voluntary and costly self-giving and humility. He presents the incarnation of the Son as the analogy par excellence for how all Christians—women and men—should relate to one another on a personal level. He writes,

> Let the same mind be in you that was in Christ Jesus,
>> who though he was in the form of God,
>>> did not regard equality with God
>>> as something to be exploited,
>> but emptied himself,
>>> taking the form of a slave. (Phil 2:5–7)

It is Christlike to willingly subordinate oneself in the service of others—and this is so for men and women.

Little has been made of this text in the contemporary debate about the status and ministry of women. Perhaps this passage points us to the most basic insight in Scripture on this matter as well. Preserving one's privileges, holding on to power, is not Christlike. What is Christlike is to subordinate oneself in the service of others, whether we are male or female. If this is the ideal, then the apostle's exhortations to women to be subordinate are to be understood simply as practical advice to women living in a patriarchal culture. These directives are temporal in nature, and the response expected is voluntary. If this is so, then Paul's words to the Philippians indicate that neither the eternal subordination of the Son nor the permanent subordination of women are endorsed by the apostle.

"Let the same mind be in you that was in Christ Jesus."

Appendix A

Trinitariograms

Two-dimensional drawings seeking to illustrate a given understanding of the Trinity are limited in their capacity to capture very much of the majesty of the triune God of revelation. Nevertheless, they can be powerful aids to conceptualization. In this appendix I want to present four models of the Trinity expressed in "trinitariograms" to illustrate the different positions we have discussed. These diagrams have only one purpose: to elucidate how the relationship between the three persons of the Trinity may be conceived.

The Hierarchical Model

In this model the Father is "above" the Son, and the Son is "above" the Holy Spirit. Figure 1 captures this understanding of the Trinity whether the hierarchy is understood in ontological terms or functional terms.

FATHER

SON

HOLY SPIRIT

Figure 1

The *Monarchē* Model

In the early church it was commonly thought that the Father alone was the *monarchē,* or the one origin, of the Son and the Holy Spirit; and most Eastern Orthodox theologians today still endorse the *monarchē* view of the Father, although some now question this idea. Many Western theologians think this way of understanding the Trinity implies a certain priority to the Father, even if the Eastern theologians who embrace the *monarchē* of the Father say they reject the subordination of the Son and the Spirit in being or action. This model of the Trinity may be illustrated by an equilateral triangle with the Father at the apex (figure 2).

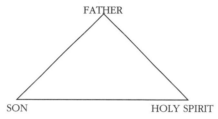

Figure 2

The *Filioque* Model

When the Western church in 589 added to the Nicene Creed the words *and the Son* (Latin *Filioque*) after the words "the Holy Spirit . . . proceeds from the Father," the idea that the Father was the sole source *(monarchē)* of the Son and the Spirit was deliberately subverted, if not excluded. Eastern theologians think this model implies the subordination of the Spirit. Western theologians reject this inference, insisting that what it underlines is the equality of the Father and the Son without questioning the equality of the Spirit. This formulation suggests a trinitariogram like figure 3.

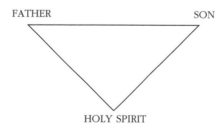

Figure 3

Symmetrical Models

As we have noted, most contemporary theologians, building on the historically orthodox tradition, prefer models of the Trinity that underline the equality of the persons and their communal unity. In the ancient church,

Athanasius came closest to seeing the Trinity in this way. Below I present three trinitariograms that attempt to capture this thought. It is to be noted they all visualize the Trinity in circular imagery.

Wayne Grudem, at the end of his discussion of the Trinity, sets out a number of trinitariograms and surprisingly favors one that is symmetrical.[1] How he equates this with his understanding of a Trinity in which the Father "has the role of commanding, directing and sending" the Son completely escapes me. Figure 4 is his drawing.

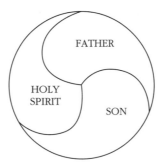

Figure 4

Figure 5 is the drawing I use when speaking on the Trinity. Many have found it helpful.

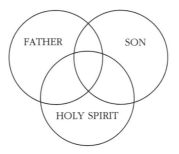

Figure 5

Professor Shirley Guthrie, whose summary of mainline contemporary trinitarianism was quoted in chapter four, offers figure 6.[2] He envisions the Trinity as

---

[1]Wayne Grudem, *Systematic Theology: An Introduction to Biblical Doctrine* (Grand Rapids, Mich.: Zondervan, 1994), p. 255.
[2]Shirley Guthrie, *Christian Doctrine* (Philadelphia: Westminster Press, 1994), pp. 91–92.

three divine persons dancing joyfully together, hand in hand, in a circle. He advocates this on what he believes is the etymology of the word *perichoresis,* the technical term that speaks of the coinherence of the three persons of the Trinity. In Greek the prefix *peri* (as in *perimeter*) means "around," and *choresis* literally means "dancing" (as in *choreography*). This etymology is disputed,[3] but the imagery is helpful.[4] In this imagery the unity of the divine persons is found in their perichoretic communion, and their equality is stressed by allowing that each may take a turn in leading the dance.

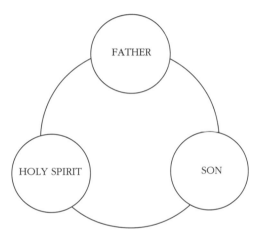

Figure 6

[3]So Thomas F. Torrance, *The Christian Doctrine of God: One Being, Three Persons* (Edinburgh: T & T Clark, 1996), p. 170 n. 8; and in more detail, R. Kress, *The Church: Communion, Sacrament, Communication* (New York: Paulist, 1985), pp. 15–22. On the development of this term see Bertrand de Margerie, *The Christian Trinity in History* (Petersham, Mass.: St. Bede, 1982), pp. 182–86.

[4]On this imagery and alternatives, see David Cunningham, *These Three Are One: The Practice of Trinitarian Theology* (Oxford: Blackwell, 1998), pp. 180–81.

Appendix B

THE 1999 SYDNEY ANGLICAN DIOCESAN DOCTRINE COMMISSION REPORT

The Doctrine of Trinity and Its Bearing on the Relationship of Men and Women

Contents

Introduction

1. The Archbishop and the Standing Committee have referred the following proposed resolution (drafted by the Rev. Narelle Jarrett) to the Doctrine Commission: "Since the doctrine of the Trinity has been used in debate to support both an egalitarian and a subordination model for male and female roles in ministry and marriage, Synod respectfully requests the Archbishop to—

(a) refer what appears to be a conflict of view on the relation of the persons of the Trinity within the Godhead to the Doctrine Commission for its consideration and report; and

(b) request the Doctrine Commission to report back to the first session of the 45th Synod."

2. The issue has been raised specifically by a paper prepared in favour of the

priesthood of women for the Conference on Women's Ministry in May 1998—

> Paul argues no priority of male and female and no subordination, only a fundamen-
> tal equality. This is all consistent with Paul's idea of headship which is based on his
> understanding of the Godhead. That God is the head of Christ means that the "Son
> is eternally begotten of the Father," or "of the same stuff as" and therefore equal to
> God. By analogy, the female is "of the same stuff as" and therefore equal to the
> male. For, in creation, God made us human, male and female. There is no order of
> subordination in this understanding of headship. ("Not Compromise," 2)

> The Athanasian Creed specifies that there is no ordered subordination or hierar-
> chy within the Godhead. The only stated subordination is that Jesus is "inferior to
> the Father, as touching his manhood." Headship within the Trinity cannot mean
> "subordinate to" or "under the authority of." Subordination is a matter of the free-
> dom of the will, not of some imposed order: it is voluntary and mutual, and for us
> in the Church, it is "out of reverence for Christ." (3)

3. An alternative view is put frequently in the literature, as by Dr Thomas R.
Schreiner, for example—

> One can possess a different function and still be equal in essence or worth.
> Women are equal to men in essence and in being; there is no ontological distinc-
> tion, and yet they have a different function or role in church and home. Such dif-
> ferences do not logically imply inequality or inferiority, just as Christ's subjection
> to the Father does not imply His inferiority. (Schreiner in Piper and Grudem, 128)

4. Both the so-called "egalitarian" and the so-called "subordinationist" accept
the equality of the sexes. The egalitarian believes that an individual may voluntarily choose to give a temporary submission in certain circumstances, without
compromising equality. The "subordinationist" regards submission in some
roles within ministry and marriage as arising from the nature of gender differences, without compromising equality. Both regard their views as being supported by our knowledge of the Trinity.

Suggested Problems with the "Subordinationist" Thesis
5. All parties in the present discussion regard both the unity and equality of the
three Persons of the Godhead as an absolute fundamental of the Christian
faith. There are not three Gods; they are not three "people"; they are not three
"parts" of God. Each partakes fully of the divine essence; each rightly receives
all praise, honour, glory and worship. Christ Jesus did not exploit his equality
with God the Father in order to use it to his own advantage and especially to
avoid his incarnation, but retained it while "being made in human likeness"

(Phil. 2:6–7). We are not saved through the work of an angel, or a secondary god. We are saved by the work of God himself: the salvation initiated by God the Father and won by God the Son on the cross, is applied to us by God the Holy Spirit.

6. In order to help emphasise this equality and unity, some theologians speak of the "coinherence" (or "perichoresis") of the Trinity, that is that each Person "indwells" the other in mutual delight and union. For the same reason, they also say that "the external operations of the Trinity are indivisible." This means that there is one God, who in all three Persons of his being is involved in all the works of God in creation and redemption. It safeguards us against any idea that there may be three different wills working in opposition. "The one God ('He') is also and equally 'they' and 'they are always together and always co-operating'" (Packer, 42). On the other hand, according to the doctrine of "Appropriation" it is permissible to refer elements of God's work pre-eminently to one or other of the Persons. Creation is "from the Father, through the Son" (1 Cor. 8:6), for example.

7. However, there has been substantial criticism of the position taken by those who like Dr Schreiner believe that along with the equality there is an element of subordination in the Godhead, and that it has direct significance in the debate about male and female relationships in the Church and the home. The three lines of criticism are as follows—

8. It is a heresy. "Subordinationism" is certainly the name given by historians of theology to a major heresy, that of suggesting that in substance or in being ("ontologically"), the Son is inferior to the Father.[1] The classic form of Subordinationism is Arianism, the doctrine which taught that the Son was a secondary god, unlike and not of the same substance or essence as the Father. But a more moderate form, in which the Son is of like substance to the Father, was also judged inadequate. The Church doctrine states that the Father and the Son and the Spirit are of the same substance, or essence, equal in power, dignity, worship and praise. The question discussed below is whether the subordinationism asserted in the current debate is the heretical form or not (see items 13–16 below). Gilbert Bilezikian claims that it is: "God and Christ are both persons within the one being of the Trinity. Nowhere in the Bible is there a reference to a chain of command within the Trinity. Such "subordinationist" theories were propounded during the fourth century and

---

[1]In this Report, the heresy of Subordination is usually spelled with a capital to distinguish it from references to any authentic subordination within the Godhead.

were rejected as heretical" (Bilezikian, 279).

9. It applies only to the redemptive work of Christ. The second criticism accepts that there is a legitimate form of subordinationism, but insists (as in the quote given in item 2 above) that it is applied only to Christ in his redemptive work. As the Athanasian Creed (a standard authority for Anglicans) says, "And in this Trinity none is afore, or after other; none is greater, or less than another; But the whole three Persons are co-eternal together and co-equal." In dealing with the Son it says: "our Lord Jesus Christ, the Son of God, is God and Man," and continues later, "Equal to the Father, as touching his Godhead; and inferior to the Father, as touching his Manhood." Thus hierarchy and subordination are features of the relationship between the man Jesus and his heavenly Father, but (it is claimed) not of the relationship between the Father and the Son before the incarnation. Another version of this criticism widens the scope by saying that the subordination is specifically to do with redemption, not the permanent inner life of the Godhead—

> . . . the subordination of the Son to the Father is not an ontological subordination in the eternal Godhead, but a voluntary act of self-humiliation on the part of the Son in the economy of redemption. As God, the Son is equal with his Father, though as Messiah he has assumed a servant role and become subordinate to his Father. The basis of the comparison between Man's being, as an "I"/"thou" fellowship of male and female, and God's being, as an "I"/"thou" fellowship of persons in the Godhead, is the doctrine of the Trinity, not the doctrine of Incarnation. (Jewett, 133 fn 105)

10. This is a matter to which direct appeal must be made to the Scriptures to see whether they throw light on the subject (see items 17 to 28 below).

11. The analogy with human relationships does not hold. There is a third problem urged from the egalitarian point of view. Even if a form of subordinationism is acceptable, and even if it applies to the eternal relations between the Persons of the Godhead, is it relevant to the subject of the relationships between men and women? Thus, since the divine Persons are not persons in the human sense (they are not "three people," for example), the analogy between God and human relations is a false one. "The subordination of individual persons within the one Trinity is quite different from a social order that encodes the subordination of one group (women/wives) to another group (men/husbands) apart from considerations of the abilities, giftedness or mission of the individuals involved." (Grenz and Kjesbo, 117) (see items 29 to 41 below)

12. In what follows, we discuss each of these points in turn.

Subordinationism as a Heresy

13. As noted already, "Subordinationism" is certainly the name given to one of the most deadly heresies ever faced by the Church. If Jesus Christ, the Son of God, is of a different and inferior essence to his Father, he cannot be the mediator between God and man, and the true revelation of God. We do not see the Father in the Son (John 14:9), and our salvation is not secure. The unity of the Father and the Son is essential for the work that Christ came to do.

14. But, despite the danger of Subordinationism, the word "subordination" is still used by orthodox theologians to describe the relation they perceived in Scripture between the Father and the Son. Thus, in the words of H. E. W. Turner, "There is an orthodox subordination in the sense that the Trinity must begin with the Father or lead up to the Father, but this is concerned with the order of thought and unity in derivation and does not affect the ontological status of the three persons." (Richardson, 329)

15. T. C. Hammond states: "In short, the full Christian doctrine demands all three of the following—

1. The unity of the Godhead
2. The full deity of the Son (who was "begotten") and the Spirit (who "proceeds" from the Father and the Son)
3. The subordination of the Son and the Spirit to the Father" (Hammond, 57)

16. Such teaching could be cited many times over. It would not be true to say, therefore, that every version of subordinationism is a heresy. There is a subordinationist element in the usual statement of the Church position.[2] It is always put alongside statements of the ontological equality of the divine persons. It maintains ontological equality and functional subordination. It usually applies to the eternal relations between the Persons and not just the order of redemption or only the manhood of Jesus. But is this type of subordinationism biblical, and in any case what does it imply?

The Meaning of "Subordination" in Orthodox Teaching

17. Its biblical roots. Pivotal to the whole revelation of the Trinity is the status of the Son of God. What we make of him determines our understanding of the nature of God. His true manhood is the explicit teaching of Scripture (1 Tim.

---

[2]Even the *Concise Oxford Dictionary* (4th edition, 1951), hardly a source of Christian Doctrine, sums up the situation with accuracy in its entry on "subordinationism": "Doctrine that second & third persons of the Trinity are inferior to the Father as regards (orthodox view) order only or (Arian view) essence."

2:5). So, too, is his deity (John 1:1). Correspondingly we read that he claimed unity and equality with God (John 10:30–33), but that he also said "the Father is greater than I" (John 14:28). In speaking of his relation with the Father, the Gospel of John refers to the way in which the world was made through him (1:3), and also the way in which he had been "sent" into the world for its salvation (e.g., 3:16–17). The Scriptures thus themselves bear witness to a subordination which belongs to the eternal relationship between the persons of the Trinity, and not only to the humanity of Jesus in the incarnation, or even in the broader work of redemption. This applies to the Spirit as well as the Son (Jn 14:26). As far as revelation permits us to see in any temporal direction—from before creation (Eph. 1:4), to creation (1 Cor. 8:6) and to redemption (Jn 3:16–17; 12:49, 50), to the gift of the Spirit (Gal. 4:6), and forward to consummation (Jn 5:25–26) and beyond (1 Cor. 15:28)—unity, equality and subordination characterise the life of the Trinity.

18. The Son's obedience to the Father arises from the very nature of his being as Son. His freedom consists in doing what is natural to him, which is to submit to his Father. He is incapable of doing other than his Father's will. The Son does not ask the Father to submit to him, for example, and cannot do so if he is to have the liberty to be true to his filial nature. The suggestion that, "Subordination is a matter of freedom of the will, not of some imposed order: it is voluntary and mutual . . ." (see item 2 above), misunderstands the meaning of freedom. The will is not free from the order imposed by the inner reality of personhood. For example, true freedom is enjoyed when a perfectly good person delights in doing good; in this case, when the Son delights to please the Father. Alternative accounts of freedom tend towards individualism and an emphasis on arbitrary choice as the essence of that freedom.

19. J. Ernest Davey sums up the evidence from John's Gospel in these words—

> The human traits in John's picture of Jesus, weariness, thirst, tears, etc., imply a creaturely dependence during the life of Christ in the flesh; but even John's picture of the eternal Son in himself retains the same subordinationist note—cf. John 14:28 . . . and cf. the Johannine Rev. 3:12, 21 and the like, where the risen Christ in Heaven not only receives gifts and dignity from the Father, but also speaks of Him as His God (four times in the one verse, and note even in our Gospel of John 20:17 after His Resurrection), i.e., even the risen and exalted Son has a God, a worship or religion in His relation to the ultimate God, the Father eternal and invisible. Indeed there is no doubt that for John the dependence of Christ upon the Father is not confined to his life upon earth; it reaches back into his pre-existence (17:24)

and forward to His exalted life as the Risen One (14:16), and is in line with the thought of Paul in such passages as 1 Cor. 15:24, 28. (Davey, 78–79)

20. Davey has given his answer as to whether the subordination of Son to Father applies only to the incarnation—he sees it as a matter of the eternal relations. Gordon Fee bears witness to the same phenomenon in his treatment of 1 Corinthians. In order to guard the unity and equality of the persons, he speaks at several points of the "functional subordination" of Son (and Spirit) to Father. In some cases, he specifically links this to the incarnation (on 11:3) and the work of redemption (on 15:28, though notice that this passage is speaking of the Son's submission in the eschatological triumph). But on 8:4–6, which speaks of creation, he refers to what he calls, "the functional subordination of the Son to the Father." He then explains, "God the Father is both the ultimate source and ultimate destiny of all things, including ourselves; the Lord Christ is the divine mediator, through whom God created all things and redeemed us" (Fee, 374). Just as clear is his reference to the "functionally subordinate" activities of both Son and Spirit (who of course has never been incarnate) in his comment on 12:6: "the unity of God dominates his thinking in such a way that the Son and the Spirit are subsumed under that unity, and their own activities are seen as 'functionally subordinate' (e.g., God gives gifts 'through the Spirit,' vv. 8–9). On the other hand, there can be little question that he thinks of Christ and the Spirit in terms of their full deity" (Fee, 588).

21. A distinction is rightly made between what is revealed to us about God in salvation (the "economic Trinity") and what we know of his own inner life (the "essential" Trinity). We may ask whether subordination is true of the inner, eternal relations of the essential Trinity, or only in the outworking of salvation. If we are to avoid agnosticism about God, however, we must assert that the economic Trinity reveals the truth, but not all that is true, about the essential Trinity. That is, when we deal with the God revealed in Scripture we deal with the real God as he is in himself and not a God whose revelation is a distortion of his reality. According to Scripture, the submission of Christ does not express a temporary and arbitrary arrangement, but the very nature of God in himself. The danger otherwise is the heresy of modalism, in which the Persons as revealed in Scripture are only the temporary manifestations of the one God. In fact, it was not the Father but the Son who was the incarnate Mediator, and it could not have been other. We never read, for example, that the Father obeys the Son or that the Son sends the Father, or that the Spirit creates through the Father.

22. The Church Doctrine of the Trinity. What distinguished the orthodox from the heretical was determination of the orthodox to do justice to the whole teaching of Scripture. The Arians over-emphasised the subordinationist elements of the NT presentation. The orthodox needed to insist on the unity and equality of Father, Son and Spirit. If the revelation in Christ was to be true, they had to say with Christ, "The Father and I are one; if you have seen me you have seen the Father." But they did not ignore or neglect the other evidence of Scripture for a relational subordination of the Son and the Spirit to the Father. With varying degrees of success they allowed room for this too.

23. In the course of Christian history there have been many attempts to state the doctrine of the Trinity. All attempts which have produced orthodox answers have followed the soteriological flow of the New Testament. In the Eastern tradition, it has been more usual to begin the process of thinking and talking about the Trinity from the Persons, and thus the priority of the Father. It is as if the Father is the source of the deity enjoyed by Son and Spirit. The danger of heresy is met by the insistence that the Son and Spirit are of one being with the Father, but the position of the Father ensures a hierarchical mode of conceiving God.

24. The Western tradition, exemplified in Augustine, has as its starting point the Triune life itself in its oneness. The emphasis falls from the beginning on the single essence and hence the unity and equality of the Persons. Even so, however, the order of the Godhead is acknowledged. This is most clearly expressed in the Catholic Creeds which assert both the equality and difference in the relations between the persons of the Godhead. The church did not conceive of the Father, Son and Spirit as just existing together. Rather they were understood as eternally related to each other in distinctive relationships of derivation and being. So the differences between the co-equal persons of the Trinity are not only voluntary or temporary, but go to each's very mode of being.

25. In the Creeds, the Son and the Spirit are asserted to be equal with the Father, but it is a derived equality. With the second and third persons, the mode of derivation and the relationship of being is distinct. The Athanasian Creed, while strongly affirming the equality of the persons, makes these differences of being most clear: "The Father is made of none: neither created nor begotten. The Son is of the Father alone, not made or created, but begotten. The Holy Ghost is from the Father and the Son, not made, nor created, nor begotten, but proceeding. . . . And in this Trinity there is none afore or after

the other; none is greater or less than the other."[3]

26. A doughty advocate of the ontological equality of the Persons was John Calvin, who insisted on the single essence of God and the self-sustaining deity ("Autotheos") of both Son and Spirit, in order to secure the point that in dealing with Son and Spirit we are dealing with God himself and not some lesser being. Even so, however, Calvin and the Calvinists (Edwards, Berkhof, Hodge, Dabney, Packer, Knox)—not to mention the neo-orthodox (Barth, Brunner) have recognised order, and "a certain subordination as to the manner of personal subsistence, but no subordination as far as possession of the divine essence is concerned" (Berkhof, 88–89). As Calvin says of the Father, "even though we admit that in respect to order and degree the beginning of divinity is in the Father, yet we say that it is a detestable invention that essence is proper to the Father alone, as if he were the deifier of the Son"; and elsewhere, summarising Tertullian, "there are thus three, not in status, but in degree" (Calvin, 152, 157).

27. Given the issues at stake in debates about the nature of human relationships, there has been a move amongst some scholars to propose a version of the doctrine of the Trinity which is "egalitarian." It has been alleged that traditional teaching undergirds political, ecclesiastical and social injustice. Mutual submission of the Persons of the Trinity takes the place of subordination in relations. One such learned work is that of Miroslav Volf (*After Our Likeness*, 1998), who shows through a consideration of two leading representatives of Orthodox (Zizioulas) and Roman Catholic (Ratzinger) theology that the mainstream of thought is "subordinationist." His own proposal, based especially on the doctrine of co-inherence, is egalitarian.

28. Nonetheless, on the basis of the considerations already given above, the Commission regards such a move as a very significant departure from Scripture and the established Church doctrine. We are troubled that a debate about the nature of humanity and human relations should have led to a move to change our established understanding of God. If this is the meaning of the paper referred to in item 2, it must be regarded as having failed to make good its contention that "There is no order of subordination in this understanding of headship."

---

[3] It is worth noting that the Athanasian Creed can be understood as expressing the main line of this doctrine. In commenting on the Creed's statement "none is afore or after other," the nineteenth century Anglican evangelical theologian E. A. Litton said: "If we remove the element of priority of time, which necessarily inheres in human relation, and conceive an eternal generation, we arrive at the catholic doctrine, that whilst a certain inequality must be admitted, the three Persons are, as regards their Deity, co-equal" (Litton, 102–3).

The Significance of "Subordination" in Orthodox Teaching

29. If we assume that subordination in the Godhead is part of orthodox Christian teaching and that it expresses the truth of Scripture, the question still remains as to its relevance to human relationships. In arguing that there is a relevance, those who hold to both equality and subordination in human and divine relationships make two uses of the doctrine. Both are significant, if justifiable, but the second is the stronger.

30. Equal and Different? In the first place, there are those who appeal to this doctrine to support the assertion that in personal life equality and subordination can co-exist. This is the view expressed by Dr Thomas Schreiner (cited in item 3 above). They argue that in the case of God a strong illustration may be found for their contention that differences in roles, even differences involving subordination, do not necessarily imply inequality of essence. In Schreiner's words, "there is no ontological distinction, and yet they have a different function or role in church or home." Thus, although in the ordering of family and church life, men are to take the lead, and women are to submit to their husbands and refrain from exercising eldership authority in the church, this in no way implies ontological inferiority, or distorts the basic truth that in Christ there is no male or female (Galatians 3:28). For this point many other cases may be found in everyday life—companies, ships, schools—wherever there is leadership, obedience, and persons who though equal in essence as human beings are subordinate in role. The fact that the inner life of God himself contains the same discernible principle is evidence that it cannot be wrong to enter such relations, and it must be possible to order life in that way with justice.

31. This line of thought is not troubled by the understanding of subordination as applying only to the order of redemption (as in Jewett, item 9 above). That God has functioned in the incarnation like this without compromising his equality, is sufficient to establish the case.

32. Dr Schreiner's position is true as far as it goes. As is shown in item 11 above, however, it may be challenged at a deeper level. While personal submission may be a pattern for instances such as individuals in work situations, it serves as an inadequate model, for "a social order that encodes the subordination of one group . . . to another group . . . apart from considerations of the abilities, giftedness or mission of the individuals involved" (see item 11 above). Subordination (with basic equality) is a common human experience. But the individual who submits does so on the basis of such matters as age, training or willingness to take responsibility. The arguments used by those who see subordination as a feature of church and home appeal to the ineradicable gender dif-

ference. They may be thought to be concluding that "all women should submit to all men." The Doctrine Commission does not accept this conclusion, but recognises that it is a key reason why the "egalitarian" contends that in the Godhead the obedience of the Son to the Father is voluntary, temporary and personal, rather than reflecting the essence of the eternal relationship between them. These deeper issues lead us to ask what bearing if any does the doctrine of the Trinity have on the relationship of men and women as such, rather than individuals from either sex?

33. God's life as a pattern for us. In the face of this challenge, a second and more profound exposition of the doctrine of the Trinity in its biblical context is required. Enough has been said to indicate that the idea that the obedience of the Son can be summed up as "voluntary, temporary and personal" is both inadequate and untrue. It relies on a view of freedom whose tendency is toward the arbitrary and the individualistic (see items 18, 20 and 24 above). The equality and subordination which "subordinationists" see in the Trinity belongs to the very Persons themselves in their eternal nature, and this has a profound bearing on human relationships. Thus Dr. D. B. Knox wrote in his addendum to the General Synod Doctrine Report of 1977, "The principle of order, of headship and subordination, is clearly seen in 1 Corinthians 15:23–28 where Christ is head over all things and yet himself is subordinate to the Father. Since Christ is both head of every man and himself subordinate to the Father he is the example (in perfect relationship) both of the exercise of headship, i.e., gratitude ("I thank thee Father") and obedience ("I do always the things that are pleasing to him")." (Knox, 31). Indeed, P. K. Jewett is also arguing a version of that case in the extract given in item 9 above.

34. The same connection is made in the Theological Statement by the (English) House of Bishops, entitled *Eucharistic Presidency* (1997). The Bishops see the ordering of the Church as reflective of the ordering of the Trinity. They therefore insist upon the equality of persons before God while regarding such equality as consistent with an asymmetrical subordination which flows from the nature of the Persons themselves—

> It is generally accepted that although there is no subordination of being, there is nevertheless differentiation of function and relationship within the Trinity. For example, it is the Son who lives in obedience to the Father and not vice versa; the Father relates to both Son and Spirit, but in different ways. So, too, there can and should be a diversity of responsibilities and relationships within the Church—a theme classically expounded by Paul in 1 Corinthians 12. (p. 22)

35. On the other hand, the word "subordination" on its own hardly does justice to the full range of the relationship of Father and Son as revealed in the Scriptures. In particular, it must be understood in the light of the mutual love and delight that each Person has in the other as is reflected in the words of Dr Knox cited above. The English Bishops speak of, "a certain 'priority' of the Father in both the acts and being of God" (22), but they are careful to describe the relation between Father and Son in these terms: "relationships within the Trinity are fully mutual and reciprocal: they are constituted by mutual interaction, giving and receiving. The obedience of Jesus to the Father is a freely given commitment, not resigned submission or servility to a greater power. . . . Likewise, within the Church, while there can be no difference of worth of persons in the sight of God, relationships of obedience and accountability between members may properly exist; and, provided that they are practised within free relationships of mutual giving and receiving, they are able to promote the fulfilment of the Church's calling" (23).

36. Nonetheless, the question remains whether the analogy presupposes that the Persons are people, and whether the revealed nature of the one God may in fact be used to illustrate or demonstrate the true relations between human beings. The life of God is very far removed from the life of humans, and the relation between three Persons dwelling perichoretically is unlike any human experience. Does the Bible itself draw any connection between the relations of the Godhead and the ordering of human life? In particular does it speak in this way to the issue of the relation between men and women?

37. It is true that the Bible carefully safeguards the distinction between God and his human creatures: "For I am God and not man—the Holy One among you" (Hos. 11:9). This is fundamental. On the other hand, there is biblical material which likens man to God: "So God created man in his own image, in the image of God he created him; male and female he created them" (Gen. 1:27). Furthermore, the new self is "being renewed in knowledge in the image of its Creator" (Col. 3:11; cf. Eph. 4:24) and it is in this new self in particular that human divisions are, in part, laid aside and "Christ is all, and is in all." Likewise, Paul speaks of "the Father, from whom every family in heaven and earth derives its name" (Eph. 3:15). Such texts demonstrate that God's pattern of creation makes it possible to draw conclusions about the nature of human life and relationships from God. To avoid mere speculation, however, we must be led by the Scriptures in our thinking. What are the implications of the relations of the Godhead?

38. In a remarkable statement, the Apostle Paul says: "Now I want you to re-

alise that the head of every man is Christ, and the head of the woman is man (NIV; the RSV gives, "the head of a woman is her husband"), and the head of Christ is God" (1 Cor. 11:3).[4] The resulting discussion depends upon this set of relations, including those between God and Christ. The passage (11:2–16) is especially germane, because the subject under review by Paul is the relationship of men and women (or husbands and wives) in the exercise of the ministry of prophecy and prayer. Women have the authority to engage in this ministry (11:10), but both men and women must do so in a way which does not blur the distinct ordering of the sexes, which is founded on God's order in creation (11:3–9).

39. Paul is particularly concerned about the symbolism of head coverings. The point at issue for him is that the head coverings in question have a symbolic purpose in distinguishing priority and reflecting relationships between the sexes (or between husband and wife): "A man ought not to cover his head, since he is the image and glory of God; but the woman is the glory of man" (11:7). The "head" plays both a literal and a metaphoric role in the passage. The covering or uncovering of the literal head is dishonouring to the metaphoric head: if a man is covered, he dishonours Christ who is his head; if a woman is uncovered, she dishonours the man, who is her head (11:3–5).[5] Paul is also at pains to point out that though man is the "head" of the woman, man and woman are interdependent: "For as woman came from man, so also man is born of woman" (11:12).

40. There are a number of exegetical questions raised about this passage: does "head" imply "source" or "authority"? Is it about men and women, or husbands and wives? Is it about the church meeting or private prophecy? Nonetheless, and this is the point at issue in the current discussion, it is clear that an aspect of the relation between God and Christ (whether "head" implies "source" or "authority") is used as the grounds of the order between man and woman (whether it means husband and wife or not) in the particular situation of ministry. This is not a matter of differentiation between individuals on the grounds of abilities, giftedness or mission (see item 11 above). It is based ultimately on the sexual differentiation, but may primarily belong to the differentiation be-

---

[4] Opinions differ whether this passage is primarily about woman and man relationships or husband and wife relationships.

[5] This explains the otherwise odd saying of Paul that man is "the image and glory of God"; he is not hereby denying that woman, too, is in the image of God, but that in relation to the man, she, by acting appropriately, manifests his glory or honor. The point is functional not ontological.

tween husband and wife made clear in Genesis 2. Furthermore, that relation is characterised by both order and interdependence, priority and equality. The point is, of course, all the clearer if, as seems most likely, the word "head" implies authority. In short, here is a key passage in the Scriptures where the ordering of the Trinity is said to have a bearing on the ordering of the sexes. It thus provides justification for those who make the claim that the subordination of the Son provides a model for that interdependence, with subordination, which is expressed in various ways in family (Eph. 5:21–33; 1 Peter 3:1–7) and church (1 Tim. 2:11–15).[6]

41. It is important to note, however, the biblical controls of the procedure. That there is an relation between the sexes which somehow reflects the divine life itself is clear (cf. Gen. 1:27). Likewise we may conclude that it has a bearing on the proper conduct of marriage and ministry. But the ordering of the sexes appropriate to home and church is not applied to business, political or professional life. While it may be argued that gender is relevant in relationships between men and women in general (cf. 1 Tim. 5:1–2), the vocabulary of "subordination" is applied to the particular context of the concrete relationships entered into in home and church. Such is the difference between God and us that we ought to apply trinitarian relations to human relations with caution. It may be best not to move beyond the applications that Scripture itself gives. In fact, the NT more often regulates relations between men and women (husbands and wives) by appeal to the present work of Jesus Christ.

Conclusion

42. The present discussion has been initiated by conflicting statements such as those referred to in items 2 and 3 above: "Headship within the Trinity cannot mean 'subordinate to' or 'under the authority of'"; and, in contrast, "Christ's subjection to the Father does not imply his inferiority."

43. It is not at all surprising that debate about the respective roles of men and women in home and church should reach the lofty heights of the doctrine of God. There may only be a few texts which deal directly with the issue of whether women may be presbyters as such, but the texts themselves are part of a whole network of material in the Bible about men and women, and about Cre-

---

[6]Professor Colin Gunton agrees with the understanding of this passage, but is unwilling to accept the consequences because of the hierarchical implications. He therefore writes: "Paul's exegesis and theology are both questionable." His is a straightforward, if inadmissible, procedure, and is preferable to an intricate exegesis which tries to turn the passage in a purely egalitarian direction (*The Promise of Trinitarian Theology* [T & T Clark, Edinburgh], 1991, 74).

ation, Redemption, the authority of Scripture and about the nature of God. Furthermore, basic ideas abut the meaning of human freedom are at stake. That is why these debates engender such passion and such interest in the church and in the community, and that is why various attempts have been made to "feminise" God and re-order the Trinity in the last decades.

44. It is inevitable, therefore, that the present dispute should raise the question of what sort of God it is who reveals himself to us. The "egalitarian" case, although not every egalitarian person, logically leads to a claim for undifferentiated equality in the relation of the three Persons. The "subordinationist" case will just as logically appeal both to elements of equality and to elements of order that are seen in the relation of the Persons.

45. The Doctrine Commission agrees that the concept of "subordination" has significant implications. It concludes, furthermore, that the concept of "functional subordination," of equality of essence with order in relation, represents the long-held teaching of the church, and that it is securely based on the revelation of the Scriptures. This teaching should, therefore, determine our commitment both to the equality of men and women in creation and salvation, and also to appropriately biblical expressions of the functional difference between men and women in home and church.

Books and Papers Referred to in the Text

Berkhof, L., *Systematic Theology* (The Banner of Truth Trust: Edinburgh), 1939. Bilezikian, G., *Beyond Sex Roles* (Baker: Grand Rapids, Mich.), 1985. Davey, J. E., *The Jesus of St John: Historical and Christological Studies in the Fourth Gospel* (Lutterworth: London), 1958. Fee, G. D., *The First Epistle to the Corinthians* (Eerdmans: Grand Rapids, Mich.), 1987. *General Synod of the Church of England, Eucharistic Presidency* (Church House: London), 1997. Grenz, S. J., and Kjesbo, D. M., *Women in the Church: A Biblical Theology of Women in Ministry* (IVP: Downers Grove, Ill.), 1995. Hammond, T. C., *In Understanding Be Men: An Introductory Handbook on Christian Doctrine* (IVP: London), 1936. Jewett, P. K., *Man as Male and Female* (Eerdmans: Grand Rapids, Mich.), 1975. Knox, D. B., *The Ministry of Women: A Report of the General Synod Commission on Doctrine* (General Synod: Sydney Square), 1977. Litton, E. A., *Introduction to Dogmatic Theology* (James Clarke & Co: London), 1960. Calvin, John. *Calvin: Institutes of the Christian Religion*, 1, McNeill, J. T. (Ed.), Battles, F. L. (Trl) (Westminster: Philadelphia), 1967 (Book 1). Mickelsen, A. (Ed.), *Women, Authority & the Bible* (IVP: Downers Grove, Ill.), 1986. Packer, J. I., *Concise Theology: A Guide to Historic Christian Beliefs* (IVP: Leicester),

1993. Piper, J., and Grudem, W. (Eds), *Recovering Biblical Manhood and Womanhood: A Response to Evangelical Feminism* (Crossway: Wheaton, Ill.), 1991. Richardson, A. (Ed.), *A Dictionary of Christian Theology* (SCM: London), 1969. Volf, M., *After Our Likeness: The Church as the Image of the Trinity* (Eerdmans: Grand Rapids, Mich.), 1998. Unpublished paper, "Not Compromise; Not Uniformity; But Liberty—A Case for the Ordination of Women to the Priesthood," May 1998.

Members of the Sydney Anglican Doctrine Commission

The Chairman: The Rt Rev Dr Paul Barnett, Bishop of North Sydney. The Rev Dr Canon Peter Jensen, Principal of Moore Theological College (Consecrated Anglican Archbishop of Sydney in 2001). The Rev Dr Peter O'Brien, Vice-Principal of Moore Theological College. The Rev Dr Robert Doyle, Senior Lecturer in Theology, Moore Theological College. The Rev Dr John Woodhouse, Rector of Christ Church, St. Ives, Visiting Lecturer, Moore Theological College (appointed principal of Moore College in 2002). The Rev Canon Robert Forsyth, Rector of St Barnabas, Broadway, Visiting Lecturer, Moore Theological College (Consecrated Bishop of South Sydney in 2000). The Rt Rev Donald Robinson, former Vice-Principal of Moore Theological College and retired Archbishop of Sydney. The Rev Dr Michael Bowie, Rector of Christ Church, St. Laurence. The Rev Stephen Williams, Rector of All Saints, West Lindfield. The Rev Narelle Jarrett, Principal of Mary Andrews College, Ordained as a Deacon.

PART 2

THE WOMAN TRADITION

Reinterpreted by Some, Rejected by Others

6

WOMEN IN THE MODERN WORLD & IN CHRISTIAN TRADITION

Determining what is the historically developed orthodox doctrine of the Trinity is an important exercise in its own right. Evangelicals can, however, learn very important lessons from studying the process by which this doctrine came to be established. These lessons are of particular interest at this time, a time when evangelicals are giving considerable thought to how to do evangelical theology and are sharply divided over what should be believed on the man-woman relationship. In the second part of this book, I argue that under the pressure of the profound change in culture, expressed in the post-1970s women's movement, all evangelicals have changed their theology of the sexes. They have broken with tradition and constructed a new theology for a new age. Cultural change has forced evangelicals to change their interpretation of the Bible. The altered social context has altered how the Bible is read. What has emerged is not one agreed-on new theology, but two competing alternatives. It is my argument that the lessons learned from the development of the doctrine of the Trinity can offer a way forward on this specific theological dispute, which now divides the church and which is stalemated.

One important matter that unites the debate on the doctrine of the Trinity and the debate on women is that in both disputes, the protagonists quote texts that initially appear to support their position. This was a problem Athanasius and Augustine had to face in the fourth and early fifth centuries and that evangelicals have had to face in the late twentieth century and are facing at the beginning of the twenty-first century. The historic answer was that one had to first determine what is central to Scripture on the issue in question and then read the whole Bible in this light. Because we are more aware today of the diversity in Scripture, we should be more aware than those who have gone before that such a theological reading of Scripture is demanded. Whatever unity there may be at a theological level, this does not eclipse the diversity in Scripture as it confronts us. This diversity alone excludes the thought that theology can be done simply by quoting proof-texts and arguing about the meaning of words and the exegesis of passages. A more mature and adequate understanding of the theological enterprise is demanded.

In the Trinity debate, the contribution of tradition—how earlier theologians had understood the Bible's teaching on the relationship of the Father, Son and Spirit—made a very important contribution. Each theologian built on the work of those who had gone before, and each new advance was codified in a creed or confession that then gave hermeneutical guidance to those following. Evangelicals on both sides of the contemporary debate about the man-woman relationship are agreed on the importance of tradition as a secondary and guiding contributor in the theological task. This is shown by those who argue for the permanent subordination of women in the church and the home. They insist on calling their theology the "traditional" or the "historic" position. They claim that they are representing the view of the church that goes right back to the apostles; their opponents are the ones who have given a new reading of Scripture and abandoned the tradition. They, of course, insist that the primary authority for their theological position is the Scriptures. The tradition simply confirms that they are the ones who are interpreting the Bible correctly.

To counter these arguments, evangelicals who want to reject the idea that the subordination of women is God's ideal for all times and all cultures have to demonstrate that the texts quoted and interpreted to prove this point are read in such a way that they counter what is theologically primary in Scripture in regard to the man-woman relationship; these evangelicals also have to prove that either the appeal to tradition is mistaken or that the tradition is to be rejected for very good reasons. In this second part of this book, I will explore these options. I will argue that the contemporary case for the permanent subordination of women is "novel," a break with the tradition; that the historic tradition on women is to be rejected for very good reasons; and that the texts quoted to prove the permanent subordination of women do not reflect the primary theological perspective on the sexes within Scripture.

Evangelicals Reformulate Their Theology of the Sexes

In the late 1960s in the Western world one of the momentous social revolutions in human history erupted: the women's movement, or women's liberation. It has transformed modern life in almost every way imaginable. The revolution has its roots in the nineteenth century, although it was only in the second half of the twentieth century that all the ingredients to make this revolution possible came to be present. Educational opportunities for women had been increasing from the 1850s, but it was only in the 1960s that women started completing high school and entering universities in large numbers. Once women were educated, it became obvious that they were not lacking in intelligence, physical endurance or leadership capabilities. However, it was the invention of "the Pill" that precipitated this monumental social revolution. For the first time in human history, women were able to control their own fertility. Educated and freed from the uncertainty of pregnancy, women entered the work force in growing numbers. This gave them, also for the first time in human history, financial independence from men. This meant they did not have to marry or to stay in marriages where they were treated poorly or disrespectfully. They could support themselves. It also meant that for marriages to work, women had to operate on more equal terms than ever before. Men could not have it all their own way. The partnership model of marriage had become the ideal.

So profound has been this revolution that all Christians have been forced to restate their theology of the sexes in this new context. Evangelicals have not been exempted. Both the evangelicals who argue for the permanent subordination of women and those who argue for the full emancipation of women have, in the last thirty years, created theologies without antecedents. They have broken with tradition, developing novel interpretations of what the Bible teaches on the manwoman relationship. *Cultural change has generated new interpretations of the relevant biblical material.* Those who oppose the full emancipation of women will clap with delight to hear me so openly confess that my position is a break with tradition. They have long claimed this. They will not be so pleased to hear me claim that this is also true of their position. It is their repeated assertion that they alone preserve the tradition. This is simply not true. The interpretations they give of their proof-texts are novel—they are a radical break with tradition. The contemporary hierarchical—or "traditional" or "historic"—case for the permanent subordination of women has been "invented" in response to what has taken place. While it is true that the traditional interpretation subordinates women to men, what I am arguing is that the way the Bible is read to support this idea and how it is selectively applied is novel. To make my case I will first outline how the great exegetes and theologians of the past have interpreted the Bible's teaching on women; then I will compare this with how scholarly, contemporary conservative evangelicals, who are committed to the permanent subordination of women, interpret the Bible's teaching on women today.

Radical reinterpretations of the Bible are common in Christian history. Tradition sometimes has to be rejected. Often this happens when a scientific or social revolution forces Christians to rethink their understanding of what the Scriptures teach. Numerous examples can be given. It was for centuries taught that the Bible forbade "usury" (lending money at interest), and texts were quoted in support. The emerging capitalism of the sixteenth century demanded this tradition be rejected. The new interpretation was that the Bible only forbade lending money at exorbitant interest—something none of the texts quoted imply.[1]

When it was believed that the sun revolved around the Earth, and the Bible could be cited in support, it was believed this was the cosmology prescribed by Scripture. Johannes Kepler and Copernicus forced Christians to abandon this interpretation of Scripture.

Once the rule of kings or emperors was the most common form of government. In the Old Testament the role of King David idealized such rule and in the New Testament, Christians are called on to obey and respect Caesar. This lead to a way of reading the Bible in support of "the divine right" of kings to rule. The ascendancy of modern forms of democracy spelled the downfall of this reading of the Bible.

The change in how creation has been understood is another example. Until the late nineteenth century, Christians believed on the basis of what is said in Genesis that the world was created in six literal days about six thousand years ago. This was largely an unquestioned tradition. The growing scientific acceptance of evolution, and of the great age of the Earth, called into question this interpretation. Most Christians now read the Genesis creation story in a very different way.

In part three of this book I will outline how Christians for nearly eighteen

---

[1]See Ex 22:25; Deut 23:19ff.; Lk 6:34–35.

centuries believed the Bible regulated *and* legitimated slavery. All Christians now think the Bible does not do this.

These examples remind us that historical, cultural, social or scientific developments can be powerful incentives for Christians to rethink how they understand and read the Bible. I will illustrate this process of reinterpretation in the "light" of profound social change in regard to women in this second part of the book and in regard to slavery in the third part. I use the word *light* deliberately because such changes seem to enable Christians to "see" in Scripture things hitherto unseen. Again I state the hermeneutical rule: *A change in cultural context often leads to a change in the interpretation of the Bible.* One interpretative tradition gives way to another.

Conservative evangelicals who work on the premise that any one text in the Bible can have only one true and correct interpretation and that there can only be one true and correct overall reading of the Bible on any particular issue explain these changes in interpretation on the basis of one interpretation being true and the other being false. In most of the above examples it is now confidently said, "Today we understand better what the Bible is teaching. Our exegesis is right, and theirs was wrong." Contemporary discussions on herme-neutics offer an alternative explanation that is far more convincing. *The historical context has determined the interpretation in each of the examples given.* It was not possible for those in earlier cultural contexts to think otherwise than of women as inferior and subordinate, of slavery as acceptable to God and of creation as taking place by the direct and immediate acts of God. In their context theologians read the Bible in the only way open to them. In another context God himself opens up other possibilities. In what follows on the issues of women and slavery, competing interpretations of the same texts are outlined, and it is argued that the change in interpretation that can be seen is due to a change in the cultural context.

Women in Christian Tradition

Across the centuries, Christian theologians have consistently appealed to Scripture to substantiate their teaching on women. Many things have been concluded, but on the issues that concern us, I have been amazed to find so much unity of thought until recent times. This is a tradition where one finds more agreement than disagreement on what the Bible teaches. The conclusions listed below were well nigh universally held until the twentieth century, even if some express themselves more starkly than others.[2]

---

[2]My main source of information for what follows is older commentaries. See also G. Tavard, *Women in Christian Tradition* (Notre Dame: Notre Dame University Press, 1973); and A. J.

God has made women as a race or class inferior to men, excluding them from leadership in the home, the church and the world. In almost every pre-twentieth-century commentary or theological text, we find theologians affirming that men are "superior" and women "inferior." Often 1 Timothy 2:11–14 is given as proof. John Chrysostom, commenting on these verses, says that God made man first to show male "superiority" and to teach that "the male sex enjoyed the higher honor . . . having pre-eminence in every way."[3] Martin Luther asserts, "This passage makes woman subject. It takes from her all public office and authority."[4] In his commentary on Genesis, he explicitly adds that the female sex is "inferior to the male sex."[5] Likewise, Calvin says this passage teaches that "women by nature (that is by the ordinary law of God) are born to obey, for all wise men have always rejected the government of women (*gunaikokratian*, γυναικοκρατιαν) as an un-natural monstrosity." In addition, a little later he adds, "The true order of nature prescribed by God lays down that the woman should be subject to the man. . . . The reason that women are prevented from teaching is that it is not compatible with their status, which is to be subject to men, whereas to teach implies superior authority and status."[6] Woman, he continues, was created "to be a kind of appendage to man on the express condition that she should be ready to obey him."[7]

John Knox, the Scottish Reformer, is of the same opinion. Appealing to the Bible and the church fathers, he concludes that men are superior and women are inferior. He maintains that "woman on her greatest perfection was made to serve and obey man."[8] The idea that a woman should be the ruler of a state, he

Schmidt, *Veiled and Silenced: How Culture Shaped Sexist Theology* (Macon, Ga.: Mercer University Press, 1989). My richest secondary source for references to check in the original was Daniel Doriani, "History of Interpretation of 1 Timothy 2," in *Women in the Church: A Fresh Analysis of 1 Timothy 2:9–15,* ed. Andreas J. Köstenberger, Thomas R. Schreiner and H. Scott Baldwin (Grand Rapids, Mich.: Baker, 1995), pp. 213–67. He argues that the position taken in this book exactly reflects the historical understanding of women, yet almost every example he quotes counts against his case! His "theology" seems to blind him to what his sources are actually saying.

[3]John Chrysostom, *The Homilies of John Chrysostom: Timothy, Titus and Philemon, Library of the Fathers,* trans. James Tweed (Oxford: Parker, 1853), pp. 63–64.

[4]Martin Luther, *Commentaries on 1 Corinthians 7, 1 Corinthians 15, Lectures on Timothy,* vol. 28 of *Luther's Works,* ed. H. C. Oswald, trans. E. Sittler and M. Bertram (St. Louis: Concordia, 1958), p. 276.

[5]Martin Luther, *Lectures on Genesis Chapters 1–5,* ed. J. Pelikan, trans. G. Schick, vol. 1 of *Luther's Works* (St. Louis: Concordia, 1958), pp. 1–5, 69.

[6]John Calvin, *The Second Epistle of Paul to the Corinthians, and the Epistles of Timothy, Titus and Philemon,* trans. T. A. Smail (Grand Rapids, Mich.: Eerdmans, 1964), p. 219.

[7]Ibid.

[8]John Knox, "The First Blast of the Trumpet Against the Monstrous Regiment of Women," in *Selected Writings of John Knox,* ed. David Laing (Dallas: Presbyterian Heritage, 1995), p. 371.

argues at length, is contrary to the interpretation of the Bible given by the Holy Ghost. It is, thus, "monstrous." The Puritans are equally adamant that women are an inferior class.[9] They believed that God set men over women by assigning, to quote William Gouge, "degrees of superiority and inferiority."[10] Similarly, Robert Bolton says God made the male body "to his superiority, and set the print of government in his very face, which is sterner and less delicate than the woman's."[11] The eloquent Matthew Henry, commenting on 1 Corinthians 11:3ff., says that women "are placed in subordination to the man; and it is a shame for them to do anything that looks like an affection of changing rank. . . . The woman was made subject to the man, and she should keep her station."[12] Repeatedly in his comments, he concludes that the Bible teaches that man is superior and woman is inferior. In America, Jonathan Edwards commends "modesty and shamefacedness in inferiors to superiors," and then quoting 1 Timothy 2:9, he applies this principle to women.[13] John Wesley says the command that women keep silent in 1 Timothy 2:11–12 was given because woman is inferior to man and because a woman is "more easily deceived and more easily deceives."[14] Robert Louis Dabney, commenting on 1 Timothy 2:9–15, says the principle stands at all times and in all situations, "man is the ruler, woman the ruled."[15] "Her race," he writes, "is a subordinate race."[16] Charles Hodge writes, "[man's] superiority . . . enables and entitles him to command. . . . This superiority of the man is . . . taught in scripture, founded in nature and proved by all experience."[17] For this reason Hodge believed that "the general good requires us to deprive the whole female sex of the rights of self-government."[18]

---

[9]See in detail J. Morgan, *Godly Learning: Puritan Attitudes Towards Reason, Learning and Education 1560–1640* (Cambridge: Cambridge University Press, 1986), pp. 142–71.

[10]William Gouge, *Of Domesticall Duties* (London: John Haviland, for William Bladen, 1662), p. 591.

[11]Robert Bolton, *Some General Directions for a Comfortable Walking with God* (London: John Legatt for Edward Weaver, 1634), p. 245.

[12]Matthew Henry, *A Commentary on the Holy Bible* (London: Ward Lock & Co., n.d.), 6:1047. He lived from 1662 to 1714.

[13]*The Works of Jonathan Edwards*, ed. C. C. Goen (New Haven: Yale University Press, 1972), 4:426–27.

[14]John Wesley, *Explanatory Notes on the New Testament* (London: John Mason, 1862), p. 327.

[15]Robert Louis Dabney, *Discussions Evangelical and Theological* (London: Banner of Truth, 1967), 2:111.

[16]Ibid., p. 107.

[17]Charles Hodge, *A Commentary on the Epistle to the Ephesians* (London: Banner of Truth, 1964), p. 312. Doriani is simply mistaken when he claims that Hodge did not think the permanent subordination of women implied their "inferiority" ("History of Interpretation," p. 255). Hodge uses this very word frequently.

[18]Charles Hodge, "The Bible Argument for Slavery," in *Cotton Is King and Pro-Slavery Arguments,*

Adam Clarke, writing in 1859 in England, says, "God designed that he [the man] should have the pre-eminence. . . . The structure of woman plainly proves that she was never designed for those exertions required in public life. In this is the chief part of the natural inferiority of woman."[19] Charles Ellicott, writing five years later, says that 1 Timothy 2:11b sets the agenda for what follows: Paul is teaching that "woman, i.e., any one of her class . . . [must be] yielding in all cases. The πᾶς (all) in 'all subjection' [is] extensive rather than intensive."[20] I can find no dissenting voice in any commentary or in the writings of any theologian until the twentieth century. All are agreed that the Bible teaches that women are an inferior class or race who are not competent to lead or exercise authority in any sphere of life. This is the tradition—this is how the Bible has been interpreted by the best of past exegetes and theologians.

Women should keep silent in public. Because women as a class were understood to be a subordinate race, inferior to men, it was maintained that they should not speak in public; they were to keep silent. Two texts were read to support this rule, 1 Corinthians 14:34 and 1 Timothy 2:11–12. Most of the comments on these texts apply them directly to a church setting, but when the public scene comes into view, it is clear that this rule is thought to apply universally. Origen wrote, "It is not proper for a woman to speak at the Assembly, however admirable or holy what she says may be, merely because it comes from female lips."[21] Chrysostom commenting on 1 Timothy 2:11 says Paul's words mean that women should "not speak at all in church" or in "public . . . for the sex is naturally somewhat talkative and for this reason he [God] constrains them on all sides."[22] Commenting on 1 Corinthians 14:34, he says women are to keep silent because by nature they are "easily carried away and light headed."[23] Jerome ruled that women should be absolutely silent in church: they were not even to sing.[24] In expounding 1 Corinthians 14:34, he takes this to mean women should be silent in all public gatherings: "It is contrary to the order of nature and of the law that women should speak in a gathering of

---

ed. E. N. Cartwright (1860; reprint, New York: Basic Afro-American Reprint Library, 1968), p. 863.

[19]Adam Clarke, *The Holy Bible with Commentary and Criticism* (London: W. Tegg), 6:448.

[20]Charles Ellicott, *The Pastoral Epistles* (London: Longman, Roberts & Green, 1864), p. 36.

[21]Quoted from George Tavard, *Women in Christian Tradition*, p. 68.

[22]Chrysostom, "Homily on 1 Timothy," in *Homilies of John Chrysostom*, pp. 69–70.

[23]John Chrysostom, *The Homilies of St. John Chrysostom on 1 Corinthians*, *Library of the Fathers*, ed. and trans. H. K. Cornish and J. Hedley (Oxford: Parker, 1853), p. 37.

[24]Jerome *Adversus Pelagianos dialogi III* 1.25.

men."[25] Thomas Aquinas concluded, "The voice of women is an invitation to lust, and therefore must not be heard in church."[26] Luther believed Paul's command that women "keep silent" applied to all "public matters," but he said, "I want it to refer to public ministry, which occurs in the public assembly of the church. There a woman must be completely quiet."[27] Calvin was of a similar opinion: interpreting 1 Timothy 2:11 he says, "Quietness means silence, they [women] should not presume to speak in public," adding that Paul bids women to "be silent and abide within the limits of their sex."[28] Knox likewise demanded that women keep silent in public. He wrote that St. Paul "names women in general excepting none."[29] This silence, he claims, is what the "Holy Ghost commands."

The Puritans also held the Scriptures taught that women should hold their tongue not only in church but also in public. Gouge, commenting on the command to silence in 1 Timothy 2:11–12, says this means that Paul "speaketh [not only] of a woman's silence in church, but also of a wife's silence before her husband."[30] Her words should be "few, reverend and meek." She is forbidden absolutely from "speaking in public assemblies and churches."[31]As late as 1890, the Southern Presbyterian Synod of Virginia forbade women to sing in church.[32]

In the nineteenth century, as women began to assert their independence and to seek enfranchisement, much of the opposition came from clergy who quoted 1 Corinthians 14:34 and 1 Timothy 2:12. In 1837 a pastoral letter was published by the clergy of Massachusetts against Angelina and Sarah Grimke, who were speaking in public gatherings in favor of the abolition of slavery. In 1840 Catherine Beecher was forbidden to speak in public on female education: her brother had to read her speeches.[33] The same opinion is given voice by the best of nineteenth-century theologians. In Germany, Heinrich Meyer interpreted 1 Corin-

---

[25]Jerome *In Primam Epistolam Ad Corinthios* 14.

[26]Thomas Aquinas *Summa Theologica,* vol. 14, *Divine Government,* trans. T. C. O'Brien (London: Blackfriars, 1975), p. 89.

[27]Luther, *Commentaries on 1 Corinthians,* p. 276. See also the discussion on this point in J. D. Dempsey, "The Image of God in Women as seen in Luther and Calvin," in *The Image of God: Gender Models in Judaeo-Christian Tradition,* ed. Kari E. Borrensen (Minneapolis: Fortress, 1995), p. 243.

[28]Calvin, *Second Epistle of Paul,* pp. 216, 217.

[29]Knox, "First Blast", p. 388.

[30]Gouge, *Domesticall Duties,* pp. 281–82.

[31]Ibid., p. 258.

[32]See Schmidt, *Veiled and Silenced,* p. 154.

[33]These stories are taken from Schmidt, *Veiled and Silenced,* pp. 154–55.

thians 14:34 to be directed against all "public speaking by women."[34] In England, Ellicott takes the command to be silent in 1 Tim-othy 2:12 as prohibiting women from speaking in church or in public. It is at "variance with women's proper duties and destination."[35] In North America, Hodge interpreted 1 Corinthians 14:34 to be forbidding women from "speaking in public, especially in church."[36] Similarly, Albert Barnes concluded that this text enjoins the complete silence of women in public: "The rule is positive, explicit and universal. There is no ambiguity."[37] Again, the tradition speaks with one voice, even if on this matter there are some minor divergences. The Bible teaches that women are to be silent in church, although most conceded that they may sing hymns. This rule is but a particular application of the general rule that women should keep their mouths shut in the public arena.

Now we consider the reasons why it was thought that the Bible taught that women were an inferior race or class, excluded from leadership in society and the church, and why they were to keep silent in public.

Women are not equally made in the image of God. The texts most often quoted in support of this idea were Genesis 1:27 and 1 Corinthians 11:7. In the second of these texts Paul calls woman "the glory of man" and omits to say she is made in the image of God. This led exegetes to ask whether the Genesis text really meant that both men and women were equally made in the image of God. In the interesting book *The Image of God: Gender Models in Judaeo-Christian Tradition,*[38] edited by Kari Borrensen, this debate is documented and discussed. Professor Borrensen argues that Augustine was the first church father who hesitated to accept that 1 Corinthians 11:7 teaches "men's exclusive Godlikeness."[39] He was puzzled by the fact that Genesis 1:27 seems to say that man and woman bear equally the image of God, whereas Paul does not say this. His conclusion is that woman only bears the image of God when united with a man in marriage.[40] Ambrosiaster, in contrast, explicitly denies

---

[34]Heinrich Meyer, *1 Corinthians* (New York: Funk & Wagnalls, 1884), p. 117.

[35]Ellicott, *The Pastoral Epistles,* p. 37.

[36]Charles Hodge, *A Commentary on the First Epistle to the Corinthians* (London: Banner of Truth, 1958), p. 305.

[37]Albert Barnes, *1 Corinthians,* vol. 5 of *Notes on the New Testament* (London: Blackie & Son, n.d.), p. 274.

[38]Kari E. Borrensen, ed., *The Image of God: Gender Models in Judaeo-Christian Tradition* (Minneapolis: Fortress, 1995). See subsequent to this book, N. V. Harrison, "Women, Human Identity and the Image of God: Antiochene Interpretation," *Journal of Early Christian Studies* 9, no. 2 (2001): 205–49.

[39]Borrensen, *Image of God,* p. 199.

[40]Ibid., p. 200.

that woman is made in the image of God.[41] This becomes the dominant tradition. Thus "between the 8th and 12th centuries, monastic exegesis and legal texts either presume or deny women's creational God-likeness."[42] Among the medieval theologians, Peter Aberlard and Peter Lombard deny that women bear the image of God, while Bonaventura argues man has it in greater measure.[43] Aquinas, like Augustine, gives a yes and a no. In the end, he concludes men more fully bear the image of God: "With reference to interior qualities, it can be said that man is more especially God's image according to the mind, since his reason is stronger."[44] Luther and Calvin both allow that woman is made in the image of God, yet they hold that she has this image in lesser measure.[45] Luther, commenting on Genesis 1, writes, "Although Eve was a most extraordinary creature, similar to Adam with respect to the image of God . . . still she is a woman. . . . She does not equal the glory and worthiness of the male."[46] Calvin, commenting on Genesis 2:18, says, "Certainly it cannot be denied that woman also, though in second degree, was created in the image of God."[47] Knox assumes a similar position: "Woman compared to other creatures is in the image of God, for she bears dominion over them. But in comparison to man she may not be called the image of God, for she bears not rule and lordship over man."[48]

Woman was created second and is therefore of second rank, inferior to man. The most enduring and most voiced argument for woman's inferiority is that because woman was created second, according to Genesis 2, she is second to man.

The premise is that the chronological order in which God created the sexes determines their status and freedoms. Chrysostom says God made man first to show male "superiority" and to teach that "the male sex enjoyed the higher honor . . . having pre-eminence in every way."[49] For Jerome the creation of women second is yet further evidence of women's inferiority:

---

[41]Ibid., pp. 191–92.

[42]Ibid., 210.

[43]Ibid., pp. 217–20.

[44]Quoted in ibid., p. 222.

[45]See in greater detail Dempsey, "Image of God," pp. 236–66. She concludes her very sympathetic account of Luther and Calvin's views on women by saying both were "deeply influenced by the tradition which sees men as more fully made in the image of God than women" (p. 260).

[46]Martin Luther, *Lectures on Genesis Chapters 1-5,* pp. 51–52.

[47]John Calvin, *A Commentary on Genesis,* trans. John Keny (London: Banner of Truth, 1965), p. 129.

[48]Knox, "First Blast", p. 397.

[49]Chrysostom, "Homily on 1 Timothy," in *Homilies of John Chrysostom,* p. 70.

There is something not good in the number two. . . . This we must observe, at least if we would faithfully follow the Hebrew, that while scripture on the first, third, fourth and sixth relates that, having finished his works of each, "God saw that it was good," on the second day he omitted this altogether, leaving us to understand that two is not a good number.[50]

Aquinas asks, does the fact that man was created first and woman second imply she is a deficient or defective male? He answers in the affirmative. He describes women as "by nature of lower capacity and quality than man."[51] In the sixteenth century, Luther argues that women are to take second place because they were created second and thus are inferior to men. In commenting on 1 Timothy 2:13 he says what is "first [is] the most preferable," and "this passage makes woman subject."[52] Calvin also based his understanding of woman's subordination on the chronological order in which she was created. This is his primary argument for the inferiority, subordination and public silence of women: "The true order of nature prescribed by God," he says, "lays down that the woman should be subject to man."[53] Then follows a startling comment that shows both Calvin's sharp logic and the importance of *chronological* order for him: "Paul's argument that woman is subject because she was created second, does not seem very strong, for John the Baptist went before Christ in time and yet was far inferior to him." Nevertheless, he argues we are to conclude that in Genesis, Moses is teaching that "woman was created later to be a kind of appendage to the man, on the express condition that she should be ready to obey him. . . . The apostle is right to remind us of the order of their creating in which God's eternal and inviolable appointment is clearly displayed."[54] English divines likewise cite the creation of women second as the primary reason given for her subordinate status, inferiority and silence in public. It is stated repeatedly in the many Puritan discussions on the family.[55] Matthew Poole concludes that Adam was created first to show that "the man had priority over the woman in God's creation."[56] In

---

[50]Jerome, quoted in Jane Barr, "The Influence of Saint Jerome on Medieval Attitudes to Women," in *After Eve: Women, Theology and Christian Tradition*, ed. J. M. Soskice (London: Collins, 1990), p. 96.

[51]Aquinas *Summa Theologica* 13, 35–36. Doriani's attempt to explain away such comments in Aquinas is not convincing ("History of Interpretation," pp. 231–32).

[52]Luther, *Commentaries on 1 Corinthians*, p. 276.

[53]Calvin, *Second Epistle of Paul*, p. 217.

[54]Ibid., pp. 217, 218.

[55]As Doriani admits explicitly ("History of Interpretation," pp. 243–46.).

[56]Matthew Poole, *A Commentary on the Holy Bible* (1685; reprint, London: Banner of Truth, 1969), 3:778.

the nineteenth century Henry Liddon writes that "Adam was formed first: then Eve. This priority in creation implies a certain superiority."[57] In America, Patrick Fairbain concluded, "For Adam was first formed . . . then Eve; the precedence in time implying superiority in place and power."[58] Writing as late as 1957, Donald Guthrie says that "the priority of man's creation places him in a position of superiority over woman, the assumption being that the original creation, with God's own imprimatur upon it, must set precedent for determining the true order of the sexes."[59] Six years later J. N. D. Kelly, in his comments on 1 Timothy 2:13–14, says, "Paul advances two arguments in support of this ban. The first is that Adam was created first and then Eve. In other words, what is chronologically prior is taken in some sense to be superior."[60]

Again, the tradition is well nigh uniform. Most exegetes, until recent times, have interpreted the Bible to be teaching that because woman was created second in chronological order, she is to take second place.

Women are more prone to sin and deception. A third exegetical tradition on which woman's subordinate status and inferiority are based builds on Genesis 3 and 1 Timothy 2:14. These passages were taken to mean that Eve is to be blamed for all evil and death and that she and all her sex are more prone to sin and error than are men. Women are subordinated as a class or race because Eve is responsible for the Fall. "Having become disobedient," Irenaeus concludes, "she [Eve] was made the cause of death, both to herself and the whole human race."[61] Tertullian is the most outspoken: speaking to women he says, "And do you not know that each of you is Eve? . . . You are the devil's gateway: you are the first deserter of the divine law."[62] Chrysostom says women are to be subject because they are "captivated by appetite."

[57]Henry Liddon, *Explanatory Analysis of St. Paul's First Epistle to Timothy* (1897; reprint, Minneapolis: Klock & Klock, 1978), p. 19.

[58]Patrick Fairbain, *Commentary of the Pastoral Epistles* (1874; reprint, Grand Rapids, Mich.: Zondervan, 1956), p. 128.

[59]Donald Guthrie, *The Pastoral Epistles* (London: Tyndale, 1957), p. 77.

[60]J. N. D. Kelly, *A Commentary on the Pastoral Epistles* (London: A & C Black, 1963), p. 68. In the final editing stage of this book, I had in hand William J. Webb's book *Slaves, Women and Homosexuals: Exploring the Hermeneutics of Cultural Analysis* (Downers Grove, Ill.: InterVarsity Press, 2001). He has an appendix listing quotes which stress woman was created second that, he thinks, mainly apply to the primogeniture of Adam. I am not entirely convinced, but I was pleased to use a couple of his examples I had not previously noted.

[61]Irenaeus *Against Heresies;* in *Ante-Nicene Fathers,* ed. Alexander Roberts and James Donaldson (Grand Rapids, Mich.: Eerdmans, 1972), 3:22.

[62]Tertullian, *The Apparel of Women,* in *Ante-Nicene Fathers,* ed. Alexander Roberts and James Donaldson (Grand Rapids, Mich.: Eerdmans, 1979), 4:33.

Their sex is "weak and fickle . . . collectively. . . . "She taught once and ruined all."[63] Commenting on 1 Corinthians 14:34–35 he describes women in comparison to men as "some sort of weaker being and easily carried away and light minded."[64] Luther says it was Eve who went "astray"—she "brought on transgression." This shows that "Adam is approved as superior to Eve" because "there was greater wisdom in Adam."[65] Calvin concludes that because the woman "seduced the man from God's commandment, it is fitting that she should be deprived of all her freedom and placed under a yoke." To woman, he says, is to be imputed "the ruin of the whole human race."[66] Puritan Poole believed that 1 Timothy 2:14 was penned by the apostle "to keep the woman humble, in low opinion of herself, and the lower order wherein God hath fixed her."[67] Matthew Henry writes, in his comments on Genesis 3, that "it was the devil's subtlety to assault the weaker with his temptations. . . . We may suppose her inferior to Adam in knowledge, and strength, and presence of mind."[68] Writing late in the nineteenth century, Liddon concludes, "The experience of all ages [is] that woman is more easily led astray than man."[69] In 1957 Guthrie is still interpreting 1 Timothy 2:14 in accord with this tradition. He says Paul has "in mind the greater aptitude of the weaker sex to be led astray."[70]

The tradition is uniform. Once more, we have seen that the best of past theologians interpreted the Bible to be teaching that women are more prone than men to sin and error.

There is little ambiguity or dissension within the tradition. Across the centuries, until very recent times, exegetes and theologians have understood the Bible to be teaching that women are a subordinate class or race who are inferior to men and, as such, are to be excluded from leadership in society and the church. They are to keep silent in public—especially in church—and they are to obey men, whom God has made superior. Women are to accept their lot in life because they were not made fully in the image of God, because they were created second and because they are more prone to sin and are more easily deceived

---

[63]Chrysostom, "Homily on 1 Timothy," in *Homilies of John Chrysostom,* p. 71.

[64]Chrysostom, "1 Corinthians Homily," in *Homilies of St. John Chrysostom on 1 Corinthians,* p. 521.

[65]Luther, *Commentaries on 1 Corinthians,* pp. 278–79.

[66]Calvin, *Second Epistle of Paul,* pp. 218–19.

[67]Poole, *Commentary on the Holy Bible,* 3:779.

[68]Henry, *Commentary on the Holy Bible,* 1:21.

[69]Liddon, *Explanatory Analysis,* p. 19.

[70]Guthrie, *Pastoral Epistles,* p. 77. For more examples of this interpretation of the Bible, see Webb, *Slaves,* pp. 263–68.

than men. Women as a "class" or "race" need men's protection and leadership. The subordination of the wife to her husband is simply a particular application of the God-given rule that women are set under men. For nineteen centuries, this is how the Bible has been interpreted.

7

WOMEN IN CONTEMPORARY HIERARCHICAL-COMPLEMENTARIAN LITERATURE

$$H$$aving outlined the authentic traditional or historic understanding of the Bible's teaching on women, I will now present the contemporary putative "traditional" or "historic" view of women, sometimes called the "complementarian" position. To be fair to those with whom I am in debate, I will limit myself to the two works that give the most informed, scholarly exposition of this case: *Recovering Biblical Manhood and Womanhood: A Response to Evangelical Feminism,* edited by John Piper and Wayne Grudem,[1] and *Women in the Church: A Fresh Analysis of 1 Timothy 2:9–15,* edited by Andreas J. Köstenberger, Thomas R. Schreiner and H. Scott Baldwin.[2]

---

[1] John Piper and Wayne Grudem, eds., *Recovering Biblical Manhood and Womanhood: A Response to Evangelical Feminism* (Wheaton, Ill.: Crossway, 1991).

[2] Andreas J. Köstenberger, Thomas R. Schreiner and H. Scott Baldwin, eds., *Women in the Church: A Fresh Analysis of 1 Timothy 2:9–15* (Grand Rapids, Mich.: Baker, 1995). See my reviews of these two books in *Evangelical Quarterly.* My review of *Recovering* appeared in *Evangelical Quarterly* 65, no. 3 (1993): 276–81; on *Women in the Church,* see my article "A Critique of the 'Novel' Interpretation of 1 Timothy 2:9-15 Given in the Book *Women in the Church,*" in *Evangelical Quarterly* 72, no. 2 (2000): 152–59. In the final editing stage of this book I had in hand Craig L. Blomberg and J. R. Beck, *Two Views on Women in Ministry* (Grand Rapids, Mich.: Zondervan, 2001), in which scholarly opinion also gets a voice. I found

It is hard to know how to designate those with whom I differ. The editors of *Recovering Biblical Manhood and Womanhood* reject the title *hierarchalist* because it "overemphasizes structural authority while giving no suggestion of equality," and they dislike the title appellation *traditionalist* "because it implies an unwillingness to let scripture challenge traditional patterns of behavior."[3] They chose the term *complementarian* to take the high ground. The trouble with this term is that egalitarians have used this word for thirty years as part of their case. The truth is that both sides are complementarians, believing God has made us distinctively women and men—the two sexes being intended to complement each other. On one side are hierarchical-complementarians who believe the Bible sets men over women in the church and the home,[4] and on the other side are egalitarian-complementarians who believe the Bible makes the ideal women and men standing side by side, equal in dignity and authority in the world, the church and the home. The editors of *Women in the Church* chose yet another name for themselves: they tell us that they are upholders of the "historic view" of men and women.[5] They repeatedly claim that their interpretation of 1 Timothy 2:9–15, a text they maintain encapsulates the biblical understanding of women, is the interpretation held by "the most profound and influential theologians" in centuries past. It is both "historic" and "traditional," argues Daniel Doriani in an essay that seeks to prove this by appeal to the sources we have just surveyed. As I cannot concede their case is traditional or historic and as I like to call myself a complementarian, I have decided to call those with whom I differ "hierarchical-complementarians" and those I represent "egalitarian-complementarians."

The Essentials of the Hierarchical-Complementarian View of Women

Men and women are equals. In the hierarchical-complementarian case, possi-

---

very little, if anything, new in this book, although the essays by Craig Keener, Schreiner and Blomberg are well informed. Schreiner and Blomberg, representing the hierarchical position, still base their case on a fixed social order given in creation, on role theory and on sexual differentiation's implying subordination.

[3]*Recovering,* p. xiv. However, Daniel Doriani calls *Recovering Biblical Manhood and Womanhood* "a traditionalist anthology" (Andreas Köstenberger, Thomas R. Schreiner and H. Scott Baldwin, *Women in the Church: A Fresh Analysis of 1 Timothy 2:9-15* [Grand Rapids, Mich.: Baker, 1995], p. 258).

[4]This is not an unfair claim because at least eight times the contributors of *Recovering Biblical Manhood* describe the man-woman relationship as a hierarchical one (Piper and Grudem, *Recovering,* pp. 67, 83, 104, 130, 162, 257, 282, 394).

[5]Köstenberger, Schreiner and Baldwin, *Women in the Church,* pp. 11, 105 n. 2, 193, 185, 213ff.

bly the most reiterated assertion is that men and women are equals. In Australia, the Sydney evangelical Anglican group opposed to the ordination of women is called "Equal but Different." The editors of *Recovering Biblical Manhood and Womanhood* tell us their hope is that everyone "who reads this book will come away feeling in his heart that women are *fully equal* to men in personhood."[6] In the next paragraph, they make the same point positively: women "are fully equal to men in status before God."[7] Later, Piper tells us men are not superior and women are not inferior.[8] In this same volume, Schreiner dogmatically asserts the Bible does not "not imply women are inferior to men."[9] Nevertheless, while equal, women and men have different roles. To quote Schreiner again, "The fundamental principle is that the sexes, although equal, are also different. God has ordained that men have the responsibility to lead, while women have the complementary and supportive role."[10] In *Women in the Church,* Schreiner says, "A difference in role or function does not imply that women are inferior to men."[11]

However, contrary to the above claims, the truly historic view of women uniformly teaches that women are inferior and men are superior. The hierarchical-complementarians uniformly deny this. On this matter, they categorically break with tradition. They reject the claim that the Bible makes man superior and woman inferior, although this view prevailed for nineteen centuries. I agree with their conclusions, but what they claim has no historical precedent. Their insistence that the Bible does not teach the inferiority of women is novel.

Men and women have different roles. In both of these books, the differences between men and women are defined almost exclusively in terms of the roles God has assigned to each sex. We are told that the allocation of different roles to men and women by God does not infer the inferiority of women. Raymond Ortland puts it this way: "There is no necessary relation between personal role

---

[6]Piper and Grudem, *Recovering Biblical Manhood,* p. xiv; the italics appear in the original.
[7]Ibid.
[8]John Piper, "A Vision of Biblical Complementarity," in *Recovering Biblical Manhood and Womanhood: A Response to Evangelical Feminism,* ed. John Piper and Wayne Grudem (Wheaton, Ill.: Crossway, 1991), pp. 38, 49.
[9]Thomas R. Schreiner, "Head Coverings, Prophecies and the Trinity," in *Recovering Biblical Manhood and Womanhood: A Response to Evangelical Feminism,* ed. John Piper and Wayne Grudem (Wheaton, Ill.: Crossway, 1991), p. 135.
[10]Ibid., p. 138.
[11]Thomas R. Schreiner, "An Interpretation of 1 Timothy 2:9-15: A Dialogue with Scholarship," in *Women in the Church: A Fresh Analysis of 1 Timothy 2:9-15,* ed. Andreas Köstenberger, Thomas R. Schreiner and H. Scott Baldwin (Grand Rapids, Mich.: Baker, 1995), p. 135.

and personal worth."[12] Paige Patterson seeks to illustrate that the assignment of roles in no way signals the worth or value of "the one in authority or the one who is subordinate." He says that Paul tells Christians "to submit to the authority of magistrates" but that this command does not suggest that those who obey are "inferior" to the magistrate.[13] Wayne House similarly argues that differing roles do not imply superiority or inferiority. We are just to accept that "God has assigned specific roles to specific people and groups of people and he expects his commands to be honored."[14] The "roles" that the Bible dictates as being the exclusive domain of men or women are, we discover, very specific. Men are given the role of leading in the home and the church; women are given the role of accepting the leadership of men. In living out these roles women and men complement each other in these two domains. Piper and Grudem insist that the role relations prescribed in creation are only for the home and the church. In the world, "God has chosen not to be specific about what roles men and women should fill."[15]

The thesis that God has assigned specific roles to women and men determines the interpretation of the key texts for hierarchical-complementarians: 1 Corinthians 11:3–16; 14:33–35; Ephesians 5:22–33; and 1 Timothy 2:11–14. Schreiner argues that in 1 Corinthians 11:3–16, Paul "utterly rejects the notion that women are inferior or lesser beings." What the apostle is teaching is the indelibility of "role distinctions."[16] "Men have the responsibility to lead, while women have a complementary and supportive role."[17] In the next chapter Donald Carson interprets Paul's command to women to be silent (1 Cor 14:34) to be a prohibition on women's sitting in judgment on prophecies given in church. This prohibition, he concludes, indicates that Paul rejects the idea that "all distinctions in roles" have been abolished.[18] The Timothy passage is also consistently interpreted in terms

---

[12]Raymond Ortland, "Male-Female Equality and Male Headship: Genesis 1—3," in *Recovering Biblical Manhood and Womanhood: A Response to Evangelical Feminism,* ed. John Piper and Wayne Grudem (Wheaton, Ill.: Crossway, 1991), p. 111.

[13]Paige Patterson, "The Meaning of Authority in the Local Church," in *Recovering Biblical Manhood and Womanhood: A Response to Evangelical Feminism,* ed. John Piper and Wayne Grudem (Wheaton, Ill.: Crossway, 1991), p. 257.

[14]Wayne House, "Principles to Use in Establishing Women in Ministry," in *Recovering Biblical Manhood and Womanhood: A Response to Evangelical Feminism,* ed. John Piper and Wayne Grudem (Wheaton, Ill.: Crossway, 1991), p. 361.

[15]John Piper and Wayne Grudem, "An Overview of Central Concerns: Questions and Answers," in *Recovering Biblical Manhood and Womanhood: A Response to Evangelical Feminism* (Wheaton, Ill.: Crossway, 1991), p. 89.

[16]Schreiner, "Interpretation of 1 Timothy," pp. 136, 137.

[17]Ibid., p. 138.

[18]Donald Carson, "Silent in the Churches," in *Recovering Biblical Manhood and Womanhood:*

of creation-given roles. Douglas Moo argues that the problem envisaged by this text is a teaching that denies "role distinctions between men and women." Paul writes "to counter the false teachers on this point."[19] Schreiner, in *Women in the Church,* likewise interprets the Timothy text as a debate about the roles of women. On the basis of the creation order, he argues that Paul forbids women from the role of teacher in the church.[20] The apostle makes childbearing "the appropriate role for women."[21]

Daniel Doriani also adopts the role interpretation of 1 Timothy 2:9–15, seeing it as a "reinterpretation" of the passage by contemporary traditionalists.[22] He is right: it is a reinterpretation, for never in the (truly) historic position do we find one word about "role" differences. Women are subordinated as a "race" or "class." Again, we have a clear and unambiguous break with tradition. In the historical interpretation of the Bible, women as women are subordinated to men because they are "inferior"; as a "race" they are ranked under men. No mention is ever made of functional subordination, and the word *role* is never used. The claim that the Bible teaches man and women as such are true equals—they are only differentiated by the roles or functions ascribed to them by God—is totally novel.

Women may speak. In *Recovering Biblical Manhood and Womanhood* and in *Women in the Church,* no one suggests that women are forbidden to speak in church or in public. The only concern is that women not teach or exercise authority in the church or the home. It is repeatedly denied that Paul's ruling that women keep silent means women are to keep completely silent in church, or that his words have any application to public life. As noted above, Carson interprets the command to silence in 1 Corinthians 14:34 to be a prohibition on women orally weighing prophecies given in church.[23] He says rather than being forbidden to speak in church, women "borne along by the Spirit were *encouraged* to do so"—though they were not to teach, he adds.[24] Moo emphatically

---

A Response to Evangelical Feminism, ed. John Piper and Wayne Grudem (Wheaton, Ill.: Crossway, 1991), p. 153.

[19]Douglas Moo, "What Does It Mean Not to Teach or Have Authority over Men? 1 Timothy 2:11-15," in *Recovering Biblical Manhood and Womanhood: A Response to Evangelical Feminism,* ed. John Piper and Wayne Grudem (Wheaton, Ill.: Crossway, 1991), p. 182.

[20]Schreiner, "Interpretation of 1 Timothy," pp. 134–35.

[21]Ibid., p. 151.

[22]Daniel Doriani, "History of the Interpretation of 1 Timothy 2," in *Recovering Biblical Manhood and Womanhood: A Response to Evangelical Feminism,* ed. John Piper and Wayne Grudem (Wheaton, Ill.: Crossway, 1991), pp. 257–59.

[23]Carson, "Silent in the Churches," p. 151.

[24]Ibid., p. 153.

restricts the silence demanded in 1 Timothy 2:11 to women's teaching men in a church setting,[25] saying that this passage does not restrict women from exercising authority or from speaking in public outside of a church setting.[26] Piper and Grudem say that when Paul asks women to be silent, he "does not mean for women to be totally silent in church."[27] In these two books, and in many others like them, the focus is almost entirely on the church and the home. It would appear that God in creation only prescribed the roles of men and women in these two domains. Virtually nothing is said about the contribution of Christian women in the world, and when something is said, the claim is made that the Bible does not restrict this in any way.

Again, we see a clear-cut break with tradition. In the historic interpretation of Scripture, we are told the Bible demands that women keep silent *in public* and that they be heard in church only when they sing hymns or say "amen." In contrast, contemporary hierarchical-complementarians read Paul to be only forbidding women from speaking in church as the teachers of men. They contradict what commentators and theologians from the past have concluded. They insist that women may speak in public and that they may speak in church so long as they do not teach men. This interpretation of the Bible is also novel.

The order of creation. In both of these books, the differing roles ascribed to men and women are consistently based on the way God ordered the man-woman relation in creation before the Fall. The fundamental reason given as to why men are allocated the leading role and why women are excluded is that this is how God structured the man-woman relationship in creation before sin entered the world. Doriani, in reviewing *Recovering Biblical Manhood and Womanhood*—what he sympathetically calls "the traditionalist anthology"—says that "nineteen of its twenty-two authors argue for their position on the basis of creation, or the order of creation, and they do so in twenty-one of the book's twenty-six chapters."[28] The editors of *Recovering Biblical Manhood and Womanhood* state that their fundamental argument for "the loving headship of husbands or the godly eldership of men [is] the created order of nature."[29] Men are to lead in ministry not because of women's "doctrinal or moral incompetence but because of God's created order for manhood and womanhood."[30] The chronological or-

---

[25] Moo, "What Does It Mean," pp. 183, 186.

[26] Ibid., pp. 187–88.

[27] Piper and Grudem, "Overview of Central Concerns," p. 71.

[28] Doriani, "History of the Interpretation," p. 258 n. 180.

[29] Piper and Grudem, "Overview of Central Concerns," pp. 73–74.

[30] Ibid., pp. 81–82.

der in which the sexes were created is sometimes mentioned, but what is determinative is the constitutive and prescriptive *social order* given by God in
creation, which, because it was established before sin entered the world, is permanent and transcultural.

The editors and contributors to *Women in the Church* likewise ground wom-
en's subordination in a constitutive and prescriptive "created order."[31] Summing
up their case, Doriani says that "for complementarians, the phrase, 'Adam was
formed or created first' refers beyond chronology to God's sovereign decree that
made males the spiritual heads of God's kingdom, churches and homes."[32] Similarly, Schreiner says Paul consistently bases his case for the subordinate role of
women on "the created order, the good and perfect world God has made."[33]
Harold Brown adds that this order, which differentiates the sexes by allocating
to them different roles, is one of a number of creation-given "*mandata Dei* that
hold good for all time and in every place."[34] Parallel to Brown's wording,
George Knight speaks of "the mandate of God about the role relationship based
on creation that speaks of the headship of men and the subordination of wom-
en."[35]

Again, we see a radical break with the historic tradition. In former centuries
commentators and theologians agreed that the Bible depicted women as a
class or race inferior to men because of the *chronological order* in which they
were created by God. Man was created first, and therefore men are superior;
woman was created second, and therefore women are inferior. In the contemporary hierarchical-complementarian case for role subordination, everything
is grounded on a *constitutive and prescriptive social order* given in creation.
This is how God has structured the man-woman relationship according to his
ideal plan and command. In no commentary prior to 1960 could I find a claim
that the Bible set women under men on the basis of a once-given, forever-
binding, *social order* given in creation. Those who discovered this idea in
Scripture, after the 1960s, discovered something no one had seen before. They

---

[31]Köstenberger, Schreiner and Baldwin, epilogue to *Women in the Church,* p. 210.

[32]Doriani, "History of the Interpretation," p. 262.

[33]Schreiner, "Interpretation of 1 Timothy," p. 134.

[34]Harold Brown, "The New Testament Against Itself: 1 Timothy 2:9-15 and the 'Breakthrough'
of Galatians 3:28," in *Women in the Church: A Fresh Analysis of 1 Timothy 2:9-15,* ed.
Andreas J. Köstenberger, Thomas R. Schreiner and H. Scott Baldwin (Grand Rapids, Mich.:
Baker, 1995), p. 204.

[35]George Knight, "Husbands and Wives as Analogues of Christ and the Church: Ephesians
5:21-33 and Colossians 3:18-19," in *Recovering Biblical Manhood and Womanhood: A
Response to Evangelical Feminism,* ed. John Piper and Wayne Grudem (Wheaton, Ill.: Crossway, 1991), p. 177.

were exegetical pioneers charting new waters.

Women are not more prone to sin. In the contemporary hierachical-comple-mentarian case, the historic claim that the Bible teaches that women are more prone to sin and more easily deceived is rejected. Thus, Piper and Grudem tell us that "the main point" of 1 Timothy 2:14

> is not that man is undeceivable or that the woman is more deceivable; the point is
> that when God's order of leadership is repudiated it brings damage and ruin. Men
> and women are both more vulnerable to error and sin when they forsake the
> order that God has intended.[36]

They also tell us categorically that "in the Bible different roles for men and women are never traced back to the fall of man and woman into sin."[37] Moo similarly rejects the view that 1 Timothy 2:14 means that "women are like Eve more susceptible to being deceived than men and this is why they should not teach." This view is unlikely, he says, because the "focus of this passage is on the role relationship of men and women."[38] Paul is warning that if the women in Ephesus seek "roles that have been given to men in the church (v. 12) they will make the same mistake as Eve made and bring similar disaster."[39] Ortland, commenting on Genesis 3, says that Eve's sin was not due to her wickedness or to a propensity to sin but to a willful rejection of Adam's headship: "Eve was not morally weaker than Adam. But Satan struck at Adam's headship. His words had the effect of inviting Eve to assume primary responsibility" in the Garden.[40] In *Women in the Church,* Schreiner says that "the proscription on women teach-ing men, does not stem from the fall and cannot be ascribed to the curse."[41] A few pages later he gives his own interpretation of Paul's words in 1 Timothy 2:14: Women should not teach because they are "less prone than men to see the importance of doctrinal formulations, especially when it comes to the issue of identifying heresy and making a stand for the truth."[42] Doriani makes the impor-tant observation that "traditionalist interpreters increasingly [are] denying that the phrase, 'Adam was not deceived but the woman was deceived,' means that women are liable to deception."[43] What Paul is teaching, he says, is that "God

---

[36]Piper and Grudem, "Overview of Central Concerns," p. 73.
[37]Ibid., p. 35.
[38]Moo, "What Does It Mean," p. 190.
[39]Ibid.
[40]Ortland, "Male-Female Equality," p. 180.
[41]Schreiner, "Interpretation of 1 Timothy," p. 134.
[42]Ibid., pp. 144–45.
[43]Doriani, "History of the Interpretation," p. 258.

created women with an orientation towards relationships more than analysis."[44]

Historically the Bible has been interpreted to teach that women are more prone to sin and deception. In contrast, contemporary hierarchical-complementarians emphatically deny that this is what the Bible teaches. Without ever admitting it, they reject this tradition. They insist that the Bible does not depict women as more prone to sin and deception. The more informed evangelicals who adopt this new approach have few other options, since contemporary experience and hard social-science research has shown that women are not more easily deceived or prone to error than men.[45]

Women are fully made in the image of God. Contemporary hierarchical-complementarians adamantly affirm that women are equally made in the image and likeness of God. In *Recovering Biblical Manhood and Womanhood,* this is emphasized. Ortland, in his study of Genesis 1, states that "man and woman are equal in the sense that they bear God's image equally."[46] Later he adds, "There is no basis in Genesis 1 for confining the image of God to males alone."[47] Schreiner, in his exegesis of 1 Corinthians 11:2–16, says categorically that in 1 Corinthians 11:7 "Paul is not denying that women are created in God's image."[48] Rejecting the argument that the Bible teaches a woman does not reflect God's image as fully as a man does is very important, as is made evident by the setting aside of a whole chapter to address this matter in *Recovering Biblical Manhood and Womanhood;* the chapter is entitled, "Men and Women in the Image of God." The author, John Frame, concludes that "men and women equally image God, even in their sexual differences with regard to authority and submission. The reason is that the image of God embraces everything that is human."[49] In *Women in the Church,* the tradition that women are not fully made in the image of God is not mentioned. It is not mentioned because it is not believed to be what the Bible teaches. I suspect, however, that Doriani has this tradition in mind when he admits, "The complementarian position has developed. Assertions of the ontological inferiority of women have become rare."[50] They certainly have! That tradition has been completely rejected.

---

[44]Ibid., p. 266.

[45]For details see William J. Webb, *Slaves, Women & Homosexuals: Exploring the Hermeneutics of Cultural Analysis* (Downers Grove, Ill.: InterVarsity Press, 2001), pp. 269–73.

[46]Ortland, "Male-Female Equality," p. 95.

[47]Ibid., p. 98.

[48]Schreiner, "Interpretation of 1 Timothy," p. 132.

[49]John Frame, "Men and Women in the Image of God," in *Recovering Biblical Manhood and Womanhood: A Response to Evangelical Feminism,* ed. John Piper and Wayne Grudem (Wheaton, Ill.: Crossway, 1991), p. 231.

[50]Doriani, "History of the Interpretation," p. 258.

Again, what is claimed today to be the biblical teaching is in diametrical opposition to what most learned and godly exegetes in the past believed the Bible
taught.

Comparisons

At this point it is possible to compare the traditional and historical interpretation of what the Bible says about women with the contemporary hierarchical-
complementarian interpretation of what the Bible says about women. We note
seven undeniable examples where the latter contradicts the former:

*The traditional position uniformly argues on the basis of Scripture that wom-
en are inferior and men are superior.* The hierarchical-complementarians uniformly deny this. They emphatically insist that women and men are equals.

*The traditional position argues that women are subordinated to men as a race
or class.* The hierarchical-complementarians reject this, arguing that the differences between women and men are purely functional: God has simply given
them differing roles.

*The traditional position maintains that all women have been excluded uni-
versally from exercising authority, the church setting being but a particular context.* Hierarchical-complementarians, in contrast, argue that the Scriptures only
forbid a wife from exercising authority in the home when her husband is
present and forbid women in general from exercising authority in the church,
especially by teaching.

*The traditional position argues that women are to keep silent in public, the
church setting being no exception.* Hierarchical-complementarians argue that
women may speak or teach in any context outside of a mixed church gathering
and that they may speak in church so long as they do not teach authoritatively.
In fact, Carson says the Spirit "encourages" women to speak in church, though
not to teach.

*The traditional position holds that women are not fully made in the image of
God.* Hierarchical-complementarians totally reject this idea.

*The traditional position consistently argues that women are subordinated to
men because they were created second.* The *chronological order* in which they
were made indicates their rank or status. Man was made first, and thus men are
first; woman was made second, and thus women are second. Hierarchical-complementarians subtly change this argument. They base their case on a constitutive and prescriptive *social order* established by God in creation that
permanently sets man over woman.

The traditional case for woman's subordination and inferiority also grounds this on the moral weakness of women. It was believed that the Bible teaches women are more prone to sin and more easily deceived, and, for this reason, women need the superintendence of men. Hierarchical-complementarians categorically reject this interpretation of Genesis 2 and 1 Timothy 2:14, despite its long history and distinguished supporters.

The editors and contributors of both *Recovering Biblical Manhood and Womanhood* and *Women in the Church* repeatedly insist that they are honestly and objectively interpreting Scripture and that their case is basically the same as the position held by the great exegetes and theologians of the past. Piper, in the book he edits, says that everything taught by him and his fellow writers is "according to the Bible."[51] The title of his book makes this explicit. The authors are giving the "biblical" understanding of manhood and womanhood. The editors of *Women in the Church* also state emphatically that they are only seeking to discover what the Bible actually says about the roles of men and women: "Scripture functions as our sole authority."[52] They want us to believe that what they teach is what the Bible says and what Christians in the past have believed. Brown, in this volume, says that the exegesis given of 1 Corinthians 14:34 and 1 Timothy 2:12 by him and his cowriters is the "clear and self-evident" meaning of these texts, which has been held "for about eighteen centuries."[53] Doriani is even more adamant. He tells us that "conservatives" simply "attempt to confirm and defend the straightforward grammatical-historical reading" of the Bible.[54] It is the egalitarians, we are told repeatedly in these two books, who give "new interpretations of the Bible to support their claims."[55] Their reading of Scripture is "putative," "Cartesian" and "novel." As "progressives" they twist Scripture to make it fit their own "liberalizing," "feminist," marriage-destabilizing, pro-gay agenda.[56]

---

[51]John Piper, "A Vision of Biblical Complementarity," p. 32.

[52]Köstenberger, Schreiner and Baldwin, epilogue in *Women in the Church,* p. 209. See also pp. 9-12, 210-11.

[53]Brown, "New Testament Against Itself," p. 197.

[54]Doriani, "History of the Interpretation," p. 257.

[55]Piper and Grudem, preface to *Recovering Biblical Manhood,* pp. xiii–xiv.

[56]See Köstenberger, Schreiner and Baldwin, *Women in the Church,* pp. 178, 257, 158, 171–90, and Piper and Grudem, *Recovering Biblical Manhood,* 71, 82–87, 91, 137, 376, 407, 473, 477, 487, 492, etc. Labeling someone a "Cartesian" is a polite way of calling a fellow evangelical a liberal. The German theologian Helmut Thielicke argued that those who radically reinterpreted the Bible to make it fit the modern worldview are beholden to the presuppositions of the philosopher René Descartes. Thielicke had in mind people such as Rudolf Bultmann. Contemporary discussions on hermeneutics suggest that no exegete can completely avoid reading the text through the cultural spectacles of her or his own culture and age. This suggests that there are only radical and conservative Cartesians.

All this is simply not true. The hierarchical-complementarians do not give the historic meaning of the text. Their interpretation is as novel as that of their opponents. They have, as Doriani admits in a slip of the pen, made "a shift away from" the historic position and given a "reinterpretation" of key texts.[57] The more emotive charges against "progressive-evangelicals" are simply unjustifiable and unfair. Like many other evangelicals who write in support of the emancipation of women, I am not seeking to undermine the Bible. Rather we want to establish its central thrust in relation to the sexes—namely, their equality in creation. Nor are we working to undermine marriage. Rather our goal is stronger marriages in which husband and wife take equal responsibility for their life together and in which men give a lead in sacrificial service to their wife and family.[58] We are also quite able to distinguish between the homosexual debate and the women's debate. The former is primarily a moral question (how people should behave sexually); the latter is primarily about the dignity and potential of women as women.[59]

If proof is needed of the hermeneutical rule that states *a changed cultural context can change how the Bible is interpreted,* then the contemporary hierarchical-complementarian reading of the Bible is that proof. What must be concluded is that, along with egalitarian-complementarians, hierarchical-complementarians have begun interpreting the Bible in a new way because a new cultural context has changed how they understand biblical teaching. In light of the profound social revolution often called "women's liberation," all Christians have abandoned the view that the Bible teaches women are inferior to men and more prone to sin and deception. All of us have discovered—just as others discovered centuries ago that the world is not flat—that seeing women in these terms is simply false. Having been allowed for the first time in history to make this discovery, Christians have returned to Scripture looking for alternative readings of the Bible.

---

[57]Doriani, "History of the Interpretation," p. 258.

[58]Most egalitarian-complementarians have no problem with male "headship" so long as it is understood in the terms of Ephesians 5:21–33 (i.e., sacrificial service). In this passage Paul is seeking to transform patriarchy. Read in its historical context, it is a liberating text.

[59]I have written many articles for Australian Christian magazines and papers over the years arguing against the ordination of practicing homosexuals. I always distinguish carefully between two questions: the modern "rights" question and the moral question. On the former, I argue homosexuals should not be discriminated against in a modern pluralistic democracy. In regard to the second, I argue that on biblical *and* theological grounds, homosexual acts cannot be judged acceptable to God any more than can adulterous acts. Thus a person, whether heterosexual or homosexual, who cannot remain celibate in singleness or faithful in marriage should not be a leader in God's church. See appendix C.

In chapter nine, I will outline the competing novel interpretations of what the Bible teaches on the man-woman relationship, but before I do this I want to examine more closely the presuppositions and exegesis of the hierarchical-complementarian case that claims to be the truly "biblical" position.

8

EXEGESIS OR EISEGESIS?

In *Recovering Biblical Manhood and Womanhood* and *Women in the Church,* there is an ongoing critique of the egalitarian-complementarian position.[1] One much-reiterated charge is that the evangelicals who have taken this approach have introduced "novel" interpretations of the Scriptures—the implication being that because they are novel, they lack credibility. We have just seen that the interpretations given by hierarchical-complementarians of the passages they select to prove their case are also novel, a break with tradition. Another charge is that egalitarian-complementarians seek to make the Scriptures say what they do not say. Now, we ask, is this in fact what the hierarchical-complementarians themselves do? The evidence that this is the case is compelling. What we have in these two books is a highly developed theological position predicated on presuppositions not found in the Bible—presuppositions that are indeed alien to the Bible. These produce an interpretative grid, or a pair of eyeglasses, through which the Bible is read. The hierarchical-complementarians frequently quote the Scriptures and carefully study key texts and the meaning of words, but in the end what is reflected are the various authors' own views on male hegemony and male privilege. This theological grid has been developed over thirty years, step by step, by a

---

[1]John Piper and Wayne Grudem, eds., *Recovering Biblical Manhood and Womanhood: A Response to Evangelical Feminism* (Wheaton, Ill.: Crossway, 1991); Andreas J. Köstenberger, Thomas R. Schreiner and H. Scott Baldwin, eds., *Women in the Church: A Fresh Analysis of 1 Timothy 2:9–15* (Grand Rapids, Mich.: Baker, 1995).

small number of highly qualified, conservative evangelical theologians. It is a sophisticated, well-honed construct. This construct, in the end, determines how key texts are interpreted; it makes possible the harmonization of the diverse comments in Scripture on women, and it provides a way of presenting the case for the permanent subordination of women that sounds acceptable to modern ears.

There are three basic ingredients to this grid, three pillars on which this whole theological construct is built: a novel understanding of what is meant by the expression *the order of creation,* a novel use of the word *role* and a novel and problematic meaning given to the word *difference.*

The Order of Creation

The most fundamental element in the hierarchical-complementarian position is that the (role) subordination of women is based on an unchanging constitutive and prescriptive *social order* given in creation before the Fall. This presents the ideal for the man-woman relationship that not even the coming of Christ challenges. Writing in *Women in the Church,* Daniel Doriani says that "nineteen of the twenty-two authors [in *Recovering Biblical Manhood and Womanhood*] argue for their position on the basis of creation or the order of creation . . . on at least eighty-one pages."[2] In *Women in the Church,* every one of the authors grounds women's permanent role subordination on the social order given in creation. That women were created second is often mentioned in this book, but what is determinative is always the constitutive and prescriptive social order given in creation. Doriani says, "for complementarians, the phrase, 'Adam was formed or created first' refers beyond chronology to God's sovereign decree."[3] Similarly, Harold O. J. Brown argues that Genesis 2 and 1 Timothy 2:13 indicate that an "ordered structure of reality . . . [was] set up by the creator" before the Fall.[4] In creation God established "explicit *mandata Dei* that hold good for all time and in every place."[5]

The creation-order argument is pivotal to the hierarchical-complementarian

---

[2]Daniel Doriani, "The History of the Interpretation of 1 Timothy 2," in *Women in the Church: A Fresh Analysis of 1 Timothy 2:9-15,* ed. Andreas J. Köstenberger, Thomas R. Schreiner and H. Scott Baldwin (Grand Rapids, Mich.: Baker, 1995), p. 258 n. 180.
[3]Ibid., p. 262.
[4]Harold Brown, "The New Testament Against Itself: 1 Timothy 2:9-15 and the 'Breakthrough' of Galatians 3:38," in *Women in the Church: A Fresh Analysis of 1 Timothy 2:9-15,* ed. Andreas J. Köstenberger, Thomas R. Schreiner and H. Scott Baldwin (Grand Rapids, Mich.: Baker, 1995), p. 201.
[5]Ibid., p. 204. See also pp. 61–62, 134–40, 192, 200–206.

case because it allows the apostolic exhortations for wives to be subordinate to their husbands and the two commands for women to keep silent in church to be read as transcultural, permanently binding rulings. Egalitarian-complementarians are not unaware of these exhortations and prohibitions; they simply do not accept that they are based on an unchanging constitutive and prescriptive social order given in creation. If it could be shown that this appeal to a transcultural, unchanging constitutive and prescriptive social order given in creation is a human construct, read back into the text of Scripture, the whole contemporary case for the permanent subordination of women would collapse. It would be seen to be an edifice without a foundation.

The expression *the order of creation* is a confusing one for it can be understood in at least four ways:

☐ chronologically—in creation, according to Genesis 2, man was created first, women second

☐ coordinately—in creation God ordered the world so that it operates harmoniously and in an orderly way

☐ constitutively—in creation before the Fall, God constituted or structured human relationships, placing the man above the woman

☐ commandingly or prescriptively—in creation God gave orders as to how human relationships should be ordered, one of which was that the man should lead and the woman obey

This fourth understanding appears whenever the orders of creation are called "mandates" or "ordinances."

In the historical tradition, when the status of women comes into view, the chronological usage predominates. Past commentators and theologians took the first of Paul's two reasons why women should not teach at Ephesus ("for Adam was formed first, then Eve," 1 Tim 2:13) to indicate their inferiority. In making this deduction, which had already been made before the time of Christ by the Jewish rabbis,[6] it seems that theologians were simply reading into the text their own cultural presuppositions.

Why should we take this to be the case? Commentators have often pointed out that being created second does not infer inferiority or subordination. There is no logical force in this argument whatsoever. In Genesis 1 man and woman are created last yet stand supreme over creation. John Calvin, with his usual clarity of thought, says, as we have noted already, "Paul's argument that woman is subject because she was created second, does not seem very strong, for John the Baptist

---

[6]See I. Howard Marshall, *The Pastoral Epistles* (Edinburgh: T & T Clark, 1999), p. 462 n. 166.

went before Christ in time and yet was far inferior to him."[7] It is true that according to Genesis 2 woman was created second, but nothing should be made of this descriptive observation because nothing is made of it in Genesis. Old Testament texts must be allowed to speak for themselves. An interpretation of an Old Testament text in the New Testament does not determine its historical meaning.[8] In any case, Paul does not explicitly draw this conclusion. He simply rules that women at Ephesus should stop teaching and, thus, exercising authority in the church "for Adam was formed first, then Eve." I, for one, would not want to make this single cryptic comment the sole basis for subordinating half of the human race, let alone suggesting their inferiority. Nowhere else in all of Scripture is there any comment on the fact that in Genesis 2 woman was created second.

In the sixteenth century, a second understanding of the expression *the order of creation* came to the fore. It was believed that before sin entered the world, the whole cosmos operated harmoniously. God in creation *coordinately* arranged the universe so that everything and everyone had its proper and gladly accepted place. Sometimes this was called "the created order," sometimes "the order of nature" and sometimes "divine order." Calvin speaks incessantly about "order." Indeed, some Calvin scholars think order is the central motif in his writings.[9] For Calvin the expressions *the order of nature* and *the order of creation* are used synonymously. This order is to be seen in the stars, the seasons, good government, family life and so on. Classic articulation of this understanding of the order of creation is given in the tenth *Homily,* published in 1562. This was a sermon to be read by clergy of the Church of England.

> Almighty God hath created and appointed all things in heaven and on earth, and waters, in a most excellent and perfect order. In heaven he hath appointed distinct and several orders and states of angels and archangels. In earth he hath assigned and appointed kings, princes, with other governors under them, in all good and necessary order. The water above is kept, and raineth down in due time and season. The sun, moon, stars, rainbow, thunder, lightening, clouds, and all birds of the air keep this order. . . . Every degree of people in their vocation, calling, and office,

---

[7]John Calvin, *The Second Epistle of Paul to the Corinthians, and the Epistles of Timothy, Titus and Philemon,* trans. T. A. Smail (Grand Rapids, Mich.: Eerdmans, 1964), p. 217.

[8]Paul's interpretation of the Exodus stories in 1 Cor 10:1–4 and his interpretation of the Hagar story in Gal 4:21–31 prove this point. Sometimes Old Testament stories are given more than one interpretation in the New Testament. This is so in regard to appeals to the story of Abraham's faith spoken about in Genesis 15. See Rom 4:1ff.; Gal 3:6ff.; Heb 11:8ff.; Jas 2:21ff.

[9]See W. J. Bouwsma, *John Calvin: A Sixteenth-Century Portrait* (Oxford: Oxford University Press, 1988); M. E. Osterhaven, *The Faith of the Church: A Reformed Perspective on Its Historical Development* (Grand Rapids, Mich.: Eerdmans, 1982), chap. 14.

hath appointed to them their duty and order: some in high degree, some in low, some kings and princes, some inferiors. . . . For where there is no right order, there reigneth all abuse, carnal liberty, enormity, sin and Babylonian confusion.[10]

The Puritans also speak repeatedly of an order given by God. However, for them social order is their key concern. Amanda Shepherd, in her important study *Gender and Authority in Sixteenth-Century England*,[11] documents this preoccupation in Puritan writings with social order, attributing it to a widespread fear that without a police force disorder in society could break out at any time. As always, she says, the social order prescribed is "culturally defined."

The *constitutive* understanding of the term *created orders* must be explained against the backdrop of its development. The idea that there are a number of divinely given structures that order social life goes back to Martin Luther, although he never actually used the terms *creation orders* or *ordinances*.[12] He spoke rather of three "orders" or "estates" of society, which were divinely given bulwarks for warding off disorder in a sinful world. These were marriage, the ministry and the state. He saw them as givens and made no attempt to ground them in the creation narratives or on anything else in the Bible. They were part of the natural law that governs the universe.

The Lutheran theologian Adolf von Harless (1806–1879), it seems, was the first to develop an orders-of-creation theology.[13] The idea was that in creation, God established a constitutive social order that governed all human relationships. Orders-of-creation theology blossomed in Germany in the 1930s, being used to legitimate the Nazi regime and the preservation of the German race. The argument was that the status quo, the social order that existed, was what God willed. Dietrich Bonhoeffer totally opposed this argument, arguing that an orders-of-creation theology so construed separated social ethics from Christ and the gospel.[14] It made "what is" into "what ought to be." Like other Europeans of this unsettled period, he wanted to believe that God had ordained social struc-

---

[10] *Certain Sermons or Homilies Appointed to Be Read in Churches in the Time of Queen Elizabeth* (London: SPCK, 1846), p. 109.

[11] Amanda Shepherd, *Gender and Authority in Sixteenth-Century England* (Ryburn, U.K.: Keele University Press, 1994).

[12] G. W. Forrell, "Luther's Conception of 'Natural Orders.' " *Lutheran Church Quarterly* 18 (1945): 166–72; W. H. Lazareth, "Luther's Two Kingdoms' Ethic Reconsidered," in *Christian Social Ethics in a Changing World*, ed. J. C. Bennett (London: SCM Press, 1966), pp. 119–31; P. Althaus, *The Ethics of Martin Luther* (Philadelphia: Fortress, 1972).

[13] He actually used the term *Schopferordnung* (the creator's order), but it is from him the whole orders-of-creation theology developed. See Adolf von Harless, "Schopfungsordnung," in *Die Religion in Geschichte und Gegenwart* (Tubingen: Mohr, 1961), 5:1492–94.

[14] Dietrich Bonhoeffer, *Ethics* (New York: Macmillan, 1955), pp. 207–13, 286–92.

turing, but he could see the danger of endorsing the status quo so that it could not be challenged or transformed by the revelation in Christ. As part of his corrective Bonhoeffer proposed that these orders be called *mandates* "because the word mandate refers more clearly to a divinely imposed task rather than to a determination in being."[15] The four mandates he lists are labor, marriage, government and church. It is God's will, he says, "that all these, each in its own way, shall be through Christ, directed towards Christ, and in Christ. God has imposed all these mandates on all men. This means there can be no retreating from a 'secular' into a 'spiritual' sphere."[16] In making this change Bonhoeffer redefined creation orders. In his thinking they were not once-given constitutive social structures but "mandates"—imperatives, commands to live in a certain way—given in creation but transformed by Christ.

In the contemporary hierarchical-complementarian case for the permanent subordination of women, the expression *the order of creation* combines the constitutive and prescriptive understandings of this expression. These creation orders give "what is" and "what ought to be" for Christians. In both *Recovering Biblical Manhood and Womanhood* and *Women in the Church* (and in virtually all other evangelical books that today argue for the permanent subordination of women), the expression *the order of creation* refers to the social order given by God before the Fall, in which men have the ruling role and women the subordinate role; and it is argued this is what God commands. It is a prescriptive order. Thus, these orders are also often called *mandates*. The chronological and the coordinative understanding of the orders of creation play no part.

Another modified theology of creation orders, lacking the dynamic and Christ-centered correctives given by Bonhoeffer, developed in the Netherlands[17] and then was adapted to support apartheid in South Africa.[18] In 1957 John Murray introduced the theology of the creation orders, or "ordinances," as he prefers to call them, into the North American Presbyterian Reformed tradition.[19] For Murray, as for the Lutherans, these orders are God-given structures governing the whole of life, not just the church and the home.[20] In orders-of-creation the-

---

[15]Ibid., p. 207.

[16]Ibid.

[17]I allude to Dooyeweerdianism, in which the "spheres" correspond to creation orders.

[18]For a brief comment, see A. Konig, *Here I Am! A Christian Reflection on God* (Grand Rapids, Mich.: Eerdmans, 1982), pp. vii–ix. See also J. de Gruchy, *Liberating Reformed Theology* (Grand Rapids, Mich.: Eerdmans, 1991).

[19]John Murray, *Principles of Conduct* (London: Tyndale, 1957).

[20]This is expressly stated by Murray (Ibid., p. 44). He says, "They touch upon every area of life and behavior."

ology it is not the autocratic state, the republican state or the democratic state that is given by God in creation, but the concept of the state itself. How the state establishes good government can differ from place to place and from time to time.

In the case of interest to us, it was marriage that was the given reality, not how marriage was ordered. Indeed, Luther insisted that in creation men and women stood side by side as equals—woman's subordinate status being a consequence of sin, part of the fallen order.[21] Something altogether new emerged when theologians started appealing to the idea of orders of creation to validate the permanent subordination of women, and then only in the church and the home.[22] These two novel ideas—woman's subordination actually being one of the unchanging orders of creation, and this subordination's being restricted solely to the church and the home—were first developed by Fritz Zerbst, a German Lutheran, who wrote soon after the Second World War opposing the ordination of women. His book was translated into English and published in 1955 under the title, *The Office of Woman in the Church*.[23] Mainly from this source, first by Missouri Synod Lutherans[24] and then by conservative evangelicals, the idea of a creation-given social order that permanently subordinated women to men solely in the church and the home took root and flourished. George Knight, in the formulating of the ideas for his influential book *The New Testament Teaching on the Role Relationship of Men and Women*,[25] seems to have assumed that what Zerbst outlined was much the same as what his mentor, Murray, had taught him, but this is not the case.[26] Murray's creation order is marriage itself, not the sub-

---

[21]Martin Luther, *Lectures on Genesis Chapters 1–5*, ed. J. Pelikan, trans. G. Schick, vol. 1 of *Luther's Works* (St. Louis: Concordia, 1958), p. 115.

[22]E. Brunner took up the Lutheran idea of orders of creation, but he rejected the thought that they were static, immutable structures. When it came to marriage he explicitly argued against the thought that the orders of creation set the woman permanently under the man (*The Divine Imperative* [London: Lutterworth, 1937], pp. 373–80).

[23]Fritz Zerbst, *The Office of Woman in the Church*, trans. A. G. Merkens (St. Louis: Concordia, 1955). A similar argument is developed in less detail by another German Lutheran: see Peter Brunner, *The Ministry and the Ministry of Women*, trans. M. H. Bertram (St. Louis: Concordia, 1971).

[24]On this see R. C. Prohl, *Women in the Church* (Grand Rapids, Mich.: Eerdmans, 1957). Prohl wrote to refute Zerbst. His book is still worth reading.

[25]George Knight, *The New Testament Teaching on the Role Relationship of Men and Women* (Grand Rapids, Mich.: Baker, 1977). His ideas first appeared in earlier articles, as he explains in the beginning of his book.

[26]In a personal letter to me (dated May 9, 1998), Dr. Knight says he thought his "indebtedness" for his understanding of the orders of creation, on which he predicated the permanent subordination of women, was to John Murray alone. From Murray came the term, but not the content. The content is Zerbst's book, which he lists in a footnote.

ordination of women; and this and his other creation orders cover all of creation, not just the church and the home, which are for him the domain of the "orders of redemption."

This observation raises a major problem for conservative evangelicals who want to ground women's permanent subordination on a constitutive and prescriptive social order given in creation. If God has in fact subordinated women to men in a created order that prescribes the unchanging ideal, then it would follow that women have been subordinated not only in the church and the home but also in the state. In classic expressions of orders-of-creation theology the basic premise is that these orders are constitutive or prescriptive of all social relations in God's creation.

On their own interpretative principles 1 Timothy 2:9–15 proves too much for the authors of *Recovering Biblical Manhood and Womanhood* and *Women in the Church* and for all others who ground women's subordination on an unchanging social order given in creation. To be consistent with their own theology, they should oppose women holding high office in the state, where they are set over men. As education opens the door to women gaining such positions of authority in the political, legal and commercial world, hierarchical-complementarians should also give themselves to opposing women's having access to higher education. Since they do neither of these things, their whole construct lacks consistency and credibility. However, this is only part of the problem faced by any appeal to a God-given creation social order that permanently subordinates women to men.

Paradoxically, at the same time conservative evangelicals began appealing to orders-of-creation theology to maintain the subordination of women, mainline Protestant theologians were abandoning creation-orders theology. Karl Barth initiated the revolt. He dismissed the whole approach as mistaken, as an attempt to preserve traditional social structuring by endorsing what is as if it were what God willed. This he saw as the reintroduction of a natural theology into Protestant ethics.[27]

Others were equally critical of orders-of-creation theology because it was invariably used by the powerful to support their privileges. It excluded justice issues by making the existing social and political order God-given and immutable. Critics noted that this theology seemed to come to the fore whenever social or political change was on the agenda. It was a reactionary construct. By the 1960s

---

[27]Karl Barth, *Church Dogmatics* 3/4, trans. Geoffrey Bromiley (Edinburgh: T & T Clark, 1955), pp. 18-46.

this static and conservative view of social order had in fact become outdated. From this time on, mainline theologians were being reminded by those who were informed by the social sciences that all social ordering and all political systems are human constructs and thus can be changed by human beings. Those who hold authority over others create and maintain the ideology and structures that keep them in power. If this is so, then God does not endorse the rule of any one class, race or sex, nor does he sanction any particular form of government. In this theological context (as orders-of-creation theology was being dismissed as a reactionary human construct), English-speaking conservative evangelicals who were searching for a way to uphold the traditional ordering of the sexes began appealing to orders-of-creation theology. Today it is the foundation of the whole conservative evangelical case for the permanent subordination of women in the church and the home. This means that those who follow this path are out of step with the best contemporary thinking on Christian social ethics, just as they are out of step with the best of contemporary Protestant and Catholic thinking on the Trinity.

It is, however, not only orders-of-creation theology that needs to be rejected. The whole idea that the creation stories establish the permanent social ideal is also to be rejected. Those evangelicals who consistently appeal to the opening chapters of Genesis to uphold the subordination of women fail to notice that the New Testament is grounded on a theology of the new creation in Christ, which looks to the transcending of the original creation.[28] "In Christ there is a new creation: everything old has passed away" (2 Cor 5:17). For this reason the apostle Paul can even annul *in some way* the creation givens of sex,[29] suggesting that being "in Christ" is of more importance than even one's sexual identity (Gal 3:28).[30] The Bible does not hold that the ideal lies in the past, in an idyllic Eden. This ideal is in the future, in the age to come.[31] Eden cannot provide the ideal

---

[28]The evangelical New Testament scholar Greg Beale argues that the new creation motif is central to New Testament theology ("The Eschatological Conception of New Testament Theology," in *Eschatology in Bible and Theology: Evangelical Essays at the Dawn of a New Millennium*, ed. K. E. Bower and M. W. Elliott [Downers Grove, Ill.: InterVarsity Press, 1999], pp. 11–52).

[29]Quoting the Greek, Paul negates the words of Gen 1:27: "[In Christ] there is no *male and female*" *(ouk eni arsen kai thēly)*.

[30]So Krister Stendahl, *The Bible and the Role of Women* (Philadelphia: Fortress, 1966), p. 34; R. Longenecker, *New Testament Social Ethics for Today* (Grand Rapids, Mich.: Eerdmans, 1984), pp. 70–93; Kevin N. Giles, *Created Woman* (Canberra, Australia: Acorn, 1985), pp. 28–32.

[31]New Testament scholars are agreed that the New Testament is profoundly orientated to the future. It is predicated on eschatology. See K. E. Bower and M. W. Elliott, eds., *Eschatology in Bible and Theology* (Downers Grove, Ill.: InterVarsity Press, 1999). In relation to created-orders

because there the devil was active and sin was possible. As the eschatological people of God, the church always looks forward and seeks to realize in its corporate life the perfection to be known in the new heaven and the new earth.[32]

The only places in the New Testament with the slightest hint that women are to be subordinated to men on the basis of some aspect of God's creative work are the disputed texts: 1 Timothy 2:13 and 1 Corinthians 11:3ff. None of the exhortations to wives to be subordinated to their husbands in the so-called Household Codes are grounded on an appeal to the creation order, however understood. Most of them make their appeal on the basis of expediency.[33] The exhortation in Ephesians 5:21ff. is grounded in a parallel between Christ and the church; the only time Genesis is quoted is to affirm that in marriage a man and a woman become "one" (Eph 5:31). In 1 Corinthians 11:3ff. we do find more than one appeal to the creation stories to enforce women's wearing of head coverings. What is to be noted in this case is that virtually everyone today agrees this dress code is culturally limited. It would seem that in this passage Paul marshals a number of ad hominem arguments that would appeal directly to his readers to enforce a local cultural practice. This reminds us that many of the details in the creation stories do not give moral or behavior norms, nor do they distinguish what is transcultural in biblical teaching. Some give the ideal, not a binding law (e.g., lifelong marriage), some are radically modified (e.g., no work at all on the seventh day), and some are ignored in good conscience (e.g., working for six days, eating only of fruit-bearing trees).[34] The truth of the matter, says William Webb, is that "original creation patterns do not provide an automatic guide for assessing what is transcultural within Scripture."[35]

None of Paul's appeals to the creation stories in 1 Corinthians 11 can be read as weighty theological reflection or as giving permanently binding instructions. Why then should it be assumed that 1 Timothy 2:13 is of this nature? It may well

---

theology, see esp. R. Prenter, *Creation and Redemption* (Philadelphia: Fortress, 1967), pp. 196–97. A. Konig argues that the authentic Reformed tradition, building on Calvin's thought, does not look back to Eden as the ideal but forward to the eschaton (*The Eclipse of Christ* [Grand Rapids, Mich.: Eerdmans, 1989], pp. 59ff.). See also the important study by Jürgen Moltmann, *The Future of Creation* (London: SCM Press, 1979).

[32]See the good discussion of this in Stanley J. Grenz and Denise Kjesbo, *Women in the Church* (Downers Grove, Ill.: InterVarsity Press, 1995), pp. 173–79.

[33]See chapter nine in this book, where I demonstrate this in some detail. See also my book *Created Woman*, pp. 42–47.

[34]I take these examples from William J. Webb, *Slaves, Women and Homosexuals: Exploring the Hermeneutics of Cultural Analysis* (Downers Grove, Ill.: InterVarsity Press, 2001), pp. 123–27.

[35]Ibid., p. 126.

be that Paul reminded the Ephesian Christians that Adam was created first solely to humble those women who were setting themselves over men as authoritative teachers of what the apostle thought was false doctrine. To find in this one comment, which has no parallel in Scripture, the basis of a God-given, immutable social order—permanently setting women under men—is to read into the text what is not there and what few in the history of exegesis have found there. What we can conclude is that Paul's sole concern in this passage is to give reasons why women should not teach *at this time* in Ephesus.

If my reasoning is correct, we must conclude then that the recently developed conservative evangelical appeal to a constitutive and prescriptive social order given in creation as the grounds for the permanent subordination of women cannot stand scrutiny. This pillar on which so much is built is made of sand. It contradicts the overall teaching of Scripture, which is eschatological; it has no long-standing or uniform historical tradition to support it; it denies the foundational premise on which orders-of-creation theology rests—namely, that these orders govern all of God's creation, not just the church and the home; and worst of all it builds a huge edifice on a single text (1 Tim 2:13) that can be interpreted in more than one way. If this is conceded, then one must recognize that contemporary hierarchical-complementarians build their whole case not on inductive exegesis or on a profound insight into what is central to Scripture in the man-woman relationship, but on a poorly attested and generally rejected theological construct that they do not apply consistently.

Role Subordination

As I read *Recovering Biblical Manhood and Womanhood* and *Women in the Church,* I got the impression that the authors used the word *role* more than they used any other term. The truly historic position spoke explicitly and frequently of the inferiority of women and the superiority of men as a class or race, implying women's ontological inferiority. Contemporary hierarchical-complementarians stress that they do not consider women to be inferior to men. The sexes are equal; they simply have different roles ascribed by God. In the Trinity, we are told, the subordinate role of the Son and the Holy Spirit in no way invalidates their personal or ontological equality with the Father, and this holds true in the man-woman relationship as well. Subordination in role or function and equality of person are not mutually exclusive ideas.

The French word *role* originated in reference to the part an actor played on stage. In the 1930s, it became a key term in functional sociology. It was only in the late 1950s and early 1960s, as the study of sociology became established in the universities, that the word began to be widely used in the English-speaking world. I can find no evidence of Christian usage of the word in theological discourse before this time. This means that its adoption by contemporary conservative evangelicals to further their case for the permanent subordination of women is also something quite novel.

The idea that women and men have been given by God differing roles or functions finds no mention in Zerbst's important 1955 study, *The Office of Woman in the Church,* or in Charles Ryrie's 1958 book, *The Place of Women in the Church,* or in Peter Brunner's 1971 monograph, *The Ministry and the Ministry of Women.*[36] Furthermore, it is not found in Larry Christenson's book *The Christian Family,*[37] first published in 1970. The word *role* occasionally appears in Christenson's book, but the reader finds no trace of the idea that women and men have been given different roles in creation. For him men as men are to lead; women as women are to be subordinate. The first theological book to give the word *role* prominence was Krister Stendahl's monograph in support of the ordination of women, which was given the English title *The Bible and the Role of Women* when it was published in America in 1966. I take it this wording was devised by the English-speaking publisher, for the original 1958 Swedish title has no equivalent to the word *role* in it, and in the translation of the book the word *role* is never used to describe how men and women are to relate to one another. It is also interesting to note that Ryrie's book *The Place of Women in the Church* was reissued in 1978 under the title *The Role of Women in the Church.*[38] In this climate it was not at all surprising that in the mid 1970s Knight took up this term and combined it with the new understanding of creation orders in his book *The New Testament Teaching on the Role Relationship of Men and Women.*

From then on women's subordinate status was redefined by hierarchical-complementarians in terms of role differentiation. Despite their profession of being those most faithful to Scripture, they embraced this new term, not noticing that they had baptized an idea and a term not found in Scripture and—it would seem to me—alien to the Bible's own teaching on the sexes. Nowhere does the Bible suggest that women and men are simply *acting out* their maleness or femaleness or that apart from procreation there are some tasks given only to men and others only to women. The defining statement of Genesis 1:27–28, which undergirds all that the Bible says about the sexes, teaches that God made us

---

[36]Charles Ryrie, *The Place of Women in the Church* (London: Macmillan, 1958).
[37]Larry Christenson, *The Christian Family* (Minneapolis: Bethany, 1970).
[38]Charles Ryrie, *The Role of Women in the Church* (Chicago: Moody, 1978). See also n. 37.

men and women. In our very being we *are* differentiated: we are not merely functionally differentiated. I personally would not want to believe that anything in Genesis 2 contradicts the basic affirmations of Genesis 1. The suggestion that Genesis 2 gives man the ruling role and woman the subordinate role is read into the text. This chapter certainly differentiates the sexes, but it does not do so according to social roles or power relations.

The climax of this highly symbolic story is given at the end, when woman and man, made of the same stuff ("bone of my bones and flesh of my flesh," Gen 2:23) stand side by side. Only at this point in the narrative is Adam man in distinction from and in relation to woman and Eve woman in distinction from and in relation to man. The subordination of women is first mentioned in the creation narratives in Genesis 3:16, where it is introduced as one consequence of the Fall.

The Bible consistently holds that our maleness and femaleness are grounded in our God-given nature, not in the things we do. The recently popularized usage of terminology and ideas drawn from the theater and humanistic sociology actually contradicts divine revelation. W. Neuer is the only hierarchical-complementarian that I know who has seen the "inappropriateness of role theory" to interpret the Bible's teaching on the differences between men and women. He concludes that "in the cause of truth we should therefore give up talking about the roles of the sexes."[39] When conservative evangelicals interpret biblical teaching on women and men in terms of role differentiation, we have to recognize they are reading into the text something that is not there and that is never mentioned prior to the 1960s. To use their own terminology, they are not being "biblical."

This novel usage of the term *role* is, however, not only unbiblical (terminologically and conceptually), it is also logically flawed. What it purports to uphold—namely, the equality of the sexes—it actually undermines. It is true that allocating someone a subordinate role does not *necessarily* imply that person's inferiority; it is not true that it *never* implies this, especially if that subordination is deemed permanent and gender- or race-specific.

An officer and a private in an army are equal in essential being even if the officer is superior in function to the private. The commanding role of the officer in no way invalidates the essential personal equality of the private. Such functional subordination or difference in roles, of which countless examples could

---

[39]W. Neuer, *Man and Woman in Christian Perspective,* trans. Gordon J. Wenham (London: Hodder & Stoughton, 1990), p. 30.

be cited, does not necessarily imply personal superiority or inferiority. This is the case because the officer's superior role is based on superior training or competence to lead and because it is possible for the private to become an officer and for the officer to be demoted. In other words, the officer's superior role is not intrinsically connected with who he is. His role is not an essential feature of his personhood. It is something transient and secondary. As such, his superior role in no way suggests that he as a person, in his essential nature or being, is superior to the private or that he is a class or race apart.

A parallel cannot be made with the complementarian-hierarchical view of women. In this case, because a woman is a woman, and for no other reason, she is locked into a *permanent* subordinate role, no matter what her abilities or training might be. Who she is determines what she can do; her sexual identity determines her role. The private can assume higher responsibilities, but a woman can never become a leader in the church and can never assume equal responsibility with her husband in the home, simply because she is a woman. Once we ask why this is this so, we must infer some permanent inability in women. It has to be understood that a woman essentially lacks something given only to men; in some way she herself is a subordinate person. Introducing the sociological term *role* in this argument for the *permanent functional* subordination of women does not negate the fact that women because they are women, and for no other reason, are subordinated. Against its usual connotation, the word *role* is recast in essential terms. Cleverly worded phraseology cannot avoid this fact.[40] If a woman's role is not essential to her nature or being, then it can change. If it cannot change because it is basic to her nature or being as a woman, then it is not just a role she performs. Thus, this novel case for the permanent role subordination of women is at best incoherent and at worst disingenuous. The assertion of equality remains just that—an assertion. It has no cash value. Construed in this way there is no way to meaningfully maintain the claim that women are created equal. The traditional exegesis was at least forthright and logically consistent on this count.

The argument that men and women are equal although they have differing roles sounds very plausible and sociologically sound, but when it is unpacked, we discover that the argument is not really addressing sociological roles at all: such as who mows the lawn, pays the bills, washes up or does the laundry— matters the Bible says nothing about. There is only one concern in mind all the

---

[40]See Rebecca Groothuis, *Good News for Women: A Biblical Picture of Gender Equality* (Grand Rapids, Mich.: Baker, 1997), pp. 27-29, 49-52, 65-67.

time: that is, the essential authority and leadership of the man and the essential subordination of the woman. The issue is not *gender roles* but essential *gender relations*. God has set men over women because they are women. The word *role* only has the effect of obfuscating this fact.

The appeal to differing roles for men and women sounds reasonable and equitable, but when we examine it we find that it contradicts biblical teaching and that it is logically flawed. It does not safeguard women's personal equality with men, it undermines it. In any case, nothing can justify Christians' defining the differences between the sexes in terms of differing roles, for this justification actually subverts what the Bible is actually saying about the sexes. "In the cause of truth," as Neuer says, "we should give up talking about the roles of the sexes." Role theory, like creation-order theology, is a pillar supporting an edifice that can bear no weight.

The Word *Difference*

Closely allied with the special use of the word *role* in these two books and in parallel literature is the special use of the word *difference*. Time and time again, we are told that women and men are "equal but different." This is the essence of the "biblical" understanding of "manhood and womanhood." The great error of evangelical egalitarians and feminists, we are told, is that they do not preserve the distinctions basic to biblical manhood and womanhood. They are accused of advocating "an unqualified equation of the sexes."[41] Harold O. J. Brown thinks the logic of his opponents' position is "total sexual equivalence."[42] Robert Yarbrough warns of those who "obliterate our God-given gender distinctions."[43] In *Women in the Church* and *Recovering Biblical Manhood and Womanhood,* such quotes abound. What their opponents are attacking, we are told, is the clear teaching of Scripture that differentiates women and men. The authors are so convinced of this that when John Piper finds Paul Jewett arguing forcibly for the differences of the sexes,[44] he takes this to be an example of the inconsistency of Jewett's

---

[41]Raymond Ortland, "Male and Female Equality and Male Headship: Genesis 1—3," in *Recovering Biblical Manhood and Womanhood: A Response to Evangelical Feminism,* ed. John Piper and Wayne Grudem (Wheaton, Ill.: Crossway, 1991), p. 99.

[42]Brown, "New Testament Against Itself," p. 200. Innumerable similar assertions can be found in both books.

[43]Robert Yarbrough, "The Hermeneutics of 1 Timothy 2:9-15," in *Women in the Church: A Fresh Analysis of 1 Timothy 2:9-15,* ed. Andreas J. Köstenberger, Thomas R. Schreiner and H. Scott Baldwin (Grand Rapids, Mich.: Baker, 1995), p. 193.

[44]Paul Jewett, *Man as Male and Female* (Grand Rapids, Mich.: Eerdmans, 1975).

understanding of biblical manhood and womanhood![45]

If egalitarians are in fact attacking differentiation between men and women so clearly taught in Scripture, then there are just grounds for concern. However, when we turn to their literature, we find not one hint of such ideas. No informed egalitarian-complementarian denies the differences between the sexes. Jewett is representative of evangelical egalitarians in underlining that sexual polarity is of the essence of "biblical manhood and womanhood." In creation, God made humankind as male *and* female. In my thirty years of involvement in this debate, I have never heard a Christian feminist deny, nor have I read a Christian book that argues against, the differences between the sexes. How could they when our differences are so observable and well documented[46] and, most importantly, so clearly taught in Scripture? The biblical teaching on the sexes is predicated on the prologue to the whole Bible, Genesis 1, which climaxes in the declaration that "God created humankind in his image, . . . male and female he created them" (Gen 1:27). In any case, why evangelical egalitarians would want to deny the differences between the sexes when many contemporary secular feminists stress the differences completely escapes me.[47] Here we may note that one of the most popular secular books on marriage in recent years is John Grey's *Men Are from Mars, Women Are from Venus*,[48] which is based on the premise that men and women are different.

What, then, is going on? One side accuses the other of denying the differences between the sexes while they stress this very thing. The answer is that for the hierarchical-complementarian, the word *difference* is a code word. It means something that the hierarchical-complementarian cannot ever say or ever admit. In the truly historic position, exegetes and theologians said God made women inferior; the contemporary hierarchical-complementarian emphatically denies this. In our age this an unacceptable idea for anyone to promulgate. The wom-

---

[45]John Piper, "A Vision of Biblical Complementarity: Manhood and Womanhood Defined According to the Bible," in *Recovering Biblical Manhood and Womanhood: A Response to Evangelical Feminism,* ed. John Piper and Wayne Grudem (Wheaton, Ill.: Crossway, 1991), pp. 33–34.

[46]For a good, readable introduction to the scholarly study on the statistical differences between men and women, see A. Moir and D. Jessel, *Brain-Sex: The Real Difference Between Men and Women* (London: Mandarin, 1989). See also Elaine Storkey, *Men, Created or Constructed? The Great Gender Debate* (Carlisle, U.K.: Paternoster, 2000). She gives a superb introduction to the debate among Christians on the differences of the sexes. Our conclusions are very similar, although she writes preeminently as a Christian social scientist.

[47]See further E. Graham, *Making the Difference: Gender, Personhood and Theology* (London: Mowbray, 1995), esp. 169–91, and Storkey, *Men, Created or Constructed?*

[48]John Grey, *Men Are from Mars, Women Are from Venus* (London: Harper-Collins, 1993).

en's revolution has forced men to give up using the word *inferior* or even suggesting the idea. What hierarchical-complementarians say instead is that God made women "different" from men. But when we ask how they are different, they mention only one matter: men have been given the ruling role and women the subordinate role in the home and the church. Women are different, therefore, because God has excluded them from exercising authority in the home and the church. The only essential difference that matters to hierarchical-complementarians is a permanent difference of authority. Headship for men and subordination for women are the defining marks of what they call "biblical manhood and womanhood." On the one hand, they want to say that the difference between the sexes is not to be identified with a difference in essence/nature/being; and on the other, they assert that this difference in role is essential to what it means to be a man or a woman. For them, since there is only one essential difference, the denial of that difference must mean the denial of all difference. Thus when they hear an egalitarian denying that women have been permanently subordinated in role, they interpret this to be a denial of what is essential in their understanding of the essence/nature/being of a woman. In reality, despite all denials to the contrary, woman is a subordinated person and for this reason is locked into a subordinate role. It is her role subordination that essentially differentiates her from a man.

We are now at the same point we reached in considering their use of the word *role.* If women—no matter what their gifts, abilities or training may be—are *permanently* excluded as a sex from leadership, it suggests they essentially lack something given only to men by God. This difference indicates that they are inferior to men in some undeniable way. Therefore, what is in contention is whether this one specific role distinction is essential to what it means to be a woman or a man.

As far as the Bible is concerned, the difference between the sexes is not based on who leads and who obeys, on differing roles or on power relationships, to be more exact.[49] In Genesis 1:27-28 the one species, humankind, is

---

[49]The temptation to find ways to define the differences between the sexes in specific terms is always present. Piper and Grudem attempt this (in *Recovering,* pp. 1–31) and end up defining men and women in the cultural terms they want to impose on others. In answer, Barth, as usual, is more perceptive than most. In *Church Dogmatics* 3/4 (pp. 149–59), he rejects all attempts to abstractly define the essence of man or woman. He denigrates such efforts as "simply opinions" and as a reflection of culture at any one time in any one place. All that can be said in the end, he argues, is that man is not woman and woman is not man. God gives their irreversible sexual identity; it is not limiting. He writes, "The summons to both man and woman to be true to themselves may take completely unforeseen forms right outside the systems in which we like to think" (p. 151).

differentiated as man and woman by God's creative act. There are two ways of being human in God's world: one is either male or female. This sexual differentiation does not imply that one is over the other. It is to man and woman together that God gives dominion and authority over his world. Woman and man are alike in their essential nature and both are made vice-regents in God's world. In their discussions of the Trinity and of the sexes, hierarchical-complementarians are wedded to the idea that difference is defined by role. We are told that if the subordinate role of the Son or women is denied, then there is no way their differences can be maintained. With the Trinity, we have seen that orthodoxy rejects this reasoning. The Father and the Son are one in being and function: they are differentiated by their personal identity and unchanging relations. In regard to men and women, it is basically the same. Men and women are one being, and their social roles do not distinguish them. Except for biological roles, the roles of men and women can overlap. Women and men, as far as the Bible is concerned, are differentiated by their God-given sexual nature. Man is man in distinction to and in relation with woman; woman is woman in distinction to and in relation with man by God's creative act. One's role is never seen in the Bible as essential to what it means to be a man or woman. If the difference between the sexes is sexual identity itself, then there is no problem with affirming the abiding differences while allowing fluidity in roles.

It may also be pointed out that in everyday life difference does not imply subordination. For example, a dog and a cat are very different creatures, yet their speciation does not determine their status or role. Size and aggression determine who rules when a cat and a dog cross paths. The examples could be multiplied. Difference does not imply or necessitate the subordination of one party.

The use of the word *difference* as synonymous with subordination and inferiority is well known. In the history of ideas those who have spoken most about the difference between people of one country and another, or the difference between one class and another, or the difference between one race and another have used this term to enhance their own privileges and power at the expense of those less privileged and powerful. The party who has most to gain by defining themselves in a way that will further or uphold their position invariably uses the word *difference* in such debates. Thus when white supremacists say, "We whites are different from blacks," they are cryptically claiming whites are in some way superior to blacks. It is not surprising, therefore, that those working for justice and equality of consideration for the oppressed, in contrast, emphasize likeness or similarity. In doing so they capture one of the most primary biblical truths: human beings, without exception, whether male or female, black or white, rich or poor, are all made in the image and likeness of God. Nothing must ever be allowed to cloud the essential equality of worth, dignity and freedom of all human beings.

The differences between the sexes are more profound than the differences between one race and another or the differences between one socioeconomic group and another because sexual identity is indelibly given by God. It is given not to disadvantage one sex but rather to enrich the life of both sexes. Sexual identity in itself does not seem to limit what men and women can or cannot do, except in procreation. Sexual differentiation in terms of role allocation simply does not fit the facts. It is true that there are statistically significant differences between the sexes. For example, most men are stronger than most women. What is not true is that all men are stronger than all women. Even if it could be shown that *most* men are better suited to be leaders, theologians, teachers or pastors than are *most* women, it would not follow that *all* women are not equipped to do these things. There are not only differences between the sexes but also profound differences among each of the sexes.

The whole idea that women are not made by God to lead is best accounted for as a culturally conditioned, androcentric premise. Moreover, it has been seriously called into question by the realities of modern life. If God has actually denied women the ability to be leaders and exercise authority, how is it that women can be so effective as queens, prime ministers, judges, doctors, business executives and even ordained ministers? Paradoxically, modern studies on sexual differences show that most women have better communication skills than most men and that most women are better at relating to others than most men—the two gifts that more than anything else make for good pastor-teachers. If this is the so, then perhaps God's revelation in nature, which never contradicts his revelation in Scripture, suggests that the differences between the sexes do not imply the subordination of women, let alone exclude them from leading or teaching in church.

In the special use of the words *difference* and *role* we have examples of what evangelical theologian Kevin J. Vanhoozer refers to as language used in the service of ideology. Words and phrases are chosen and developed by those holding the reins of power to preserve their privileges, to exclude others and to make what they say sound acceptable to modern ears. "Ideology legitimates ruling-class domination," writes Vanhoozer, "by making its ideas and norms appear natural, just and universal."[50] Once we recognize this, we can see on almost

---

[50]Kevin J. Vanhoozer, *Is There Meaning in the Text? The Bible, the Reader and the Morality of Literary Knowledge* (Grand Rapids, Mich.: Zondervan, 1998), p. 173. His discussion on these matters is highly commended. See especially pp. 166–68, 174–75. See also J. Plamena-

every page of the books we are considering the ideology of male hegemony at work. It determines not only the language used but also the texts selected as normative, how the texts are to be interpreted and the theology adopted to integrate the material into a theological position. Because ideology rules, no refutation is ever given serious consideration.[51] Counter arguments or rebuttals are ignored, stigmatized or emotively dismissed.[52] Ideology can never be overthrown by rational argument.

Again, we must conclude that this third pillar in the case for the permanent subordination of women cannot bear the load placed on it. Women and men are differentiated by God's creative initiative, but this differentiation exists within their shared humanity. Hierarchical-complementarians, in defining the differences between the sexes solely in terms of differing roles, not only contradict what the Bible teaches on the sexes but also deny what modern life has made so evident. God-given sexual identity gives amazing freedom to women and men in what they can do and achieve, while allowing each to make a distinct contribution to our common tasks. Such differentiation neither constrains human potential nor necessitates prescriptive roles. What the Bible in fact suggests—and the social sciences confirm—is that social ordering is always a human construct and, as such, human beings can change it when they have the will.

Examples of Eisegesis

When these three novel and unbiblical ideas are welded together as an interpretative grid, eisegesis follows. Although texts are carefully studied and dissected, the presuppositions of the interpreters triumph because this grid determines how the Bible is read. This can be seen happening in several ways: in the use of carefully crafted obfuscating language; in a reading into the text of what is not there; and sometimes in a rejecting of what is there. Usually all these things go hand in hand.

---

taz, *Ideology* (London: Macmillan, 1970), for a more broad-ranging discussion of ideology. He argues that ideology creates an "illusion" that the position advocated is rationally and factually based.

[51]I speak from twenty-five years of experience in debating these issues with my fellow graduates of Moore Theological College, Sydney.

[52]A classic example is found in Köstenberger, Schreiner and Baldwin, *Women in the Church,* where Yarbrough counters my arguments that the "biblical" case for slavery is stronger than that for the subordination of women ("Hermeneutics of 1 Timothy," pp. 185-90). For my reply to him see "A Critique of the 'Novel' Contemporary Interpretation of 1 Timothy 2:9–15, Given in the Book *Women in the Church,*" part 1, *Evangelical Quarterly* 72, no. 2 (2000): 157–58.

In the (truly) historic case for women's subordination, the language is stark and unambiguous. When interpretations of passages mentioning women are given, what is being said is plain: women are inferior; they are "a subordinate class"; they "are born to obey" (Calvin); they are to keep silent in public; they are responsible for sin, being "weak and fickle" (Chrysostom); and they will be saved so long as they concentrate on bearing children. Larry Christenson, in *The Christian Family,* also speaks in the plainest of language: "Upon man is laid the authority to rule." "A woman is normally not equipped by nature to sustain . . . psychological or emotional pressure." "Wives, rejoice in your husband's authority over you! Be subject to him in all things."[53]

In contrast, the language used by the contemporary hierarchical-complementarian is euphemistic, obfuscating and often misleading. The wording is carefully chosen to make what is culturally unacceptable sound acceptable and to support the case being presented. We have just seen this in the use of the words *role* and *difference.* In hierarchical-complementarian writings these terms are used in a way that has no parallels in any other literature. These terms are given a special meaning to conceal what is actually being argued and to make the case presented sound plausible and acceptable to modern ears. One euphemistic turn of phrase that made me smile is provided by Robert Yarbrough: instead of saying men are to rule in the home and the church, which is the essence of his case, he says, "Men must bear a few strategic burdens that women normally do not."[54] One can also see their ideological use of language in their avoidance of certain terms and denials of what is obvious. For example, the word *subordination* is avoided as much as possible. We are told the only issue at stake are the different roles of men and women. Men and women are equal. Yarbrough criticizes me for calling the complementarian position the case for "the subordination of women."[55] In fact, I invariably call it the case for "the permanent subordination of women." In doing this I name their position accurately, something they can never come to do. Their use of the word *complementary* is another example. To claim one's position enshrines the complementary view of the sexes sounds attractive. The trouble is that egalitarians have consistently upheld the complementarity of the sexes. This term on its own does not distinguish the two positions. What distinguishes them is how they understand the relation between the sexes. One side places the man over the woman; the other has the woman and man standing side by side. In politics, making bad news sound

---

[53]Christenson, *Christian Family,* pp. 40, 45, 54.
[54]Yarbrough, "Hermeneutics of 1 Timothy," p. 195.
[55]Ibid., p. 185.

good is called putting a "spin" on things. The writers of these two books are "spin-doctors" in this sense. The contemporary hierarchical-complementarians' deliberate use of ambiguous, euphemistic and misleading language does not help them get to grips with the teaching of the Bible, it prevents them hearing what the Bible is really saying.

Specific examples of eisegesis abound. In his exposition of what he tells us is the plain meaning of Genesis 3, Raymond Ortland concludes Moses is teaching that "Eve usurped Adam's headship and led the way into sin. . . . Adam for his part abandoned his post as head. Eve was deceived; Adam forsook his responsibility." Their sin was "sex role reversal."[56] The text just cannot bear this interpretation. The Bible never suggests that God-given roles are the basis of sexual differentiation. Genesis insists God has made us in our very being women and men, not two sexes who have different roles. The idea that their sin was "role reversal" has never been suggested before 1970. Most orthodox theologians have concluded Adam and Eve's sin was willful disobedience of the command of God. Furthermore, nowhere in Genesis 2 or in the first part of Genesis 3 does it say that Adam was the one responsible for every decision in the Garden. The rule of the man is made a consequence of the Fall and is thus mentioned for the first time in Genesis 3:16. The word *headship* is not used anywhere in Genesis 1–3. Clearly much more than a straightforward reading of the text is determinative in this interpretation of the story of the Fall.

In outlining his interpretation of Ephesians 5:21ff., Doriani tells us Paul is teaching that "the male, the husband and father, lead the home and the marriage. . . . He must bear final responsibility for making decisions."[57] Again, whatever one thinks of these ideas, one must note that they do not come from the text of Scripture. Paul says the husband is "the head of the wife," not the head of the home, and he is completely silent on who has final responsibility for making decisions. What he actually teaches is that the headship of the husband involves costly self-sacrifice and self-giving *agape* love.

Possibly no single text in all of Scripture has had so much built on it as 1 Timothy 2:13—"For Adam was formed first, then Eve." On the basis of this one text, half the human race is subordinated to the other half. For nineteen centuries these words were interpreted to teach that because woman was created second, women as a race or class are inferior to men, excluded from holding authority in any context. Since the 1970s, hierarchical-complementarians have

---

[56]Ortland, "Male-Female Equality," p. 107.
[57]Doriani, "History of the Interpretation," p. 260.

consistently given another interpretation.

They tell us Paul's words indicate that in creation God instituted an *unchanging social order* that gives men the leading role in the home and excludes women from leading or preaching in church. Paul's words actually teach neither of these things. His reason for appealing to the fact that in Genesis 2 man is created first would seem to have a far more modest aim. He wants to achieve just one thing: to stop women from teaching and exercising authority in the heresy-ridden church at Ephesus. He gives two reasons for this new ruling, this being the first: women should not teach or exercise authority in the church "for Adam was formed first." In other words, women are not to claim they are "first," that they are above men. To take this to mean that women are inferior to men or that in creation God instituted a unchanging social order setting men over women is to read into the text far more than what Paul actually does say.

The hierarchical-complementarian interpretation of 1 Timothy 2:13 is predicated on a selective reading of the New Testament. It ignores or denies that elsewhere Paul adopts a nondiscriminatory theology of ministry (Rom 12:3–8; 1 Cor 12—14; Eph 4:11–12); that he usually speaks positively of women's ministry, including their leading verbally in church (1 Cor 11:5); and that his theology is grounded on the new creation in Christ that in some ways transcends the first creation (2 Cor 5:17). Nothing is made of Adam's being created first in all of Scripture apart from 1 Timothy 2:13, which clearly has a limited aim.

The second reason Paul gives as to why women should stop teaching at Ephesus is that "Adam was not deceived, but the woman was deceived and became a transgressor" (1 Tim 14). Historically, these words were taken to mean that woman was responsible for the Fall; thus all women are more easily led into sin and error and, for this reason, should not hold authority or speak in public. The more theologically aware, contemporary hierarchical interpreters of this text want to avoid at all cost suggesting that women are subordinated because they are responsible for the Fall and avoid the socially unacceptable idea that women are more prone to sin and error than men.[58] In seeking to avoid these two things several very creative and differing interpretations of the apos-

---

[58]Schreiner ("An Interpretation of 1 Timothy 2:9-15," p. 134) is typical: "The prescription on women teaching men, then, does not stem from the fall and cannot be ascribed to the curse" (on women in Gen 3:16). Some, however, are less careful. In this same volume, T. David Gordon argues in a passing comment that Paul "grounds" women's permanent subordination "in the entire created and fallen order" ("A Certain Kind of Letter: The Genre of 1 Timothy," in *Women in the Church*, p. 61.

tle's words are given, each of which claims to be what Scripture itself teaches.

Doriani says Paul's words do not "mean that women have less capacity than men, but they have different inclinations. . . . God created women with an orientation towards relationships more than analysis."[59] Thomas Schreiner concludes Paul is teaching that

> women are more relational and nurturing and men more prone to rational analysis and objectivity. Women are less prone than men to see the importance of doctrinal formulations, especially when it comes to the issue of identifying heresy and making a stand for the truth. What concerns [Paul] are the consequences of allowing women in the authoritative teaching office, for their gentler and kinder nature inhibits them from excluding people from doctrinal error.[60]

Whatever one thinks of Schreiner's sermonic words, one thing is clear: this interpretation is read into the text. Professor I. Howard Marshall, quoting this example says, "There is no evidence that such a thought was in the author's mind, and therefore it must be judged totally irrelevant to the exegesis of the passage."[61]

John Piper and Wayne Grudem have yet another interpretation. They tell us "the main point" of 1 Timothy 2:14 is

> not that man is undeceivable or that the woman is more deceivable; the point is that when God's order of leadership is repudiated it brings damage and ruin. Men and women are both more vulnerable to error and sin when they forsake the order that God intended.[62]

These varying interpretations of 1 Timothy 2:14 may sound plausible to those who believe God has subordinated women to men, but to those of another opinion how the authors found these ideas in this text is a complete mystery. Paul speaks of Adam's not being deceived and of Eve's being deceived; he does not speak of their different "inclinations," or of either's inability to maintain doctrinal nonnegotiables, or of the dangers of reversing male and female roles. These ideas are simply not in the text. What Paul actually says is that women should stop teaching at Ephesus, and as one of two reasons he gives for this locally determined ruling, he reminds the church that it was Eve who was first

---

[59]Doriani, "History of the Interpretation," p. 266.
[60]Schreiner, "An Interpretation of 1 Timothy," p. 145.
[61]Marshall, *Pastoral Epistles,* p. 466.
[62]John Piper and Wayne Grudem, "An Overview of Central Concerns," in *Recovering Biblical Manhood and Womanhood: A Fresh Response to Evangelical Feminism* (Wheaton, Ill.: Crossway, 1991), p. 73.

deceived. This would have the effect of warning any women who thought otherwise that they were not above being misled and mistaken in their views—a logic similar to his first point. Women are not to think of themselves as superior to men.

One good example of a hierarchical-complementarian's reluctance to hear what the text of Scripture may be actually saying is seen in Schreiner's treatment of 1 Corinthians 11:10.[63] Following normal word usage and syntax, Paul here says, "a woman ought to have a symbol of authority on her [own] head." Nowhere in all of Greek literature is the word *authority (exousia)* ever used in the passive sense of an authority to which one must submit. The word always alludes to the authority that someone exercises. Thus in 1 Corinthians 7:4 Paul speaks of the authority the wife exercises over her husband's body. Nevertheless, Schreiner summarily dismisses the view that in this passage Paul envisages a woman's having a God-given authority, although Paul's endorsement of women's praying and prophesying in the congregation would seem to imply just this. Despite the grammar, Schreiner gives seven reasons why what the text seems to say must be otherwise.

Whenever the word *role* is introduced, the reader must recognize that the author is doing eisegesis, not exegesis, and that he is using this word to interpret every key text in these two books. By using this word as a hermeneutical key, the hierarchical-complementarians distort what the Bible is actually saying and reach conclusions that are in fact contrary to what the Bible says about the sexes. It is exactly the same when appeal is made to a constitutive and prescriptive social order given in creation as the grounds for women's permanent subordination. The Bible does not give any support to this idea. Neither the narrative of Genesis 2 nor Paul's words in 1 Timothy 2:13 teach this. What Paul himself emphasizes is that in Christ there is a new creation.

We must conclude therefore that although the books *Recovering Biblical Manhood and Womanhood* and *Women in the Church* claim to be exegetical studies setting out what the Bible actually says, what we have, in fact, are two highly developed theological and ideological books in support of male "headship." The conclusions reached are not truly biblical at all.

---

[63]Thomas R. Schreiner, "Head Coverings, Prophecy and the Trinity: 1 Corinthians 11:2-16," in *Recovering Biblical Manhood and Womanhood: A Response to Evangelical Feminism,* ed. John Piper and Wayne Grudem (Wheaton, Ill.: Crossway, 1991), pp. 134–36.

9

AN EGALITARIAN-COMPLEMENTARIAN THEOLOGICAL READING OF THE BIBLE

Having outlined both the historic and the contemporary hierarchical-complementarian interpretation of what the Bible teaches on the man-woman relationship, it is now time to present a third option. This option argues that the Bible can be read to endorse the full emancipation of women—indeed, I would say, to demand the full emancipation of women *in our age and culture*. In the same thirty-year period during which some evangelicals have been developing a case for the permanent subordination of women, other evangelicals have been developing a theology that affirms the social equality of women. Egalitarians share a great deal of common ground, but as the doctrine of Scripture is inherently related to this question, they reflect considerable diversity as well. The main divide is between those who think the only solution allowed to evangelicals is an exegetical one and those, like myself, who think that exegesis alone can only take us so far. In the end, we come up against hermeneutical questions: most notably, what is theologically primary and secondary in the diverse scriptural comments on women, and what in this diverse teaching applies in our age? When one takes only the exegetical path, some strained interpretations appear as one attempts to get the biblical authors to speak as if they held a modern perspective on women. The approach I represent holds that "doing" evangelical (systematic) theology is a far more complex process than simply gathering and exegeting certain texts. In attempting to discern what God is saying to the church *in our age* on any matter (which is what theology is all about), we must weigh the varied comments in Scripture related to the particular issue, determine their relevance and applicability to a different historical context, evaluate the force of the tradition, hear the opinions of Christians of differing opinion and consider the outcomes of the conclusions reached. On this understanding of theology the debate about the man-woman relationship is not so much over the historical meaning of this or that text but about what the Spirit is saying to the church on this matter *in our age and culture* in the Scriptures.

I have just confessed that I come to the Bible with the presuppositions that there is diversity in biblical teaching on many important matters and that not everything in Scripture applies or is to be obeyed in our age—presuppositions I believe are thoroughly consistent with an evangelical commitment. Before moving forward, however, the force of our presuppositions in the reading of Scripture needs to be reiterated. Modern studies in the art and science of hermeneutics have made it clear that everyone reads the Bible through a metaphorical pair of eyeglasses that are called *presuppositions*.[1] The presuppositions we bring with us to the text include informational assumptions (e.g., early Christian worship was very like worship today), cultural assumptions (e.g., the early Christians thought slavery was an evil), doctrinal assumptions (e.g., Presbyterian polity reflects the polity of the early church) and ideological assumptions (e.g., the free enterprise system is "the Christian" way to run a country). We usually recognize the presuppositions others bring to the text, especially in the writings of Third World theologians and of those who differ from us in the man-woman relationship debate. We are less cognizant of our own presuppositions. If we are middle-class, educated, theologically informed, twenty-first century Western theologians and we are male, then we too bring a host of presuppositions to the text. We take these ways of seeing the world for granted. No one can escape having presuppositions. We now recognize that cultural presuppositions were powerfully at work in the traditional reading of Scripture on the man-woman relationship. For nineteen centuries the best of theologians believed the Bible taught that women were inferior to men, that women were more prone to sin and deception and that women were devoid of leadership potential. These

---

[1]See the excellent discussion on presuppositions in D. S. Ferguson, *Biblical Hermeneutics: An Introduction* (London: SCM Press, 1986), pp. 6–22.

views exactly reflected the presuppositions of their age. In part three of this book, we will find this was also the case with slavery. For eighteen centuries, virtually everyone believed that the Bible regulated and legitimated slavery. The institution of slavery was, they thought, endorsed by the Bible. This reading of the Bible again perfectly matched the cultural presuppositions that everyone held until modern times.

The contemporary hierarchical-complementarian position is also shaped by presuppositions. It could not be otherwise. The problem with this position is not that presuppositions play a part, for they do in all biblical interpretation; the problem is that it denies this is so.[2] Those who take this position want us to believe that they are outlining exactly what the Bible is teaching on the sexes, what Christians have always believed—the tradition.[3] And conversely, they charge, it is the egalitarian-complementarians who are reading the Bible in a novel way determined by the presuppositions of the modern world. I gladly admit that there is a large measure of truth in their counter claim. At this point, I simply want to stress that the contemporary hierarchical-complementarian position reflects many presuppositions that are not acknowledged, as has been shown. It is a reading of the Bible based on the presupposition that God has given leadership in the home and the church to men. This may be denied, but the truth of this assertion stands.

Evangelicals in tune with Western culture's new high estimation of womanhood have felt very uneasy about this subordinating theology. They have felt it devalues and demeans women. In reply they have highlighted texts that speak of the equality and dignity of women and have sought to find alternative interpretations of the texts highlighted by their opponents. Sadly, this has simply led to a "textjam."[4] It is now obvious that this theological dispute cannot be resolved by reading the Bible on the flat, as if every verse made an identical contribution to a given issue. There are texts that can be quoted by both sides to "prove" their position. I want to argue that if this theological debate among evangelicals is to be resolved, a more sophisticated hermeneutic is required. This will de-

---

[2]One pleasing exception to this rule is seen in Thomas R. Schreiner, but his acceptance that presuppositions are important does not affect his essay in any significant way ("Women in Ministry," in *Two Views on Women in Ministry,* ed. Craig L. Blomberg and J. R. Beck [Grand Rapids, Mich.: Zondervan, 2001], pp. 178–79).

[3]These ideas dominate in the books *Recovering Biblical Manhood and Womanhood: A Response to Evangelical Feminism,* ed. John Piper and Wayne Grudem (Wheaton, Ill.: Crossway, 1991), and *Women in the Church: A Fresh Analysis of 1 Timothy 2:9–15,* ed. Andreas J. Köstenberger, Thomas R. Schreiner and H. Scott Baldwin (Grand Rapids, Mich.: Baker, 1995).

[4]As Blomberg and Beck so honestly admit in their book, *Two Views on Women in Ministry,* p. 13.

mand two things: an honest and open acknowledgment of our presuppositions and a better understanding of what is involved in doing evangelical theology. I begin with the latter.

Going Backward: Athanasius and Augustine on the Theological Reading of Scripture

The historic debate on how the Bible should be read in regard to the Trinity has already been dealt with in some detail.[5] It is agreed there are texts in the New Testament that speak of some kind of subordination of the Son to the Father (e.g., Jn 14:28; Heb 5:8; 10:5–10) as well as texts that mention the Son's obedience to the Father (e.g., Mk 14:36; Jn 4:34; 5:30; 6:38) and the Son's being sent by the Father (e.g., Jn 3:17, 34; 5:36). What Athanasius saw so clearly was that to read these texts as though they were speaking of the *eternal* relationship between the Father and the Son undermined the full divinity of Christ and jeopardized our salvation, for only God can save. Athanasius's theology could not allow this. In reply, he argued that the Arians did not embrace the "scope" of Scripture—what we would call today the overall drift, or the theological center, of the Bible. For Athanasius, the Bible gave a "double account" of the Son, and two passages provided the key to the correct reading and relating of these two perspectives in Scripture. These texts (Jn 1:1, 14; Phil. 2:6–8) disclosed the two truths basic to the incarnation: "the Word was God" and "the Word became flesh." Nothing in Scripture could counter the full divinity of the Son—"the Word was God." Rather than being embarrassed by the texts that spoke of the subordination of the Son and of his obedience to the Father, Athanasius emphasized them. For he held that they proved the reality of the incarnation—"the Word became flesh." In his incarnate person, the Son willingly, *for our salvation,* subordinated himself to the Father. Athanasius could not, however, convince the Arians. They were sure the Bible was on their side. The subordination of the Son, of which the Bible spoke, was eternal. Athanasius, in contrast, said the full divinity of the Son was eternal and his subordination was temporal. Quoting texts and arguing about interpretations could not settle the matter, so Athanasius gave his support to the use of the extrabiblical Greek word *homoousios* to exclude the Arians because he concluded that this word captured what was foundational

---

[5]For substantiation of what immediately follows, and for what is said on Athanasius and Augustine, the reader should refer back to the discussion on the Trinity, especially the sections on these two church fathers in chapter two, where the original sources are documented in the footnotes.

to the New Testament understanding of Christ, the Son of God: that Christ is *one in being or substance* with the Father. In endorsing the use of this word, Athanasius allowed that theology could follow the trajectory in which Scripture pointed. It could go beyond what was actually said in the Bible. At the council of Constantinople in 381, the bishops who were assembled endorsed Athanasius's reading of the Bible, which is now enshrined in the Nicene Creed.

Early in the fourth century, Augustine, in his monumental work *De Trinitate,* returned to the question of how Scripture should be read in constructing a theology of the Trinity. He laid down a number of "rules" for a "canonical" or theological reading of the New Testament. The first rule is that the proper starting point is the many passages that speak of the full divinity of the Son (e.g., Jn 1:1; 5:21; 1 Cor 1:24; 1 Tim 6:14–16). These affirm the eternal equality of the Father and the Son. The second rule is that all texts which speak of the Son's subordination refer exclusively to his earthly ministry, when he willingly took "the form of a servant." For Augustine one text (Phil 2:6) summed up orthodox Christology, showing the correct way to read Scripture. In this verse, Paul speaks of the Son's being equal with God, his emptying himself, his taking the form of a slave and his being born in human likeness. In reply to those who drew attention to the fact that Jesus was "sent" by the Father—which, in "error," they argued proved that Jesus was "less than the Father"—Augustine introduces a third rule for the correct theological reading of Scripture: the temporal mission of the Son is a revelation in time to be distinguished from the procession of the Son that is eternal. What Augustine does in his second and third rule is completely exclude the option of reading the New Testament's teaching on the Son's subordinate status and work, seen in the temporality of the economy of salvation, back into the eternal Trinity. In the Athanasian Creed what is basically Augustine's theology of the Trinity is said to be the catholic faith, to be believed if salvation in Christ is to be enjoyed.

Arius and his followers mounted an impressive biblical argument supporting the eternal subordination of the Son. Any seemingly incompatible text quoted could be integrated into this "biblical theology." What Athanasius and Augustine, two of the greatest theologians of all times, had to do in reply was show that despite the impressive number of texts quoted, Arian theology did not reflect the fundamental drift of Scripture. By taking the whole of Scripture and its overall emphasis and foundational elements seriously, they found a way to refute the Arian reading of the Bible. They showed that what the Arians "proved" from Scripture actually stood in opposition to what was central to Scripture—

namely, the full divinity of Christ. In taking up this line of thinking and in constructing the ecumenical creeds on this basis, the early church established a theological center, a christological and evangelical hermeneutic, that was to guide all the church's interpretation of the Bible. All particular texts and interpretations must conform with what is central to Scripture. Interpretations that do not conform to this center were to be regarded, as we now say today, as being taken out of context and improperly interpreted.

From this story we learn that the theology we bring to Scripture can determine how we read Scripture. In other words, "our theology" is a presupposition. Only if the theology that we bring to Scripture rightly grasps what is fundamental to Scripture will the outcome reflect the "scope" of Scripture, the mind of God revealed in the Bible. What Athanasius and Augustine recognized before all others is that if the Bible is to shape and inform theology, then theology must also shape and inform exegesis. If these two things are not dynamically related, the Bible will become merely a source of texts that can prove whatever the clever theologian wants them to prove.

Confessing One's Presuppositions

I now confess my own primary presupposition on the question of the man-woman relationship. I believe that men and women should be regarded as equals in social life, including in the home and the church. I reject the idea that God's ideal is the subordination of women, however expressed. How have I come to this conclusion, you ask? To start, I have done so in the same way that Athanasius and Augustine came to the conclusion that texts which spoke of the Son's subordination should not be interpreted to speak of the eternal subordination of the Son. To eternally subordinate the Son, they believed, was to devalue the Son. I believe that to permanently subordinate women devalues women. In my reading of the Bible, especially the Gospels, I became convinced that there is something basically wrong with the thesis that Scripture permanently subordinates women to men. Surely if the subordination of women is one of the most important distinctives in God's perspective on the man-woman relationship, then Jesus would have raised this matter. The fact that Jesus says not one word on the subordination of women or wives—and that he says and does much that suggests the contrary—convinces me that it is not God's ideal.[6] In other words, my reading of the Gos-

---

[6]See the good outline on Jesus and women by D. M. Scholer, "Women," in *Dictionary of Jesus and the Gospels,* ed. Joel B. Green, Scot McKnight and I. Howard Marshall (Downers Grove, Ill.: InterVarsity Press, 1992), pp. 880–86. Most of the books in favor of women's per-

pels lead me to believe that any theology that devalues women in our world is in opposition to the mind of Christ revealed in Scripture.

However, it is not just my reading of the Bible that has led me to reach this conclusion. My life experiences also have influenced me profoundly. I was raised in a home where traditional patterns of male headship prevailed. I trained at a theological seminary where authoritative male headship was taught, and I accepted this teaching and its concomitant belief that this excluded women from ordination. When I married in 1968, I chose the Anglican marriage service in which the wife promised to obey her husband. Then the world began to change. Once married, I first discovered that determining who made decisions was far more complex than the teaching of male headship suggested. If my wife, Lynley, and I were to jointly own decisions, I found we had to make them together. The partnership model of marriage worked best. I saw this also in other marriages. The best and most rewarding marriages were partnerships of equals, where important decisions were made conjointly and amicably.[7] I also came to discover that women made excellent leaders. I saw women leading as ministers of state, judges, lawyers, school principals, teachers, doctors and generals in the Salvation Army.[8] I saw, too, inconsistency in the church. Women were sent out as missionaries to found and lead churches overseas, but when they came home they could not speak from the pulpit. Likewise, women who were leaders in the community were relegated to making tea and teaching children in Sunday school when they came to church. When I heard men telling women how important these jobs were—when they themselves did not want to do them—I was unconvinced. I could not help but conclude that this teaching and practice devalued the contribution of women.

Thirdly, I came to think that all the assertions of male headship by men are self-serving. They inflated the delicate male ego at the expense of the female ego.

---

manent subordination say very little on Jesus and women. When I pick up a book on the women issue, I always look at the contents page first and can tell immediately which side the author is on by the attention given to Jesus and the Gospels. Those on the hierarchical side ignore or say very little about Jesus; egalitarian books generally stress the importance of Jesus' stance towards women.

[7]No casting vote by the husband is needed. Usually with prayer and good will, every problem can be worked out to the satisfaction of both parties; and it is no problem if sometimes the husband concedes to the wife, for on another occasions she will gladly give way to his stronger wishes. In group discussion with those committed to the belief that the man must have the final say, time and time again I have found that when questioned, all happily married couples admit that often the wife is the wiser in knowing what is best for the family and the husband usually recognizes this. In other words, what couples say about headship often has no basis in how they interact and make decisions.

[8]I am thinking of Eva Burrows.

This theology demeaned and devalued women. In this new cultural context, women were granted equality of consideration; but when they came to church so often their pastor told them, "God wants you to remain subordinate to the men." Not surprisingly in this confused situation thousands of women have been hurt and wounded by this teaching. Its consequences have been destructive and its outcomes unjust and unfair. Good old Christian commonsense cried out, "There is something profoundly wrong with this whole approach." No quoting of texts can convince me otherwise. Hierarchical-complementarian theology devalues women. If this were my opinion alone, I would need to show great caution, but it is not mine alone. I dare to claim that this is basically the conclusion that most Western Christians have reached. The old subordinating theology no longer makes sense of their marriage, church life or much of what traditionalists claim the Bible says, and it sounds like one big male putdown of women.

It was at this point in my thinking that I began writing this book. I was conscious that my primary presupposition (God's ideal is equality of consideration) was challenged by the hierarchical-complementarians' growing insistence that both their primary presupposition (God's ideal is the subordination of women) and the claim that the correct starting point for any study of the Bible on this question is 1 Timothy 2:11–12 were confirmed by the orthodox doctrine of the Trinity. They were arguing that divine relations are a model for human relations, especially the man-woman relationship. Just as the Father is head over the Son, so husbands are head over their wives in the home and men are head over women in the church. If the persons in the Trinity are hierarchically ordered, as this argument presupposes, I would need to accept that my position was only one possibility or even concede my case altogether. My study of the orthodox doctrine of the Trinity has, however, not necessitated this. Indeed, it has confirmed absolutely my presupposition. I have been able to show that historical orthodoxy rejects the subordination of the Son in being or function. The Athanasian Creed affirms that "in this Trinity, none is afore or after other; none is greater, or less than another; . . . the whole three Persons are . . . co-equal." The creeds and the reformation confessions of faith make subordinationism in any form a heresy. If the orthodox doctrine of the Trinity in fact emphasizes that the Father and the Son are one in being and act/function, then on the hierarchical-complementarian premise that divine relations should be the model for man-woman relations, the egalitarian position is given the ultimate imprimatur. Equality of consideration is not one possible premise or presupposition on which to begin reading the Bible, it is the one God himself has revealed. Any other presupposition is wrong.

It almost seems that through the change in culture God is screaming out to us, "I have set women free in this period of history. I am the God who liberates and lifts up the downtrodden. I want you to read the Scripture afresh and discover that equality of consideration is my revealed will. I have made women and men alike in my image and likeness, and I have given them authority in my world. Change your ways. If your theology devalues women, it does not reflect my mind."

In seeking to read the Bible with this assumed premise or presupposition, I first rejected that the place to begin in working out what the Bible taught on the man-woman relationship is 1 Timothy 2, for starting there seems to immediately weigh the case in favor of the permanent subordination of women. Where else could the quest begin? I noted many began with Galatians 3:28, the so-called Pauline charter for emancipation, but as there was no agreement on the force of this text, I did not follow this route. At first I chose the teaching and example of Jesus. This is an excellent starting point, but in recent years I decided that the correct starting point is the one given in canonical revelation, Genesis 1:26–28. This primary affirmation of the equal dignity of women and men and their equal authority as rulers in God's world sets the stage for all that follows. Then in the last year, as I was completing my study of the historical development of the Trinity, I came to see that this starting point opened up the way to read the Bible according to three hermeneutical principles, modeled on those developed by Athanasius and Augustine, that would resolve this debate once they were accepted.

Rule 1. The proper staring point in any discussion on the man-woman relationship is the starting point given in canonical revelation, Genesis 1:26–28. At the climax of the prologue to the whole Bible, we are told God made one species, humankind, differentiated not by roles but by their God-given nature, who alike are made in the image and likeness of God and alike are given the mandate as rulers of God's world. This rule demands that nothing in Scripture be read to undermine or call into question the differentiated equality of the sexes as God's perfect will.

Rule 2. The Bible is always to be interpreted in line with its own primary forward-looking eschatological perspective. This means that God's ideal for the man-woman relationship is to be seen not in the Garden of Eden, where the devil was present and sin was a possibility, but in the perfection of the new creation in Christ that will be consummated in the last day. This rule demands the rejection of normative orders-of-creation theology because in looking backwards it contradicts what is foundational to biblical theology.

Rule 3. From these two hermeneutical rules the most important rule follows:

All texts that imply the equality of the sexes speak of God's ultimate eschatological ideal; all texts that speak of the subordination of women are culturally limited, time-bound, practical advice to women living in a culture that took for granted the subordination of women. This rule means that all the exhortations to women to be subordinate do not apply in our age and culture. If these texts have on-going relevance, they are simply reminders that in personal relationships Christians should gladly subordinate themselves to one another (Eph 5:21).

Adopting these theologically sound hermeneutical rules immediately illuminates biblical revelation. It discloses how the Bible may be read and should be read in a culture that has liberated women and accorded them equality of consideration. In outlining this way of reading the Bible I am not offering a possibility to be considered, I am arguing that *this is how the Bible should be read in our age* if we are to grasp its liberating moral and christocentric thrust, which affirms the equal value and potential for leadership of men and women. It is my belief that this is how God himself wants us to understand the Scriptures today. It is he who has liberated women in our time, and it is he who asks us to look in Scripture afresh to discover that equality of consideration for women and men in the world, the church and the home has always been his ultimate will. This is a theological reading of Scripture predicated on the belief that the equality of the sexes is the ideal revealed in the Bible and made possible in recent times by God's own work in history.

An Egalitarian-Complementarian Reading of Scripture

In summary form I now outline such a reading of Scripture.[9]

1. In creation, God made woman and man equal in dignity and status, giving to both authority and dominion over creation (Gen 1:27–28). They are male and female, differentiated by divine act, yet equal in essence/nature/being and in authority. Genesis 2 seeks to picturesquely elaborate on the polarity of the sexes. The solitary Adam on his own ("alone") is helpless, incomplete. No animal can meet his need for companionship. God's solution is to make woman, an equal partner, for the solitary Adam. In this creative act for the first time the two sexes stand side by side. Without Eve, Adam is not man distinct from woman; without Adam, Eve is not woman distinct from man. He cannot be, for man is man in distinction from and in relation to woman, just as woman is woman in

---

[9]I spell out this reading in more detail in my book *Created Woman* (Canberra, Australia: Acorn, 1985). There is nothing novel in this outline. Every point has good scholarly support, although each point is contested by those who begin with the presupposition that the Bible permanently subordinates women to men.

distinction from and in relation to man. It is not conceded that anything in Genesis 2–3 teaches that woman is subordinated to man before the Fall. Yet even if a hint of this can be found in some mute detail in the story, it would not be of any theological consequence. The whole Bible is determined by a forward-looking eschatology that sees perfection in the future.

2. The hierarchical ordering of the sexes is a consequence of the willful disobedience of Adam and Eve (Gen 3:16). Man's superordination and woman's subordination reflects the fallen order, not the creation order. This is not a tradition to be lightly dismissed. Luther taught that the subordination of women was introduced as a consequence of the Fall,[10] and the Roman Catholic Church today endorses this interpretation of the opening chapters of Genesis.[11]

3. Nowhere in the Gospels does Jesus ever speak of the subordination of women, and he says and does much to deny their subordination. This is amazing given that Jesus lived in a thoroughly patriarchal culture. It is true the twelve apostles were all men, but this is a mute historical detail and of no surprise in that cultural context.[12] However, no teaching is based on this fact. In any case, it would seem the twelve had to be men because the twelve were the counterpart of the twelve male patriarchs, the founding fathers of the new Israel, and because their main work was to be "witnesses" of the life, ministry, death and resurrection of Jesus (cf. Acts 1:21–22), something women could not legitimately do in Jewish society at that time.[13]

4. Luke makes Acts 2 programmatic for the new age that dawned with the gift of the Holy Spirit to all believers. In the new Spirit-endowed community, Luke, quoting the prophet Joel, says, "Your sons and your daughters shall prophesy," and then he repeats the point (Acts 2:17–18). In the patriarchal world of the first century, Luke accurately records that men assumed most leadership positions in the Jerusalem church and in the Pauline mission churches,

---

[10]Martin Luther, *Lectures on Genesis Chapters 1–5,* ed. J. Pelikan, trans. G. Schick, vol. 1 of *Luther's Works* (St. Louis: Concordia, 1958), p. 115.

[11]See John Paul II, *On the Dignity of Women* (St. Paul, Minn.: Homebush, 1988), pp. 32–46. In this exposition of the biblical teaching on women, the starting point is Genesis 1, and anything said on the status and dignity of women is tested against Jesus' teaching. In this theological study, women's subordination is explicitly grounded in the Fall.

[12]I do not, of course, hold that Jesus was a modern-day "women's libber." He was a man of his age and culture, as were all the Gospel writers. In that culture men did have precedence, and this is reflected in the Gospels by the prominence of men in the narratives. What is so amazing is that Jesus never endorsed these cultural values and sometimes challenged them.

[13]As Josephus explicitly states (*Jewish Antiquities* 4.219). See likewise Rabbi Akiba *m. Yevamot* 15:1.

but this in no way negates what he highlights as the essence of Spirit-endowed communal life. When the Spirit is present men and women may proclaim the word of the Lord in power. For Luke, *prophecy* is a term that can cover all Spirit-inspired speech.[14]

5. Paul's teaching on the ministry of the body of Christ presupposes that the Spirit can bestow the same gifts of ministry on women and men. These gifts of ministry, given to both sexes, are to be exercised in the congregation (Rom 12:3–8; 1 Cor 12—14; Eph 4:11–12). His practice, as a general rule, perfectly matches his theology. He speaks positively of women's prophesying, leading house churches and ministering in other undefined ways. He even commends a woman apostle (Rom 16:7). She is to be understood not as one of the twelve but as one of the larger number of missionary apostles, whom God has appointed in the church to be "first" (1 Cor 12:28; cf. Eph 4:11–12). The examples may be few, but their presence and number in this patriarchal cultural context are very significant. They show that, wherever possible, Paul put his nondiscriminatory theology of ministry into practice.

6. In 1 Corinthians 11 Paul insists that men and women be differentiated when they lead in prayer and prophecy by what they have or do not have on their head. There can be no dispute that Paul's primary reason for penning these words was to insist that when women lead in the congregation they do so as women and men do so as men. Whether or not Paul subordinates women to men in giving reasons for his primary concern is an insoluble question because both the language and the logic of his argument is unclear. He first says the man is the "head"[15] of the woman, and then he allows that as long as a woman has her "head" covered she can lead in the congregation in prayer and prophecy. Charles Hodge rightly points out that "praying and prophesying were the two principal exercises in the public worship of the early Christians."[16] Next Paul differentiates woman and man by their differing glory, which again could be read to imply woman's subordination, if he had not

---

[14]See my article "Prophecy, Prophets, False Prophets," in *Dictionary of the Later New Testament and Its Development,* ed. Ralph P. Martin and Peter H. Davids (Downers Grove, Ill.: InterVarsity Press, 1997), pp. 970–77.

[15]The force of this word in this context continues to be disputed. See the most recent discussion by Anthony C. Thiselton, *The First Epistle to the Corinthians* (Grand Rapids, Mich.: Eerdmans, 2000), p. 816. He concludes that while the Greek word *kephalē* (head) may not mean "source" in this context, it does not "denote a relation of 'subordination,' or 'authority over.' "

[16]Charles Hodge, *A Commentary on the First Epistle to the Corinthians* (London: Banner of Truth, 1958), p. 208. For a similar opinion by a recent commentator see Thiselton, *First Epistle,* p. 826.

gone on to speak of the "authority" of woman (1 Cor 11:10). In making these comments he says woman was made "for the sake of man" only then to add, "Nevertheless, in the Lord woman is not independent of man or man independent of woman. For just as woman came from man, so man comes through woman" (1 Cor 11:11). One of the few things we can be certain of in this passage is that here Paul endorses the public verbal ministry of women and men in the congregation. This is highly significant, for Paul judges prophecy to be the "second" most important ministry given by God to the church, behind apostleship and before teaching (1 Cor 12:28).

7. In Ephesians 5:23 Paul calls the husband the "head" of the wife, using the Greek word *kephalē* unquestionably in the sense of "boss." The word, however, is given new content. To be the "head" of one's wife, he explains, involves not rule but sacrificial, self-giving, *agapē* love. Jesus exemplifies this kind of leadership in his self-giving on the cross. It is the leadership of the servant who is willing to serve even to the point of giving one's life for the other. Not one word is said in this passage about who makes the final decision on important matters or about family management. In Ephesians 5:21ff. Paul is seeking in his cultural setting to transform patriarchy, not endorse it. When first read it would have been the men in that church who felt threatened by the countercultural teaching Paul enunciates. In its original historical context, this was a liberating text and should be read in this way today.

8. The apostolic exhortations to wives to be subordinate parallel the exhortations to slaves to be subordinate.[17] These admonishments stand side by side and are not to be distinguished in character or purpose. In both cases, practical advice is given to people living in the first century, where patriarchy and slavery were social norms. Nothing suggests that the exhortations to women alone are timeless precepts. Not one of these exhortations is grounded on an appeal to the creation stories. The only time Genesis is quoted in Ephesians is to affirm that in marriage husband and wife are one (Gen 2:24; Eph 5:31).[18]

9. The call to silence in 1 Corinthians 14:34–35, many scholars argue,[19] is to be seen as a later addition to the text; but if it is genuine, Paul is only asking wives to desist from asking questions in church. Paul's advice is, "If there is anything they desire to know, let them ask their husbands at home" (1 Cor 14:35).

10. The prohibition on women's exercising authority and teaching in church

---

[17]This will be substantiated in detail in part three of this book, which addresses slavery.

[18]Again, for proof see the following discussion on slavery.

[19]So Gordon D. Fee, *God's Empowering Presence* (Peabody, Mass.: Hendrickson, 1994), pp. 272-81.

in 1 Timothy 2:11–12 is addressed to a particular situation.[20] This text is to be understood against the backdrop of false teaching that had erupted in Ephesus, which had led both men and women astray. Women had been allowed to teach in church, since Paul first founded the church several years previously, but now he forbids them from doing so.[21] He changes his policy to meet the specific challenge facing the church. What the women had been teaching had deceived many. The reasons he gives for this exceptional command reflect the exceptional problem addressed, although we do not know exactly what it was. Women are not to claim to be first for Adam was created first, and they are not to teach for it was Eve who was first deceived. These are ad hominem arguments that were telling and applicable to the problems found in that church at that time. They were meant to counter the arrogance of some women and their opportunities to give false teaching. Elsewhere, in more theological passages, Paul insists that "in Christ, there is a new creation: everything old has passed away" (2 Cor 5:17) and that Adam is responsible for sin (Rom 5:12ff.). In 1 Corinthians 11:3ff. Paul uses similar ad hominem arguments based on the creation stories to establish a case for women's covering their heads when leading in prayer and prophecy in the church and for men's leaving their heads uncovered—a cultural practice virtually no one thinks is binding today.

One should note in this reading of the Bible that the canonical ordering of what is given in biblical revelation is followed. The starting point is where the Bible starts: Genesis 2—3 is read in the light of Genesis 1. In the New Testament, the starting point is Jesus and the Gospels. Acts comes next, followed by the early Paul, and the late Paul in the Pastorals comes last. On this preferred reading of the Bible on the man-woman relationship, the one difficult passage (1 Tim 2:11–15) comes last, and in this place it appears as a problem text to be explained in the light of all the teaching that has preceded it. In this position it stands out like a proverbial sore thumb.

In this reading of the Bible, 1 Timothy 2:11–15 is taken to be a classic example of the text in tension with the overall drift of Scripture. Such a text in tension can be found when one seeks to work out what the Bible teaches on any major doctrine. If one gives prominence to isolated comments that do not match up with the dominant teaching of Scripture, then theological error invariably re-

---

[20]The best exposition of 1 Tim 2:11–14 is given by I. Howard Marshall, *The Pastoral Epistles* (Edinburgh: T & T Clark, 1999), pp. 437–67.

[21]1 Tim 2:11–12 presupposes that women were teaching in church. This means that there was no apostolic prohibition in force before this epistle was written. Paul does not remind them of his policy; he gives a new ruling.

sults. For example, James 2:14–26 taken in isolation could be used to prove salvation is by works; Acts 8:4–24 could be used to prove that everyone needs a second work of the Spirit to be a Spirit-filled Christian; and Revelation 20:1–3 could be used to prove that there will be a literal thousand-year period on earth, in which Satan is vanquished, before the end. Years ago the Reformed New Testament scholar Oscar Cullmann, in discussing this phenomenon in relation to Romans 13:1–7, which was quoted by some Christians to prove that complete and unquestioning allegiance to the state was demanded of Christians, said reading Romans 13 in isolation made this text stand in

> flagrant contradiction to the teaching of Jesus. It would also contradict the opinion of other New Testament authors as well, chiefly that of the author of the Johannine apocalypse. Above all, Paul would contradict himself.[22]

From this observation he formulated the general rule that "the fountainhead of all false biblical interpretation and all heresy is invariably the isolating and absolutizing of one single passage."[23] Cullmann describes exactly what has happened by making the Timothy passage the defining text in the debate over the man-woman relationship.

Which Theology of the Sexes Is to Be Endorsed?

Now we are at the point where we can ask the question, which of the two contemporary competing theologies of the sexes is to be endorsed *in our day and age?* From Athanasius and Augustine we have learned that when different biblical texts can be used to support competing theologies, we must first get our basic theology right, if we are to "hear" aright the Scriptures. The proper way to read the Bible has to be established first.

The hierarchical-complementarian position is to be rejected because it presupposes a certain theology of the sexes, which it then uses to interpret problematic biblical material. It comes to Scripture assuming that God instituted in creation a permanently binding social order that set men over women in the church and the home, and then it finds proof-texts to substantiate this opinion. It brings in an appeal to the eternal subordination of the Son to the Father to give added support to this social ordering. Just as the Father is the head of the Son, so men have been given headship over women in the church and the home. This position cannot be right because of the reasons outlined below:

☐ It contradicts the basic biblical premise that woman and man alike are made

---

[22]Oscar Cullmann, *The State in the New Testament* (London: SCM Press, 1963), p. 46.
[23]Ibid., p. 47.

in the image and likeness of God and alike are given dominion over the earth.

☐ It presupposes that the ideal lies in the past, whereas as far as the Bible is concerned the ideal lies in the future—in the perfecting of the creation on the last day.

☐ It ignores the noble vision of women held by Jesus.

☐ It interprets certain texts in such a way that they stand in conflict with other texts.

☐ It subverts the orthodox doctrine of the Trinity.

☐ Moreover, in the end it demeans women. It implies that in some way women are inferior to men, for God has not given them potential for leadership. *In our age and culture,* this teaching is unjustifiable and unjust.

A wrong reading of the Bible results because those who argue this position begin with wrong theology. Their conclusion is a case justifying male hegemony and privilege, supported by proof-texts and the promulgation of a doctrine of eternal subordination of the Son, whom the Bible confesses is the Lord. By appealing to the Bible, they attempt to turn back the clock, although God's work in history has moved on and led us to see what beforehand was hidden to human eyes—namely, that men and women are equal in status, dignity and potential for leadership. God has made us women and men, differentiated but not hierarchically ordered in being or function.

What makes me particularly suspicious of this case is its attempt in a period of profound social change to give biblical support to a social ordering that has been undermined by God's work in history in recent times and by his work in Jesus Christ in past times. It maintains that God has appointed men to lead women and that to oppose this social order is to oppose God. However, the Bible and the best of sociology suggest that all social ordering is in fact a human construct. The nation of Israel could freely decide to move from a twelve-tribe alliance to monarchy and later to high priestly rule. In the flow of history, forms of government change; oppressive oligarchies are overthrown; and the way men and women relate in the world, the church and the home change, as we have seen happen in the last thirty years.

Five things positively indicate that the alternative reading of Scripture outlined above is the one to be preferred and endorsed by Christians today.

☐ The egalitarian-complementarian reading embraces the "scope" of Scripture better than any other position. This reading of the Bible, as I have set it out, is more comprehensive in scope and it integrates far better the diverse comments about women in the Scriptures than any other reading. It makes the best sense of everything the Bible says about women. It makes primary what the Bible puts first: man and woman alike made in the image and likeness of God and together given dominion in God's world. In particular it gives rightful emphasis to the teaching and example of Jesus, who anticipated the emancipation of women by never suggesting that they were subordinate to men. With Paul's epistles it brings into harmony his theology of Spirit-given ministry that is not gender-specific and his practice of ministry. He accepts that women prophesy in church, he commends a woman apostle, he speaks of women house-church leaders, and for many years he allowed women to teach in church at Ephesus, until he introduced his prohibition toward the end of his life (cf. 1 Tim 2:11–12).

☐ It captures the moral vision of the Bible, in which everyone is to be treated fairly and equitably. This insight must never be ignored in the hermeneutical quest. An interpretation of the Bible cannot be right unless it leads to right action.[24] The Bible demands that all human beings be treated fairly and equitably because all are made in the image and likeness of God. This truth is most consistently worked out in the words and works of Jesus. He insisted that God loved and valued every human being equally.

☐ It mirrors the orthodox understanding of the God of Christian revelation, the most fundamental of all Christian doctrines and the one that should inform all other doctrines. This depicts the triune God as three persons equal in divinity, majesty and authority, abiding together in a bond of loving communion and harmony, none being before or after the other: they are one in being and action. Such is their self-giving that after the resurrection the Father makes the Son the head of all things. Since God made man and woman in his image, we assume the relations between the sexes as God originally intended should reflect something of the relations within the Godhead. Divine relations set the ideal.

☐ It is a reading of Scripture that can provide a Christian perspective on the sexes that is meaningful and helpful for the world in which we find ourselves. It emphasizes the God-given dignity, freedom and leadership potential of women and men; it affirms the differences between the sexes; and it underlines the complementarian nature of the man-woman relationship. This theology stands in opposition to those who would demean women, reject God-given sexual polarity or devalue marriage as the supreme expression of how woman and man complement and enrich each other in the most intimate life-long union.

---

[24]See Roger Lundin, Anthony C. Thiselton and Clarence Walhout, *The Responsibility of Hermeneutics* (Grand Rapids, Mich.: Eerdmans, 1985).

☐ It makes human beings, not God, responsible for social ordering. In history, time and time again, Christians have appealed to the Bible in support of the status quo. In arguing that God himself has instituted a social order that sets men over women in the home and the church, contemporary hierarchical-complementarians are making a mistake that has been made many times in the past. This argument is always expounded by those who hold the reins of power. It was once voiced by kings and aristocrats opposed to democratic forms of government. It was heard in the American Old South in support of slavery. And it was expressed by Reformed Christians in South Africa in support of apartheid. It is an ideology of self-interest. A responsible social ethic accepts that social ordering is always a human construct and that as such human beings can change it. God wants the oppressed liberated.

PART 3

THE SLAVERY TRADITION

Rejected by All—Some in Ignorance, Some in Painful Awareness of Its Past Consequences

10

THE PROSLAVERY TRADITION

The Bible Endorses the Institution of Slavery

Contemporary hierarchical-complementarians want to completely separate the discussion on slavery from the discussion on women, but this is not possible, for there are close parallels between them. Both the Old and New Testaments accept slavery and the subordination of women as facts of life without direct criticism. In the Epistles, women and slaves are exhorted to be subordinate in the same context on several occasions. Paul relates the two when he declares, "There is no longer Jew or Greek, there is no longer slave or free, there is no longer male and female; for all of you are one in Christ Jesus" (Gal 3:28). In addition, for many centuries after the New Testament was completed, the realities of slavery and the subordination of women were taken for granted and endorsed by Christians. Virtually no one questioned either matter. No one argued that the subordination of women or slavery should be repudiated. Then cultural values made a seismic shift. First slavery came to be seen as inherently unjust, and then later the same happened for women's subordination. In these changed cultural contexts, theologians of all persuasions have had to consider afresh what they thought the Bible taught about slavery and, later, women. Some broke with the tradition and pioneered new ways of reading the Bible; others sought to uphold the status quo by an appeal to the Bible. In this chapter, we are going to outline how the slavery tradition came to be rejected and how evangelicals have dealt with this change. I hope that from this historical example of a change in the interpretation of the Bible generated by a change in cultural values, we will learn something that may inform us on the present debate on the relationship of the sexes.

In arguing, as I will, that virtually no difference can be seen in the way the Bible discusses slavery and the subordination of women, I am not arguing that the Bible suggests wives should be treated like slaves or that those who today endorse the permanent subordination of women support the ill treatment of women. We are agreed that the Bible values men and women equally and teaches men to respect and love their wives. The "headship" of men can be and often is used to justify verbal, emotional and physical violence against women,[1] but evangelical theologians who write in support of this doctrine always condemn such behavior. The parallel I want to underline is not between the realities of slavery and the social life of women but between how the Bible speaks of slavery and the subordination of women. In both cases I argue that the Bible takes for granted these two things—never directly questioning them—and it can be (and has been) read to endorse them.

Slavery Defined

Before progressing further, it should be made clear what is involved in slavery. Many conservative evangelicals, as part of their apologetic for the Bible's apparent acceptance of slavery, tell us that slavery is only a form of ordinary work. Robert Yarbrough, in *Women in the Church,* clearly outlines this approach, which is common among evangelicals. "The modern equivalent of slaves has not disappeared," he maintains. "It is present in the form of those who work for a living . . . which means virtually everyone."[2] He then spells out his case further:

> The same curse that decreed sweat from the brow and thorns from the earth and that lay behind the social expression that was slavery in the ancient Near East

---

[1] See J. B. Brown and C. R. Bohn, eds., *Christianity, Patriarchy and Abuse* (Cleveland: Pilgrim, 1989).

[2] Robert Yarbrough, "The Hermeneutics of 1 Timothy 2:9-15," in Andreas J. Köstenberger, Thomas R. Schreiner and H. Scott Baldwin, eds., *Women in the Church: A Fresh Analysis of 1 Timothy 2:9–15* (Grand Rapids, Mich.: Baker, 1995), p. 187. Yarbrough is responding to my article "The Biblical Argument for Slavery: Can the Bible Mislead? A Case Study in Hermeneutics," *Evangelical Quarterly* 66, no. 1 (1994): 3–18. This chapter is a rewrite of that article's material, developing the argument differently. Other evangelicals who equate slavery and work include George Knight, *The New Testament Teaching on the Role Relationship of Men and Women* (Grand Rapids, Mich.: Baker, 1977), p. 24; Susan Foh, *Women and the Word of God* (Phillipsburg, N.J.: Presbyterian & Reformed, 1980), p. 141.

takes the form of a much different social order today—and yet is very similar in essence. A few still reign, and most still serve them with the best efforts of their productive years. . . . In reality the abolition of serfdom and slavery was only the abolition of an obsolete form of slavery that had become unnecessary, and the substitution for it of a firmer form of slavery, and one that holds a greater number of people in bondage.[3]

These assertions strike me as a very negative view of work to come from a Christian. But the point I wish to contest is the claim that slavery is only one form of human labor that involves virtually everyone. Scholars who have critically studied the phenomenon of slavery are of a completely different mind. They set in stark contrast slavery and all other forms of work, even forced labor. All are agreed that slavery is a "peculiar institution," but what is distinctive about slavery continues to create debate. D. B. Davis gives three defining characteristics of a slave: slaves in their person are the property of another human being, their will is completely subject to their owner's authority, and their labor is obtained by coercion.[4] The idea of the legal status of the slave as property is the chief distinguishing mark that goes back to antiquity. M. I. Finley, while noting a number of characteristic features of slavery, still thinks the defining element is that the slave is always considered property: he or she is "owned" by someone.[5] The slave

> suffered not only total loss of control over his labor but also total loss of control over his person and his personality: the uniqueness of slavery, I repeat, lay in the fact that the laborer himself was the commodity, not merely his labor or labor power.[6]

This debate moved forward with the publication of *Slavery and Social Death: A Comparative Study,* the very important sociological and historical study of slavery published in 1982 by Orlando Patterson.[7] He agrees that the slave is always the property of someone, but he argues that defining a slave simply in

---

[3]Yarbrough, "Hermeneutics of 1 Timothy 2:9-15," pp. 187–88.
[4]D. B. Davis, *The Problem of Slavery in Western Cultures* (Cornell, N.Y.: Cornell University Press, 1966), p. 31.
[5]M. I. Finley, *Ancient Slavery and Modern Ideology* (London: Chatto & Windus, 1980), p. 77. On defining slavery see also L. B. Scherer, *Slavery and the Churches in Early America 1619–1819* (Grand Rapids, Mich.: Eerdmans, 1975), pp. 13–17; J. A. Harrill, *The Manumission of Slaves in Early Christianity* (Tübingen: Mohr, 1995), pp. 13–14.
[6]Finley, *Ancient Slavery,* pp. 74–75.
[7]Orlando Patterson, *Slavery and Social Death: A Comparative Study* (Cambridge, Mass.: Harvard University Press, 1982).

these terms is inadequate. His starting point is that "all human relationships are structured and defined by the relative power of the interacting persons."[8] Three essential elements in the power relationship between the master and the slave distinguish slavery from all other forms of domination and all other forms of work. These are as follows:

Slavery is distinctive in the extremity of power conferred. The master's total domination over the slave is normative and a constituent feature of this relationship. Slaves are coerced to work by the threat or exercise of violence against them. Patterson says, "There is no known slaveholding society where the whip was not considered an indispensable instrument."[9]

Slavery is distinctive because it involves "natal alienation."[10] The slave is a socially dead person. She or he is alienated from her or his family of origin and has no right to establish a family with ongoing relationships. Slave couples can not have an exclusive, lifelong union; and if they have children, these can be sold like one would sell a calf. Slavery for women involves sexual availability. Patterson says, "Natal alienation goes right to the heart [of slavery]. . . . The loss of ties of birth in both ascending and descending generations. . . . This is true, at least in theory, of all slaves, no matter how elevated."[11]

Slavery is distinctive in that the slave is a "dishonored" person. Slaves can have no honor as human beings because they have no power and no independent existence. Owning a slave or slaves bestows honor on the master and degrades the slave. Patterson says that slaves consistently spoke of "the crushing and pervasive sense of knowing that one is considered a person without honor and there is simply nothing that can be done about it."[12]

A number of differences between slavery in the Roman Empire in the first century and slavery in America's Old South in the eighteenth and nineteenth centuries may be noted,[13] but in both contexts the three constituent elements

---

[8]Ibid., p. 1.
[9]Ibid., p. 4.
[10]Ibid., p. 5.
[11]Ibid., p. 7.
[12]Ibid., p. 12.
[13]S. Bartchy, *Mallon Chresai: First-Century Slavery and the Interpretation of 1 Corinthians 7:21* (Missoula, Mont.: Scholars Press, 1973), pp. 67–82, discusses these differences, three of which have great significance: in the Roman world slavery was not based on color, slaves could expect manumission one day, and the vast majority of slaves were captives rather than born into slavery. These things were not true of nineteenth-century slavery in the Old South. Much is made of the differences between slavery in these two contexts by Brian Dodd in *The Problem with Paul* (Downers Grove, Ill.: InterVarsity Press, 1996), pp. 85–91. Recent specialized comparative studies of slavery stress the similarities and relativize the differences. See, for example, Patterson on race and color (*Slavery and Social Death,* pp. 177–79).

given by Patterson were present. Modern comparative studies of slavery like Patterson's have completely overthrown the idealistic view that somehow slavery in the first century was a humane and kindly institution.[14] In the first century slaves in the Roman Empire, if they were not born into captivity, were captured in war, taken away in chains, sold naked in slave markets and often branded with a hot iron. Whatever their origin they were forced to work by the threat of violence to their person, and the women were used sexually. In both the Roman Empire and in the Old South, the way slaves were treated could differ greatly. Some had humane and kindly masters, some did not. Some were forced to work until they dropped, others were not. However, these variations in no way limited the awfulness of slavery as an institution.[15] Slaves were, in the first instance, property owned by someone who could do with them as they wished, and the threat or use of violence secured their labor. The primary instrument to "break" slaves in the Roman Empire and in the Old South was the whip.

Slavery is to be contrasted, not compared, with working for a living—no matter how backbreaking the work or poor the conditions. It is a distinctive expression of human domination in which the worker is considered to be property and in which his or her labor is achieved by coercion.

The Historical Tradition: The Bible Regulates and Legitimates Slavery

The evidence from tradition is consistent and transparent. Until modern times, most Christians believed that the Bible regulated and legitimated slavery.[16] This is the tradition—the way the Bible had been understood for almost nineteen centuries. The apostolic fathers, the Apologists, Clement of Alexandria, Origen

---

He demonstrates that race and color were significant in Roman slavery. In regard to manumission he notes that the rate of Roman manumission in the country where most slaves labored was "very low" and was "high" in urban areas (pp. 274, 282). See also his description of slavery in the Old South, which indicates its similarity with Roman slavery (pp. 206–7).

[14]Bartchy, following many older classicists' studies, adopts this idealized view of slavery in the first century. On the realities of slavery in the Roman empire, see also the important symposium "Slavery in Text and Interpretation" (ed. A. D. Callahan, R. A. Horsley and A. Smith, *Semeia* 83/84 [1998]). See esp. Horsley's essay "The Slave Systems of Classical Antiquity and Their Reluctant Recognition by Modern Scholars," pp. 19–66. See also See M. I. Finley, ed., *Slavery in Classical Antiquity: Views and Controversies* (Cambridge: Cambridge University Press, 1960), and Murray J. Harris, *Slave of Christ: A New Testament Metaphor for Total Devotion to Christ* (Leicester, U.K.: Apollos, 1999).

[15]On the slave trade and the phenomenon of black slavery from the fifteenth to nineteenth centuries, see the definitive study by H. Thomas, *The Slave Trade: The History of the Atlantic Slave Trade 1440–1870* (London: Papermac, 1997).

[16]Davis, *Problem of Slavery*, pp. 87–89; Thomas, *Slave Trade*, pp. 12, 29–30, 35, 65, 71–72, 124–25, 146–56, 449, 464, 582, 665.

and John Chrysostom all wrote in support of slavery.[17] In A.D. 362 the Council of Gangrae laid an anathema on "anyone [who] under the pretense of godliness should teach a slave to despise his master, or withdraw himself from his master."[18] The early church fathers endorsed slavery on the basis that the apostles had accepted slavery. However, they also argued that one's station in life was of minimal importance. What was important was to be a believer, "a slave of Christ."

In Augustine the justification of slavery was given a more profound basis. He argued not only that slavery, along with other hardships in life, was a consequence of the Fall but also that God appointed both the master and the slave to their positions in the prevailing social hierarchy. In depicting the reigning social order as fixed and given by God, Augustine baptized into Christianity a view of social ordering that owed more to Plato and Aristotle than to the Bible.[19] This conception of a social order that justified slavery dominated from this time on and was given classic expression by Thomas Aquinas, who argued mainly on this basis that slavery was acceptable to God.[20] This same conservative understanding of social ordering, with its concomitant endorsement of slavery, is seen in Martin Luther, John Calvin[21] and many of the Puritans.[22] Cotton Mather, George Whitefield and Jonathan Edwards owned slaves with good conscience.[23] The evidence is overwhelming. Until the middle of the eighteenth century, slavery was accepted as a fact of life; virtually no one thought of it as evil or sinful, and the theologians who wrote on this topic argued that slavery was acceptable to God and legitimated by the Bible.

It was only late in the eighteenth century that for the first time in human

---

[17]On the apostolic fathers, see the good summary of the evidence by S. Bartchy, "Slave, Slavery," *Dictionary of the Later New Testament and Its Developments,* ed. Ralph P. Martin and Peter H. Davids (Downers Grove, Ill.: InterVarsity Press, 1997), pp. 1098–1102. On the others mentioned, see A. Rupprecht, "Attitudes on Slavery Among the Church Fathers," in *New Dimensions in New Testament Study,* ed. R. N. Longenecker and M. C. Tenney (Grand Rapids, Mich.: Zondervan, 1974), pp. 261–77.

[18]Davis, *Problem of Slavery,* p. 89.

[19]Rupprecht, "Attitudes on Slavery," pp. 271–73; Davis, *Problem of Slavery,* pp. 88–89, 90, 93.

[20]Davis, *Problem of Slavery,* pp. 94–97.

[21]Rupprecht, "Attitudes on Slavery," p. 273. For substantiation see *John Calvin's Sermons on Ephesians* (London: Banner of Truth, 1973), pp. 633–47. See also John Calvin *Institutes of the Christian Religion* 2.8.46, ed. J. T. McNeil, trans. F. L. Battles (London: SCM Press, 1960).

[22]Davis, *Problem of Slavery,* pp. 105–6, 247, 199–205. On the New England Puritans in particular, see Scherer, *Slavery and the Churches,* pp. 33–39, 66–67.

[23]On Mather see Scherer, *Slavery and the Churches,* p. 64. He speaks of "scores of New England ministers" owning slaves. On Whitfield see Davis, *Problem of Slavery,* pp. 148, 213, 385, 387–89; on Edwards see p. 388.

history people began to question the morality of slavery and to suggest that it
was both evil and sinful. We will discuss later this revolution in thought on slavery. At this point, I want to outline the most detailed attempt to justify slavery
by appealing to the Bible this world has ever seen. Just as voices were growing
in ever-stronger tones against slavery, a small group of privileged evangelical
and Reformed theologians in the Old South gave themselves to creating what
might be called a "biblical theology of slavery." When other evangelical Christians were increasingly denouncing slavery as sinful and the case for abolition
was growing in strength, these men applied their able minds to perfecting a
theology that endorsed slavery and maintained the status quo, almost entirely
by appeal to the Bible. They deliberately and defiantly set themselves against
this profound step forward in human social awareness that the case for abolition represented. Those who made the biggest contribution in this exercise
were the best evangelical and Reformed theologians and biblical scholars of
the day: Robert Louis Dabney, James Henry Thornwell and the learned Charles
Hodge of Princeton—fathers of twentieth-century evangelicalism and of the
modern expression of the doctrine of biblical inerrancy.[24] As late as 1957 John
Murray of Westminster Theological Seminary was still arguing that these men
were basically correct in their understanding of the Bible. He too argues that
the Bible endorses the institution of slavery.[25] He speaks of it as "a divine institution."[26]

In the protracted debate with other Christians, these evangelicals were able
to refine their "biblical" arguments for slavery to such a point that they could
summarily dismiss any counter arguments made by appeal to the Bible. They
were totally convinced that the Bible was on their side. Because these defenders
of slavery had the very highest doctrine of Scripture and developed their argument in the face of unmitigated opposition, what they concluded is very significant.[27]

---

[24]See D. F. Wells, *Reformed Theology in America* (Grand Rapids, Mich.: Eerdmans, 1985).

[25]John Murray, *Principles of Conduct* (London: Inter-Varsity Press, 1957), pp. 93–102. Murray
accepts that Scripture endorses slavery, but to safeguard himself he takes up the argument
popularized by Thornwell that slavery is only the property of one man in the labor of
another, not the property of man in man. This is special pleading. Slavery by definition
involves owning the person and his labor.

[26]Ibid., p. 96.

[27]See H. Shelton Smith, *In His Image, But . . . : Racism in Southern Religion, 1780–1910*
(Durham, N.C.: Duke University Press, 1972). See also W. S. Jenkins, *Pro-Slavery Thought in
the Old South* (Chapel Hill: University of North Carolina Press, 1935); Willard Swartley, *Slavery, Sabbath, War and Women: Case Issues in Biblical Interpretation* (Ontario: Herald, 1983),
pp. 31–66.

The defenses of slavery written with the pens of these evangelicals are legion and should be read in the original. The most accessible original sources are the collection of essays in the book *Cotton Is King and Pro-Slavery Arguments*[28] and the Banner of Truth reprints of the writings of Dabney,[29] Thornwell[30] and Hodge.[31] No one can appreciate how certain these evangelicals and others were that the Bible endorsed slavery or appreciate the force of their argumentation unless something from their writings is read. I can only give a pale reflection of their righteous zeal for "the biblical case for slavery."

The Biblical Case in Summary

The exegetical case made to justify the institution of slavery can be summarized in five points.

1. Slavery established. "The curse on Ham" (Gen 9:20–27) was taken to be the divine initiation of slavery.[32] The Genesis text tells us that when Noah woke from a drunken stupor and discovered one of his sons, Ham, had seen him naked, he cursed him saying, "Lowest of slaves shall he be to his brothers" (Gen 9:25). In the first instance this story was quoted to prove that God himself instituted slavery. Thus Alexander McCaine, a Southern evangelical minister, quite

---

[28]E. N. Cartwright, ed., *Cotton Is King and Pro-Slavery Arguments* (1860; reprint, New York: Basic Afro-American Reprint Library, 1968).

[29]Robert Louis Dabney, *Discussions: Evangelical and Theological,* 3 vols. (London: Banner of Truth, 1981); T. C. Johnson, ed., *The Life and Letters of Robert Louis Dabney* (Edinburgh: Banner of Truth, 1977). Dabney's biblical arguments for slavery can be found in volume 3 of his *Discussions,* pp. 33–38. In volume 2 he outlines his opposition firstly to the ordination of women and secondly to the ordination of Negroes. The parallels in his arguments are instructive. Archibald Alexander, the great Reformed scholar, called Dabney "the best teacher of theology in the United States, if not in the world." (This quote is taken from the dust jacket of the reprint of Dabney's *Discussions.*) I was not able to obtain his "full biblical case for slavery," entitled *The Defense of Virginia and the South,* to which he refers in the above works.

[30]*The Collected Writings of James Henry Thornwell,* ed. D. M. Palmer, 4 vols. (London: Banner of Truth, 1986). His defense of slavery is mainly found in *Collected Writings,* 4:387–436. He also refers to other writings of his on this matter that were not available to me.

[31]Dabney and Thornwell argue that the Bible endorses the institution of slavery and that therefore it is pleasing to God. Hodge is more moderate in his wording. His extended defense of slavery is found in his essay "The Bible Argument for Slavery," in *Cotton Is King and Pro-Slavery Arguments,* ed. E. N. Cartwright (1860; reprint, New York: Basic Afro-American Reprint Library, 1968), but it is also given briefly in his *A Commentary on the Epistle to the Ephesians* (London: Banner of Truth, 1964), pp. 365–66.

[32]See further on this text, L. R. Bradley, "The Curse of Canaan and the American Negro," *Concordia Theological Monthly* 42, no. 2 (1971): 100–110; G. P. Robertson, "Current Questions Concerning the Curse of Ham (Gen. 9:20–27)," *Journal of the Evangelical Theological Society* 41, no. 2 (1998): 177–88; R. Hood, *Begrimed and Black: Christian Traditions on Blacks and Blackness* (Minneapolis: Fortress, 1994), pp. 129–30, 155–63.

typically concluded that Noah "spoke under the impulse and dictation of heaven. His words were the words of God himself, and by them was slavery ordained. This was an early arrangement by the Almighty, to be perpetuated for all time."[33]

Professor Murray is of the same opinion. This text, he says, "is the first overt allusion to slavery in the scripture. It is apparent that it is a curse upon the sin perpetuated by Ham." But even if slavery originated because of sin, Murray adds, this does not make it "intrinsically wrong": slavery is "a divine institution."[34] God himself initiated and established slavery.

The second deduction drawn from this passage was that this curse made Negroes a slave people. Ham was taken as the father of the Negro race, Shem was the father of the Semites, and Japheth was the father of the white race. The opinion that this passage instituted slavery is a very old tradition: the tradition that singles out Negroes as a race of slaves appears much later, gaining a hearing only from the sixteenth century onwards. Much of the nearly four hundred pages of the Reverend Josiah Priest's book *Bible Defense of Slavery*, first published in 1855, is given to proving this connection, as we read here:

> The appointment of this race of men to servitude and slavery was a judicial act of God, or, in other words, was a divine judgment. . . . We are not mistaken in concluding that the Negro race, as a people, are judicially given over to a state of peculiar liability of being enslaved by other races.[35]

Priest held that the fulfillment of this curse was found in the subjection of Negroes by white Americans (the descendants of Japheth) with "God's permission and blessing."[36] It needed to take place, he argued, to establish the truthfulness of the Holy Scriptures.

> "The servitude of the race of Ham, to the latest era of mankind, is necessary to the veracity of God Himself, as by it is fulfilled one of the oldest of the decrees of the Scriptures, namely that of Noah, which placed the race as servants under other races."[37]

Many commentaries early in the twentieth century were still endorsing these two deductions. Among twentieth-century evangelicals who wrote in support of

---

[33]Alexander McCaine, "Slavery Defended from Scripture," quoted in Smith, *In His Image*, p. 130.
[34]Murray, *Principles of Conduct*, p. 96.
[35]Josiah Priest, *Bible Defense of Slavery* (1855; reprint, Detroit: Negro History Press, 1969).
[36]Ibid., p. 289.
[37]Ibid., p. 393.

these views, we can list not only John Murray but also Arthur Pink, Basil Atkinson and Griffith Thomas.[38] Here we need to recall that until very recently, most white people thought that they were ordained by God to lead the black races, and for this reason this interpretation of the Noah story went unquestioned. In South Africa, the Reformed Church, until the overthrow of apartheid, also repeatedly appealed to this text to support the right of whites to rule over blacks.

2. *Slavery practiced.* The fact that all the patriarchs had slaves was taken to be of great significance. Abraham, "the friend of God" and "the father of the faithful," brought slaves from Haran (Gen 12:5); armed 318 slaves born in his own house (Gen 14:14); included them in his property list (Gen 12:16; 24:35); and willed them to his son Isaac (Gen 25:5). What is more, Scripture says God blessed Abraham by multiplying his slaves (Gen 24:35). In Abraham's household, Sarah was set over Hagar, a slave. The angel tells her, "Return to your mistress, and submit to her" (Gen 16:9).[39] Joshua took slaves (Josh 9:23), as did David (2 Sam 8:2, 6) and Solomon (1 Kings 9:20–21). Likewise, Job, whom the Bible calls "blameless and upright," was "a great slaveholder."[40] If these godly men held servants in bondage, it was impossible, therefore, to consider slave holding a sin. To argue otherwise was the sin. A. B. Bledsoe says the "sin of appalling magnitude" is not slave holding but the claim by the abolitionists that slave holding is a sin. To suggest such a thing was "an aggravated crime against God."[41]

3. *Slavery sanctioned and regulated by the moral law.* The fact that slavery is twice mentioned in the Ten Commandments (the fourth and tenth) was seen to be very important in revealing the mind of God. The ceremonial law was temporary, but not the moral law—this perfectly reflected the mind of God. Here as elsewhere it was pointed out that God himself regulated slavery by legislating how masters were to behave toward their slaves. The question was thus put to the abolitionists, would God regulate by legislation what he thought was intrin-

---

[38]Arthur Pink, *Gleanings in Genesis* (Chicago: Moody Press, 1922), p. 126; Basil Atkinson, *The Pocket Commentary on the Bible: Genesis* (Chicago: Moody Press, 1957), p. 97; Griffith Thomas, *Genesis: A Devotional Commentary* (Grand Rapids, Mich.: Eerdmans, 1953), pp. 95–99.

[39]See A. B. Bledsoe, "Liberty and Slavery" (pp. 338–40), and T. Stringfellow, "The Bible Argument, or Slavery in the Light of Divine Revelation" (pp. 464–72), in *Cotton Is King and Pro-Slavery Arguments,* ed. E. N. Cartwright (1860; reprint, New York: Basic Afro-American Reprint Library, 1968), or in more detail, J. H. Hopkins, *A Scriptural, Ecclesiastical and Historical View of Slavery, from the Days of the Patriarch Abraham to the Nineteenth Century* (New York: W. J. Moses, 1864), pp. 76ff.

[40]So Stringfellow, "Bible Argument," pp. 470–71. He refers to, e.g., Job 1:15–17; 3:19; 4:18; 7:2; 31:13—where Job speaks of his slaves.

[41]Bledsoe, "Liberty and Slavery," p. 340.

sically wrong? In replying to their own question, they said that the existence of this legislation indicated God approved of slavery. The importance of these references to slavery in the Decalogue are seen in the address "To all the churches of Jesus Christ," published by the General Assembly of the Presbyterian Church of the Confederate States of America in December 1861. It began, "God sanctions slavery in the first table of the Decalogue, and Moses treats it as an institution to be *regulated,* not abolished; legitimated and not condemned."[42] The sanctioning of slavery in the Law was a fundamental element in the biblical case for slavery. The argument was that the specific apostolic commands to slaves to accept their lot in life were not simply practical advice to slaves living in the first century, they were timeless, transcultural directives predicated on the moral law.

And it was not simply that God permitted slavery, he commanded it. In Leviticus 25:44–46, where God is said to be speaking, the Jews are told, "It is from the nations around you that you may acquire male and female slaves. . . . You may keep them as a possession for your children after you, for them to inherit as property." The Reverend James Smiley, an old-school Presbyterian, took this to mean that God had given "a written permit to the Hebrews, then the best people in the world, to buy, hold and bequeath, men and women, in perpetual servitude."[43] Hodge summed up the conclusions of these evangelicals when he wrote, "The fact that the Mosaic institutions recognized the lawfulness of slavery is a point too plain to need proof, and is almost universally admitted."[44]

4. Slavery accepted by Jesus. The Gospels do not record a single word spoken by Jesus that could be read to explicitly endorse slavery, a point the abolitionists were quick to note. However, the Southern evangelicals who adamantly held that the Bible sanctioned slavery found this objection no problem. They noted that in the Gospels the specific term for a slave *(doulos)* is found over seventy times. In some of the best known parables, slaves are prominent characters (e.g., Mt 13:24–30; 18:23–35; 22:1–14; Lk 12:35–40; 14:15–24); and Jesus often encountered slaves (e.g., Lk 7:2–10; 22:50), yet he offered not one word of criticism of slavery. He was quick to attack moral evil, but not slavery. His silence, rather than being a criticism of slavery, these Southern evangelicals argued,

---

[42]Quoted in Smith, *In His Image,* p. 196. I have italicized the word *regulated,* which in this sentence implies approval. Slavery is "legitimated" by God himself. Contemporary evangelicals also speak of God's "regulating" slavery, implying that God does not approve of slavery, he only regulates it.

[43]Quoted in ibid., p. 132. For a similar opinion see also Bledsoe, "Liberty and Slavery," p. 340, and Stringfellow, "Bible Argument," p. 476.

[44]See Hodge, "Bible Argument for Slavery," p. 859.

showed that he approved of slavery. T. Stringfellow sums up the case thus:

> I affirm then, first (and no man denies) that Jesus has not abolished slavery by
> prohibitory command: and second, I affirm, he has introduced no new moral
> principle which can work its destruction, under the Gospel dispensation: and the
> principle relied on for this purpose is a fundamental principle of the Mosaic law,
> under which slavery was instituted by Jehovah himself.[45]

But even if the Gospels did not contain any explicit endorsement of slavery,
it was pointed out that Paul sanctioned slavery on the basis of Jesus' teaching.
In 1 Timothy 6:1–3 slaves are told to accept their status and obey their masters
because this is commanded by "our Lord Jesus Christ." In reply to those who
claim Jesus did not endorse slavery, Stringfellow says this verse proves otherwise: "If our Lord Jesus Christ uttered such words, how dare we say he has been
silent? If he [were] silent, how dare the apostle say these are the words of our
Lord Jesus Christ?"[46]

5. *Slavery endorsed by the apostles*. Although the Gospels may not say anything explicit about slavery, the Epistles are different. In no fewer than seven
passages the apostles demand that slaves accept their lot in life, often adding
that masters should treat their slaves kindly (1 Cor 7:20–21; Eph 6:5–9; Col 3:22–
25; 1 Tim 6:1–3; Tit 2:9–10; Philem 10–18; 1 Pet 2:18–19). For many evangelicals
who felt their conscience was bound by the letter of Scripture, it was clear that
the apostles endorsed slavery. In most instances, their instructions to slaves
were given in parallel to instructions to wives to be subordinate and children to
be obedient. They reasoned that to reject the comments about slavery called into question the authority of husbands and parents. It was obvious that the apostles held these matters to be of equal force.[47] In commentating on the related
exhortations in Ephesians, Hodge reasons,

> What the Scriptures teach, is not peculiar to the obedience of the slave to his mas-
> ter, but applies to all the other cases in which obedience is regulated. . . . It
> applies to children in relation to their parents and wives to their husbands. Those
> invested with lawful authority are the representatives of God. The powers (i.e.,

---

[45]Stringfellow, "Bible Argument," p. 480.

[46]Ibid., pp. 488–89.

[47]Modern-day supporters of the permanent subordination of women claim the exhortations to
slaves are profoundly different from those to wives and women, an argument we will
explore in due course. This claim was opposed by the proslavery theologians. They were
united in seeing these exhortations as of one kind. See, e.g., Bledsoe, "Liberty and Slavery,"
p. 354; Stringfellow, "Bible Argument," pp. 480–81; Hodge, "Bible Argument for Slavery," pp.
848–49; Thornwell, *Collected Writings*, 4:386.

those invested with authority) are ordained by God.[48]

The instructions to slaves, Hodge noted, were grounded on weighty theology. Slaves were to be subservient and content with their lot because this is how they were to serve Christ (Eph 6:5; Col 3:22), honor God (1 Tim 6:1; Tit 2:10) and learn the Christian virtue of suffering (1 Pet 2:20-21). The example of Onesimus, which the abolitionists were wont to quote, was shown to point in the opposite direction. Paul's sending this Christian slave back to his Christian master proved that the institution of slavery was sacred to the apostle.[49]

All the discussions on slavery in the Old South point out that the Pauline texts played a pivotal part in the biblical case for slavery. Texts from Paul were the passages on which white preachers based their frequent sermons on slavery. When addressing white congregations, preachers quoted Paul as endorsing slavery; when addressing black congregations, preachers quoted Paul as demanding that slaves accept their lot in life if they wanted to please Christ and be saved. Brian Dodd says, "Thousands of expository sermons were preached on these texts, sending many of the half million Southern soldiers to their deaths confident that God was on their side."[50]

The essence of "the biblical argument for slavery" was that "human bondage" is grounded in the unchanging moral law, accepted by Jesus and unambiguously endorsed by the apostles. If slavery was depicted in the Bible as pleasing to God, it could not be sinful to buy, own or sell slaves. Behind these "biblical" arguments lay two premises or presuppositions thought also to be biblical: God instituted and maintained the social order, and the Negro was a subservient race, created for bondage. On the second matter little needs to be added. We have already noted how the story of the curse of Ham was understood to make the Negroes a slave race. We are thus not surprised that Dabney concludes, "The Negro . . . is a subservient race; he is made to follow, and not to lead,"[51] and that Alexander Stephens, the vice president of the Confederate States, wrote that "the Negro is not equal to the white man; slavery—subordination to the su-

[48]Hodge, *Paul's Epistle,* p. 366. Hodge was not alone in arguing this way. See C. Martin, "Somebody Done Hoodoo'd the Hoods Man: Language, Power, Resistance and the Effective History of Pauline Texts in American Slavery," in *Slavery in Text and Interpretation,* ed. A. D. Callahan, R. A. Horsley and A. Smith, *Semeia* 83/84 (1998), pp. 216–17.

[49]This would seem to be the historical meaning of Paul's letter. See J. M. G. Barclay, "Paul, Philemon and the Dilemma of Christian Slave-ownership," *New Testament Studies* 7 (1991): 161–86; M. Barth and H. Blanke, *The Letter to Philemon* (Grand Rapids, Mich.: Eerdmans, 2000). So also Dodd, *Problem with Paul,* pp. 102–5.

[50]Dodd, *Problem with Paul,* p. 84.

[51]Dabney, *Discussions,* p. 203.

perior race—is his natural and normal condition."[52] The only other thing we
need to note is that this premise discloses the racial prejudices of these Southern
evangelicals. They assumed that white people were superior to blacks. In modern terms, they were racists.

The premise that social ordering is established and sanctioned by God and
thus is inviolable plays an important part in the contemporary evangelical case
for the permanent subordination of women, as we have already noted. This idea
is also foundational to the biblical case for slavery as evangelicals in the Old
South developed it. These supporters of slavery thought civilization would be
brought to its knees if the prevailing, God-given social order were called into
question. Dabney described "[social] order as heaven's first law"; he believed
that subordination of women and Negroes "is the inexorable condition of peace
and happiness, and this as much in heaven as on earth."[53] "Men are not naturally
equal, in strength, talent, virtue, or ability," he continues, "and different orders
of human beings naturally inherit different sets of rights and franchises."[54] Social
order, he insisted, is "founded in the unchangeable laws of nature."[55] In a similar
vein Thornwell called social order "an ordinance of God."[56] Finally, we quote
Hodge, who wrote, "Order and subordination pervade the whole universe, and
is essential to its being. . . . If this concatenation be disturbed in any of its parts,
ruin must be the result."[57]

For all these men the essence of this ordering was its hierarchical character.
At the top of the social hierarchy stood free white men, then white women and
finally black slaves. God himself ordered society, placing "masters and servants
[i.e., slaves], each in their respective spheres."[58] Because this hierarchical social
order was established by God, it could not be thought to be unjust or unfair.
The slave has been, according to Thornwell, "assigned to a particular position
in this world by the Almighty."[59] In the conflict over the abolition of slavery,
Thornwell held that on one side stood "the friends of order," such as himself,
and on the other stood "Atheists, Socialists, Communists, Red Republicans and
Jacobins."[60] These "friends of order" believed the Bible taught that hierarchical

---

[52]Quoted in Smith, *In His Image,* pp. 183–84.
[53]Dabney, *Discussions,* p. 112.
[54]Ibid., p. 116.
[55]Ibid.
[56]Thornwell, *Collected Writings,* 4:406.
[57]Charles Hodge, *A Commentary on the First Epistle to the Corinthians* (London: Banner of
  Truth, 1958), p. 206.
[58]Thornwell, *Collected Writings,* 4:428.
[59]Ibid., 4:430.
[60]Ibid., 4:405.

social ordering was God-given and unchanging. They were unaware that this conception of inviolable social order had its roots in Greek philosophy, not the Bible. Because the prevailing social order gave them an advantage, they were not able to see that the Bible allowed changes in social ordering and that the Bible itself called on men and women to be instruments of social change when confronted by social sin, such as the slavery before their very eyes.

The force of this cumulative argument for slavery, based primarily on biblical exegesis, is impressive. Those who propounded this "biblical theology" thought it was irrefutable. In 1835, the Presbyterian Synod of West Virginia fiercely assailed the case for abolition, calling it "a dogma" contrary "to the clearest authority of the word of God."[61] In 1845, the Old School Presbyterian Assembly decreed that slavery is based on "some of the plainest declarations of the Word of God."[62] Thomas Smith added, "Upon this rock [the Bible] let the South build her house, and the gates of hell shall not prevail against it."[63] Thornwell, in an even more combative spirit, said, "Our policy is to push the Bible argument [for slavery] continually, drive abolitionism to the wall, to compel it to assume an anti-Christian position."[64] Hodge assumed a similar stance, writing, "If the present course of the abolitionists is right, then the course of Christ and the apostles was wrong." To call slavery sinful, he added, was "a direct impeachment of the Word of God."[65] Finally, I quote Albert Bledsoe:

> The history of interpretation furnishes no examples of more willful and violent perversions of the sacred text than are found in the writings of the Abolitionists. They seem to consider themselves above the Scriptures: and when they put themselves above the Law of God, it is not wonderful that they should disregard the laws of men. Significant manifestations of the result of this disposition is to consider their own light a surer guide than the Word of God.[66]

Such quotes could be multiplied many times over. These Southern evangelicals, steeped in Reformed theology, committed to the authority of Scripture, were totally convinced that the Bible endorsed both the practice and the institution of slavery. Nothing upset them more than the repeated attacks by those wanting to abolish slavery. How could anything clearly taught by Scripture possibly be wrong, let alone sinful, they asked. The only conclusion they could

---

[61]Smith, *In His Image*, p. 79.
[62]Quoted in Murray, *Principles of Conduct*, p. 260.
[63]Quoted in Smith, *In His Image*, p. 172.
[64]Quoted in ibid., p. 136.
[65]Hodge, "Bible Argument," p. 849.
[66]Bledsoe, "Liberty and Slavery," pp. 379–80.

draw, when the abolitionists attacked them for enslaving the Negro, was that the abolitionists did not stand under the authority of Scripture. Frequently they called them "heretics" and "infidels."[67] When war broke out between the North and the South, large numbers of the Southern clergy took up arms against the "infidel" Yankee because they believed the authority of Scripture was at stake. Dabney was chief of staff for Thomas Jonathan ("Stonewall") Jackson.[68] These men were willing to kill or be killed because, for them, the authority of Scripture was the fundamental issue. The loss of the war did not change their mind. Southern evangelicals, until fairly recently, remained virtually united in their belief that the Bible sets whites over blacks and endorses and legitimates slavery. Sadly, it must be admitted that the Scriptures interpreted through the eyes of self-interest led them astray.

The evidence is clear. For almost nineteen centuries, Christians believed that the Bible endorsed and legitimated both the institution and the practice of slavery. In the nineteenth century the best Reformed theologians developed this tradition into an impressive biblical theology of slavery. They quoted extensively from the Old and New Testaments, they argued lucidly and convincingly, and they were able to integrate scriptural teaching into a coherent system. If it is held that Christians should believe that every word in the Bible is timeless truth—to be obeyed in every age, excepting those parts abrogated by the death of Christ—and that Scripture always speaks with one voice, then it is hard to see how this case can be overthrown. As noted above, Murray was arguing in 1957 that theologians who wrote in support of slavery were correct in their reading of the Bible. "No scripture," he says, indicates "the intrinsic wrong of slavery."[69] Indeed "the uniform witness of the New Testament . . . recognizes not only the fact of slavery, but its *legitimacy*."[70] It is "a divine institution."[71]

This "biblical" case for slavery, which is almost universally regarded now as mistaken and self-serving, is far stronger than the case for the permanent subordination of women put forth by some evangelicals today. Their case basically rests on one text, 1 Timothy 2:11-14. Even if they maintain that several other texts support their case, the truth remains. The "biblical" case for slavery is far more impressive than the "biblical" case for the permanent subordination of women.

---

[67]Smith, *In His Image*, pp. 187–97; Thornwell, *Collected Writings*, 4:405.
[68]See details in Smith, *In His Image*, pp. 189ff.
[69]Murray, *Principles of Conduct*, p. 100.
[70]Ibid., p. 102; italics added for emphasis.
[71]Ibid., p. 96.

The Southern evangelical understanding and interpretation of the Bible blinded these men from seeing the evil of slavery before their eyes.

There were some unique elements to slavery in the Old South, such as its permanency and the color factor. In the Roman Empire of the first century, the master could be black and the slave white, or vice versa, and the slave could expect to be emancipated one day. Some slaves in the Roman Empire were also well educated. Nevertheless, slavery is slavery, and there were more similarities than contrasts between slavery in the first century and slavery in the nineteenth century. In the Old South, as a general rule, slaves experienced far less thought- less cruelty than did those in the Roman Empire, for the South was a predomi- nantly Christian community. There were no mass killings of slaves, nor were slaves used in gladiatorial fights. Nevertheless, slavery in the Old South was as cruel and dehumanizing as it was in the Roman Empire: blacks did not have any control over their own life, they were slaves in perpetuity, their children were born into slavery, they were forbidden formal education, they were severely punished for any act of disobedience, their families were commonly split up as children were sold off, and the women were always vulnerable to the sexual advances of white men, whom they were powerless to resist.[72] This is to say nothing of frequent whippings and many other forms of punishment. Slavery in the Old South was a "heinous sin," as the abolitionists repeatedly claimed. These evangelical and Reformed theologians opposed gross cruelty to slaves and the sexual exploitation of the women, but they did not oppose the institution itself. In supporting the institution so strongly by appealing to the Bible, they allowed for the worst of the abuses to continue unchecked. Though this terrible injustice was constantly before their eyes and their fellow Christians were crying out to them to show some insight and compassion, these men remained steadfast, holding on to their understanding and interpretation of the Bible. Somehow, the Bible blinded them from seeing the evil of slavery.

The Presuppositions Behind This Theology
Behind this biblically grounded endorsement of slavery lay a number of inter- locking theological presuppositions:

☐ The God of the Bible has established and sanctioned the existing social

---

[72]There are several excellent collections of original documents that describe slavery in the Old South. The most significant is Theodore Weld's *American Slavery as It Is: A Testimony of a Thousand Witnesses* (1839), republished in *Slavery in America,* ed. R. O. Curry (Itasca, Ill.: Peacock, 1972). See also W. L. Rose, ed., *A Documentary History of Slavery in North America* (Oxford: Oxford University Press, 1976); N. R. Yeldman, ed., *Life Under a Peculiar Institution* (New York: Reinhart & Wilson, 1970).

order. He appoints both the master and the slave to their allotted positions. To rebel against the God-given social order prescribed by the Bible is to rebel against God.

☐ The social order instituted and endorsed by God cannot be sinful or immoral. In any case, social ordering is not a moral issue. Sin is an individual breach of the moral law.

☐ The Negro race is a subordinate race. Negroes are inferior to whites. They are not equipped by God for leadership.

☐ The Bible is the word of God,[73] and what Southern biblical scholars say it says is what God says.

☐ Because God is always of one mind, the Bible's teaching on any issue is uniform.

☐ What the Bible says applies in exactly the same way in every age and culture, and what it says must be obeyed. In other words, the Bible's message in its entirety is transcultural, transparent and prescriptive.

☐ Theology is simply an ordered account of what the Bible says.

To overthrow this theology of slavery, four things were needed:

☐ The repudiation of the presuppositions on which the theology of slavery was built.

☐ The rejection of what the proslavery theologians insisted was the primary question: Can the Bible be read to legitimate slavery or not? Proslavery theologians were able to convincingly answer this question in the affirmative, as we have shown, because as a historical document, the Bible reflects the ideas of those who came from an age when slavery was a taken-for-granted reality. The primary question that the nineteenth-century evangelical supporters of slavery needed to ask was in fact this: Can slavery be legitimated *in our age and culture* when abolition is a possibility, when the cruelty and injustice of slavery cannot be denied and when other evangelical Christians are telling us that we are using the Bible to serve our own ends?

☐ The realization that the Bible often speaks with more than one voice on impor-

---

[73]I confess, naturally, that the Bible is the Word of God, but this confession can mean different things to different people. I personally am sympathetic to the explanation given by Donald G. Bloesch, *Holy Scripture: Revelation, Inspiration and Interpretation* (Downers Grove, Ill.: InterVarsity Press, 1994), particularly pp. 40–44, 120. In contrast to the scholastic view, which equates the words in the text with God's words, and the liberal view, which separates them, Bloesch advocates a sacramental-like connection. The words of Scripture are human words that communicate the word of God. He says, "The Bible is not in and of itself the revelation of God but the divinely appointed means and channel of this revelation" (p. 57). See also Stanley J. Grenz and J. R. Franke, *Beyond Foundationalism: Shaping Theology in a Postmodern Context* (Louisville, Ky.: Westminister John Knox, 2001), pp. 57–92.

tant issues. The theological quest is not finding texts that support what is believed but working out what is primary and secondary in Scripture at a theological level. ☐ The recognition that interpretative outcomes that degrade and devalue other human beings are always wrong. The principle is that biblical interpretation cannot be right if it does not result in right action.

In nineteenth-century America's Old South, virtually no one was willing to consider these options, and as a result, a terrible civil war was needed to bring emancipation. In the twentieth century, a new way of reading these slavery texts developed. And now, in the twenty-first century, as I am about to show, evangelicals cannot believe that other evangelicals so recently quoted the Bible to endorse slavery. The tradition is deliberately ignored or denied for apologetic reasons. Many evangelicals do not want to face the fact that some of the best of evangelical theologians in the nineteenth century convincingly interpreted the Bible to prove that slavery was pleasing to God.

11

THE REJECTION OF THE
PROSLAVERY TRADITION

F rom the very beginning of the Christian faith a tension existed between
slavery and the freedom promised by the gospel. The good news was that in
Christ, believers gained universal emancipation from bondage of one kind or
another. Jesus spoke of his ministry in terms of setting people free (Lk 4:18–19;
Jn 8:36). Similarly, Paul asserted frequently that the gospel liberates people
(Gal 5:1; cf., e.g., Rom 8:15; 1 Cor 7:22–23; Gal 1:4; 2:4; 4:31). However, neither Jesus nor the apostles ever condemn slavery. They said much that would
condemn treating slaves cruelly, but challenging abuses is not the same as
challenging the institution itself. It would seem that both Jesus and the apostles
accepted slavery as a fact of life, as did everyone else in their time. There were
no movements for the abolition of slavery in the ancient world.

This tension—between slavery and freedom in Christ—reflects the eschatological tension that underlies the whole New Testament. In the coming of Christ
the new age dawned, but the final and complete realization of the new age is
yet to come. In between what is now and what is yet to come sin continues,
and one way sin is manifested is in the subjugation of the weak. Jesus and the
apostles lived with this tension between the "now" and the "not yet" but never
abandoned it. Galatians 3:28 is the clearest indicator of this tension in Paul. In
this verse Paul speaks of a oneness in Christ that places on an equal footing Jew
and Greek, slave and free, male and female. In regard to the Jew-Gentile relationship, Paul saw barriers broken down in his time by the gospel, which

formed one new community, the church (Eph 2:11–22). For the slave-free and man-woman relationships, he sought simply to alleviate the worst abuses. He apparently could not imagine a world in which such social ordering could be transcended. Thus he gave instructions to husbands and wives, as well as masters and slaves, on how to conduct themselves as Christians living in a culture that accepted the subordination of women and the institution of slavery. It is thus not surprising that subsequent Christians living in cultures that accepted slavery saw only the more common and extended apostolic teaching that could be interpreted to legitimate slavery. When the assumption was added by Augustine that social ordering was God-given and inviolable, it was virtually impossible for anyone to think that the Bible might question rather than endorse the institution of slavery.

God himself had to act in history to open the eyes of people to the cruelty and injustice of slavery. He needed to change cultural values so that the hints in Scripture that slavery was part of the fallen order, doomed to pass away, could be seen. This change took place in a particular moment in human history—early in the second half of the eighteenth century. At that time a small number of men came to the conclusion that slavery was a terrible evil, and they began to attack it, seeking to abolish it from the face of the earth. Christians of various persuasion—Quakers, latitudinarians and evangelicals—and the leading exponents of Enlightenment ideals came to this realization at roughly the same time.[1]

The first to denounce slavery as sinful and abhorrent to God was Benjamin Lay, a Quaker who published a tract condemning slavery in 1736, in which he called it "a hellish practice . . . the greatest sin in the world."[2] Within fifty years, Quakers in England and America came to agree with Lay, and they pioneered the cause of the abolition of slavery. In 1774, after reading a Quaker tract denouncing slavery, John Wesley followed their lead and wrote against slavery. He had seen the awful degradation of the Negro slaves firsthand in the American colonies, and he needed little convincing. For him the God revealed in Jesus Christ was a God who was opposed to injustice, cruelty and the denial of human freedom. Soon other English evangelicals came to the same conclusions and began working for the abolition of slavery. This discovery of the social conscience among Christians found its secular counterpart in the great Enlightenment think-

---

[1] D. B. Davis, *The Problem of Slavery in Western Cultures* (Cornell, N.Y.: Cornell University Press, 1966), and H. Thomas, *The Slave Trade: The History of the Atlantic Slave Trade 1440–1870* (London: Papermac, 1997), tell this story in some detail.

[2] Quoted by Davis, *Problem of Slavery,* p. 291.

ers of that time. The grand figure of the Enlightenment was, of course, Voltaire, who laughed at "those who call themselves white . . . [but] proceed to purchase blacks cheaply in order to sell them expensively in the Americas."[3] He also mocked the Roman Catholic Church for having accepted slavery. However, D. B. Davis believes it was Charles-Louis Montesquieu who "did the most to undermine the pro-slavery" case.[4] Montesquieu argued that there was a law higher than the law of any land—a law of nature that excluded, among other things, slavery because it was contrary to the public good. It debased one group of people, exalted another and corrupted public morals.[5] It is to be noted, nevertheless, that Montesquieu's views were somewhat confused. He seems to have accepted the propriety of enslaving the black races, which he thought were not fully human.[6] This was not the case with Jean-Jacques Rousseau, who rejected slavery absolutely, describing it as the final manifestation of the degrading and idiotic principle of authority.[7] He argued that all were born free and equal and that to deprive people of their freedom was to deny them their humanity. Rousseau's concerns were wider than slavery: he, like other Enlightenment thinkers, wrote to free the European mind from the shackles of tradition, authority and superstition. He attacked slavery because it was a classic example of where the existing social order was justified contrary to reason and at the expense of the disenfranchised.

It was not, however, the great Enlightenment thinkers who gave themselves unreservedly to the abolition of slavery. It was Christians, particularly evangelical Christians. In England, Wesley's stand against slavery inspired a small number of gifted and influential evangelicals, known as the Clapham Sect, led by Sir William Wilberforce, to commit themselves to the cause of abolition. They faced relentless opposition from the most influential and powerful of their day, including some of the bishops of the Church of England, but this did not deter them. As a result of their efforts, the slave trade was abolished in the British Empire in 1807 and outlawed in 1833. In the United States, evangelicals likewise led the opposition to slavery. Charles J. Finney, the greatest evangelist of his day, was untiring in his opposition to slavery. He preached that the gospel condemned not only individual sin but also social sin. As far as he was concerned, the worst

---

[3]Quoted by Thomas, *Slave Trade*, p. 462.
[4]Davis, *Problem of Slavery*, p. 402.
[5]Charles-Louis Montesquieu, *The Spirit of Laws* (Cambridge: Cambridge University Press, 1989), bk. 15, p. 246, 251.
[6]Ibid., bk. 15, p. 250.
[7]See the excellent discussion of Rousseau's views in Thomas, *Slave Trade*, p. 464.

social sin of his day was slavery. As a young man Theodore Weld was converted by Finney's preaching. The abolition of slavery became for him an all-consuming passion. In his book, *The Bible Argument Against Slavery,* he argued that the basic principles the Bible enshrined were in direct opposition to slavery:

> Slavery seeks refuge in the Bible only in its last extremity. . . . Goaded to a frenzy in its conflicts with conscience and common sense . . . it courses up and down the Bible, "seeking rest and finding none." The law of love, glowing on every page, flashes through its anguish and despair.[8]

John Newton (1725–1807), who composed "Amazing Grace" and many other wonderful hymns, lived through this time of cultural and moral change. His story is an instructive example of how Christians came to change their thinking on slavery in this brief period of history. He was dramatically converted in 1748 but continued as the captain of a slave ship until 1754, when he left the sea because of ill health. After his conversion he introduced prayers twice on Sundays for the crew, but he thought nothing of the slaves in chains below deck, and it never crossed his mind that what he was doing might be displeasing to almighty God. He accepted what most men of his time took as axiomatic: Negroes were a subordinate race created by God to be slaves. As Marcus Loane writes,

> He felt no sense of scruple at this wretched traffic in human life; he was the child of an age which saw no scandal in that hateful market of murder and man-stealing. . . . No voice had yet reached his conscience to condemn the horrors of the slave trade.[9]

As late as 1764, when Newton published *An Authentic Narrative,* the account of his dramatic conversion, he showed no remorse for having been involved in the horrors of the slave trade he would later describe so vividly. He lists the sins that made him fear hell, but they are all personal and individual sins: blasphemy, the ridicule of Scripture, coarse language and possibly sexual immorality.[10] His change of thought on slavery and the slave trade comes to light for the first time some thirty-nine years after his conversion, in 1787, when he wrote

---

[8]Theodore Weld, *The Bible Argument Against Slavery* (1865; reprint, Detroit: Negro History Press, 1970), p. 13.

[9]Marcus Loane, *Oxford and the Evangelical Succession* (London: Lutterworth, 1950), pp. 98–99. Exactly the same conclusion is drawn by D. B. Hindmarsh in *John Newton and the English Evangelical Tradition: Between the Conversion of Wesley and Wilberforce* (Oxford, Clarendon, 1996), p. 22.

[10]See further on this Hindmarsh, *John Newton,* pp. 57–58.

Thoughts on the African Slave Trade.[11] This moral awakening came not through the study of Scripture or through personal revelation, but through the effect of the growing weight of opinion, especially among his evangelical friends, that slavery was both evil and sinful. In this new cultural and social context he changed his mind.

The English evangelicals who led the crusade against slavery believed that the gospel had the power to transform the individual *and* society. For them sin was not simply an individual transgression displeasing to God, it also had a social dimension. Human selfishness—the essence of sin, for them—manifested itself in social sins, epitomized in slavery. In a special sense they were "universalists." They believed in the universal sinfulness of human beings, in the universal love of God and in the universal provision of salvation for all who believed in Christ. No class or race was thus to be treated differently, and in particular Negroes were not to be thought of as inferior to whites. Instead of seeing Africa as a place where heathen savages were to be bought as slaves, they thought of the Negroes, like themselves, as those for whom Christ had died. They began sending missionaries to Africa to proclaim the gospel.

It is to be noted that they believed "doing" theology was far more than gathering together texts from the Bible to support what one believed. For Wesley and subsequent evangelicals committed to the abolition of slavery, the horrors of the slave trade and the brutality of slavery were the starting point for theological reflection. What condemned slavery was the most basic command in the Christian faith: to love one's neighbor as one's self. All other passages in Scripture bearing on Christian behavior had to be interpreted in the light of this one fundamental rule. No text could ever be read to negate this law. This meant that, for them, the Christian faith laid down principles which spelled the downfall of slavery. They saw their time as the season God had appointed to abolish slavery once and for all. Humankind had invented slavery, and with God's help, they believed they could eradicate this evil from the face of the earth.

Slavery in Evangelical Thought Today: Regulated but Not Legitimated

The overwhelming majority of contemporary evangelicals—along with virtually all other Christians—accept the condemnation of slavery that came after the 1750s. It is agreed that slavery is an evil. To take from those who have done nothing wrong their freedom, to force them to work by coercion, to be free to

---

[11]John Newton, *Thoughts on the African Slave Trade,* republished in vol. 6 of *The Works of John Newton* (London: Banner of Truth, 1985), pp. 521–48.

punish them without constraint if they do not obey, to sexually use them at will if they are female and to deny them basic rights—this would be sinful. Most Christians, in fact, think the Bible condemns slavery, and nowhere is this more strongly asserted than in conservative evangelical literature. Sherwood Wirt in his book *The Social Conscience of the Evangelical* says, "The New Testament (considers) trafficking in human lives . . . on a level with impure drinking water, highway robbery, and leprosy. Slavery . . . is an evil."[12] He makes much of evangelicals' contribution to the battle to abolish slavery, but he neglects to mention that for many centuries Christians generally supported slavery and that evangelicals in the nineteenth century led the campaign in America against the abolition of slavery.[13] Similarly, Thomas Schreiner, writing in 2001, concludes that "slavery is an evil human institution."[14]

The editors of and the contributors to *Recovering Biblical Manhood and Womanhood* never mention that until modern times most Christians thought that the Bible legitimized and endorsed slavery. On each of the book's 566 pages, this fact is ignored. In contrast to the tradition, the argument put forth by the editors holds that the Bible unambiguously disapproves of slavery, that it lays down the grounds "for slavery's dissolution."[15] In reply to those who connect the emancipation of women and slaves, the editors say that even if "some slave holders in the nineteenth century argued in ways parallel with our defense of distinct roles in marriage, the parallel was superficial and misguided."[16] Surely, this is a slight overstatement. The case for slavery was defended not by "some slave holders" but by the best evangelical theologians of the day; and even if it was "misguided," it certainly was not "superficial." Later in this same volume, we are told the Bible does not "approve" of slavery, it only "regulates" an existing institution, just as Moses regulated divorce.[17]

The editors of and contributors to *Women in the Church* similarly ignore or dismiss the tradition. It is true that Robert Yarbrough, in response to my case

---

[12]Sherwood Wirt, *The Social Conscience of the Evangelical* (London: Scripture Union, 1968), p. 17.

[13]Ibid., pp. 17, 35–36, 39, 88.

[14]Thomas R. Schreiner, "Women in Ministry," in *Two Views on Women in Ministry,* ed. Craig L. Blomberg and J. R. Beck (Grand Rapids, Mich.: Zondervan, 2001), p. 216.

[15]John Piper and Wayne Grudem, eds., *Recovering Biblical Manhood and Womanhood: A Response to Evangelical Feminism* (Wheaton, Ill.: Crossway, 1991), p. 65; cf. p. 159.

[16]Ibid., p. 66.

[17]George W. Knight, "Husbands and Wives as Analogues of Christ and the Church: Ephesians 5:21-33 and Colossians 3: 18-19," in *Recovering Biblical Manhood and Womanhood: A Fresh Response to Evangelical Feminism,* ed. John Piper and Wayne Grudem (Wheaton, Ill.: Crossway, 1991), p. 177.

that the best of nineteenth-century Reformed theologians endorsed slavery, admits they "deserve criticism" and their arguments deserve "not a little . . . rejection." However, he then muddies the water by adding that

> if Southern reformed "historic" hermeneutics should be blamed for endorsing the
> social order of its day with all its attendant ills, then Giles' theology, which
> defends and enshrines the modern liberal social order of emancipation, must
> share the guilt of the wars, the injustices and inequities . . . in the modern world.[18]

The charge is so absurd I can think of nothing to say in reply. This same deliberate passing over of tradition and denial that the Bible may be, and has been, read to support and legitimate slavery is seen in Murray J. Harris's book *Slave of Christ*.[19] He insists that while the Bible accepts slavery as a fact of life, it cannot be read as approving of it in any way. We are led to assume that no one has ever thought otherwise. The tradition is ignored. Again, we are told the Bible only "regulates" an existing institution as it regulates divorce without ever implying approval—not a very convincing argument.[20]

In all the books advocating the permanent subordination of women we see the same thing: the slavery tradition is ignored or denied; and we are told the Bible cannot be read to give any support to slavery, that indeed it implies the sinfulness of slavery. George Knight, in his formative 1977 book, *The New Testament Teaching on the Role Relationship of Men and Women,* argues exactly in this way.

> Does Paul's instruction for slaves and masters mean that the scriptures regard this
> relationship as a God-ordained institution to be perpetuated? The answer with
> which we must respond . . . is no. The apostle Paul instructs men and women in

---

[18]Robert Yarbrough, "The Hermeneutics of 1 Timothy 2:9-15," in Andreas J. Köstenberger, Thomas R. Schreiner and H. Scott Baldwin, eds., *Women in the Church: A Fresh Analysis of 1 Timothy 2:9–15* (Grand Rapids, Mich.: Baker, 1995), p. 186.

[19]Murray J. Harris, *Slave of Christ: A New Testament Metaphor for Total Devotion to Christ* (Leicester, U.K.: Apollos, 1999).

[20]Ibid., pp. 61–65. To argue that the Bible only regulates slavery does not prove anything. Everyone agrees the Bible regulates slavery. For nearly nineteen centuries, Christians thought the Bible regulated *and thus* legitimated slavery. Today many evangelicals argue the Bible regulates slavery but does not legitimate it. The example of divorce does not help. In this case the Bible definitely regulates divorce but never legitimates it: "I hate divorce, says the LORD" (Mal 2:16). When the Pharisees quoted Moses' regulation on divorce, Jesus annulled Moses' concession. He insisted that lifelong fidelity was the creation ideal. He refused to regulate what he did not approve. Where, we might ask, does the Old Testament say God hates slavery or where does Jesus suggest it is an expression of the hardness of the human heart? The way the Bible treats divorce and the way it treats slavery are better contrasted than compared.

the situation in which they find themselves without implying that he as the spokesman for God desires to perpetuate this situation.[21]

Similarly, James Hurley, in his book *Man and Woman in Biblical Perspective,* says the Bible "does not endorse slavery, but rather regulates it and indicates its undesirable nature."[22] In her book *Women and the Word of God,* Susan Foh says "slavery is a social institution created by sinful men; as a purely human invention, it can be obliterated. Because the relationship [of master and slave] can be erased, the commands (to slaves) should be considered conditional or obsolete."[23] And as we have noted above, Schreiner tells us the Bible depicts slavery as "an evil human institution."

In agreeing with virtually all other contemporary Christians that to enslave someone in our cultural context would be sinful, these conservative evangelicals come to the right conclusion and rightly break with the tradition. They accept the modern evaluation of slavery: slavery is evil and sinful. They recognize that to enslave someone is to degrade them and that this is counter to ultimate creational and gospel values: All are made in the image and likeness of God. All are loved by God. In Christ there is neither slave nor free. This is not to say, however, that one can commend the way they arrive at this conclusion. It is neither helpful nor honest to imply or directly claim that Christians have never thought the Bible endorsed slavery and to argue that nothing in Scripture would suggest that slavery (at least in what is now a past cultural context) was acceptable to God.

This way of explaining the many seemingly positive biblical statements about slavery, which has been adopted by many conservative evangelicals, raises more problems than it solves. It presupposes that the biblical writers had a modern view of slavery unknown in the ancient world. They thought slavery was an evil when no one else had reached this conclusion. It also demands arguing that the apostolic fathers, who lived in the same social world as did the apostles and the best of theologians across the centuries—including John Calvin and, more recently, professor John Murray—were wrong in their exegesis. They thought the Bible legitimated and endorsed the institution and practice of slavery when in fact it condemned slavery and saw it as sinful.

As a second line of defense to this conservative evangelical apologetic for the

---

[21]George Knight, *The New Testament Teaching on the Role Relationship of Men and Women* (Grand Rapids, Mich.: Baker, 1977), p. 22.

[22]James Hurley, *Man and Woman in Biblical Perspective* (Leicester, U.K.: Inter-Varsity Press, 1981), p. 159.

[23]Susan Foh, *Women and the Word of God* (Phillipsburg, N.J.: Presbyterian & Reformed, 1980), p. 142.

many positive comments on slavery in the Bible, we are told that although the
literal commands to slaves can no longer be applied today, the abiding spiritual
principles these texts imply are still binding on Christians and are applicable in
our cultural setting.[24] That is, today these texts inform the employer-employee
relationship. Behind this argument lies a particular doctrine of Scripture which
holds that everything in the Bible, other than what is abrogated by the coming
of Christ, is to be obeyed in every age. To allow that the commands to slaves
and masters is apostolic teaching not applicable today—that they are not binding on the Christian conscience in our culture—would overthrow this doctrine
of Scripture and allow the possibility that the parallel commands to women to
be subordinate are also not binding. The practice of footwashing is often quoted
to illustrate the argument. The literal command to wash one another's feet, we
are told, is obeyed when the spiritual principle is followed—namely, when we
gladly serve others. Schreiner cites Paul's specific command to drink a little wine
to alleviate stomachache as another illustrative example. He says the apostle's
literal command is obeyed in principle when "we use an antacid or some other
medicine."[25]

We can agree that a general principle stands behind most, if not all, biblical
commands or exhortations; but it is disingenuous to say that following the perceived principle is the same as obeying Scripture. The truth is that we do not
obey Jesus' command to wash one another's feet nor Paul's command to take a
little wine for our upset stomachs—and many other specific commands in Scripture. No play on words can get around this. Some commands in Scripture are
time-bound and culturally limited. However, even if it is conceded that we may
presume a theological principle is behind most biblical commands, agreeing on
the principle implied is difficult, if not impossible, especially when the particular
principle is not prescribed by Scripture, as is usually the case.

Let me give an example. We all agree that Jesus' command to his disciples to
wash one another's feet need not be literally obeyed in our culture. Presupposing
my egalitarian theology I could take the undisclosed principle to be that the leader, the one with headship, should gladly subordinate himself in service to those

---

[24]Robert Yarbrough, "Hermeneutics of 1 Timothy," p. 187. One of Andreas J. Köstenberger's
major criticisms of my review of this book is that I do not understand this hermeneutic and
therefore reject it. See his article "Women in the Church: A Response to Kevin Giles," *Evangelical Quarterly* 73, no. 3 (2001): 210–13. See my reply in the same issue of this journal,
entitled "Women in the Church: A Rejoinder to Andreas Köstenberger," pp. 227–28.

[25]Thomas R. Schreiner, "An Interpretation of 1 Timothy 2:9-15: A Dialogue with Scholarship,"
in *Women in the Church: A Fresh Analysis of 1 Timothy 2:9-15*, ed. Andreas J. Köstenberger,
Thomas R. Schreiner and H. Scott Baldwin (Grand Rapids, Mich.: Baker, 1995), p. 121.

under him. I could quote Philippians 2:6–11, Ephesians 5:21 and many other texts as clear justification for this principle, but would hierarchical-complementarians agree to what I make the abiding principle? I think not. The great danger of this distinctive evangelical hermeneutic is that at this point exegesis can easily become creative theologizing. Given enough time and enough clever theologians, we could devise a principle behind any problematic text to match our theologies.

Surely, it is much more convincing to agree that slavery is not the equivalent of working for a living. The slave's person is owned by the master: the master has absolute power over his slave, and the slave is forced to work by the threat or use of violence. No modern-day employee is in this situation. The apostolic exhortations to slaves command them to be obedient to their masters no matter how badly they are treated. Employers and employees are not in a master-slave relationship. They have mutual rights and responsibilities. Employees work because they are rewarded, not because they the fear the whip or worse forms of punishment. Slavery and working for a living are better contrasted than compared. We find obvious, monumental problems in these efforts to explain the Bible's many positive comments on slavery by arguing that they give unchanging spiritual principles to direct the employer-employee relationship. In his book *Slaves, Women and Homosexuals,* conservative evangelical theologian William Webb discusses this hermeneutic several times. His comments on it when applied to the master-slave relationship are caustic. He says that it

> produces grotesque, mutation-like applications. Imagine taking the words of Peter and advising modern employees to accept physical beatings by their employers for the sake of the gospel (1 Pet 2:18–25). Or, think about instructing contemporary employers from the Pentateuch that, should they limit beatings of their employees to within a hairbreadth of their life, they would not be guilty of legal reprisal (Ex 21:20–21). Or, maybe our modern world should consider handing out lesser penalties for sexual violation against an employee (= slave) than in the case of sexual violation against an employer or self-employed person (= free) (Deut 22:25–27; cf. Lev 19:20–22).[26]

Contemporary Scholarly Studies on Slavery

Modern-day scholarly studies of slavery in the Bible are of no help to those who want us to believe that the Bible consistently depicts slavery as a form of human social ordering that has never been acceptable to God. Contemporary critical

---

[26]William J. Webb, *Slaves, Women and Homosexuals: Exploring the Hermeneutics of Cultural Analysis* (Downers Grove, Ill.: InterVarsity Press, 2001), p. 36-37; see also pp. 54–55.

studies on slavery in the Old Testament are agreed that slavery was taken for granted in every period in Israel's history, although Israel was never a slave-based economy.[27] Two kinds of slavery were recognized: Jewish "debt slavery," where bondage was temporary, and foreign "chattel slavery," where bondage was permanent.[28] Israel's laws governing slavery were distinctive in that they addressed the concern that all slaves should be treated kindly and be included in the religious life of Israel, particularly so if they were Jewish slaves in bondage to Jewish masters. Thus the Israelites were to rest their male and female slaves on the sabbath (Deut 5:14) and set Jewish slaves free after six years (Lev 25:39–41; Deut 15:12–18). They were to recall that they too had once been slaves in Egypt (Deut 5:15). However, having noted these injunctions, which were intended to give some protection to slaves, four points need to be made.

☐ In Israel slavery was still slavery.[29] Slaves were often taken in war (Gen 14:21; Deut 20:14; 21:10–14; 1 Sam 4:9; 2 Chron 28:8); they were regarded as property to be bought and sold or bequeathed (Gen 17:12–13; Lev 25:44–46; Eccles 2:7); a master could beat his slave to the point of death, and if he killed him, it was not a capital offense (Ex 21:20–21); the law valued free Jews differ-

---

[27]See G. C. Chirichigo, *Debt-Slavery in Israel and the Ancient Near-East* (Sheffield: Sheffield Academic, 1993), and the articles on slavery in any of the well-known Bible dictionaries. An excellent article on Old Testament slavery by K. A. Kitchen is found in *The New Bible Dictionary*, ed. J. D. Douglas (Leicester, U.K.: Inter-Varsity Press, 1992), pp. 1121–24. See also R. De Vaux, *Ancient Israel: Its Life and Institutions* (London: Darton, Longman & Todd, 1962), pp. 80–90.

[28]I note, however, that D. E. Callender lists three forms: chattel slavery, debt slavery and forced labor. See his article "Servants of God(s) and Servants of Kings in Israel and the Ancient Near East," in *Slavery in Text and Interpretation*, ed. A. D. Callahan, R. A. Horsley and A. Smith, *Semeia* 83/84 (1998), pp. 73–77. On chattel slavery, see Kitchen, "Slavery," in *New Bible Dictionary* par. (e), p. 1123.

[29]Webb argues that the Bible anticipates the emancipation of slaves and women by its "redemptive movement hermeneutic" (see *Slaves*). It gives clues that slavery and the subordination of women are not God's ideal by mitigating their more oppressive and hurtful characteristics. There is much in Webb's book with which I would agree, but to prove his point he would have to show that the moderating comments on slavery and women in Scripture were unique to the Bible. Comparative studies on slavery and the subordination of women seem to indicate more similarities than contrasts. From time to time and from place to place, non-Jewish and non-Christian humane legislators gave some protection to women and slaves. In any case, I cannot see how this argument really helps on its own. The primary question is, why did Christians not see this redemptive motif in Scripture on slavery for eighteen centuries and on women for twenty centuries? Was it not a change in culture that allowed Christians to see in Scripture what had hitherto been hidden to them? The redemptive motif did not bring the change, it was the change that brought to light the redemptive motif. I also think the homosexual question is distinguished primarily from the woman and slavery debates by being an essentially moral question. It relates to how people behave, which is not the case in the other two examples, which are about the worth of people as people. See appendix C for more on the homosexuality issue.

ently than it valued slaves (Ex 21:20–21, 32; Lev 19:20–22); and female slaves were sexually available to their masters, even if there were safeguards for Jewish female slaves (Gen 16:1–4; 30:3–4; Deut 20:10–14; 21:10–14; Judg 5:30).[30]

☐ Much of the more positive legislation protecting slaves seems to apply specifically to Jewish slaves.

☐ There is a great difference between legislating to protect slaves and legislating to abolish slavery. The Old Testament does the former, not the latter.

☐ We should not make the mistake of thinking that because there are humane laws in the Old Testament that slaves were always treated humanely in Israel, or that the minority who were Jewish slaves were always set free after six years.[31] Once humans are given absolute power over others, laws and exhortations seldom, if ever, eradicate the abuses of power that follow. The evangelical Old Testament scholar K. A. Kitchen says, "The treatment accorded to slaves (in Israel) depended directly on the personality of their masters. It could be a relationship of trust (cf. Gen. 39:1–6) and affection (Deut. 15:16), but discipline might be harsh, even fatal (cf. Ex. 21:21)."[32]

The Old Testament includes innumerable references to slavery and the taking or making of slaves. In the Pentateuch, legislation on slavery is invariably depicted as being given directly by God. To suggest that these laws and instructions only "regulate" an institution of which God disapproves stretches the imagination beyond belief (e.g., Ex 20:10; 21:2–11, 20–21, 26–27, 32; Lev 25:6, 47–54; Deut 15:12–18; 20:10–14). In these passages God legislates slavery without making one negative comment. What is more, in Leviticus 25:44–46 and Deuteronomy 20:10–14, God commands the Israelites to take slaves from the nations around them. Nowhere in the Old Testament is it ever suggested that God viewed the institution of slavery as an evil or that he desired that all slaves be set free.

The situation in the New Testament is not dissimilar, although far less is said on slavery. The apostles accepted the institution of slavery as a fact of life, never suggesting that it is evil or sinful. They offer not one word of criti-

---

[30]It is to be noted that the legislation allowing a Jewish man to sell his daughter as a slave does not also allow her master to sell her later to a foreigner. See Ex 21:7–11.

[31]See Jer 34:8–14. See also Orlando Patterson, *Slavery and Social Death: A Comparative Study* (Cambridge: Harvard University Press, 1982), p. 275; M. Barth and H. Blanke, *The Letter to Philemon* (Grand Rapids, Mich.: Eerdmans, 2000), pp. 96–97.

[32]Kitchen, "Slavery," p. 1123. In Prov 29:19–21 the advice seems to be that masters should treat their slaves very firmly, possibly harshly. Because slaves were often treated poorly by Jewish masters, runaway slaves were a problem. See 1 Sam 25:10; 30:13-15; 1 Kings 2:39–40; cf. Sirach 33:31-33.

cism of the institution nor one word of reproach to slave holders, although they would have seen firsthand how cruelly slaves could be treated.[33] Rather, they tell slaves to accept their lot and serve their masters no matter how harsh—for they are serving Christ (1 Pet 2:18-21). Their exhortations are all based on weighty theology: slaves are to obey their masters "as you obey Christ" (Eph 6:5); "fearing the Lord" (Col 3:22); in obedience to "our Lord Jesus Christ" (1 Tim 6:1-3); in conformity with Christ's own suffering (1 Pet 2:18-21). Nothing in this wording suggests the apostles were only "regulating" an institution or a practice they thought was sinful and transitory. Marcus Barth and H. Blanke say that in the Household Codes, Paul seems to be enunciating "a more or less timeless ethic."[34] Morton Smith concludes that the apostles "not only tolerated slavery . . . but helped to perpetuate it by making the slaves' obedience to their masters a religious duty."[35] This is true, yet it also needs to be said that the apostles commanded masters to treat their slaves "justly and fairly" (Col 4:1). They did not oppose the institution of slavery, but they wanted Christian slave owners to behave with benevolence, which no doubt some did and some did not. We are not told whether the "harsh" masters mentioned in 1 Peter 2:18 were Christians. They probably were, if they had Christian slaves. Often the religion of the master was that of the slave (cf. 1 Tim 6:2; Philem 2). Brian Dodd writes:

> We want to find Paul saying to Christian masters, "Free your slaves." Instead, we hear the opposite message when he says to slaves, "Be content in your bondage." What the Abolitionists would have given for a single statement in Paul that echoed Moses' heart-cry for his enslaved people: "Let my people go" (Ex 5:1). Sadly, the pages of Paul contain nothing like this.[36]

No one in the ancient Near East in Old Testament times or in the Greco-Roman world of the first century opposed the institution of slavery or argued that it was an evil. There were no movements for the abolition of slavery and no moral philosophers arguing that the institution of slavery was morally bankrupt.

---

[33]To suggest that Paul only ever experienced the more humane household slavery is special pleading. In his extensive travels by land and sea in the Roman Empire, Paul would have seen the worst and the best of Roman slavery.

[34]Barth and Blanke, *Letter to Philemon,* p. 161.

[35]Morton Smith, "Slavery," in *What the Bible Really Says,* ed. Morton Smith and R. R. Hoffman (Buffalo: Prometheus, 1989), p. 145. In Col 3:25 Paul designates a slave's disobedience to a master as "sinful wrong doing *(adikeō)*." This is the same term Paul uses of sexual immorality, idolatry, adultery and so on in 1 Cor 6:9-10.

[36]Dodd, *Problem with Paul,* pp. 84-85.

We would thus expect, unless there were clear indicators otherwise, that the biblical writers as men of their time held the same views on slavery as everyone else. They did not think slavery to be inherently evil. It was simply a fact of life. In their cultural context they believed that slavery was more pleasing to God than other options. It was better for destitute Jews to sell themselves into slavery than to starve to death; and when prisoners were taken in war, they were kept as slaves rather than killed. Prisoner-of-war camps were unknown. In other words, in that cultural context, slavery can be seen as serving a social good, albeit of a very mixed kind, from our perspective.

This critical reading of what the Bible says about slavery and the comments on the social values of the biblical period imply that history should be taken seriously. It presupposes that what is of most importance in understanding the text is not our cultural values nor what we as moderns think of slavery in particular, let alone what would preserve our doctrine of Scripture, but what is actually in the text. Our primary question in the exegetical quest is, what did the original writers and readers think about slavery, and what did they say about it? When we put aside our altogether-modern presupposition that slavery is an evil, it is hard to avoid the fact that as men of their age, they saw slavery as a fact of life, acceptable to God and not inherently evil. Contemporary critical scholars who have specialized on slavery in biblical times differ very little on matters of exegesis from theologians of past times. Where they differ is on the applicability of this biblical teaching. Unlike their predecessors they think that what the Bible says on slavery is *not prescriptive* for those living in another age and cultural context. For the modern critical scholar what the Bible says on slavery is *descriptive* of the practices of and the prevailing cultural presuppositions about slavery held by the biblical writers and nothing more. If there is a distinctive element in what the Bible says on slavery, it is the attempt to make the lot of individual slaves less dehumanizing by commanding masters to act in a kindly way. The institution of slavery as such is unquestioned.

Where Do We Go from Here?

If, then, there is much in the Bible that can and has been read to endorse the institution of slavery yet we cannot endorse slavery today, where does this leave evangelicals? I would answer, in exactly the same position as we find ourselves in today in regard to the subordination of women. We are faced with the fact that there is teaching in Scripture that cannot be applied in our day and age; indeed, to do so would be wrong and unjust. Our responsibility in this situation is not to do exegetical handstands to make the Bible say what it does not say so that by clever "exegesis" we make the Bible support our modern viewpoint on slavery (or women). Our task, rather, is to return to Scripture to see whether other teaching in the Bible actually calls slavery (and the permanent subordination of women) into question. It is to ask this: is there teaching in the Bible that was hidden to the eyes of those living in cultures that accepted slavery but that God, the ultimate author of Scripture, now wants us to see in the new context in which he has placed us?

Much in the Bible can be read to endorse slavery, but also within Scripture is teaching of great theological weight that calls into question all forms of human domination and discrimination. Thus in the canonical prologue to all of Scripture, we are told that every human being is made in the image and likeness of God and given dominion over the earth (Gen 1:27–28). This noble vision of man and woman teaches that every human being is of equal dignity and worth and is equipped by God for leadership in his world. In the New Testament, Jesus clearly reveals a God who loves and values every human being, who sees none as intrinsically second-class citizens (Mt 19:19; Mk 12:31; Jn 3:16; 13:14). The equal dignity of all human beings is also embraced by Paul, who declared that in Christ "there is no longer Jew or Greek, there is no longer slave or free, there is no longer male and female" (Gal 3:28). This grand biblical view of the equal worth and dignity of every person corresponds with the fundamental Christian doctrine, the doctrine of God. The Christian God of revelation is three persons living in perfect communion and love, in whom "none is afore, or after other; none is greater, or less than another; . . . the whole three Persons are . . . co-equal."[37]

In arguing in relation to slavery, as I did with the subordination of women, that within Scripture particular commands and teaching are secondary to more profound theological motifs, I find that Willard Swartley, in his important book *Slavery, Sabbath, War and Women: Case Issues in Biblical Interpretation,* comes to much the same conclusion. It is his thesis that no resolution on what the Bible teaches regarding the four topics he examines can be found unless this tension within Scripture is recognized. He thus concludes,

> The interpreter should give priority to theological principles and basic moral imperatives, rather than to specific counsel on particular topics when these two contradict. This is part of the effort to determine how the Bible functions norma-

---

[37]Quoted from the Athanasian Creed.

tively for believing communities removed from the history and culture in which it was written. It is related also to the concern that we follow the "spirit of scripture" and not become legalistic in interpretation.[38]

Behind what might be called a "contextual evangelical hermeneutic" lie five presuppositions:
□ The Bible has the power to address new situations that it does not anticipate.
□ When cultural values change, often how the Bible is interpreted changes.
□ Not everything in Scripture is applicable in every age. Some teaching in the Bible is time-bound and culturally limited.
□ The Bible is multifaceted in its story line—there is diversity within Scripture.
□ The way forward in most, if not all, disputes over what the Bible teaches is to determine from the words of Scripture what is theologically primary in Scripture—to grasp what Athanasius called the "scope" of Scripture—and then interpret particular passages in this light.

In other words, the challenge constantly before the church is to find a way to read Scripture theologically in the historical and cultural context in which we find ourselves.

A contextual evangelical hermeneutic is not a hermeneutic *determined* by culture. It is a theology which acknowledges that God places his people in an ever-changing world, which is continually throwing up new questions. Change and disputation always drive us back to Scripture to re-read what it says. Finding ourselves in a new cultural context—and possibly challenged by other Christians who disagree with us—we invariably discover things we had hitherto not seen before in Scripture. This reminds us that, as we've seen in church history, the Scriptures, inspired and illuminated by the Holy Spirit, can speak afresh in every age. The Bible can give answers to questions it does not directly address, and it can give new answers to old questions. The Dutch Reformed theologian G. C. Berkouwer sums up the point I am making more eloquently than I have:

> The Word has to be free to remake and reform the Church over and over again. The moment the Church loses interest in working the mines of the Word because it thinks it has seen all there is to see, that moment the Church also loses its power and credibility in the world. When the Church thinks it knows all there is to know, the opportunity for surprising discovery is closed. The Church then

---

[38]Willard Swartley, *Slavery, Sabbath, War and Women: Case Issues in Biblical Interpretation* (Ontario: Herald, 1983), p. 230.

becomes old, without perspective, and without light and labor and fruitfulness.[39]

The Evidence Is Compelling

The Bible can and has been read as legitimating slavery. We cannot simply condemn all theologians until the middle of the eighteenth century for wrongly interpreting the Bible. They did have good biblical support for their position, even if they failed to see other teaching that called slavery into question. It is hard to imagine how they could have read the Bible otherwise, given that they lived in cultures that took slavery for granted. It was only when God moved in history to bring social change that for the first time in human history, people became conscious of the awfulness of slavery—an evil so plain to us today. Only at that point were theologians able to see in Scripture the teaching (hitherto unseen) which disclosed that God's ideal was emancipation, setting the oppressed free. At this level the parallel between slavery and the subordination of women exactly corresponds. It is only in the last hundred years or so, especially in the last thirty years as our culture has changed, that the subordination of women has been called into question. In this altogether new context, most Christians now reject interpretations of the Bible that endorse the permanent subordination of women, no matter how subtly the argument is put. If we all agree that in our culture we should not read the Bible to endorse slavery, why cannot we agree on the same with the subordination of women? Why can we not say, God's work in history cries out to us to change, to repudiate once and for all the idea that the Bible makes the subordination of women the ideal?

In reply, we are told that in the New Testament the subordination of women and the institution of slavery are dealt with in altogether different ways. The former is grounded on profound theology and as such cannot be repudiated, whereas the latter is simply practical advice, open to change. Is this really true? To this question we now turn.

---

[39]G. C. Berkouwer, "Understanding Christianity," *Christianity Today* 14 (1970): 40. This is an old quote but it is right up to date. I first used it in my first book, *Women and Their Ministry* in 1977.

12

THE PARALLEL
EXHORTATIONS TO
SLAVES & WOMEN
TO BE SUBORDINATE

Conservative evangelicals who argue for the permanent subordination of women want to sharply differentiate the apostolic exhortations to slaves to be subordinate from the apostolic exhortations to wives to be subordinate—exhortations that are generally paired in the New Testament. If it were agreed that these parallel exhortations are of the same kind, then the contemporary hierarchalists' whole case would collapse. The problem arises because contemporary hierarchalists adopt the novel and problematic idea that the Bible cannot be read to endorse or legitimate slavery, even tacitly. They tell us that slavery is a sinful institution created by humans and that the apostles only give practical advice to masters and slaves living in a culture that accepted slavery. Thus in our culture, this teaching is no longer "literally" binding on Christians. I agree with these statements, but this reading of the apostolic exhortations to masters and slaves creates a major problem for evangelicals who wish to maintain the permanent subordination of women. They cannot concede the same for the parallel apostolic exhortations to husbands and wives. They need to argue that these exhortations are permanently binding and transcultural because they are grounded on the unchanging constitutive and prescriptive order given in creation. They are *unlike* the exhortations to masters and slaves, which are simply practical guidance for men and women living in the first century, when slavery was practiced. Contrasting these paired apostolic exhortations is a constituent element in the novel post-1970s argument for the permanent subordination of women.

John Piper and Wayne Grudem, the editors of *Recovering Biblical Manhood and Womanhood,* claim that the connection between the exhortations to women and slaves is "superficial and misguided."[1] In this same book George Knight says, "There is a great divide between (the exhortations to) husbands and wives . . . on one side of this list of household relationships, and masters and slaves on the other side"; to compare the two is like "comparing apples and oranges."[2] The roles in marriage are "a permanent and absolute institution," but those between masters and slaves are not.[3] In *Women in the Church,* Robert Yarbrough is given a chapter to refute "Western culture's liberalizing views on women, the putative meaning of Galatians 3:28, *and the alleged tie between women's subordination and slavery.*"[4] I am singled out for criticism for having tied together the apostolic exhortations to women and slaves with "more comprehensiveness and verve" than either F. F. Bruce or Krister Stendahl.[5] More recently, Thomas Schreiner rejects this connection but in doing so makes the important admission that

> if the egalitarians are correct in saying that the admonitions to wives and the restrictions on women in ministry are analogous to the counsel given to slaves, then I would agree that the restrictions on women in ministry are due to cultural accommodation and are not required of believers today.[6]

Most commentators, both past and present, have argued that these paired exhortations are of the same nature, and the nineteenth-century American evan-

---

[1]John Piper and Wayne Grudem, "An Overview of Central Concerns: Questions and Answers," in Piper and Grudem, eds., *Recovering Biblical Manhood and Womanhood: A Response to Evangelical Feminism* (Wheaton, Ill.: Crossway, 1991), p. 66.

[2]George Knight, "Husbands and Wives as Analogues to Christ and the Church: Ephesians 5:21-33 and Colossians 3:18-19," in John Piper and Wayne Grudem, *Recovering Biblical Manhood and Womenhood: A Response to Evangelical Feminism* (Wheaton, Ill.: Crossway, 1991), p. 177.

[3]Ibid. See exactly the same argument in Susan Foh, *Women and the Word of God* (Phillipsburg, N.J.: Presbyterian & Reformed, 1980), p. 141.

[4]Robert Yarbrough, "The Hermeneutics of 1 Timothy 2:9-15," in Andreas J. Köstenberger, Thomas R. Schreiner and H. Scott Baldwin, eds., *Women in the Church: A Fresh Analysis of 1 Timothy 2:9-15* (Grand Rapids, Mich.: Baker, 1995), p. 159, italics added.

[5]Ibid., p. 185.

[6]Thomas R. Schreiner, "Women in Ministry," in *Two Views on Women in Ministry,* ed. Craig L. Blomberg and J. R. Beck (Grand Rapids, Mich.: Zondervan, 2001), p. 216.

gelicals who argued in support of slavery emphasized this. They insisted that the three sets of apostolic exhortations that stand side by side in the so-called Household Codes reflected the unchanging mind of God. If one were to believe that Paul's exhortations to slaves were not expressive of the ever-binding Word of God, then the subordination of wives and the obedience of children would be undermined.[7] They reasoned that rejecting the comments about slavery called into question the authority of husbands and parents, not only masters. For them these apostolic directives were of equal force and were to be obeyed until the end of the world.[8] In commentating on the related exhortations in Ephesians, Charles Hodge wrote:

> What the Scriptures teach, is not peculiar to the obedience of the slave to his master, but applies to all the other cases in which obedience is regulated. . . . It applies to children in relation to their parents and wives to their husbands. Those invested with lawful authority are the representatives of God. The powers (i.e. those invested with authority) are ordained by God.[9]

The assertion by contemporary hierarchical-complementarians that these parallel exhortations to women and slaves to be subordinate are to be contrasted is an entirely novel idea, never heard before the 1970s and rejected universally by critical scholarly studies of the Household Codes or Rules.[10] These rules are given in their fullest form in Ephesians 5:21—6:9 and Colossians 3:18—4:1, where three paired groups are addressed: husbands and wives, masters and slaves, fathers and children. In 1 Peter 2:18—3:7 masters disappear from view, as they do in the Pastorals, where fathers and children are also not mentioned (1 Tim 2:8–15; 6:1–2; Tit 2:1–10). In the Pastorals, the reciprocal element is missing: women and slaves are addressed, but their counterparts are not. These in-

---

[7]See Charles Hodge, *A Commentary on the Epistle to the Ephesians* (London: Banner of Truth, 1964), p. 366; Hodge, "The Bible Argument for Slavery" (pp. 848–49), A. B. Bledsoe, "Liberty and Slavery" (p. 354), and T. Stringfellow, "The Bible Argument, or Slavery in the Light of Divine Revelation" (pp. 480–81), in *Cotton Is King and Pro-Slavery Arguments,* ed. E. N. Cartwright (1860; reprint, New York: Basic Afro-American Reprint Library, 1968); *The Collected Writings of James Henry Thornwell,* ed. D. M. Palmer, 4 vols. (London: Banner of Truth, 1986), 4:386.

[8]See Hodge, "Bible Argument," pp. 848–49; Bledsoe, "Liberty and Slavery," p. 354; Stringfellow, "Bible Argument," pp. 480–81; Thornwell, *Collected Writings,* 4:386.

[9]Hodge, *Commentary on the Epistle,* p. 366.

[10]On the Household Codes see the good summary articles on the state of research at this time by D. L. Barch, "Household Codes," in *Greco-Roman Literature and the New Testament,* ed. D. E. Aune (Atlanta: Scholars Press, 1988), pp. 25–50; James D. G. Dunn, "The Household Rules in the New Testament," in *The Family in Theological Perspective,* ed. S. C. Barton (Edinburgh: T & T Clark, 1996), pp. 43–63.

structions on the good ordering of the extended patriarchal family have parallels in Greek, Hellenistic and Jewish writings. The New Testament versions are distinguished by seeking to make the gospel affect the prevailing social structuring of that time. This distinctive element is most clearly seen in Colossians and Ephesians. In Colossians, Paul adds a reference to "the Lord" seven times.[11] By doing this, he is indicating that the Christian extended family should be ordered traditionally, but in a Christian manner with Christian motivation. In Ephesians, he seeks to transform the patriarchal understanding of marriage by, among other things, defining male headship in terms of sacrificial loving service.

The profound difference between these parallel exhortations, according to the hierarchical-complementarians, is that whereas the exhortations to women are based firmly on an unchanging order given in creation before the Fall, the ones to slaves are not. This difference makes the exhortations to women permanently binding and those to slaves not binding. If the apostles held to this profound difference, we would imagine it would be clearly observable by comparing the two sets of exhortations in these Household Codes.

However, as already noted, none of the scholarly studies on the Household Codes finds any differences in substance between these exhortations. On this they agree with the tradition, with how the Bible has been understood in the past. To prove this point, tables 12.1 an 12.2 set the two sets of exhortations will be set similar to the schema given by David C. Verner in his book *The Household of God: The Social World of the Pastoral Epistles*.[12] Presented in this way, the reason given for each exhortation—first to wives and then to slaves—is highlighted.

In three of the six passages detailed in table 12.1, the reason given for the exhortations is one of expediency or appropriateness: "as is fitting in the Lord" (Col 3:18); "so that the word of God may not be discredited" (Tit 2:5); so that unbelieving husbands may be won for Christ (1 Pet 3:1). In 1 Corinthians 14:34 the reason is because "the law" demands it. As no Old Testament law demands that wives or women be subordinate,[13] some have argued that the law in this

---

[11]"As is fitting in the Lord" (Col 3:18); "your acceptable duty in the Lord" (Col 3:20); "fearing the Lord" (Col 3:22); "as done for the Lord" (Col 3:23); "from the Lord you will receive" (3:24); "you serve the Lord Christ" (Col 3:24); "you also have a Master [the Lord] in heaven" (Col 4:1).

[12]D. C. Verner, *The Household of God: The Social World of the Pastoral Epistles* (Chico, Calif.: Scholars Press, 1981), p. 88.

[13]Gen 3:16 does say that as one consequence of the Fall, the man will rule over the woman. This is not a demand that women be subordinate. Old Testament scholars have usually seen this as a descriptive comment, not a prescriptive one. If the appeal is to this text, then women's subordination is grounded on the fallen order, not the ideal created order.

context alludes to the Jewish oral law.[14] Others have suggested that the issue in this text is not the subordination of wives to husbands but of women to the prophets.[15] There is also the question of the authenticity of this text.[16] But whatever is concluded on any of these questions, one thing is clear: this exhortation is not grounded on an appeal to a creation order established before the Fall; the appeal is to "the law."

Table 12.1. The Exhortations to Wives

Passage	Persons Addressed	Imperative	Reason
1 Cor 14:34	women	be subordinate (also be silent)	as the law also says
Eph 5:22	wives	be subject to your husbands	for the husband is the head of the wife
Col 3:18	wives	be subject to your husbands	as is fitting in the Lord
1 Tim 2:11–14	women	learn in silence with full submission	for Adam was formed first, then Eve; and Adam was not deceived, but the woman was deceived.
Tit 2:4-5	young women	be submissive to their husbands	so that the word of God may not be discredited
1 Pet 3:1	wives	accept the authority of your husbands (RSV "be submissive to")	so that, even if some of them do not obey the word, they may be won over without a word by their wives' conduct

Ephesians 5:21-33 is the most theologically grounded of all the material in the Household Codes. Here wives are exhorted to subordinate themselves to their husbands, their "head," while husbands are exhorted to love their wives as their own bodies. In making these demands on men *and* women and in depicting Christian marriage as a dynamic relationship—*a process* rather than *a structure*—that has as its goal the union of both parties, Paul seeks to transform

---

[14]S. Aalen, "A Rabbinic Formula in 1 Corinthians 14:34," *Studia evangelica II* (1964): 513–25.

[15]Donald Carson, "Silent in the Churches," in John Piper and Wayne Grudem, *Recovering Biblical Manhood and Womanhood: A Response to Evangelical Feminism* (Wheaton, Ill.: Crossway, 1991), pp. 140–53.

[16]See Gordon Fee, *God's Empowering Presence* (Peabody, Mass.: Hendrickson, 1994), pp. 272–81.

the patriarchal understanding of marriage without attacking it directly. In this passage, Andrew Lincoln concludes, "submission and love can be seen as two sides of the same coin—selfless service of one's marriage partner."[17] The ground for the appeal is christological and the paradigm ecclesiological. The only time the creation narratives are mentioned is in Ephesians 5:31, where the making one of man and women in marriage is the issue.

In the *one instance* where there is an appeal in these Household Codes to the creation narratives of Genesis—1 Timothy 2:13–14—the man's being created first is one reason given for women's subordination, and the second reason is that "Adam was not deceived, but the woman was deceived." Earlier in this book I argued that these two reasons why women should not teach at Ephesus are ad hominem arguments directed at a specific error. They are not weighty theology. If they are read as weighty theology, then they stand in tension with Paul's own new-creation theology (2 Cor 5:17; Gal 6:15) and his insistence that Adam is responsible for the sin in the world (Rom 5:12ff.). In 1 Corinthians 11:3–16, Paul also appeals in several ways to the creation stories to bolster his argument that when women lead in prayer and prophecy in church, they should do so with heads covered, whereas men should do so with their heads uncovered. However, no one lists this passage among the Household Codes, and no one argues that the teaching on head coverings, grounded on the creation narratives, is universally binding. The evidence is compelling: there is no common appeal to the creation order, however understood, in the Household Codes. At best there is *one example* of an appeal to the *chronological* ordering of the sexes in creation, matched by an appeal to the responsibility of the woman for the Fall (1 Tim 2:13–14). This means that the appeal to creation is *the exception to the rule,* not the pattern. Where there is a second example of an appeal to the creation narratives to ground an apostolic ruling on head coverings (1 Cor 11:3–16), no one thinks the ruling is universally binding.

The exhortations to slaves usually follow those addressed to women. This in itself would suggest that the exhortations are of the same nature and force. These parallel exhortations follow the same schema. Again, they are best analyzed by separating the constituent parts and viewing them in a table.

The reasons given for slaves to be subordinate are more consistent and weightier than those to women, for there is a repeated christological appeal

---

[17]Andrew Lincoln, *Ephesians* (Dallas: Word, 1990), p. 393.

Table 12.2. The Exhortations to Slaves

Passage	Persons Addressed	Imperative	Reason
Eph 6:5	slaves	obey your earthly masters	as you obey Christ
Col 3:22	slaves	obey your earthly masters	fearing the Lord
1 Tim 6:1	all who are under the yoke of slavery	regard their masters as worthy of all honor	so that the name of God and the teaching may not be blasphemed
Tit 2:9–10	slaves	be submissive to their masters	so that in everything they may be an ornament to the doctrine of God our Savior.
1 Pet 2:18-21	slaves	accept the authority of your masters with deference (RSV "be submissive")	for it is a credit to you if, being aware of God, you endure pain while suffering unjustly . . . because Christ also suffered for you

(Eph 6:5; Col 3:22; 1 Pet 2:18-21). In the 1 Timothy passage Paul tells his younger assistant to "teach and urge these duties . . . [according to] the sound words of our Lord Jesus Christ" (1 Tim 6:2–3). It is certainly hard to find any indication that the apostles were only "regulating" something they thought was displeasing to God. Nevertheless, one can conclude that these exhortations are basically of the same nature and force as those addressed to women. They speak not to those who are locked into a permanent, God-given hierarchy, but to free men and women—members of the new community founded by Christ—who, while having equality in Christ, are asked to follow the example and teaching of their master and submit themselves to others. The most common ground for *all* the exhortations, whether to women or slaves, is the example of Christ, who willingly subordinated himself in the incarnation and taught that the great in his kingdom would be those who assumed the ministry of servants (Mk 10:45; Lk 22:25–26). In a social setting totally different from the setting in which they were given, the exhortations to slaves should not be read as an endorsement of slavery; nor should the exhortations to wives be read as the endorsement of a fixed, hierarchical structure in which men are set over women in marriage or the church.

If, therefore, there is no significant difference between the exhortations to slaves to be subordinate and those to women or wives, then there is no reason why we should think that only the exhortations to women apply in our historical context. We are free—indeed, encouraged—by the agreed understanding of the slavery texts to read the women texts (like the slavery texts) as time-bound advice. Paul asked women and slaves in his cultural setting to be subordinate. In our cultural setting, his exhortations no longer apply.

13

LESSONS TO BE
LEARNED & CONCLUDING
THOUGHTS

T he study of history is supposed to help human beings avoid the mistakes of the past. Tradition, as it has been defined in this book, is a particular kind of history, the history of interpretation. From it we learn how Christians in the past have understood the Bible. It is dangerous to ignore this voice of tradition. It should always be listened to with the greatest attention and only rejected when the reasons are compelling. The tradition of slavery is an example where it had to be rejected. What is so tragic is that few evangelicals were aware of the repudiation of this tradition when the women's movement began in the late 1960s. They had been led to believe the fiction that the Bible only regulates slavery, depicting it as evil, and that evangelical Christians with one mind had led the forces of emancipation. Thus, when the women's movement erupted, they did not have the rich theological resource of a recent example of a profound social change that had forced theologians to reject the tradition and re-read the Bible. Once again, in a little more than a hundred years after the American Civil War that ended slavery, conservative evangelicals took a reactionary stance that was theologically, morally and intellectually bankrupt. They sought by appeal to the Bible to hold back the tide of history and positive social change, resisting attempts to read the Bible in the cause of liberation and justice. New ways to restate the old subordinating theology were developed, which convinced many of their fellow evangelicals but no one else. As the years have passed, however, even evangelical support has waned. It is obvious to all but a few that there is something profoundly wrong with a theology that permanently subordinates women in a culture that has emancipated women.

If evangelicals had known from the 1970s onward that for most of Christian history the Bible had been read to regulate and legitimate slavery, and that the most adamant supporters of slavery in the nineteenth century were conservative evangelicals who made their case by appeal to the Bible, I very much doubt that we would be where we are now in the women's debate. From history we would have learned these lessons:

No social order should be taken as God-given and inviolable.[1] In the history of Christianity, whenever political or social change has been mooted, some Christians have argued that the present social order is established by God and should not be changed. Socially conservative Christians, appealing to the Bible for support, opposed democracy, republicanism, the abolition of slavery and the downfall of apartheid; and today they oppose the emancipation of women in the home and the church. What we have learned in recent years is that social ordering is always a human construct. Invariably it reflects the values of those who hold the most power in any community. As a human construct it can either be supported or rejected. Change is always possible given the will.

Culture is forever changing. Both the nineteenth-century evangelicals who wrote in support of slavery and those who now write in support of the permanent subordination of women want their readers to believe the cultural world of the Bible and our own culture are much the same. If there are differences, they are of no great importance. The undeniable truth is that a great gulf separates the cultural world of the Bible and that of modern times. Slavery and the subordination of women are two compelling examples of this fact. Once both these were taken for granted as social realities that reflected prevailing societal values, but now they are not. It is true that all people are forever sinners in need of God's grace, but all people in all places do not live in the same cultural world the Bible addresses. Change the culture, and how the Bible is interpreted may well change.

Theology divorced from social ethics is bound to be erroneous. In the herme-

---

[1]It is, of course, theologically correct to think of certain social structures or institutions as God-given and sanctioned: e.g., the state, marriage, the polarity of the sexes. What is theologically incorrect is to think that one particular historical expression of how these givens are ordered is God-given and permanent.

neutical quest no interpretation can be right if it does not lead to right action.[2] The evangelical theologians of the Old South were convinced that if there were texts supporting slavery, then slavery must be pleasing to God because what Scripture said in every instance, one for one, was God's final word on the subject. The realities of the terrible suffering and the gross injustices slavery perpetuated were daily before their eyes, but because they could find many passages in the Bible that on face value suggested God approved of slavery, they could not believe it was evil or sinful. For them, upholding what they understood to be revealed truth was the most important thing to do. The call to express love of neighbor and justice was not heard because their concern for what they thought was truth muffled everything else.

The Bible should not be read as though it were a set of timeless, transcultural precepts all saying virtually the same thing. The Bible is a historical revelation, much of it in narrative form; it is usually addressing specific situations, and therefore it is quite diverse. Evangelical theology is not about accumulating texts and giving one's interpretation of them to prove what one already believes, nor is it simply reiterating what "sound" theologians tell us these texts mean. It is about thinking deeply and long about what is the primary theological thrust or "scope" of Scripture, a process invariably sharpened by listening to other Christians with whom we differ. It involves critically reading and studying the tradition—how the Bible has been understood on this matter in the past. It demands a deep awareness of the questions and presuppositions of the contemporary scene. Theologians are always seeking to address the present. They are asking what God would have his people believe or do in this period of history, in this cultural context.

It is possible for evangelicals with the Bible in their hand to get the wrong answer from the Scriptures to the questions facing them in their age. Appealing to texts and giving one's interpretation of them does not guarantee either that the scope of Scripture has been correctly grasped or that its teaching is being applied correctly in a cultural setting very different from that of the biblical writers. The great Reformed theologians of the Old South were totally convinced that the slavery they supported was acceptable to God because they found biblical teaching that seemed to endorse slavery. Since for them the very words of Scripture were the unchanging words of God, they concluded slavery must always be pleasing to God. The historical nature of Scripture was eclipsed by their

---

[2]This point is eloquently made by Roger Lundin, Anthony C. Thiselton and Clarence Walhout, *The Responsibility of Hermeneutics* (Grand Rapids, Mich.: Eerdmans, 1985); see particularly p. ix.

"high" view of Scripture, and they never considered the possibility that self-interest was corrupting their theologizing.

One must take great care not to undermine or deny explicitly or implicitly the equal dignity, worth and potential of every human being. It could be argued that the next most important doctrine to the doctrine of God is the doctrine of humanity, or "Christian anthropology," as it was called in the old theological textbooks. Fundamental to this doctrine is the revelation given right at the beginning of the Bible as a kind of prologue to all that follows: *all human beings* are made in the image and likeness of God and are given dominion over the earth (Gen 1:27–28). To deny or subvert this truth is to fall into error. Both the proslavery theology of nineteenth-century evangelicals and the prosubordination-of-women theology of contemporary conservative evangelicals do this. The evangelicals of the Old South were perfectly straightforward in stating their belief that Negroes are a subordinate race, inferior to whites. Contemporary evangelicals who argue for the permanent subordination of women are not so straightforward and honest. They tell us they believe men and women are equal yet different. None could deny this, but when their case is analyzed and unpacked, we find the word *different* is actually a code word meaning "subordinate." The one essential difference between men and women is that men have been given "headship" and women are to accept this. They are permanently allocated a subordinate role. This means they lack the capacity to lead or a mandate to lead. In other words, in some way they are inferior to men.

Significant Parallels

Let me now outline the many parallels between the case for the permanent subordination of women developed in recent years by some evangelicals and the case for the endorsement of slavery put by the learned evangelical theologians of the Old South.

Both theologies were developed during the collapse of the cultural context that had supported the social reality they wanted to maintain. The "biblical theology" of slavery was developed in the early and middle years of the nineteenth century, when the abolition of slavery was gaining ascendancy. The "biblical theology" for the permanent subordination of women was developed in the post-1970s period, when women's liberation was turning the world upside down. Thus both theologies are reactionary—attempts to maintain the status quo.

Both theologies are predicated on the belief that the present social order is sanctioned by God. They reflect a profoundly socially conservative ideology. They oppose social change by appealing to the Bible, insisting that to endorse the liberation of slaves or women is to oppose the social order God has established and sanctioned.

Both theologies were constructed and promulgated by those who held power and privilege. They are theological constructs developed by the powerful at the expense of the less powerful. In this sense, they are self-serving theologies.

Both theologies are grounded in an erroneous doctrine of humanity. One posits the inherent superordination of white men, the other the inherent superordination of men. The first is racist, the second sexist. Both devalue human beings who are somehow different from the authors of these theologies.

Both theologies are authoritarian. They presuppose that one party is obviously and uniquely endowed by God to lead: whites in relation to blacks, men in relation to women. In both cases, defenders warn of the dire consequences of allowing blacks or women to exercise authority.

Both theologies refuse to consider ethical or justice issues. We are told that if the Bible endorses slavery and the subordination of women, then these things must be ethical and moral in God's sight in every age. Empirical evidence on the consequences of the doctrine held are not taken into consideration, or they are dismissed with emotive countercharges. It is assumed that spiritual equality need not work itself out in social equality. One does not anticipate the other. (I am not suggesting that slavery and women's subordination are equally cruel or degrading. I am suggesting that in both cases one party unjustly treats and demeans another party and that this is unethical.)

Both theologies take little note of changing cultural values and structures. The Bible is read in every part as if it gives timeless, transcultural directives to unchanging social realities. Thus because the Bible depicts slavery and the subordination of women as unchallenged realities, the authors of these theologies assume that texts regulating these forms of social ordering are binding in every age. They are forever prescriptive rather than descriptive of another age and culture.

Both theologies argue that the individual texts on which the case is grounded rest on an unchanging theological foundation. In the case of slavery, this foundation is the moral law, and in the case of women it is the creation order. These are attempts by well-informed theologians to make what is obviously reflective of a past culture, and thus secondary in Scripture, into weighty theology.

Both theologies opposing emancipation were developed by evangelicals and vigorously rejected by other evangelicals. Those who opposed emancipation in both cases would not listen to their critics, whose doctrine of Scripture, they insisted, was defective. It was not a debate over how to read the Bible or over what is fair and just, but an issue of biblical authority. For this reason, no matter what texts those working for emancipation pointed to in the Bible, they were deemed to be wrong by definition. This made dialogue impossible.

Both theologies produced anthologies seeking to establish their position as the only one to be considered "biblical." The first, published in 1860, is called *Cotton Is King and Pro-Slavery Arguments*, and the second, published in 1991, is called *Recovering Biblical Manhood and Womanhood: A Response to Evangelical Feminism*.

One major difference between these theologies is that while the "biblical theology" constructed to justify slavery by the best of nineteenth-century Reformed theologians has now been universally repudiated, the "biblical theology" in support of the permanent subordination of women still has supporters, although the number of informed evangelicals endorsing this position continues to decline as each year passes.

The Harmony Line

This book began as a short article on the growing tendency among evangelicals to speak of the eternal subordination of the Son to the Father, and it grew into a major study on the historical development of the orthodox doctrine of the Trinity. I became interested in this issue because of my interest in the question of women's subordination, in which I have been involved for thirty years. I was convinced that seeking to ground and explain women's permanent role subordination on the basis of the supposed eternal role subordination of the Son is a theologically dangerous trend. In reading Athanasius and Augustine, I discovered that one of the greatest challenges they faced was how to answer those who were quoting and interpreting the Bible to prove what they themselves thought was heresy. Once I recognized this, I immediately saw that the debate on the doctrine of the Trinity and the debate on the subordination of women were connected at yet another level: in both cases theologians were quoting the Bible, giving their interpretations and reaching diametrically opposed conclusions. Athanasius and Augustine had to determine, therefore, a way to read the Bible so what is theologically primary in Scripture triumphs. In doing this they disclose how the Bible should be read to inform the theological quest on any matter. I thus went on to apply what I had learned from these two magisterial theologians, first to the debate on the man-woman relationship and then to slavery.

Discovering helpful insights on theological method in studying the Trinity was one unexpected reward for my work, but there were others. I also gained a new appreciation of the importance of tradition—how the Bible has been understood by the best of past theologians. I came to see how this helps us interpret the Bible in the present and to understand how Christians in other historical periods and cultural contexts dealt with issues now facing the church in our present historical period and cultural context. In the development of the doctrine of the Trinity, tradition played an important part. Each theologian built on the work of those who came before, and gradually an agreed way of reading the Bible emerged in the East and West that was codified in the Nicene and Athanasian Creeds. These traditions differed on some details, but each stressed that the three divine persons are one in being and work. This trinitarian tradition, in which the three divine persons are taken to be "co-equal," was reaffirmed by the sixteenth-century Reformers and is endorsed by most Christians today. It is a very weighty tradition. The traditions on women and slavery, on the other hand, are "light." They are nothing more than reflections of the cultural norms that prevailed until modern times. In neither case do they grasp the primary thrust of Scripture.

In coming to see that tradition may simply reflect past cultural norms, I was able to appreciate at greater depth than I had before one of the key insights of the contemporary discussion on hermeneutics: historical and cultural contexts contribute to how Scripture is interpreted and understood. When the culture changes profoundly, things hitherto not seen in Scripture come to light. Old interpretations are abandoned and new ones are formulated. On the women's subordination question and on slavery, it is hard to deny that this is exactly what has happened. There are opposing points of view on the issue of women's subordination, but I have shown that the new post-1970s cultural context has led all evangelicals, without exception, to change their interpretation of the key texts in the debate.

Thus, although it was never planned, these three things—how to read the Bible theologically so it is not simply a source of texts that can be used to prove what is already believed; the contribution of tradition in the theological enterprise; and the culture's effect on interpretation—are like a musical harmony line behind the melody line of the Trinity, women's subordination and slavery. I hope what I have discovered and presented on these three interrelated topics is of help to those who read this book, but I also hope that the three matters that have emerged along the way, and are now what I call the harmony in the background, contribute to evangelical thinking on theological method that is also on the evangelical agenda at this time. (See appendix C for an example of how to apply these three matters.)

The Bankruptcy of the Old Approach

For evangelicals who were taught to believe, as I was, that theology is nothing more than the gathering together of what the Bible teaches on any matter, this more inclusive and wider understanding of what is involved in "doing" evangelical theology might sound rather dangerous. It suggests that simply appealing to the Bible cannot settle complex theological or ethical disputes. This is the problem. It cannot. Let me give three examples to make the point. First, quoting texts and giving one's interpretation of them never resolves theological disputes among evangelicals. For every text quoted, other texts that seem to say something different can be found. This methodology generates more division than unanimity in the evangelical community (consider, e.g., the issues of election, baptism, eschatology, spiritual gifts, the Trinity).[3] The diversity in Scripture means that for almost anything asserted to be "biblical," a verse or a passage that seems to teach otherwise can be identified. Second, it is possible to find numerous texts on some matters and to give their plain meaning (consider, e.g., that the Son is subordinate to the Father, that salvation is earned by what one does, that the sun revolves around the Earth) and come to a conclusion that other evangelicals judge to be totally mistaken. Then third, there is the problem that the Bible is totally silent on many of the most pressing questions of our age (e.g., using drugs, gambling, abortion, euthanasia). This suggests that "doing" theology demands we do more than simply gather texts from the Bible and give "our" interpretation of them. No example more forcibly illustrates this truth than the work of the learned evangelicals of the Old South. Their cumulative biblical case for slavery was impressive in every way, but it was totally wrong *for that time and in that cultural setting.* Their theology sanctioned the institution and the practice of slavery when God, by his own work in history and in human consciousness, had revealed slavery to be a terrible sin against humanity.

These men began with a doctrine of Scripture that depicted the Bible as a compendium of timeless, transcultural precepts or propositions which only had to be systematized to give a divinely authoritative answer to any question. The answer gained was to be thought of as "revealed theology" because it was nothing other than an ordered account of what God said in the Bible. The possibility of theologians' reading the Bible in the wrong way or of their not grasping fully what is theologically primary and what is secondary—and so failing to discern

---

[3]For an extended list, see the titles of the evangelical series Two Views On, which are given in the front pages of Craig L. Blomberg and J. R. Beck, eds., *Two Views on Women in Ministry* (Grand Rapids, Mich.: Zondervan, 2001).

how some particular directives contained in the Bible may not apply in another cultural context—never crossed their minds.

This doctrine of Scripture led them to read the Bible on the flat, as if all texts were of equal theological weight, as if all said much the same on any given topic and as if all were timeless transcultural precepts to be obeyed at all times and in all places. The diversity within Scripture was staring them in the face, but they were not able to see it because they thought their belief in its unity demanded belief in unqualified uniformity in what it taught. Once they had accumulated their texts in support of slavery, they could not conceive that within Scripture there might be other texts that called into question all forms of human oppression and domination. In hindsight, we now see how they went wrong. They made absolute the many comments on slavery in Scripture that are best understood as temporal or "culturally bound" advice to those living in a culture that accepted slavery, and they made relative or ignored the few key passages of much greater theological weight that spoke of the equality and dignity of all human beings.

It has been my argument that from the 1970s onward, evangelicals have made exactly the same mistake in relation to women as was made by evangelicals just over a hundred years ago in relation to slavery. They have given themselves to proving, by appeal to the Bible, that women are permanently subordinated to men. They have had far less biblical material to work with than the proslavery theologians had, but they have developed a case that they feel is compelling. They argue that the texts in the New Testament asking women to be subordinate are binding on Christians in every age. These passages, they say, give timeless and transcultural truth; the social ordering prescribed is pleasing to God and should be endorsed by us today. In reply I have argued that this "theology" is to be rejected not only because it devalues and demeans women but also because it counters what the Bible itself makes primary. In the climactic comment in the prologue to the whole Bible (Gen 1:27–28) and in the teaching and example of Jesus, man and woman are depicted as being of equal value and dignity, neither having precedence over the other. In these texts God's ideal is revealed. This is what will prevail when the new creation is consummated, and this ideal corresponds with what is revealed of the triune God we worship. Each divine person in the Trinity is differentiated from the other, yet each is of equal dignity and authority: "none is afore, or after other; none greater, or less than another; . . . the whole three Persons are . . . co-equal."[4] This means that

---

[4]Quoted from the Athanasian Creed.

comments in Scripture on the subordination of women *must* be taken as temporary practical concessions to the fallen order. They reflect nothing more than the social ordering assumed in a cultural setting where patriarchy prevailed. They do not apply in a society that has emancipated women and has granted them equality of consideration. So I have posited the rule for a correct theological reading of Scripture on the man-woman relationship: *All texts that imply the equality of the sexes speak of God's ultimate eschatological ideal; all texts that speak of the subordination of women are culturally limited, time bound, practical advice to women living in a culture that took for granted the subordination of women. They do not apply in our age.*

APPENDIX C

HOMOSEXUALITY

A Test Case

In response to my argument that theology cannot be done simply by appeal to texts and that when culture changes a change in how the Bible is interpreted may follow, my critics immediately respond, "Well what about homosexuality? Your position must mean the acceptance of homosexuality, since contemporary Western culture now accepts gays and lesbians." This objection would be fair if I had argued that culture should *determine* theology, but I have not. My argument is that the impact of culture on the biblical writers and on all subsequent Christians should never be ignored in the theological enterprise.

It is vitally important that I respond to this objection; not to do so would allow those who are deeply committed to the permanent subordination of women to dismiss cavalierly the arguments presented in this book and others of a similar nature. In footnotes I have already pointed out that there is a huge difference between the woman debate (and its parallel, the slavery debate) and that about homosexuality (p. 167, note 59 and p. 244, note 29). The first is exclusively about the dignity and freedom of women as women, a matter of equity and justice; the second does involve equity and justice concerns but is primarily an ethical question: are same-sex sexual relations acceptable in God's sight?

A detailed discussion of homosexuality cannot be given in this book. I think, however, that I should show how the homosexual debate, rather than counting against my case, is another telling example of what I have been arguing.

☐ It illustrates the fact that quoting texts and giving one's interpretation of them never settles complex theological debates—and cannot.

☐ Instead of proof-texting, one must work out what is central and foundational to the scriptural revelation on any issue and theologize from that standpoint.

☐ A change in culture often leads to a change in how the Scriptures are interpreted.

☐ A change in culture often demands that the tradition—how the Scriptures were understood in the past—be evaluated and reappropriated.

☐ For these reasons theology is the unending task of the church. It has to be "done" time and time again.

The Tradition and Contemporary Thinking

For long centuries Christians believed that those who were guilty of homosexual behaviour should be punished and that such behavior was to be absolutely condemned.[1] The proper response should be both punitive and judgmental. Good biblical support could be given for this stance. The book of Leviticus demands the death penalty for anyone caught having sex with someone of the same sex (Lev 20:13), and it calls such behavior an "abomination" (cf. Lev 18:22). In the New Testament homosexual acts are also condemned in very strong language (Rom 1:26-27; 1 Cor 6:9-10; 1 Tim 1:9–10).

The demise of this tradition was spelled out with the publication of the 1957 Wolfenden Report, which argued that most homosexual behavior reflects a homosexual orientation, and for this reason, and because modern democratic societies are pluralistic in their values, it should not be a punishable offense.[2] Gradually these two conclusions have won over most people, including most evangelicals. Christian discussions on homosexuality, whatever conclusion they reach, usually reject a punitive response and a totally judgmental attitude. In other words, by the late twentieth century Western Christians had generally abandoned the tradition on homosexuality as it was expressed for centuries. One reason is that until the twentieth century it was not understood that most homosexual behavior is expressive of a homosexual orientation. This orientation is not freely chosen. It is the cumulative result of—in varying importance from person to person—genetic factors, the home environment while growing up, early sexual experiences, labeling by others, friendships and other forces.[3] Once the homosexual identity is well established, it seems it can never be erad-

---

[1]Richard F. Lovelace, *Homosexuality and the Church: Crisis, Conflict, Compassion* (Old Tappan, N.J.: Fleming H. Revell, 1978); pp. 17–27 outlines and documents this tradition.

[2]This study issued recommendations for laws governing sexual behavior. Published in 1957 by the Committee on Homosexual Offences and Prostitution in Great Britain, it was named for Sir John Wolfenden, chair of the committee. Drawing on the work of psychologists and social scientists, it clearly showed that homosexual orientation is a fact of life for some people. It recommended that private homosexual acts between consenting adults be legalized. This report led to a liberalizing of the laws on homosexuality in almost every Western country. See *The Wolfenden Report,* introduction by Karl Menninger (New York: Lancer, 1964).

[3]Thomas F. Schmidt, *Straight and Narrow? Compassion and Clarity in the Homosexual Debate* (Downers Grove, Ill.: InterVarsity Press, 1995), pp. 131-59, helpfully outlines the various forces that are thought to lead to a homosexual orientation.

icated completely. Even when the behavior is rejected, possibly under the transforming power of Christian conversion, the orientation remains, at least to some degree. Many see a parallel with alcoholism. The drinking can be stopped, but not the temptation to drink.

In the light of this new understanding of homosexuality, the traditional punitive and condemnatory response to homosexuality has been abandoned by most Christians. Very few Christians now believe that the state should punish homosexuals. Seldom if ever is it acknowledged, but it has been agreed that the Bible's command to put to death those who commit homosexual acts does not apply in our cultural context. In laying aside the biblical teaching that advocates punishment of those involved in homosexual acts, Christian theologians have agreed that compassion, not punishment, should be shown to those caught up in homosexuality.

However, most Christians today, including most evangelicals, reject not only punitive action against homosexuals but also a totally condemnatory stance. All but the most homophobic of contemporary Christians desire to be charitable toward homosexuals. As a general rule, the more informed on this matter one is, the less likely one is to be condemnatory. The sin may be hated, but not the sinner.

A Contemporary Theological Evaluation

For some Christians, the rejection of homosexuality is of great concern. It is thus often hard for them to appreciate that the Bible says very little on this matter. What so many believe is so important is discussed in only seven passages (Gen 19:1–11; Lev 18:22; 20:13; Rom 1:26–27; 1 Cor 6:9–11; 1 Tim 1:9–10; Jude 7), and some of these references are not of great significance. For example, the horrible story of the attempted homosexual pack rape of Abraham's guests (Gen 19:1–11) depicts a sin that all should condemn. It does not condemn homosexual acts as such. Indeed all seven texts can be read not to condemn consensual sexual relations between adult homosexuals. Careful and detailed exegesis of the relevant passages has to be undertaken to show their applicability to the homosexuality of our age.[4]

But even when this is done, some may reply, "Well, I don't accept what the Bible says on this matter," or "I don't accept your exegesis." At this point the parties can agree to differ, or the Christian objector to homosexuality can progress from quoting texts to doing theology. Virtually all evangelicals today

---

[4]This is done well by Schmidt, *Straight and Narrow?* pp. 64-99.

do this, thereby conceding that simply quoting texts and giving one's interpretation of them cannot settle profound theological and ethical issues.[5]

In seeking to make a reasoned response to the issues raised by homosexuality in contemporary society, the informed evangelical theologian would want to make the following points.

1. There is an important difference between homosexual orientation and homosexual acts. The Bible condemns same-sex sexual relations: it does not condemn people for having a homosexual orientation any more than it condemns people for being prone to anger. This distinction is vital for any contemporary Christian attempt to articulate a response to homosexuality, but it is to be noted that the Bible does not address sexual orientation. The existence of homosexual orientation is a discovery of modern social sciences.

2. Once this distinction is made, the fundamental objection to sex between men and men or women and women can be raised. The primary issue is not that a few texts condemn homosexual behavior; it is that same-sex sexual relations stand in opposition to God's creational pattern making sex the creative bond between man and woman (Gen 1:27–28). Men and women are made by God to complement one another. Their sexual polarity makes their union qualitatively different from that of two men or two women. Only in a heterosexual union can the procreational mandate given by God can be fulfilled; it cannot be in a homosexual union.

3. As this book has shown, there is teaching in Scripture that calls into question both slavery and the subordination of women. There is nothing in Scripture that might suggest that homosexual behavior is pleasing to God. The Bible consistently evaluates homosexual behavior negatively.

4. To add support to their appeal to the Bible at a theological level, most evangelical theologians draw on scientific data showing that long-term, exclusive relationships between homosexuals, especially males, are rare and that male homosexual practices involve serious risks to health.[6] It is true that many marriages today break down, but over the lifetime of the vast majority of heterosexuals, they have relatively few sexual partners, not comparable with the number of sexual partners for most male homosexuals.

5. It is appropriate to appeal to the unified tradition that has understood the

---

[5]Schmidt's book clearly illustrates this fact. It is an argued case drawing on many authorities beside the Bible. See also the excellent discussion of homosexuality by Stanley E. Grenz, *Sexual Ethics: An Evangelical Response* (Louisville, Ky.: Westminster John Knox, 1990), pp. 223-35.
[6]Again see Schmidt, *Straight and Narrow?* pp. 100-130.

Bible to depict homosexual behavior as displeasing to God. This tradition, one should add in this instance, has been radically reinterpreted but not rejected in toto as in the case of slavery.

Practical Outcomes

On the basis of these conclusions, a contemporary evangelical theological response to homosexuality can be formulated that suggests the following practical outcomes.

1. Christians should agree that homosexual sexual relations are not pleasing to God. They are not a sin worse than any other sin, but they are sinful.

2. Christians should not advocate punitive action by the state against practicing homosexuals. Indeed some evangelicals would argue that Christians should be advocates for homosexual rights in our pluralistic society.

3. Christians should not be judgmental and dismissive of homosexuals. They are human beings made in the image and likeness of God and loved by him. Only if we are without sin should we cast a stone at those who often have been sinned against more than they have sinned.

4. The local church should be welcoming of those struggling with homosexuality. The church is the home of sinners who know they desperately need the grace of God.

5. The church should not ordain practicing homosexuals; those who would lead God's people need to be "above reproach" (1 Tim 3:2). If anyone is not in control of such things as their temper, their drinking or their sexuality, they should not be ordained. In regard to sexual morality the same nondiscriminatory rule should apply to all: celibacy in singleness, faithfulness in marriage.

This contemporary theological response to homosexuality, it is to be noted, reflects to some degree the prevailing cultural estimation of homosexuality yet at the same time offers a critique of it. The change in culture has influenced how the Bible is understood, but it has not *determined* the evangelical theological evaluation of homosexuality.[7]

---

[7]For a very fine discussion of the Bible's teaching on homosexuality and the hermeneutical issues it raises for Christians today, see also Richard B. Hays, *The Moral Vision of the New Testament* (San Francisco: HarperSanFrancisco, 1996) pp. 379-406.

Author Index

Subject Index

analogy, 90-91, 109
apartheid, 224
Arian, Arianism, 1, 4, 14-
  15, 35-36, 38-39, 41, 44,
  63-64, 80-81, 129, 197
Arminians, 65, 71, 74
begotten, 14, 34, 42, 48,
  51, 64-69, 103
being of God, 4, 13
canonical rule, 46
chain of command, 22,
  38, 100, 113
Clapham Sect, 236
complementarians, 157
Confessions
  Belgic, 59
  Reformation, 1, 7, 33,
    59-60, 73
  Second Helvetic, 59
  Westminster, 11
Councils
  of Chalcedon, 45
  of Constantinople, 15,
    45
  of Florence, 50
  Fourth Lateran, 50
  of Gangrae, 220
  of Lyons, 50

of Nicea, 13, 26, 84
of Toledo, 119
Creeds
  Athanasian, 1, 7, 15,
    29, 31, 33 ,43-44, 50-
    52, 59, 123, 125, 267
  Nicene, 1, 7, 13, 15,
    29, 31, 33, 43-44, 50,
    59, 65, 73, 80
cultural context, 8-9, 11,
  25, 141, 143, 145, 167,
  194, 203, 235, 259-60,
  266
De Trinitate, 46-50, 73,
  198
difference (the term), 77,
  183-88
differences between
  men and women based
  on roles, 158-60, 163,
  165, 179-83
differentiated by authority (the Father and the
  Son), 47, 55, 63-64, 72,
  77, 82-83, 89, 100, 105
divine unity, 12, 42, 48,
  51, 54, 72, 78, 99, 103
divine will, 38, 47, 64, 83
Eastern Orthodoxy, 2,
  15, 21, 45, 50, 84, 98-

100
egalitarians, 7, 61, 79,
  157
eisegesis, 166, 188-93
Enlightenment, the, 235-
  36
eschatology, 177, 234
Father, two uses of the
  title, 43, 49
Filioque, 45, 50-51, 87,
  89, 98, 119
Fundamentals, the, 108
harmony line, 264-65
head (kephalē), 6, 16-17,
  24, 49, 56, 78, 81-83,
  134, 205-6, 255
headship, 1, 16, 24, 57,
  77, 105, 109, 112, 161,
  190, 200, 216
hermeneutics, herme-
  neutical, 5-6, 8-11, 32-
  33, 45-46, 53, 110, 145,
  167, 244
hierarchy, hierarchal, 6,
  24, 41-42, 44, 47, 49,
  55, 61, 71-72, 74, 77-80,
  105, 111, 118, 125, 202,
  204, 228
hierarchalists, 7, 157
Holy Spirit, 11-13, 18, 31,